Amelia Stone Quinton and the Women's National Indian Association

Women and the American West
Renée M. Laegreid, Series Editor

Amelia Stone Quinton and the Women's National Indian Association

A Legacy of Indian Reform

Valerie Sherer Mathes

Foreword by Lori Jacobson

UNIVERSITY OF OKLAHOMA PRESS : NORMAN

Publication of this book is made possible through the generosity of Edith Kinney Gaylord.

Library of Congress Cataloging-in-Publication Data

Names: Mathes, Valerie Sherer, 1941– author. | Jacobson, Lori, 1973– other.
Title: Amelia Stone Quinton and the Women's National Indian Association : a legacy of Indian reform / Valerie Sherer Mathes ; foreword by Lori Jacobson.
Description: Norman : University of Oklahoma Press, [2022] | Series: Women and the American West ; vol. 2 | Includes bibliographical references and index. | Summary: "An account of Amelia Stone Quinton (1833–1926) and the organization she cofounded, the Women's National Indian Association (WNIA), that offers a nuanced insight into the intersection of gender, race, religion, and politics in our shared history. Shows how Quinton was a true force for reform and progress who was nonetheless constrained by the assimilationist convictions of her time"— Provided by publisher.
Identifiers: LCCN 2021036089 | ISBN 978-0-8061-8027-4 (hardcover)
ISBN 978-0-8061-9291-8 (paperback)
Subjects: LCSH: Quinton, Amelia S. (Amelia Stone), 1835?–1926 | Women's National Indian Association (U.S.) | Indians of North America—Cultural assimilation. | Women—Political activity—United States—History—19th century. | Women political activists—United States—History—19th century. | Women social reformers—United States—History—19th century.
Classification: LCC E98.C89 M38 2022 | DDC 320.0820973—dc23/eng/20211007
LC record available at https://lccn.loc.gov/2021036089

Amelia Stone Quinton and the Women's National Indian Association: A Legacy of Indian Reform is Volume 2 in the Women and the American West series.

The paper in this book meets the guidelines for permanence and durability of the Committee on Production Guidelines for Book Longevity of the Council on Library Resources, Inc. ∞

The manufacturer's authorized representative in the EU for product safety is Mare Nostrum Group B.V., Mauritskade 21D, 1091 GC Amsterdam, The Netherlands, email: gpsr@mare-nostrum.co.uk

Contents

Foreword

Lori Jacobson

These pages on the life of Amelia Stone Quinton offer compelling insights into the labor and leadership required of women engaged in benevolence work in the nineteenth century. Quinton's schedule was demanding: near-constant travel and public speaking, meetings and conferences, correspondence with influential women and men, the writing of articles and pamphlets, and the creation of independent branch associations and missions across the country. Quinton was singularly focused on the goal of establishing "a just, protective, and fostering Indian policy," and she maintained that focus for decades. This biography reveals Quinton to be a woman in motion, a woman whose energy and effort shaped public sentiment and transformed the political landscape in a time when women had little political capital and were refused the vote.

But this positive narrative of women's public work comes with caveats.

Quinton was an assimilationist. She was at the forefront of a movement to protect Indians from a host of powerful forces that were aligned against them, and she had to persuade lawmakers and others in power that the indigenous people of America were worthy of their care. Like almost everyone around her, she took it on faith that assimilation was the most logical path. In Quinton's view, the way to overcome hatred of Indians and inspire a sense of moral culpability in powerful white Americans was to transform native people, eliminating their cultural traditions and inculcating them with white, middle class, Protestant values. She saw Indians as potential Christians, farmers, laborers, homemakers, and citizens. The native people she held up as success stories epitomized these roles. Tribal sovereignty and the preservation of indigenous cultures and languages were anathema to Quinton's worldview.

Quinton steered the Women's National Indian Association (WNIA) toward good-faith efforts to amend the corruption, negligence, and other systemic failures that denied Indians their treaty rights. She recognized that government policies had led to Indian dispossession and displacement, and she believed that better policies could make amends. Her role in the creation and passage of the Dawes General Allotment Act grew from this desire to use government as a force for good. The fact that allotment led to further dispossession and displacement was both unanticipated and unacknowledged by Quinton.

The WNIA under Quinton also worked to address the palpable needs of tribal groups living in devastating poverty. These reformers provided healthcare and education, built homes and supplied domestic goods, subsidized farming equipment, and delivered clothing and books. These efforts to meet pressing daily needs served the WNIA's more fundamental goal of spreading the tenets of civilization and Christianity among native people. Quinton's organization was above all devoted to traditional missionary work where necessities were delivered in equal measure with Christian teachings.

Benevolence work opened career paths to white, middle- and upper-class women, granting them the means to engage in public and political discourse. But this public presence remained constrained by nineteenth-century gender norms, and women performing this work had to align it with traditional notions of femininity. As a result, women's Indian reform work was presented as an extension of the maternal work of the home. WNIA members believed that their power to inspire change resided in their moral influence. Helen Hunt Jackson's books *A Century of Dishonor* and *Ramona*—inspirational to the Indian reform movement—spoke to the need for a national moral reckoning to address the "Indian problem." WNIA women responded accordingly but firmly within their spheres of influence. The concurrent women's suffrage movement was controversial among conservative WNIA members primarily because it was so disruptive to the social order under which they operated. Women on this side of the suffrage divide generally believed that the benefits of enfranchisement would be offset by a loss of feminine forms of moral persuasion.

Quinton had a gift for this kind of persuasion. That fact emerges clearly from the important archival work performed by Valerie Sherer Mathes in this book. Motivated both by her religious affiliations and by her strong sense of justice, Quinton saw clearly that the people with power in America were failing to live up to their individual and national obligations. In turning her prodigious organizational and leadership skills toward the work of Indian reform, Quinton demonstrated how women could take on public leadership roles that served a moral purpose. This biography provides rich source material for future scholars who wish to analyze the history of women's labor, social networks, and organizational strategies. More importantly, it presents opportunities to understand women's complicity in and resistance to the colonial narrative in America.

Preface

My research on Amelia Stone Quinton began decades ago at a time when Helen Hunt Jackson was my primary focus. Quinton and the Women's National Indian Association had continued Jackson's work among the Mission Indians in Southern California; so, while pursuing additional research on the WNIA's work elsewhere in California for my book *Divinely Guided,* I became aware of the pivotal role that Quinton played within the late-nineteenth-century reform movement and believed she deserved her own biography. Yet, despite decades of research, I found little on her life prior to her WNIA years.

Although Quinton's early years still remain a mystery, there was sufficient material to provide an insightful glimpse into the life and legacy of this remarkable woman, who cofounded and guided an organization which, while openly promoting the government's policy of assimilation, through their petition drives, literature, and the activities of numerous state auxiliaries, also provided schools, housing, and hospitals, thus improving the lives of those Indians living near the association's more than sixty mission stations.

What follows is a narrative history—generally chronological, more descriptive than critical, and almost exclusively of her WNIA years—using Quinton's letters in the Papers of William Henry Weinland at the Huntington Library in San Marino, California; the National Archives; and at the Cornell University Library. This latter collection, still not catalogued, was discovered decades ago in a box in the basement of the Phillips Free Library in Homer, New York, where Quinton grew up. In later years, she had returned to Homer, at one time buying a home there. When she left for the final time, she either forgot or deliberately left the box behind where it was found by the town librarian who fortuitously moved into that same home. Among more than five hundred items were copies of letters written by Quinton between 1902 and 1906, responses, and family correspondence from two of her brothers with several from her stepson. This collection was formally transferred from Homer to Cornell University in July 2020.

Other sources included Quinton's articles, newspaper accounts, and WNIA literature, such as annual reports, trustee reports, and issues of their monthly paper *The Indian's Friend,* as well as the papers and reports of the Indian Rights Association and of the Lake Mohonk Conference.

Without Quinton's story, the history of the late nineteenth- and early twentieth-century Indian reform movement is incomplete. It is my intention to let her words and those of others she worked with speak for themselves. Our great challenge today is the passage of the last hundred plus years and a, sometimes dramatic, change in views of assimilation and its impact. Understanding Quinton's motivations and actions within the context of their time can provide insight into her, the WNIA, and the Indian reform movement. This era is part of our collective history and acknowledging both the positive and the negative help us write a more accurate biography. It is my particular hope that future scholars will build on this work, expanding our understanding of her nuanced role within the movement and comparing her achievements to that of equally exceptional women leaders in other reform movements.

My lengthy effort has resulted in obligations to the staffs of many institutions including, but not exclusive to, The Huntington Library, Art Museum, and Botanical Gardens, San Marino, California; the Pennsylvania Historical Society, Philadelphia, Pennsylvania; the Carl A. Kroch Library, Cornell University, Ithaca, New York; the National Archives and Records Center, Washington, DC; the Morgan County Archives, Madison, Georgia; and the Cortland County Historical Society, Cortland, New York. I also want to thank Alessandra J. Tamulevich, my editor at the University of Oklahoma Press; Renée M. Laegreid, series editor; and Susan Walters Schmid, my copy editor. Thanks also go to Patricia Heinicke and Lori Jacobson for their insightful comments. Special thanks to Homer Town Historian, Martin A. Sweeney, who alerted me to the existence of the box of Quinton letters in the Homer Library, and to Phil Brigandi, who until his untimely death in December 2019, was, from the very beginning, on this lengthy journey with Quinton and me.

Abbreviations

ABHMS	American Baptist Home Mission Society
BIA	Bureau of Indian Affairs
BIC	Board of Indian Commissioners
CIA	Cambridge Indian Association
IRA	Indian Rights Association
ITKPA	Indian Treaty-Keeping and Protective Association
LMC	Lake Mohonk Conference
MIA	Massachusetts Indian Association
NIA	National Indian Association
NYCI	New York City Indian Association
OIA	Office of Indian Affairs [predecessor of BIA]
RIA	Redlands Indian Association
SCIA	Southern California Indian Association
WABHMS	Woman's American Baptist Home Mission Society
WBHMS	Women's Baptist Home Mission Society
WCTU	Woman's Christian Temperance Union
WNIA	Women's National Indian Association

Introduction

When Amelia Stone Quinton died in Ridgefield Park, New Jersey, on June 23, 1926, she was almost ninety-three. Two days later the *New York Times* noted her passing, simply mentioning her parents' names and that she was a writer and a founder of the Women's National Indian Association (WNIA). Yet, Quinton was far more than that mere three sentence blip in the *Times* suggested. Its brevity and the fact that there were no other prominent reformers who responded to her death was in no way a reflection on her accomplishments; she simply had outlived most of her contemporaries. For almost three decades during the late nineteenth and early twentieth centuries, she served as the public face of the WNIA, a volunteer organization of upper-and middle-class Christian women that she had cofounded with Mary Lucinda Bonney. In the words of Mary Lowe Dickinson, a contemporary and fellow WNIA member, the WNIA became "a most potent adjunct in the solving of the social problems that press upon the enlightened conscience in this day of grand endeavors for the uplifting of the [Indian] race."[1]

Although Quinton was the most prominent female reformer of her day within the Indian reform movement, her contributions are generally not recognized by scholars of women's history, unlike those of, for example, Frances Willard, a founding member of the Woman's Christian Temperance Union or Jane Cunningham Croly, who formed the General Federation of Women's Clubs. Although Willard and Croly were Quinton's contemporaries, they both have a place in the National Women's Hall of Fame at Seneca Falls while Quinton does not. A possible explanation may be that historians have generally allowed this reform movement to remain within the realm of Indian history. After all, the WNIA's primary goal, explicit even in their various name changes, was to "secure the adoption of a just, protective and fostering Indian policy."[2] It may also be true that the WNIA's resistance to women's suffrage and their wholehearted embrace of assimilationist doctrines have made their approach to activism difficult to reconcile with the larger story of women's history in America.

Nevertheless, Quinton and the organization she cofounded are significant to women's history. The WNIA originated within the Women's Home Missionary Society of the First Baptist Church of Philadelphia in the summer of 1877 when members expanded their work beyond prayer and philanthropy to actively engage in Indian reform. The association would help to shape and then promote the U.S. government's Indian policy. Quinton was at the helm, initially as its first secretary, and then as its third president. When she finally retired, she remained chairman of the Missionary Department and the association's Honorary President but continued to organize, speak before various groups, and write articles for the association's monthly magazine, *The Indian's Friend*. A month after her death the magazine praised her organizational skills, speaking ability, and leadership, declaring that she had made the WNIA "one of the foremost missionary agencies of the country working for the spiritual and material welfare of the Indians."[3]

Quinton worked successfully in an arena dominated by male reformers, creating a professional, and at times personal, relationship with them as well as with successive commissioners of Indian affairs, secretaries of the Interior, and various prominent congressmen. And, because the WNIA was the first of the assimilationist Indian reform organizations, its goals and methods—initiated and promoted by Quinton—influenced other reformers. She left behind a remarkable personal legacy as well as an association that at the time of her death had been engaged in Christian missionary work among Indians in the United States for almost half a century.

Quinton was respected by her fellow reformers during her lifetime. In 1914, the Society of American Indians—the first pan-Indian reform organization founded three years earlier by a progressive group of mostly middle-class Indian men and women—praised her in their quarterly journal. In an essay discussing the "staunch and unselfish friends" of the Indians, the journal editor concluded: "We may not forget the earnest women who have given their lives in the service of the Indian—women like Helen Hunt Jackson and Amelia S. Quinton."[4] It was appropriate that the Society praised both women, for Quinton and the WNIA had continued Jackson's legacy among the Mission Indians of Southern California.

Quinton received one of the highest of compliments from Henry Roe Cloud, a Nebraska Winnebago Indian. Roe Cloud was the first Indian to graduate from Yale University and he had first met Quinton in 1906 while he was a student there, and later they visited a number of times. Three years after Quinton's death, Roe Cloud was invited to the WNIA's golden anniversary luncheon on December 7, 1929. Unable to attend, he sent a letter to be read in which he wrote: "I recall vividly now her inspiriting personality, [and] her untiring devotion to the welfare of the Indian people." He described her inspirational leadership, which had enabled her to "overcome one obstacle after another, so that the work of the Association itself long ago became one of the outstanding pieces of constructive and redeeming work for the Red Man in America." She had "helped to lay the foundations that meant the future freedom and security of the Indian race in the nation," he continued, praising the long list of pioneer missionary stations started and nurtured by her association before being turned over to a Christian missionary society to operate. He was personally familiar with this work, having visited the Rocky Boy band (Chippewa-Cree) station in Montana.[5] Indeed, Henry Roe Cloud himself personified exactly what the WNIA had for decades been working towards—an assimilated American Indian.

Margaret Jacobs in her *White Mother to a Dark Race*, winner of the 2010 Bancroft Prize, described Quinton as one of three white women who stood out as "powerful spokespersons" for the Indian reform movement. Jacobs concluded that, "Together these three women created, reinforced, and promoted images of Indian women and families that gained wide currency in both popular culture and government circles and wielded significant influence over the direction and implementation of Indian policy in the late nineteenth and early twentieth centuries."[6]

The organizational foundation that Quinton had helped build enabled the WNIA to continue its missionary efforts for another twenty-five years after her death. When it finally disbanded in 1951, it had completed almost seventy-five years of work on behalf of America's Indian population and had founded over sixty mission stations from Florida to California.[7] As early as 1901, Quinton had seen the handwriting on the wall, declaring in her presidential address that they were working on their "last needed reforms." The association had already lasted far longer than anyone had intended.[8] In her 1908 presidential address, incoming president Mrs. Walter R. Brooks openly explained that she and others had been expecting that by this time their work would be taken over by an "interdenominational union of the evangelical missionary societies."[9] The association's original reason for existing, that of supporting and promoting the federal government's policy of individualizing and Americanizing the Indians as a means of assimilating them into mainstream culture, was no longer viable. According to historian Francis Paul Prucha, after 1900 the nineteenth-century belief of Christian reformers that the Indians would be "abruptly and dramatically transform[ed]" and the "Indian problem" would rapidly disappear gradually changed with the Progressive Era into a more practical approach of "self-support and self-reliance."[10] The fact that the association lasted until 1951 is a credit to Quinton's early decisions and her foundational work.

The "Indian problem" was a serious social issue during Quinton's day. Following the Civil War, settlers flooded into the Trans-Mississippi West where, eager to exploit the region's natural resources, they overran the Indian inhabitants, who fought back to save their homelands. A dozen years of intense warfare followed. Working with the government, a reform movement emerged that became part of the solution once peace came. Described by Prucha as "a tight little group of dedicated men and women," they played an influential role in promoting the government's new assimilationist policy. Quinton and fellow reformers together shaped a solution to the Indian problem and worked harmoniously to realize it, drawing upon church support and on what Prucha calls "a common philanthropic and humanitarian outlook expressed in Christian terms." They used various forms of propaganda to educate the American public, Congress, and government officials, with the aim of shaping Indian reform policy at a federal level.[11]

American society during Quinton's time was dominated by evangelical, revivalist Protestant Christianity, which molded many of its citizenry into what William McLoughlin described as "a unified, pietistic-perfectionist nation" and spurred them to "heights of social reform, missionary endeavor, and imperialistic expansionism which constitute the moving forces of our history in that century."[12] Middle- and upper-class women like Quinton were, however, further burdened by society's expectation that to achieve the desirable role of "true womanhood," they had to be pious, pure, submissive, and domestic, with their home viewed as their "proper sphere." With these four "cardinal virtues," women would have happiness and power; without them, "all was ashes."[13] However, historian Helen M. Bannan concludes that as "real women responded to the 'true woman' model," they got down off of their pedestal, left the home, and because they were viewed "as moral guardians of society," they joined various reform movements and engaged in charity and missionary work.[14] Quinton, along with her fellow female reformers, unknowingly were fulfilling the dictates of Rev. J. F. Stearn, who decades earlier had declared that women were not only the "mainspring" of society but were "fitted by nature" to the cause of Christian benevolence.[15]

Driven by a duty to save others and a desire to live up to society's high expectations, many women concluded, like their male counterparts, that the power of the Christian religion could transform American Indians into "civilized" citizens. Reformers inspired by this possibility organized themselves into gender-specific associations: women joined the Women's National Indian Association (WNIA), the oldest of the assimilationist associations, and men joined the Boston Indian Citizenship Committee (Boston Committee) or the Indian Rights Association (IRA). Once a year a select number from each group were invited to come together at the Lake Mohonk Conference of the Friends of the Indians to discuss and determine Indian policy.

Quinton succeeded in this male-dominated Indian reform arena for a number of reasons. She had been raised with three brothers in a predominantly male household and obviously had learned from a young age how to navigate within that unit. Also, Quinton's grounding in the Baptist faith was extremely strong. At age nineteen she had been baptized into the Homer (New York) Baptist Church, where her grandfather's brother had been the founding pastor and her father served as a senior deacon, and she later married a Baptist minister. Quinton became a member of the First Baptist Church of Philadelphia and it was out of that church's Women's Home Missionary Society that the WNIA had grown. Quinton's experiences left her uniquely fitted for success in this reform movement.

As we will see, what we do know of Amelia Stone Quinton's life suggests she was destined to become who she was—a leading member of a group of Christian reformers who came to dominate the late nineteenth century Indian reform movement.

1

Quinton's Early Years

Childhood

Amelia C. Stone was born in Jamesville, New York on July 31, 1833, and raised in Homer, Cortland County, about 140 miles from Albany. Homer had been settled in 1791 by religious migrants from Connecticut, described as "industrious, frugal, and moral." By 1837, following the New England pattern, the townspeople had designed a village green surrounded by four churches and a school, the Cortland Academy. Within three years the population had grown to 3,572, large enough to support three taverns, ten stores of various kinds, a large woolen factory, two grist mills and two sawmills, a nail factory, a brewery, and a tannery. By 1860 a gazetteer listed six churches, a printing office, and the only cotton factory in the county. Nine years later the village was described as pleasant with broad streets and walks "ornamented with beautiful shade trees, which add much to the general appearance of the village." Eventually it became a station on the Syracuse, Binghamton, and New York Railroad.[1]

The first of the Stone family to move to Homer was Thomas Stone Jr. and his wife, Polly Webb Stone. They had accompanied Thomas' brother, Nathan Stone, from Monson, Massachusetts, in 1801, settling on the hill east of Homer village. The *Homer Republican* described the brothers as "men of the best New England type [who] were largely influential in building up the institutions of society on a right basis." On December 8, 1803, Quinton's father, Jacob Thompson Stone, was born to Thomas and Polly Stone. Although he worked long days on the family farm, Jacob acquired sufficient education to be considered "well informed on many current topics and matters of general information." On December 7, 1826, he married Mary Bennett, the daughter of Chloe Grow Bennett and Asa Bennett, a deacon in the Homer Baptist Church. The ceremony was performed by Alfred Bennett, pastor of the church and Quinton's grandfather's brother.[2]

Amelia Stone Quinton co-founder and longtime president of the WNIA in an 1898 photograph taken by G. J. Pruden, a Homer, New York photographer. She gave this photograph on September 16 to Rev. and Mrs. William Henry Weinland.
William H. Weinland Collection, The Huntington Library, San Marino, California (photCL 39 [202]).

The couple had four children. Amelia C. was their second child and only daughter.[3]

Jacob Stone provided for his family by farming until asthma forced him to seek less strenuous work. In 1845 he was elected Homer's justice of the peace and four years later was appointed the town's postmaster.[4] By this time his wife's elderly mother and her sister Amelia had joined the household. Jacob's continued failing health forced the family to take in boarders. The 1850 federal census revealed twelve people living in the household, including five non-family members, one of whom was identified as a teacher and two as teenagers—these three presumably were affiliated with nearby Cortland Academy. The 1855 state census revealed eleven residents, including six boarders. Five years later the federal census listed the elder Stone as operating a boarding house, with two boarders identified as teachers. In 1870, with all the Stone children out of the house, four of the occupants were still boarders. The 1880 City of Homer census listed Jacob and his wife, he as an asthmatic and she as suffering with rheumatism.[5] At Jacob's death on January 12, 1884, the *Homer Republican* described him as "generous and magnetic," possessed of a "conscientious and of a deep religious nature," and respected for his integrity and loyalty.[6]

Cortland Academy

Two Homer institutions played a prominent role in the lives of the Stone family, and especially in Quinton's—the Baptist Church and Cortland Academy, where at least three of the Stone children studied. Presumably they all had attended the one-room school on the Homer Green. The Cortland Academy, initially incorporated in 1819 and educating only male students, opened its doors to female students in 1821. The Stones' twelve-year-old daughter was listed as a student in the school's 1845–1846 catalogue. The "Course of Instruction," designed to be thorough, combined "a rigid intellectual training with that which is practically useful," preparing the students for college admission or for work in various businesses, and providing Quinton with an educational experience that enabled her to cofound and run the WNIA for decades. The catalogue's author also admonished parents "not to indulge their children in the free use of money—nothing has a more direct tendency to produce dissipation and idleness, and to ruin the moral and intellectual character of the scholar."[7]

Quinton and fellow students faced a vigorous curriculum: mathematics; natural philosophy; Latin, Greek, or French; natural sciences (botany, chemistry, geology, mineralogy, natural history, and physiology); and a course of study entitled "moral, intellectual and political science," which included criticism, history, logic, natural theology, philosophy, rhetoric, and an analysis of poetry. She may have begun writing poetry herself as she had two poems published decades later. She also excelled in composition, later putting this skill to good use as the WNIA's general secretary.[8] Piano lessons, bookkeeping, and surveying courses were also available as was the use of an "elegantly" arranged library with more than one thousand volumes in literature and science, provided by the town of Homer.[9]

Religion was also crucial to Quinton's future. She was a member of the Homer Baptist Church, where her grandfather's brother, Alfred Bennett, had served as first pastor from 1807 to 1828. Her father served as senior deacon from the time he formally united with the church in his forties until his death in 1884.[10] On February 1, 1852, at age nineteen, Amelia was baptized into the church. Then three years later, on January 6, 1855, married and living in Georgia, she was granted a formal dismissal.[11]

Sojourn in the South

Little is known of Quinton's personal activities after she left Homer, or even when and why she left. From a late nineteenth-century publication we learn that she had served as a "preceptress" at an unidentified academy near Syracuse before supposedly accepting a teaching position in an unnamed Georgia seminary.[12] It was quite common for young Northern women to go South to teach, for Southern women generally did not pursue educational careers. Mary Lucinda Bonney, Quinton's future WNIA cofounder, had taught in South Carolina.

Although there is no record of an arrival date or of an educational institution that employed her, Quinton moved to the vicinity of Madison, Georgia, some time prior to 1854 because late in that year she married James Franklin Swanson, a local resident.[13] In the 1840s, Madison, in Morgan County, was described as "the wealthiest and most aristocratic village on the stage-coach route between Charleston and New Orleans."[14] By 1852 the county had a population of 10,896, of which 66 percent were African American slaves.[15]

Quinton left behind no record of her life in the South, but it seems reasonable to assume that the presence of so many slaves made her uncomfortable, since upstate New Yorkers tended to be antislavery. Curtis D. Johnson, in *Islands of Holiness*, writes that Cortland County "residents had few economic ties to the South, a very small black population, and a deep commitment to personal liberty and republican principles." Some Homer residents "castigated the 'peculiar institution' as early as 1821," and by the late 1820s the Homer Baptist Church was supporting the American Colonization Society. Based on this evidence, Johnson concluded that "Cortland County was fully in the antislavery camp."[16]

Prosperity had come to Morgan County with the cotton boom of the first half of the nineteenth century, and many of its wealthy plantation owners built homes in Madison to take advantage of its educational institutions for their children. In addition to several private academies, there were two women's colleges chartered by the state legislature: the Madison Collegiate Institute (later the Georgia Female College) founded by the Baptists (1849), and the Madison Female College founded by the Methodists (1850), both offered a well-rounded academic education. If Quinton did indeed teach in Georgia, it would more than likely have been at the Baptist-affiliated Georgia Female College. None of the college's extant catalogs listed her as a faculty member; however, the 1850 catalog listed her future husband, James Franklin Swanson, as a member of their board of trustees.[17]

Frank Swanson

James Franklin "Frank" Swanson was born January 27, 1825, in Morgan County. He was the eleventh of fourteen children born to John Swanson, a deacon of the Antioch Baptist Church in Godfrey, Morgan County, and his wife, Elizabeth B. Tuggle Swanson. Originally from Pittsylvania County, Virginia, the Swansons had moved to Morgan County about 1808.[18] By 1811 John Swanson owned eight slaves and 202 1/2 acres near Indian Creek, north of Godfrey and eleven miles south of Madison. Over the years he added to his land, purchasing a forty-acre parcel in Cherokee County in 1838. By 1842 he owned forty slaves and 1,522 1/2 acres near Indian Creek.[19] At the time of his death in 1847, his planation was described as "mostly in a fine state of cultivation," with two thirds cleared and the remainder in woodlands, with a good dwelling home and kitchen, a gin house, and all other buildings necessary for a proper farm.[20]

Frank's parents had died before Quinton arrived in Madison—his mother on October 30, 1843, and his father on August 12, 1847. John Swanson had bequeathed his second wife, Francis McClendon Hearn Swanson, the use of his houses and four hundred acres. The remainder of his estate was divided among his children. Frank, who received $1,150 in cash, served with two of his brothers as executors. The inventory, appraisal, and sale of the property reflected the holdings of a middling Southern planter. John Swanson's twenty-seven slaves, down from forty, alone were valued at $12,800 ($406,211 in 2021 dollars).[21] Frank, by no means wealthy, nevertheless in 1849 owned one slave, a four wheeled carriage, and forty acres in Cherokee County, presumably the same property his father had purchased in 1838. By 1858, four years after his marriage to Quinton, he owned 302 acres in Morgan County, valued at $2,200 and one slave, valued at $900, with an aggregate property value of $4,105 ($130,237 in 2021 dollars).[22]

According to Frank's biographer, Jessie Harrison Campbell, little is known of his youth "beyond the fact that it displayed the manliness, modesty, generosity and thrift which characterized him when grown." When Frank was about twenty, he left the family home and moved to Madison, where in August 1848, along with Jesse W. Fears and Parmenius R. Thomason, he purchased the American Hotel. Two years later in March, his declining health forced him and Fears to sell out to Thomason. Also in 1848, Frank had partnered with Fears in founding Fears & Swanson, a successful mercantile business selling "Staple and fancy dry goods," such as shoes, hats, hardware, crockery, tobacco, eventually family groceries, and in March 1856, Steinway & Son's pianos. In 1856, again health issues forced the closure of this profitable business, and Frank turned to the less strenuous job of teaching at the Georgia Female College.[23]

By this time he was married, having on December 24, 1854, wed twenty-one-year-old Amelia C. Stone in a ceremony performed by Rev. Charles M. Irwin. Campbell described the bride as "a highly accomplished Christian woman, who conferred on [her husband] the heritage of great happiness." Their union was "'pure" and "congenial" and "productive of spirituality and usefulness." Although they had no children, "each was the complement of the other."[24]

Presumably Quinton and her husband shared faith in the main Baptist tenets, although there were differences between Northern and Southern Baptists, with the major issue being slavery.[25] Frank, however, seemed to have had a more enlightened view because soon after what Campbell refers to as his "conversion," he began "working for the salvation of the negroes, and continued it with so great ardor that an unquenchable desire to preach the gospel to all men was developed." Frank, who was active in the Madison Baptist Church, leading the choir and teaching Sunday school, had been baptized in October 1848 by Reverend Irwin. His ardor to preach led to his ordination on March 18, 1859. Although continuing to teach at Georgia Female College, Frank began preaching "to country churches and in destitute neighborhoods." His first permanent pastoral duties were at the Bethlehem Baptist Church (later Apalachee Baptist Church) located seven miles northeast of Madison.[26] The Civil War broke out one year later.

Impact of the Civil War

The Civil War years saw Quinton and Frank living apart. She moved to New York, ostensibly for health reasons in December of 1860, returning in the summer of 1865.[27] Since she lived into her nineties, illness or even the climate may not have been the sole reason for this move. It may well have been that Quinton's upbringing and exposure in upstate New York to the abolition movement caused friction within her marriage and with the extended Swanson family. But a lack of any records makes it impossible to know for sure. She may possibly have been thinking about moving as early as the spring of 1860, for Frank visited two churches near New York City at that time, but for unknown reasons declined offers from both churches. Instead, according to Campbell, driven by "his deep sense of personal responsibility" and following the truth that "to do good to others, we must first be good," Frank committed himself to helping Southern African Americans, accepting a pastorate at the Second Baptist Church in Augusta, in the heart of the conflict.[28]

Frank remained in Augusta for a year before an unidentified "long and severe illness" (probably tuberculosis) forced him to seek a healthful location near Cedar Town (today Cedartown), northwest of Atlanta, where in March 1862 he became pastor of the local Baptist church. Cedar Town, where the Creek and later the Cherokee Indians had lived, was known for its large natural limestone spring with healing powers. He also served the Cave Spring Church located a short distance to the northwest. Described as an influential pastor, he moved "from house to house as a godly man, warmly welcomed, greatly beloved, and gladly leaving his benediction upon all." His condition worsened, forcing him in January 1863 to resign the Cave Spring Church, but he remained as the pastor in Cedar Town until the end of 1865. By this time his wife had returned home.[29] On October 28, 1869, James Franklin Swanson died and was buried in the cemetery overlooking Rome, Georgia, north of Cedar Town. He had drawn up his will three days prior to his death, naming his wife as his sole heir.[30]

The Stone family in Homer, New York, also endured a family split. Frail health had forced Amelia's twenty-year-old brother Lucius Bennett Stone to seek a milder climate and he moved to Georgia around 1855. According to the 1860 federal census, he was living in the Macon household of Thomas Jefferson Swanson, the youngest in the Swanson clan. At the outbreak of the war, Lucius joined the Confederate army, enlisting on January 23, 1861, in Jackson's Battery, Georgia State Troops, transferring in April to the Second Georgia Battalion of Infantry, concluding his career in the Forty-Ninth Georgia Infantry as a drill master and later as an ordnance sergeant. His younger brother, George Whitefield Stone, who had just been admitted to the New York State bar in 1861, became the first man in Cortland County to enlist in the Union cause, joining the Twelfth New York Volunteers. Although elected a captain in the army, he switched to the navy, where he served as a judge-advocate, remaining until war's end. The oldest brother, Seymour Henry, became a lieutenant in the

Fifty-first Regiment, New York National Guard.[31] Little else is known of the brothers' lives.

For no reason that forty years of research has been able to uncover, Quinton never mentioned in any future correspondence, speeches, or articles that she had once lived in Georgia or that she had been married there. Even for her life after living in the South, what we do know of her personal life and views is revealed only in her writings related to her work and her business dealings.

2

Early Social Reform Activities and the Birth of the WNIA

After the war, while her brothers sought their own paths, Quinton, now widowed, returned to the North. A brief sketch in *A Woman of the Century* (1893) has her teaching at Chestnut Street Seminary in Philadelphia, founded by WNIA cofounder Mary Lucinda Bonney, but the few extant seminary records reveal no record of such employment. The same source says that she moved from Philadelphia to New York City, where she "turned to the religious and philanthropic work to which she has given the best years of her life." Volunteering among the poor, she worked in unidentified prisons, almshouses, and a women's reformatory. Then a December 1873 issue of the *Sailor's Magazine* described a Mrs. A. C. Swanson, of the Bethany Institute, holding a weekly Bible class that "was exceedingly attractive and profitable." A month later the *Cortland County Republican* reported that Mrs. Amelia Swanson, whose parents lived in the county, had "been spending the past few months among the poor in New York City. She finds a vast amount of suffering there and has been the means of affording much relief." During a visit home she had met with a number of local women and "laid before them the facts which she has learned. Much interest was felt and measures were taken to aid her in her good work."[1]

Quinton and the WCTU

From this work, Quinton went on to serve during the latter half of the 1870s as an organizer for the Brooklyn branch of the Woman's Christian Temperance Union (WCTU); she would later bring with her to the Indian reform movement considerable organizational skills learned from this time. Temperance was a logical path considering her upbringing in upstate New York, known for its involvement in reform movements and her father's membership in a Homer temperance society.[2] Her Baptist upbringing also may have led to this choice. According to historian Anne Firor Scott, the Baptist church, although more conservative in their view of women's rights, encouraged an expanded role for women in some benevolent causes, especially the temperance crusade, "as long as these efforts remain dissociated with the feminist agitation and politics."[3]

The earliest evidence of Quinton's WCTU membership dates from 1876.[4] However, she could easily have been among the founding members who met in rooms provided by the YMCA on March 16, 1874. Thereafter Brooklyn women immediately began making hundreds of saloon visits, distributing temperance literature and Bibles, and holding daily prayer meetings all over the city. The first national WCTU president, described these meetings as "filled nightly with the same changing class, from the jails and saloons, the gutter and the homes of wealth, all bitten by this serpent of sin, intemperance." Members also held meetings in local jails, "inebriate asylums," in private homes, and in churches across the city. When a local saloonkeeper invited them to speak before his patrons and lead a Sabbath evening prayer meeting, hundreds attended. Before long, members in Brooklyn, for example had organized a flourishing juvenile society, and in the first saloon they put out of business, they founded a restaurant and inn that became an important part of their work, providing free meals and lodgings. Some saloons were closed and no liquor was sold on Sundays in others.[5]

Subsequent references to Quinton's temperance activities are scant. In an 1877 temperance publication, she was described as "a faithful worker" presenting the association's message in "every town and village in [New York] state." That same year in the *Third Annual Report* of the Brooklyn branch, she was listed as a member of the executive committee. The previous June, she had served as a delegate to the International Temperance Conference in Philadelphia.[6] Presumably she engaged in traditional organizing work, preparing propaganda, giving addresses, encouraging others to join, and leading an occasional prayer meeting. In January 1877, identified as Mrs. A. C. Swanson, she gave an evening Bible reading at the Tabernacle Baptist Church.[7]

The society in which she lived expected women in Quinton's position to become involved in benevolent work. According to Lori D. Ginzberg, "middle-and upper-class women of the antebellum era shared a language that described their benevolent work as Christian, their means as fundamentally moral, and their mandate as uniquely female." Some women attacked liquor, others eradicated slavery, yet others established "training programs and shelters."[8] Although conceived decades earlier, this belief still dominated American society. Quinton recognized its significance in her 1892 WNIA address when she wrote that the "duty of freeing Indians from their disabilities . . . touched upon the centuries-old and divine call to women, often to lead and always to share in moral movements."[9] Ginzberg notes "the ideology of female moral superiority was a central component of nineteenth-century domesticity, or the 'cult of true womanhood,'" with one of women's duties to be religious. They were "duty bound to cling to religion as the only safeguard against vice." Thus they were viewed as more fit to guard the morals of home and society. After the founding of voluntary associations, women assumed "a unique responsibility to disseminate Christian virtues and counter the materialism and greed of the nineteenth-century male."[10] Quinton, who easily fits Ginzberg's description, embraced her responsibility to use her skills to better society.

Mary Lucinda Bonney [Rambaut] cofounder of the WNIA and founder of the prestigious Chestnut Street Female Seminary in Philadelphia.
The Huntington Library, San Marino, California (RB 482860).

Exhausted by her organizing work, or possibly seeking distant new fields in which to spread her temperance message, sometime late in 1877 Quinton sailed for England. On board she met Englishman Richard Linton Quinton, a professor and lecturer on historical and astronomical topics, who at the time was living in London. They married in All Saints Church in Highgate, London, on February 21, 1878.[11] Then the new Mrs. Quinton gave a number of temperance lectures in English homes and churches. Months later, accompanied by Richard's twelve-year-old son, George Henry Quinton, the couple sailed for America, settling in Philadelphia, where sometime later Quinton fortuitously affiliated with Philadelphia's First Baptist Church, which had a long and illustrious history of engaging in missionary work. The church's minister, Rev. George Dana Boardman, was the son of Baptist missionaries. Born in Tavoy, Burma, in 1828, he was educated at Brown University and Newton Theological Institution. Because of his missionary upbringing, Boardman and his wife, Ella Covell Boardman, encouraged their parishioners to engage in missionary work. On May 17, 1877, Mrs. Boardman had organized a missionary circle, the Women's Home Missionary Society of the First Baptist Church, to pursue humanitarian work on behalf of the American Indians.[12] At the time Quinton joined the circle, Mary Lucinda Bonney was its president.

Birth of an Indian Movement

Half a century earlier, on January 20, 1819, the 1,500-member congregation of the First Baptist Church had sent a memorial petition to Congress, calling attention to Indian traders who continually defrauded the Indians, corrupting their morals and leading "them to the most contemptible ideas of civilization and religion." The memorialists requested that Congress establish regulations "to secure to the Indians a supply of such articles as they need, by fair and honorable trade," and "prevent the continuance of this base and corrupt intercourse." Signers additionally requested that provisions and appropriations be made for Indian education, "instructing them in the arts of civilized life, as the importance of the case demands."[13] Congress appointed a special committee that in January 1819 reported the need for a better system to regulate trade and to civilize the Indians. In March the Civilization Fund Act was passed, setting aside $10,000 annually to be spent by "benevolent societies" to introduce "habits and arts of civilization" to Indian tribes to provide against their "further decline and final extinction."[14]

Now almost six decades later this same First Baptist Church would once again take up Indian reform work, establishing its Women's Home Missionary Society circle, an activity about which Ginzberg observes that "denominational organizing remained the most common form of grassroots activity among women" during the nineteenth century.[15] Ella Boardman had formed her circle following an illustrated lecture delivered at the church on May 1, 1877, by George Washington Ingalls, the General Missionary to the Indians for the American Baptist Home Mission Society (ABHMS).[16] Four months earlier, on February 1, 1877, at the Michigan Avenue Baptist Church in Chicago, women had gathered to listen to Ingalls urge them to work among Indian women and children. As a result, they had founded the Chicago-based Women's Baptist Home Mission Society (WBHMS) with a call to organize affiliates. Boardman's Philadelphia missionary circle was one of many such affiliates.[17]

Three months after their initial organization, the WBHMS met in a general meeting with the male dominated ABHMS.[18] Ingalls again "presented the claims of Indian women, showing their deep degradation without the gospel." His appeal and that of others led to a resolution that the WBHMS would "carry forward the work of Christian women for the evangelization of the heathen and semi-heathen people and homes" in the country. During their first annual meeting in Cleveland in May 1878, Chicago Baptist women again resolved to undertake "work by women in homes for the elevation and Christianization of the families of the most degraded populations" in the country. During their second annual meeting in Saratoga, New York, on May 27, 1879, they took the next logical step, becoming politically involved by sending a petition to the president and Congress calling for the fulfillment of treaty provisions and the prevention of "a violation of justice and of humanity in our treatment of the Indians of the [Indian] Territory."[19]

Sixteen Philadelphia churches, including First Baptist, formed the Philadelphia Union, which supported this new WBHMS work. First Baptist member Elizabeth Arms Wayland served as its recording secretary. Her husband, Rev. Heman Lincoln Wayland, was the current editor of the *National Baptist*, which had begun publishing in 1865 to sustain denominational interests for Baptists in Pennsylvania and New Jersey. Wayland, who served as editor from 1872 to 1894, wrote and published articles and editorials on Indian affairs and played an important role in the early years of the WNIA.[20]

The Woman's American Baptist Home Mission Society (WABHMS), a rival to the Chicago group, was organized in Boston's Tremont Temple on November 14, 1877, to engage in "evangelization of the women among the freed people, the Indians, the heathen immigrants, and the new settlements of the West."[21] The all-male ABHMS, short of funds, conspired with these Boston women in 1879 to dissolve the Chicago board, placing it and its treasury under a new body administered by them. Quinton and Bonney, actively involved in the WBHMS, were in attendance at a special meeting in January 1880 to discuss this radical proposal—the disbanding of all existing women's societies and the formation of a new one in New York City to unify the work of the Home Missions. This idea had initially been proposed during the second annual WBHMS meeting in May. During their January meeting, Bonney spoke at length, deploring "the organization of a society that would relieve the woman of any part of the responsibility imposed upon them in this Society."[22] Members of the Philadelphia Union, even angrier about the loss of their Women's Society, were quoted in the December 4, 1879, issue of the *National Baptist* as being "against its motives, its spirit, and its method," describing the step as "so momentous and so revolutionary" that it was to them "unprecedented." If the Chicago group ceased to exist, they would, as Christian women, "enter upon any fields of Woman's Work for Woman through Woman, which the Providence of God may open."[23] In an almost unanimous vote, it was resolved that the Chicago and Boston societies would remain independent and hold their own annual meetings, coming together only for an annual joint meeting.[24]

A week later Quinton reported in a *National Baptist* article on an informal conference in New York City, noting representatives from both the Chicago and Boston group hashed out details, including a division of territories. Boston would be in charge of New England states; and the Chicago Society the rest of the country.[25] With major issues negotiated, their first joint meeting took place on May 27, 1880, during which Quinton described their work as "the cry of mothers to mothers," writing that the "needs of millions of unsaved mothers and homes in this land cannot appeal in vain."[26]

Three weeks earlier, on May 5, Quinton, Bonney and two other women, formally separated from the Chicago society and formed a "Committee of Ways & Means" within their Philadelphia church circle to support their own Indian work and to distribute petitions and leaflets. This small step was the beginning of what would eventually become known as the Women's National Indian Association. Why they separated is unknown, maybe to be in charge of their own work and protect monies raised, or simply out of a displeasure in any appearance of a conflict between the Chicago and Boston societies.[27] However, in mid-November to assure the press and public that there was no longer any animosity between the WBHMS and the WABHMS, Quinton, still active within the former group, wrote an article declaring harmony, fellowship and cooperation between the two societies "as inspiring to both as if there were a formal" union of the two.[28]

Thus, in the summer of 1880, Quinton and Bonney had taken the first tentative steps in the formation of their Christian women's volunteer association. Quinton would spend the next several years growing the WNIA, engaging in large scale petition drives, organizing outside of Philadelphia and adopting education as a major goal. In a Methodist Episcopal Church publication, she explained that what was also needed "along with the regular operation of law" was "at least one first-class mission in every tribe which shall include night schools for those beyond school age, domestic art and industrial teaching, medical and hospital help, instruction in gardening, farming, and the mechanic art." It would be a mission "for constant and earnest Christian teaching on week-days and on Sunday." Her challenge to her followers was "Let the patriotic Christian women who are newly ready to help this work be now heard from."[29]

3

WNIA Growth and Missionary Work, 1880–1884

Quinton's Critical Role

In an article in *Woman's Work in America* (1891), Quinton described "the labor, self-sacrifice, and heroism of women in connection with the various missionary organizations in behalf of the red man." In this piece she focused on the work of three early WNIA members, author Helen Hunt Jackson, anthropologist Alice Cunningham Fletcher, and association cofounder Mary Lucinda Bonney. After recognizing their efforts, Quinton described in great detail the early WNIA petition drives and shared with her readers a statement of praise by Henry B. Whipple, the first Protestant Episcopal Bishop of Minnesota, who described the women of WNIA as building "better than they knew."[1] What Quinton did not include was her own contribution.

It is fair to say that without Amelia Stone Quinton there would have been no WNIA. Quinton shaped the WNIA, initially as secretary, setting precedents and often determining the direction of the infant association. As president she assumed the entire burden of organizing auxiliaries and establishing mission stations from coast to coast; delivering addresses to social gatherings, women's groups, missionary societies, and church associations; conferring with government officials; writing petitions and their accompanying memorial letters as well as letters to Indian Office (Office of Indian Affairs [OIA]) officials requesting support for missionary work; and writing many articles for the association's monthly periodical, *The Indian's Friend*. In fact, Quinton also served several different times as the periodical's editor, determining its direction. In 1883 she took on an additional role, that of secretary of the Missionary Committee, and later its chairmanship, requiring her to not only visit WNIA mission stations, which she did for the first time in the Indian Territory in 1884, but to write the lengthy annual missionary reports. She selected mission sites and wrote Indian Office officials for land grants or whatever else she felt was necessary for the work. She did not hesitate to travel to Washington, DC, to visit Indian commissioners or secretaries of the interior in their offices to reinforce earlier requests. Quinton's organizing tasks required extensive travel, especially as she expanded the association beyond Philadelphia's city limits and visited mission sites. For 1884 alone she traveled more than 10,000 miles throughout Pennsylvania and neighboring states.[2]

Through her critical and voluminous correspondence, Quinton supervised the building of missionary cottages and chapels, and supported government teachers and field matrons, and WNIA-sponsored physicians and missionaries on Indian reservations. She often determined which missionary society should be involved and handpicked WNIA missionaries when possible, then summarized their letters for *The Indian's Friend*, deciding what information should be passed on to the membership. She confronted Indian agents who blocked her efforts and forged cordial working relationships with Indian commissioners and Interior secretaries. She gave informative reports before the prestigious U.S. Board of Indian Commissioners (BIC) and the Lake Mohonk Conference and officiated at annual WNIA meetings. She had no equal in the association.

A New Origin Story

According to all its institutional literature, the WNIA was founded in 1879. But, in fact, it had actually begun two years earlier.[3] In a brief autobiographical sketch written in 1894, Mary Lucinda Bonney reminisced that the WNIA had been founded when she learned from newspapers that Missouri Senator George V. Vest had been pressing Congress for more than a dozen years to open up Indian-held lands in Oklahoma for settlement. Surprised that a Senator would urge "this moral wrong upon our government," she had turned to Quinton, and together they pledged to "awaken the conscience of Congress and of the people." In her sketch, Bonney clearly stated that the year was 1879, and that became, for all institutional literature, the founding date of the Women's National Indian Association.[4] Bonney never once mentioned G. W. Ingalls, the General Missionary to the Indians for the ABHMS, or the Chicago-based WBHMS, founded in 1877, although clearly both she and Quinton had been inspired by Ingalls's call to action and had participated in these earlier meetings. Neither Ingalls nor the WBHMS ever appeared in any WNIA publication. Although no reason is given, a hint may be found in a *New York Times* article singling out Ingalls for actions as agent that could have been either negligence or fraud, depending on how one viewed it. Although between $40,000 and $50,000 had been disbursed to him while agent, his successor, A. J. Barnes, said he "could not find any results," which left him with no money or means as creditors clamored for payment.[5] Even though absolved, Ingalls was dismissed by the ABHMS as its missionary.[6]

The official founding of the WNIA was viewed as occurring during the April and May 1879 meetings of the Women's Home Missionary Society of the First Baptist Church, when Bonney informed the membership of Senator Vest's activities in the Indian Territory. Viewing his action as creating "a vast hindrance to Indian missions," and as a "great injury to the moral sense" of the country, she had then requested that Reverend Wayland prepare a protest petition to be taken to Congress. When the petition copies were left unnoticed in the pews and the missionary society adjourned for the summer, Bonney turned to Quinton for assistance. Thus, the WNIA was born, according to its official history.[7]

Whatever its origin, the partnership formed by Quinton and Bonney was a natural one. They were both born in the Burned-over District of upstate New York, known for evangelical revivals and social reforms; each had likely taught school in the South and had married a Baptist clergyman.[8] Both also joined Philadelphia's First Baptist Church and had a lengthy history of earlier reform and benevolent work. Bonney was a member of the Woman's Union Missionary Society of America for Heathen Lands and the Women's Home Mission Society of her church while Quinton had volunteered in charity asylums, infirmaries, prisons, and almshouses and had organized for the WCTU. Sharing a friendship, faith, experience, and values, they founded the WNIA, expanding women's sphere to include work in the public arena, spreading the virtues of "true womanhood" to American Indian women. Bonney's profitable boarding school, the Chestnut Street Seminary, provided funding while Quinton handled all the necessary daily details.

Early WNIA Petition Drives

In Quinton and Bonney's earliest efforts to secure for the Indians "a just, protective and fostering Indian policy," they turned to petitioning, a "feminine tactic" that did not require "women to step out of the normal circle of their private lives."[9] According to Susan Zaeske, a petition, by its very nature was "characterized by a humble tone," sent by a subordinate to a superior to redress grievances, obligating officials to receive and respond regardless the subject; its "supplicatory nature held radical potential for women."[10] Decades earlier, Catharine Beecher, educator, author of *A Treatise on Domestic Economy,* principal of the Hartford Female Seminary, daughter of prominent Presbyterian cleric, Lyman Beecher, and sister to Harriet Beecher Stowe, had initiated the first women's national petition drive to protest Cherokee removal. Moved by the Cherokee's acceptance of "civilized ways," in late 1829 she wrote a petition hoping to convince Congress that President Andrew Jackson's Indian removal policy was misguided. Believing that the shaping of the American character was women's responsibility, she articulated their stand against removal as a question of piety and benevolence, building "a case for women's national political advocacy" without demanding political rights.[11]

Unlike Beecher, whose petition was sent anonymously, Quinton sent her petition openly. In the summer of 1879, she mailed a one-page flyer, *Earnest Work Needed*, to women's missionary groups and other benevolent societies. With her name in bold print, Quinton reminded the petition's recipients that the presentation of this petition to Congress "for righteous dealing, by covenant-keeping with that oppressed people" was drawing near, and encouraged them to hold popular meetings, complete with reports to the local press, to help "swell the plea to Congress, which the great perils of a helpless people and the crimes of this nation against them imperatively call forth."[12] Like Beecher, Quinton deferred to men, explaining that the women were not suggesting "any political policy to be pursued, leaving such matters to wise statesmanship." The petition was printed at the bottom with a note that it could "be copied on sheets of ruled foolscap for signatures."[13]

The petition was presented to President Rutherford B. Hayes on February 14, 1880, by missionary circle members Bonney, Mrs. Mariné J. Chase, and Ella Covell Boardman.[14] Measuring 300-feet long with 13,000 signatures from fifteen states and addressed to the president and Congress, it "earnestly" requested that officials take steps to prevent the encroachment upon the Indian Territory and to guard Indian rights guaranteed by the "faith of the nation." As an accompanying memorial letter, Quinton had written *An Earnest Petition Needed: A Few Historical Facts*, a three-page leaflet presenting facts of the government's mistreatment of the Five Civilized Tribes, inquiring if "the 30,000 Indian Christians of the Territory and of our western frontiers [should] look in vain to us to plead their righteous cause?"[15] Three days later Quinton and Bonney spoke before the Philadelphia Union of the Women's Home Mission Society, Bonney giving her account of the interview between President Hayes and her missionary circle members during the presentation, and Quinton appealing for cooperation in the Indian work.[16]

On May 5, 1880, Bonney suggested to Quinton, Boardman, and Chase that they form a Committee of Ways & Means within the missionary circle and broaden their support by securing a release from the First Baptist Church, becoming nonsectarian. Thus, by their first formal meeting on December 11, 1880, calling themselves the Central Indian Committee, the eight committee women represented five different Protestant denominations. Chase served as chair, Quinton as secretary, and Boardman as treasurer. During the December 31 meeting, Quinton suggested they change their name to the Indian Treaty-Keeping Association, and by the January meeting they had become the Indian Treaty-Keeping Committee.[17]

Quinton and Chase carried the group's second petition, signed by 50,000 people from all thirty-eight states and several territories, to Washington in late January 1881. The petitioners requested honorable governmental dealings with all Indians, the prevention of white encroachment upon reservations, and the recognition of Indian treaties unless changed by the consent of both parties. Quinton, in her memorial letter, described the signatories as representing all occupations and ranks of society, evidence that "the *moral* sentiment of those classes who largely make and control public opinion already requires governmental faithfulness to our Indian treaties."[18] Massachusetts Senator Henry Laurens Dawes, chair of the Senate Indian Committee, presented the petition and letter to the Senate, while four days later Gilbert De La Matyr, a Methodist Episcopal minister from Indiana, made a similar presentation to the House of Representatives.[19] The day before Dawes's appearance, New England author and poet Helen Hunt Jackson had placed a copy of *A Century of Dishonor* on the desk of every congressman, challenging them to be the first Congress to "redeem the name of the United States from the stain of a century of dishonor!"[20] She then joined Quinton to listen to Senate debates, and together, they called upon various congressmen to support the WNIA petition.[21] Jackson had participated in both petition drives, securing signatures at John Hopkins University, Fisk, and Harvard for the first petition, and during two days in December had obtained one hundred signatures for the second one. In mid-January she informed Quinton she had just sent in a roll with about four hundred additional signatures.[22]

Several months later, on March 12, 1881, Quinton thanked Senator Dawes for his support, enclosing a copy of their newest pamphlet, hoping for his approval. She inquired if in his judgment her association should continue their efforts to help form public opinion "to hasten justice & mercy in the fulfillment of our national covenants to helpless peoples." Dawes recommended they continue their efforts, offering the women the use of his congressional franking privileges to send their literature for free. Early the following month she accepted his offer.[23] Quinton and her small but determined group of women had just succeeded in attracting the support of one of Washington's most powerful senators.

Author and reformer Helen Hunt Jackson inspired the WNIA to establish a missionary station among the Mission Indians of Southern California, which they called the Ramona Mission after her novel *Ramona*.
C.C. Pierce Collection, The Huntington Library, San Marino, California (photCL Pierce 08629).

The fledgling WNIA continued to undergo change. In mid-March 1881, over-burdened with other Christian work, Chase resigned and Bonney was unanimously elected to succeed her. Quinton, praised for "awakening public sentiment in favor of justice to [the] Indians" during her first two years of service, remained as general secretary. She was recognized for her "earnestness, devotion

& perseverance" bringing a vitality to their Indian work, and for her "rare ability, discrimination & judgment" in integrating facts from government records into their official pamphlets, leaflets, and various circulars. With a new leader at the helm, the committee vowed to pursue their work with renewed energy, relying on God's "promises to overthrow all injustice & to lift up the oppressed."[24]

On June 3, 1881, during the fifth meeting of the executive committee, Quinton recorded the adoption of a new constitution to awaken "a Christian public sentiment which shall move our Government to just dealing with the Indian tribes among us," as well as a name change to the Indian Treaty-Keeping and Protective Association (ITKPA). Their goal remained the same—to circulate organizational literature; send memorials to Congress; hold parlor and public meetings; appeal to Christian clergymen, editors, churches and societies; and send out press articles. Bonney remained president, Quinton continued as general secretary, and Ella Boardman became treasurer. The executive board, representing eight Protestant denominations, would remain in Philadelphia, but the association would expand to include new auxiliaries outside the city.[25]

In late June, Quinton began organizing in Amsterdam and Gloversville, New York, then in Western New York and in neighboring states. In October, she attended a meeting of the Association for the Advancement of Women in Buffalo, New York, taking the opportunity to give a brief talk and become a member.[26] By mid-November she had visited Hartford, Connecticut; Providence, Rhode Island; and Boston, Massachusetts, soon adding New Jersey, and on February 1, 1882, organized a state committee in Wilmington, Delaware. Wasting little time, in between her organizing efforts she answered her correspondence and wrote press articles and circulars to be sent to state committees. Unfortunately, this rapid growth soon began to drain the association's finances, prompting Quinton to suggest that dues be set at an annual fee of $1, with $10 for life membership, and $25 for honorary membership.[27]

Quinton's first two petitions had been in defense of Indian rights, but as she dug deeper into the history of treaties and the government's Indian policy for her leaflets, pamphlets, and flyers, she gradually came to see what she perceived as the negative influence of the communally held reservation system. Thus, along with her usual demand for the maintenance of treaties, recognition of Indian rights, and common and industrial schools, she included a provision in her third petition to break up reservations into smaller individual parcels—an individualizing of land holding—a fee-simple title of at least one hundred and sixty acres granted to reservation Indians and to be held in severalty (owned by an individual), inalienable for twenty years.[28] In her accompanying memorial letter, Quinton described her fledgling association as composed of "patriotic Christian women" calling upon Congress to pay attention to the "suffering of undefended, ever-endangered Indian women and children." She described "the plea of Indian women for the sacred shield of law" as that of "all womanhood, indeed, on their behalf to you as legislators and as men." Years later she viewed this petition as a new departure in the government's treatment of the Indians—one including "the features of later government policy." Dawes went further, declaring the new federal Indian policy that was emerging as "born of and nursed" by the WNIA.[29]

This petition, circulated in late 1881 in every state and territory, measured 400 feet long and was wrapped in white bunting tied with red, white, and blue ribbons.[30] It was signed by 100,000 individuals, from nearly 1,000 churches, including the entire ministry of three protestant denominations in Philadelphia; presidents, professors, and students from theological seminaries, colleges and universities, including Yale, Harvard, Cornell, Washington and Lee, and Brown; editors of leading periodicals; boards of hundreds of missionary and benevolent societies; members of art, literary, and social clubs; prominent judges; and governors John D. Long of Massachusetts and John P. St. John of Kansas.[31] Quinton and Harriet Ward Foote Hawley, president of the association's Washington, DC, auxiliary and wife of Connecticut senator Joseph R. Hawley,[32] and Eliza Stout Keifer, wife of Joseph Warren Keifer, seven-term congressman from Ohio and speaker of the House, presented the petition on February 21, 1882, to President Chester A. Arthur. It was then carried to the Senate Marble Room where Quinton and her companions listened to Dawes's presentation followed by an extremely heated debate. Four days later it was presented to the House.[33]

Senators Preston B. Plumb of Kansas and Henry Teller of Colorado vehemently criticized the women's message as much too simple and sentimental, prompting Dawes to come to their defense. Residents of Kansas and Colorado had continually overrun Indian lands, resulting in Indian reprisals, and therefore the views of these western senators contrasted sharply with those of eastern reformers far removed from Indian wars. Years later Quinton described Dawes's defense as "brilliant" and "of thrilling eloquence" in telling of "outrages upon Indians by the Government and white settlers." Merely viewing the "animated conversation" of Dawes, Plumb, and Teller as an occasion "of great interest," Quinton recognized the senators' fervent opinions as "Western impatience with Indians, and antagonism to Eastern sympathy."[34]

Because the debate was printed in the *Congressional Record*, Quinton remained in Washington for three weeks to secure its reprinting in pamphlet form for distribution to editors, pastors, and members of state committees. While in the capital, she took the opportunity to address several drawing-room meetings; conferred with Senator Dawes, Secretary of the Interior Samuel Kirkwood, and other congressmen; organized an associate committee in Washington; interviewed a Choctaw chief; and attended a reception where she met prominent ethnologist Frank Hamilton Cushing and a delegation of Zuñi Indians. On the way home she organized a state committee in Baltimore.[35] Quinton was never one to waste time.

More Institutional Changes

From mid-March to mid-May 1882, a reenergized Quinton wrote a leaflet entitled "A Letter to You," and articles for the *Council Fire &Arbitrator*, the *National Baptist*, the *Cherokee Advocate* (published in the Indian Territory), and the *Philadelphia Inquirer.*[36] She interviewed a number of pastors and editors; spoke before two social gatherings; made several visits to Germantown, Pennsylvania to organize an auxiliary; and addressed the students at Bonney's Chestnut Street Seminary, four church missionary meetings, a literary club, and a drawing-room meeting. She also recruited women to serve as association officers, raised several hundred dollars, and sent out an official article to sixty editors. In mid-May she organized the Philadelphia Indian Association.[37] Then several days later, accompanied by Bonney, Quinton attended the third joint anniversary meeting of the WBHMS and WABHMS in New York City, remaining until May 27 to attend the fifth annual meeting of the WBHMS, as she continued to serve as head of its resolutions committee.[38]

Wearing many hats, Quinton kept to a grueling schedule, juggling not only her obligations to the Women's Home Mission societies but driving her own association forward. During their October 3, 1882, meeting, the ITKPA executive committee held two important votes. The first was to change the mode of circulating their petitions, relegating the work to the state committees instead of to Quinton, thereby freeing her to concentrate on her organizing efforts. The second change was the inclusion of educational work, requiring a revision of their constitution to reflect this new undertaking. Now calling themselves the National Indian Association, they described themselves as Christian women "deeply deploring the long catalogue of unjust dealings of [the] Government with the Indians," intent on awakening public sentiment to force the government to adopt a policy of "equity and justice" and to engage in educational and missionary work among the Indians to hasten their "civilization," Christianization, and enfranchisement.[39]

During November 1882, Quinton addressed fourteen Indian meetings, reviewed or organized auxiliaries in Wilmington, West Philadelphia, and Germantown, and spoke before the Bi-Centennial Anniversary of the Peace Society and at the Annual Meeting of the Women's Foreign Mission Society of the Methodist Episcopal Church. Her address was so compelling that the Methodist Society not only endorsed the aims of the WNIA but passed a resolution resolving to sign the association's current memorial to Congress.[40] And to promote the association's adoption of Indian education as a new goal, Quinton had written an article on the Carlisle Indian Industrial School for the *National Baptist.* Then on December 4 she organized the Brooklyn Indian Association, followed the next day by the New York City Indian Association (NYCIA) at the home of Mrs. William Earl Dodge.[41]

WNIA Missionary Work

In December 1882, the work of the WNIA changed markedly with the founding of the Indian Rights Association (IRA). This male-dominated reform group was better positioned to exert political pressure on Congress to bring civil rights, general education, "civilization," and citizenship to the Indian population, largely because they employed Charles C. Painter as a full-time lobbyist (agent) in Washington, DC.[42] "In hearty accord as to their objects," several months later IRA founder Herbert Welsh asked Quinton to prepare "resolutions of moral union" for their combined efforts. The two associations resolved to appoint a mutual advisory board, send an executive board representative to one another's meetings, and make formal presentations at one another's conventions. With an agreement that the IRA would not allow female members, the women changed their name to the Women's National Indian Association, adopting a new constitution on October 27, 1883.[43] WNIA members and officers praised the arrangement. Bonney, WNIA president at the time, acknowledged the IRA's ability to pursue the "very objects which had previously wholly occupied" the women's attention, while months later, her successor, Mary Lowe Dickinson, described the IRA as a strong younger brother massing "its forces against the legal and political barriers in the way of Indian elevation."[44] The IRA in turn credited the women with planning and executing the work which they were now pursuing.[45]

With the IRA and Painter assuming much of the women's political burden, with the exception of petitioning, the WNIA returned to its former mission-circle roots and began missionary work among Indian women, ministering to "their great sufferings from barbarism," enlightening "their physical, mental, and spiritual ignorance," teaching them "of a Saviour longing to help them."[46] To implement this new task, Quinton set guidelines for mission stations at the February 13, 1883, board meeting. "With entire unanimity" the board adopted the work, resolving to not duplicate that of existing societies or to aid government schools. Instead, they would concentrate on funding pioneer schools and engage in mission work among some of the sixty-eight tribes listed in Indian Commissioner Hiram Price's 1882 report as having no resident missionary. As Quinton explained a decade later, their plan was "to get land, by purchase or gift, to build the cottage and chapel, [and] to establish workers in them." Once a mission was completed, the WNIA would then turn it over to a society "desirous to take the mission for permanent care." She had concluded: "How often, too, has woman's inspiration led the way, or clasped behind the throne the sceptered hand that, lifted by her lesser grasp, has opened a royal gate to a new age."[47]

According to Helen Wanken some members challenged this divergence from "the goal of trying to guarantee civil rights for the Indians," but Quinton, who had written the initial resolution and a second one in mid-October, was in the driver's seat, "aggressively" pushing missionary work, and showing her "biases for the type of work she wanted accomplished and the kind of missionaries she wanted to accomplish it."[48] The original intent to employ missionaries and teachers only from evangelical Protestant churches drew strong objection from the Massachusetts Indian Association (MIA), whose members included Unitarians who practiced a more liberal theology. The executive board compromised, rewriting the resolution to replace "evangelical" with "Christian."[49]

Bonney, now almost seventy, was appointed to chair the new Missionary Committee with Quinton as secretary, responsible for writing the reports and visiting stations. When Quinton took over as chairman in December 1885, she acquired even more control over the work, making this committee the most recognized of all the WNIA departments. In 1951 when the association disbanded, it had established more than sixty mission sites from Florida to California, with more than fifty founded under Quinton's direction.[50]

Initial WNIA missionary work began in 1884, when the board voted to work among the Ponca, Otoe, and Pawnee Indians in the Indian Territory. In May, a Miss Howard was sent to the Poncas and a Miss McGlashan to the Otoes. Early work among the Pawnee was transferred that July to the Women's Methodist Episcopal Board while the other two stations were transferred in June 1887 to the

Women's Methodist Episcopal Home Missionary Society.[51] The Indian Office, recognizing that the WNIA's "civilizing" and Christianizing efforts matched its own goals, opened up reservations to these resourceful women, granting them land for the building of missionary cottages and chapels and offering them free use of abandoned federal buildings for housing and educational work.

Although the Missionary Committee was the most enduring, the WNIA had established an efficient organizational framework with a number of standing committees or departments. A Committee on Petitions distributed auxiliary-written articles and organized petition drives, while the Indian Home Building Department provided loans for the building of modest Indian homes, and the Indian Education Committee offered off-reservation training. The Young People's Department encouraged an interest in Indian reform, with older children raising money and their smaller companions making scrapbooks and other items to be sent to Indian children. There also was an Indian Civilization Department, a Hospital Department, and a Committee on Indian Libraries. The Committee on Temperance Appeals, established in 1893, served as a clearinghouse to send literature to agents, missionaries, and teachers.[52]

Quinton's 1883 Activities

On January 2, 1883, Quinton began her year's organizing efforts by establishing the New Jersey Indian Association at Newark.[53] By year's end, the WNIA had circulated "a million pages of information and appeal[s] on behalf of justice to Indians." And as early as March, Quinton had founded twenty-six auxiliaries in Maine, New Hampshire, Massachusetts, Connecticut, New York, New Jersey, Pennsylvania, Delaware, Maryland, Ohio, and Michigan, and the District of Columbia. She eagerly encouraged women to invite their friends from every religious denomination in their city, town, or village to meet either at home or in a church parlor and organize into a branch of an existing state association, of the national association, or to form an "Indian committee." The latter was the least complicated, with no constitution or regular meetings, simply bringing members together occasionally for specific work or to hear a speaker. To aid organizers, the WNIA published several pamphlets with tips, including an order for business meetings as well as practical suggestions for topics. In her pamphlet, Quinton suggested that auxiliaries establish libraries and include her friend Helen Hunt Jackson's expose of the government's Indian policy, *A Century of Dishonor*. In later pamphlets Quinton would add Jackson's California Indian novel, *Ramona*, to the list.[54]

The WNIA's adoption of education as a goal prompted Quinton to spend August 9 to 12 at Ocean Grove, New Jersey, attending the second meeting of the National Education Assembly. She was one of eleven reformers invited to address the Indian issue.[55] The Assembly had been organized the previous year in part because of Congress's failure to pass Interior Secretary Henry Teller's educational bill but also to provide a platform for the country's Christian educators, party leaders, and churches to gather annually and encourage public sentiment in favor of the education and elevation of the "illiterate and degraded masses."[56] This year more speakers had been invited and the range of topics had been broadened. Included among the speakers on Indian issues were two members of the recently formed Indian Rights Association, Henry S. Pancoast and Herbert Welsh. Pancoast addressed the Indian's legal status, while Welsh spoke on the issue of Christianity and its relationship to Indian "civilization." A third association member, Charles C. Painter, who was also the corresponding secretary of the National Education Committee, presented his committee's work for the year.[57] One can image that Quinton, fairly new to Indian reform, took this opportunity to become acquainted with all three IRA members. Two years later during her first Lake Mohonk Conference she would listen to Painter address the present condition of the Indian question. In an association pamphlet, she described his address as "stirring" as he demanded that "obstacles in the way of Indian progress must be swept away, and the hands of legislators must be untied." His strong stand must have resonated with Quinton for over the coming years she was continually forcing aside obstacles.[58]

During her August 1883 National Education Assembly address, Quinton emphatically declared that "woman's work and heart" was needed to solve the Indian problem, "and *because* these are *needed*, *God* has already employed both." Her association, she explained, now representing ten Protestant denominations with auxiliaries in twenty states, was cooperating with hundreds of churches, publishing articles in religious and ordinary newspapers, and circulating and presenting an annual petition to Congress. The WNIA, initially drawn to this work by sympathy toward Indian women and children, had in late 1882 broadened their goal to include the promotion of Indian education. They intended to organize reservation mission schools to "teach Indian children and young parents how to speak English," keeping them "in civilized and Christian fashion," and providing knowledge and self-support to those unable to attend Eastern boarding schools, preventing them from growing up in "barbarism." She informed her audience that "where the barbarism, squalor, vice, suffering, and dense ignorance are, there should the Christian teacher be with the remedies of 'light.'" Once when an Indian agent declared that any lady would shrink from these Indian "savages," Quinton had assured him "not if she had a really Christian spirit," denouncing the idea that Indians were "naturally more revengeful and cruel than other races." Quinton exclaimed: "The Christian lady is solemnly covenanted to such work, and the history of missions assure the success of it."[59]

Drawing on past histories, Quinton reminded her audience that such tragedies as the Sand Creek massacre in 1864 and the Northern Cheyenne odyssey of Dull Knife and Little Wolf a decade later were acts perpetrated by whites, not by Indians. "That the Indian is a man of force and character is overwhelmingly proved by the fact that he has survived our treatment of him," she continued. "Not even death can daunt him." Women could do much to secure righteous legislation on their behalf by "circulating information about our past unjust and imbecile Indian policy" and by bringing attention to Secretary Teller's educational demands. Pastors, philanthropists, educators, statesmen, and thoughtful people were endorsing their movement. If only ten thousand Christian women would send for WNIA leaflets and join them, the helpless Indians would be given a fair opportunity to grow "into manhood, citizenship, and Christian character," she concluded.[60]

Quinton Tours the West, 1884

Although only hundreds, not the thousands that she had called for in her August 1883 address joined the WNIA, Quinton remained undaunted, delivering addresses almost every week in 1884, speaking before ninety-nine different groups, in Protestant churches, private homes, YMCA meetings, Baptist Home Missionary Societies, and ministers' meetings, establishing a pattern for the next two decades. She also organized ten new state branches that year and wrote at least one pamphlet, *A Few Facts*, in which she called the government's policy "a despotism without republic," describing the Indian's lack of legal rights, subjected to the whims of their agents with removal at any time. She pleaded that "every Christian pray and labor, expressing moral power in all the needed acts of consecrated Christian citizenship."[61]

Quinton had started 1884 with a late January address before a ladies meeting in the Broadway Tabernacle in New York City before quickly moving through Connecticut, Rhode Island, Maine, New Hampshire, Washington, DC, and Delaware addressing Indian associations, missionary societies, and church union meetings before speaking to the Brooklyn Indian Association on April 4; then a public meeting of the NYCIA at Calvary Baptist Church on April 8; the yearly meeting of the NYCIA in the chapel of the Broadway Tabernacle on November 13; and ending with an address in Brooklyn in mid-December.[62]

In what must have been a highlight of the year, from late June to early September Quinton ventured west for the first time. An organizing tour took her to Minnesota, Dakota Territory, Iowa, Nebraska, the Indian Territory, and Kansas, visiting several reservations and enduring primitive travel accommodations. Accompanied by several unidentified individuals, she began with an address in Minneapolis in the home of Mayor George A. Pilsbury on June 30, having organized in both that city and St. Paul several days earlier. From there she headed to the Great Sioux Reservation to visit the mission station of Oahe, founded by Rev. Thomas L. Riggs in the early 1870s at Peoria Bottom on the Missouri River's eastern side in modern day South Dakota. Upon arriving, Quinton viewed what she described as the "mysterious seemingly trackless 'Great Sioux Reserve,'" anxiously awaiting seeing her first "wild Indians."[63]

Quinton met with Mary C. Collins, a Congregational missionary, who had been in residence at Oahe since 1875. They attended an Indian prayer meeting in the mission's chapel, led by Yellow Hawk, a Christian Indian pastor. On Friday, July 4, Quinton gave a Bible reading to the Indian women while Collins interpreted, and on Sunday they attended Yellow Hawk's sermon, listening to familiar hymns sung in Lakota. Then Quinton and her party spent four days traversing the reservation. They began with a small iron skiff ride across the Missouri River, transferring to a wagon that had been taken apart and reassembled on the other side. She described her pleasure viewing the hills and buttes, experiencing an unbelievable spectacle in the night-time sky camping under a full moon, then sleeping beneath their wagon, wrapped in buffalo robes. They visited several villages, made house calls, and attended a meeting with Indian women and girls, sitting in a circle outside an Indian lodge. At Cherry Creek they slept in a new lodge constructed around twenty-foot poles. A now reinvigorated Quinton returned to Pierre and organized the Dakota Women's Indian Association on July 14.[64]

On August 1, 1884, Quinton was driven from Bancroft, Nebraska, to the Omaha Reservation to pay a visit to Thomas Henry Tibbles, whose eastern speaking tour had resulted in the formation of the Boston Committee, and his wife, Susette La Flesche, Standing Bear's interpreter. Two days later Quinton gave a Bible reading and met with father, Joseph La Flesche, the last Omaha chief.[65] Later in council with Joseph and other tribal members, Quinton listened to them explain why they were capable of handling their own affairs, a sentiment they had clearly expressed in "a petition they desired to send to Washington." Moved by their earnest argument

Congregational missionary Mary C. Collins, who served in the Oahe mission station on the Great Sioux Reservation in modern day South Dakota. She hosted Quinton during her 1884 visit. *South Dakota State Historical Society.*

and the "reasonableness" of their demands, Quinton agreed to carry this petition to Washington for them. After leaving the reservation, she went on to Omaha where, on August 7, she organized the Women's Indian Association of Nebraska before traveling on to the Indian Territory (modern-day Oklahoma), where she would witness "the squalor, the helplessness, the heathenism, of unused, and in some cases fine capabilities," describing "unspeakable needs of many kinds," especially Christian instruction.[66]

Leaving the Omaha Reservation in early August 1884, Quinton set out for the Indian Territory for her first visit to the WNIA mission among the Poncas. She needed to see for herself the condition of these Indians, forcibly exiled from their Nebraska homeland in 1877—their numbers further reduced by Standing Bear and his followers' flight to Nebraska. "We saw them, a helpless looking hungry horde of men and women, gathered at the agency headquarters for their rations," she wrote. "What a spectacle it was in the last quarter of the nineteenth century, in a Christian land," she continued. She was sickened by the "starvation, abject helplessness, misery and degradation" she witnessed, describing the women and children holding up their ration tickets on poles to attract the official's attention. From the Ponca station Quinton traveled the nine miles to the WNIA Otoe station, there witnessing the Indians in council with their agent, and then headed for their former Pawnee mission. During her stay she conferred with the WNIA missionaries and visited several Indian homes.[67] With this initial visit to the first WNIA stations, Quinton would establish a precedent she followed for the remainder of her presidency, that of visiting every new station at least once if at all possible. At times, while traversing the western landscape on other tours, she also selected sites for potential stations.

Quinton departed the Indian Territory on August 22, and three days later established a branch association at Topeka, Kansas. In Chicago on September 12 and 13, she described WNIA's missionary work before the Women's Congregational Board and the Women's Presbyterian Board, inquiring if their boards were willing to take over one of these Indian Territory stations. Several days later she organized in Indianapolis and near the end of September visited both Cleveland, Ohio, and Rochester, New York. She returned to Philadelphia in November, having traveled a total of 10,000 miles.[68] In mid-November she addressed the NYCIA describing her recent tour.[69] And then on November 19, 1884, she attended the WNIA's annual conference at St. George's Hall in Philadelphia along with the delegates from nine states. The speaker for their evening meeting was Herbert Welsh of the IRA, who described his association's Indian work. Fifty Indian students from Lincoln Institute provided entertainment.[70]

Under the expert guidance of Quinton, the WNIA had grown and prospered during its first half dozen years. Originating from within a missionary society in a Baptist church, Quinton, Bonney, and the handful of other members had declared their independence from any particular church, immediately broadening their appeal to other Christian women. Their well-organized petition drives were successful and their third one generated 100,000 signatures. With the founding of the male-dominated IRA, in late 1882, the WNIA adopted missionary work as the men took over much of their political work. But it was Quinton's organizational skill that had pushed the association forward, out of Pennsylvania, with her first two auxiliaries in June 1881 in New York State. By the time of their November 1884 annual meeting, Quinton had founded thirty-eight auxiliaries, twenty-seven of which were state branches.[71] Her influence continued to expand over the next handful of years, with the WNIA benefiting. One benefit was the

WNIA advisory board, which appeared for the first time in the 1887 annual report but was built on years of personal connection and support Quinton had nurtured and inspired from the beginning.

Quinton and the WNIA Advisory Board

As the WNIA was the only Indian reform association solely run by women, Quinton and her membership chose some of the most powerful men in the country to join their all-male advisory board. Because the WNIA had emerged from within a Christian missionary society, it was logical that half of the members of the first board in 1887 would be clerics. They included Rev. Lyman Abbott, author and editor-in-chief of the *Christian Union* and successor to Henry Ward Beecher of the Plymouth Congregational Church in Brooklyn Heights, New York; Rev. George Dana Boardman, pastor of Philadelphia's First Baptist Church; and the Rt. Rev. William Hobart Hare, Episcopal Bishop of South Dakota and missionary to the Sioux. Rev. William Hayes Ward, Congregational pastor and editor of the New York *Independent* joined the following year.[72]

From the beginning, Quinton scheduled many addresses in Protestant churches in and around Philadelphia, presumably depending upon the ministers' good will. Using these venues was brilliant as they were easily accessible for public meetings and good locations from which to address local missionary societies, church union meetings, or minister's conferences. As she expanded beyond Philadelphia, she could count on finding churches en route whose ministers willingly opened their doors to her. Occasionally, in out of the way places, she would hold a meeting in the home of the local minister. Using a church also enabled her to recommend that those willing to establish an auxiliary "hold the monthly meeting of the local Indian Association in some central church-parlor or vestry, as all then feel at liberty to attend, and thus larger meetings are gathered."[73] In 1882, she made a public plea to pastors of all churches to support the WNIA by endorsing their current petition and handing out their leaflets. "The Association earnestly begs the above aid, because of the wrongs and sufferings of Indians," she wrote, requesting their support "by prayerful effort, to end our nation's long record of loss, suffering, and guilt from our treatment of Indians."[74]

To further support their goals of reforming the government's Indian policy and providing Indian education, the WNIA also selected prominent educators, reformers, and government officials to be on their advisory board. Educators included Samuel Chapman Armstrong, founder of Hampton Normal and Agricultural Institute, which educated African Americans and later Indians, and General

Clinton B. Fisk, founder of Fisk University. Merrill E. Gates, former president of Rutgers and Amherst colleges joined in 1890. The most prominent political figure was Massachusetts senior Senator, Henry Laurens Dawes. Reformers included Albert K. Smiley, founder of the Lake Mohonk Conference of Friends of the Indian, who was joined in 1890 by Herbert Welsh, the influential leader of the Indian Rights Association (IRA).[75] The presence of Smiley and Welsh on the board enabled Quinton to seek advice and also work more efficiently with them and their respective organizations to promote WNIA goals.

Smiley was a member of the Board of Indian Commissioners (BIC), a powerful group of philanthropists and humanitarians nominated by major Protestant denominations authorized, among other powers, to exercise joint control with the Interior department in the disbursement of Indian appropriations and in the purchase and inspection of Indian supplies.[76] Smiley, displeased with the limited time the BIC had to deal with issues brought before them, had founded the Lake Mohonk Conference. Every autumn from 1883 to 1916, reformers, educators, government officials, and others interested in Indian reform gathered as a forum. To provide a link to the government's Indian policy, the BIC held one of their official sessions at Lake Mohonk. More important, Smiley ensured that certain traditions of his Quaker faith were practiced at the conference, including female equality, affording Quinton, who first attended in 1885, and other WNIA members equal access to conference activities.[77] Every fall Quinton looked forward to her personal invitation from Smiley to Lake Mohonk, where she ably presented the WNIA's annual missionary report.

Welsh's presence on the WNIA advisory board was of great importance, especially because the IRA was also headquartered in Philadelphia. Although most of the founders of the IRA were Episcopalians, Quinton's influential pastor, George Dana Boardman, was at the founding meeting, drawing her even closer to the IRA.[78] More significantly, the founding of this male-dominated association enabled the women of the WNIA to return to their original missionary roots. Founded as a "non-partisan, non-sectarian organization," the IRA had goals similar to those of the WNIA.[79] Although Welsh had hoped to emulate Quinton's WNIA structure, the few IRA branches instead merely raised "funds, distribute[d] literature, and inspire[d] letters and petitions in behalf of causes identified by the Philadelphia leadership."[80] Welsh also followed Quinton's lead in running a central office, addressing public meetings, organizing branches, and making extensive tours of western reservations, leaving his clerk, Matthew K. Sniffen, to handle administrative affairs.[81]

Initially Quinton had far less contact with the Boston Indian Citizenship Committee and none of their members served on the WNIA advisory board. However, once she had founded auxiliaries in Boston and Cambridge, WNIA members began to work closely with Boston Committee members, holding joint meetings, joined by IRA members from their Boston and Cambridge branches; the president of the latter was Rev. Samuel Longfellow, younger brother of Henry Wadsworth Longfellow. The Boston Committee had been organized by prominent politicians, lawyers, businessmen, clergymen, and philanthropists, following a July 1879 eastern fundraising tour by Omaha journalist Thomas Henry Tibbles on behalf of Ponca Chief Standing Bear and his small band of followers.[82] Tibbles sponsored a second tour with Standing Bear and his interpreter, Susette La Flesche, daughter of Omaha Chief Joseph La Flesche, as speakers. While in Boston they were supported by the Boston Committee.[83] Well-attended public meetings drew prominent local citizens including poet Henry Wadsworth Longfellow, whose daughter, Alice Mary Longfellow, became president of the WNIA-affiliated Massachusetts Indian Association (MIA), and New England poet and writer, Helen Hunt Jackson, who in *A Century of Dishonor*, included a chapter on the forced Ponca removal.[84]

From the beginning, Quinton had formed a congenial working relationship with members of the three male-dominated reform organizations, mostly by choosing their leaders to be a part of the WNIA advisory board. But she still had to forge a relationship with officials of the Indian Office, especially commissioners of Indian affairs and secretaries of the Interior. One avenue was through the BIC which shared certain joint controls with the Interior department. Fortunately, three members of the WNIA advisory board were also BIC members—Albert K. Smiley, Clinton B. Fisk, and Merrill E. Gates. And as a representative of a missionary organization, Quinton was entitled to attend their annual meetings. Therefore, not only her personal reputation but that of the WNIA grew through her participation in all these various meetings and conferences.

4

Quinton as Organizer, 1885–1890

During her tenure as general secretary, Quinton had set and maintained a hectic pace. In 1885 she added two additional tasks: presenting the WNIA's Indian work before the Board of Indian Commissioners (BIC) and at the Lake Mohonk Conference. Even after assuming the presidency in 1887, she continued as the primary organizer, prompting Helen Wanken to write that the WNIA's "success in attracting auxiliaries began to rise and fall in direct proportion to the amount of time she was able to spend on the road recruiting." Describing Quinton as a "hustler who thrived on over-extending himself," Wanken draws this conclusion: "Secretly enjoying the thought that she was considered irreplaceable, she would never voluntarily relinquish any of her jobs."[1] Whatever the psychological motivation, it is clear that Quinton was a powerhouse. In addition to her organizing activities, she cheered the passage of the 1887 Dawes Act and threw the full force of her association behind legislation to prevent the removal of the Southern Utes, strongly supporting Herbert Welsh's IRA efforts.

New Opportunities in 1885: The BIC and Lake Mohonk

Quinton began 1885, with an address on January 7 before the WNIA's Washington, DC, auxiliary at the home of its president, Harriet Foote Hawley. The following day, she attended her first BIC meeting in the historic Riggs House, joining representatives of other religious societies and Indian associations engaged in missionary work among the Indians. Quinton was by no means intimidated by the prominent attendees, who included her own pastor, Rev. Boardman, and Welsh and Painter of the IRA. This was her maiden opportunity to acquaint the representatives from other missionary boards with her association's Indian work, and to explain their recent addition of educational and missionary work.[2]

Between this meeting and her first attendance at Lake Mohonk in October, Quinton continued her hectic pace. By year's end, the WNIA had grown to fifty-six branches in twenty-seven states and territories. Under her supervision, the membership had circulated hundreds of IRA pamphlets, no fewer than 20,000 association-sponsored leaflets, and the annual report, as well as signing petitions, writing personal letters to congressmen, sending letters to 170 newspaper editors with association news, and collectively holding more than 450 meetings, including 130 public gatherings. Quinton personally delivered eighty-three addresses before auxiliary meetings and missionary societies and in private homes and churches. To spread her message more widely, during that spring she began contributing to the *Southern Workman*, the Hampton Institute school newspaper, and wrote articles for similar publications.[3] She traveled far less than she had the previous year, going only as far west as St. Louis, Missouri, where she organized an Indian association, one of fourteen auxiliaries that year.[4] WNIA missionary work was on going, the association was poised to establish its first California mission among the six small tribes at Round Valley—the Concow, Ukie, Pitt River, Potter Valley, Little Lake, and Red Woods; it already had a fledging mission in Dakota Territory.[5]

In early October, Quinton traveled to New Paltz, New York, to attend her first Lake Mohonk Conference, beginning a long tradition of explaining the WNIA's work to this diverse, well-connected gathering of reformers, humanitarians, and philanthropists. In 1885 some fifty men and women gathered for three days, attending two daily sessions with afternoons free to explore Albert Smiley's mountain estate, where the conference was held. Over the years those who received Smiley's personal invitation included congressmen, Indian commissioners, interior secretaries, representatives from various religious societies, clergymen, members of congressional Indian committees, army officers, heads of Indian schools, presidents of universities and colleges, members of national Indian reform associations, and editors of secular and religious newspapers. Although new to the conference, Quinton was acquainted with a number of the attendees and was elected to the business committee along with Philip C. Garrett, a Philadelphia lawyer and executive board member of the IRA; Rev. Lyman Abbott of the *Christian Union*, who in 1887 would become a member of the WNIA advisory board; and Charles C. Painter.[6]

The October 8 morning session was devoted to "Woman's Work for the Indian." Mrs. Elizabeth Keller Shaule Crannell, secretary of the Eastern New York Indian Association, a WNIA affiliate, opened the session with a brief account of their work.[7] Quinton followed, addressing the growth, methods, and work of the parent association, explaining they no longer engaged in the "great popular petitions" of the past. Instead, they used Christian instruction through Bible reading, domestic teaching, and visits to Indian homes, as well as encouraging the Indian women to visit an association-sponsored missionary's home "to set them coveting Christian homes instead of a tent." She explained that the WNIA's latest goal was her organizational tour through the South.[8] At the conclusion, attendees unanimously approved a platform calling for enlarging Indian education, allotting reservation land in severalty, granting immediate citizenship to those adopting modes of "civilized" life, and opposing the removal of Indians from improved homelands. A committee of nine, including Quinton and three other women, was appointed to prepare a formal address and to present their platform to President Grover Cleveland. On November 10 they met with Cleveland and Secretary of the Interior Lucius Q. C. Lamar. Unfortunately, Quinton left behind no report of this meeting.[9]

A week later, Quinton joined nearly two hundred women at the fifth annual WNIA meeting at the First Baptist Church in Philadelphia. As general secretary, she related the past year's work—literature distributed, petitions circulated, meetings held, and editorials and articles sent to newspapers—and as Missionary Committee chair, she read excerpts from missionaries' and teachers' letters. Her combined reports took up almost half of the annual report. General Clinton B. Fisk, BIC chairman, presided over the evening public mass meeting, during which anthropologist Alice C. Fletcher described her land allotment work among the Omaha Indians.[10]

Four days later Quinton resumed her speaking engagements, addressing a gathering in New Haven, Connecticut, and organizing another association. The main speaker that evening was Senator Henry L. Dawes, whose severalty bill was moving through congressional conferences and hearings. Quinton and Fletcher both urged its passage.[11] Then on December 18, Quinton addressed the weekly prayer meeting at the Plymouth Congregational Church in Brooklyn Heights on a topic that its minister, Rev. Henry Ward Beecher, described as "that most interesting, neglected, and abused portion of our people." At the conclusion of her address, Beecher explained that the old president of Amherst College had once addressed the downtrodden Indians in one of his sermons and it had stirred in him his own abolitionist fire. With Quinton's address and Beecher's support, the congregation raised hundreds of dollars to support the missionary work of the WNIA's Brooklyn branch.[12]

Quinton's Organizational Work of 1886

Quinton addressed the Poughkeepsie auxiliary on January 6, 1886, and the following day spoke before the Niobrara League in New York City before heading to Massachusetts. Unlike the previous year, she did not attend the annual BIC meeting, addressing instead the annual meeting of the MIA in Boston, and then organizing a new auxiliary in neighboring Cambridge.[13] After three more addresses, on January 31, she spoke before the Homer Congregational Church. In February she gave eight addresses, cutting back to a monthly average of four until August when she spoke at nine different venues, including public meetings and Indian associations, and organized four new auxiliaries.[14]

Part of the reason for fewer speaking engagements was the need to spend more time writing association pamphlets and handling correspondence with Indian office officials about missionary activities. Her correspondence regarding the WNIA mission in Round Valley, California, provides a good example of this work. On June 17 Quinton wrote Indian Commissioner John D. C. Atkins thanking him for past favors, and informing him that two Baptist missionaries, Claudia J. White and Anna L. Boorman, had begun their work at Round Valley. She requested use of an unoccupied agency government building for a temporary headquarters "where Indian women may come for instruction in domestic arts, as well as for religious, physiological & other teaching."[15] On October 25, Helen R. Foote, WNIA assistant secretary, informed Atkins that the association was ready to build their mission cottage in Round Valley and only awaited the grant of several acres he had "kindly promised them for this purpose." When he did not respond, Quinton reminded him in a December 10 letter of his earlier "kind assurance of aid to [their] civilization & missionary work among Indians," requesting three or more acres. Then a week later she asked that he sign the land over to the Executive Board of the Women's Baptist Home Missionary Society of Chicago, which would soon be taking over the station. On December 23, the acting secretary of the Interior department ordered Atkins to permit the Round Valley agent to make a selection of not more than three acres. By year's end, three of the six WNIA mission stations had been turned over to denominational societies, activity that required similar rounds of correspondence on Quinton's part.[16]

The year also included the usual work related to national meetings. On October 13, Quinton, Bonney, and other WNIA members attended the Fourth Mohonk Conference.[17] Quinton's brief remarks on the final day were followed by presentations by representatives of two WNIA affiliates: Mrs. Sara Thompson Kinney, chair of the Committee on Home Building of the Connecticut Indian Association, and Elizabeth Crannell, secretary of the Eastern New York Indian Association, who gave an account of her Albany society.[18] The following month Quinton presented her secretary's report and that of the Missionary Committee before the ninety delegates from twelve states attending the annual WNIA meeting on November 18 and 19 at the Broadway Tabernacle in New York City—their first meeting outside of Philadelphia. A well-attended evening mass meeting followed with the public and members listening to addresses by meeting chairman General Fisk, Merrill E. Gates, and Rev. Dr. Lyman Abbott, all members of the WNIA advisory board.[19]

Although Quinton had limited her engagements in 1886 to only forty-six in four states, she had established twenty-three new branches, including an Indian committee in Rockville, Maryland, bringing the total to eighty-three in twenty-eight states and territories.[20] She had also written a number of pamphlets under her own name, including *Indians and Their Helpers*, *Suggestions to Friends of the Women's National Indian Association*, and *Indian Territory Exclusion*, the latter more widely distributed through a Lend A Hand reprint in February. She supervised the distribution of sixty-five petitions to Congress supporting various Indian bills, and the publication of fifteen pamphlets and leaflets—a total of 49,000 pieces of association-sponsored literature were circulated that year.[21] In the meantime, on April 27, the two young Baptist missionaries had arrived at Round Valley, California; the WNIA message was reaching a larger audience with more articles appearing in the *Southern Workman;* and the WNIA's home-building department had constructed two houses for Indian families.[22] Quinton later wrote that from within such safe, happy homes, Indian women "shall preside with skilled hands, [and] disciplined mind—a home from whose sacred precincts her sons shall go forth strong men, gentle and well taught, men of integrity, law abiding citizens and Christian patriots."[23] The WNIA, through their missionary efforts, was now providing Christianity, education, and homes for America's Indians at an increasing number of mission stations.

This work did not go unnoticed. The IRA began to see the value of the women's efforts. During the summer, Welsh had become alarmed because Painter, the IRA's Washington, DC, agent, had expressed grave concern that IRA-sponsored legislation might be crowded out during the current congressional session. Therefore, Welsh had turned to Quinton, asking that she "sound the alarm throughout" her association. Her immediate response prompted him to describe her as representing the Indian work of "the good women of this country."[24]

The Dawes Legislation and the Presidency of the WNIA, 1887

By the opening of 1887, Quinton had been the association's general secretary for almost a decade. She would be rewarded for her longevity and hard work with the presidency during a year that started, like many others, with her attendance at the annual BIC conference. On January 6 she was joined by more than a dozen women, including Kate Foote of the Washington Auxiliary. Quinton reported that the WNIA had over eighty auxiliaries with visible success including petition campaigns, mission stations, and newspaper work through 800 different periodicals. However, she stressed the importance of the work of "an unrecordable character, being done by private conversations, and by private correspondence." Their newest department, the Indian Home Building Department, had lent money to two Christian Indians who had already built their cottages; three more were planned. She concluded that WNIA members were "more earnest to-day than ever before."[25]

The year also brought changes to the association. To strengthen their commitment to Indian work, on February 26, officers incorporated under Pennsylvania state law,[26] and to expand membership, Quinton embarked on her first organizing tour in the South, spending April 24 to June 3 in Virginia, North Carolina, South Carolina, Georgia, Alabama, Tennessee, Kentucky, and West Virginia, organizing auxiliaries in all but Alabama. She had arrived in Richmond on April 27 armed with letters of introduction to the governor of Virginia, then met with the new officers of these Southern auxiliaries, describing them as "women of ability, influence, and often, of historical families."[27] However, the most significant organizational change was Quinton's unanimous election to the presidency at the October executive board meeting. Previously she had been vice president as well as secretary. At the annual November WNIA meeting, she accepted the new role despite the death of her husband, Richard L. Quinton, just weeks earlier. She would hold this position for almost the next two decades.[28]

The year also witnessed, on February 8, the passage of the General Allotment Act, more commonly known as the Dawes Act after its sponsor, Henry Laurens Dawes. The law dealt a devastating blow to the Indian communal way of life, for its intent was to individualize the Indians, paving the way for their future assimilation. Under its provisions, reservations were broken up by special allotting agents, and plots—varying from 160 acres to heads of households, and 80 or 40 acres to various classes of individuals—were allotted in severalty. Citizenship was conferred upon allotment, and surplus lands opened to white settlement, resulting in the loss of ninety million acres of Indian-held lands.[29]

Allotment had deep roots. As early as 1633 the General Court of Massachusetts had decreed that certain Indians should receive them. By the early 1800s, treaties began to include the concept, and in 1875, congressional legislation enabled Indians to homestead public lands, although few did so because it required they relinquish tribal affiliations. In 1879 Indian Commissioner Ezra A. Hayt had drafted legislation calling for allotment, announcing it at that January's BIC meeting. The bill's failure prompted new ones including one introduced in May 1880 by Texas Senator Richard Coke, chair of the Committee on Indian Affairs. His legislation required the consent of two-thirds of the males of each tribal group before implementation. Its alternative, the Dawes version, excluded this provision.[30]

Although there were critics, many reformers, especially those who opposed tribalism and communally held lands, cheered its passage because they believed it promised Indian assimilation into mainstream culture. Merrill E. Gates, BIC president, described it as "a mighty pulverizing engine for breaking up the tribal mass," while the IRA viewed it as a "vital and important step" and as a "definite and comprehensive" Indian policy. Quinton called it the "Indian Emancipation Act," for "every Indian within our national limits may become a citizen of the United States, with all the privileges of such citizenship, and thus also enter the great brotherhood of nations." During her presidential address, she accepted credit for its passage. "It is not a vain boast" to say that its passage "is largely due to the tide of popular sentiment started eight years ago by the work which began the history of this Association," she declared, noting that their third petition had pushed for allotment in severalty. She praised Dawes for welcoming the WNIA's efforts and their petitions and for being an adviser and helper ever since. At the October 1885 Lake Mohonk Conference he had even described the present Indian policy as "born of and nursed by" the WNIA.[31]

In September at the fifth Lake Mohonk Conference, Quinton again would present her association's work. General Fisk, conference chairman, in calling the session to order, described the gathering as "a happy combination of elements, combining representatives of the various religious bodies who are active in Christian and educational work among the Indian Tribes." Recognizing the work of each of the Indian reform organizations present, he praised the WNIA for responding "to the cry of the most needy of our tribes, and whose devotion to the Indian women and Indian homes ought to receive the God-speed and hearty support of all who would uplift the Indian race." Quinton once again was appointed to the business committee along with Alice Mary Longfellow, an MIA member and eldest daughter of Henry Wadsworth Longfellow.[32]

During her address on "Woman's Work among the Indians," Quinton strongly emphasized how earnest women could effect change, noting there were now more than a hundred WNIA branches spread across the country, including the recent ones she had founded during her Southern tour. During the year, auxiliaries had held four hundred meetings, circulated 4,900 pamphlets and leaflets, and sent sixty-five petitions to Congress and press releases to eight hundred periodicals. Their missionary work had been fruitful, with special attention paid to industrial, sanitary, and domestic needs, although Christian instruction was the "center and crown of all work attempted," she emphasized.[33]

Leaving Lake Mohonk, Quinton returned to her schedule, delivering five addresses during October, one before the Philadelphia Baptist Association, representing eighty-five churches. Then on November 30, 1887, she gave her first address as WNIA president, at the Washington Avenue Baptist Church in Brooklyn. Described in the *Brooklyn Eagle* as "an able and comprehensive statement" of her association's progress "in formulating public opinion on the Indian causes in the education of Indians and their children,"[34] her presentation listed the year's work, discussing proposed Indian legislation that had failed, praised the passage of the Dawes Act, describing it as ending "the notorious wrong of taking the Indian's land by fraud or force," and called for the continued establishment of night schools and other schools as well as "medical, hospital, and dispensary work." She praised God as the "leader in all redemptive work," reminding members to "blazon this fact on every banner, and plant it deeply in every heart as our wisdom, solace, strength, and *go forward*."[35] Quinton and the WNIA had each had a good year. She had given fifty-eight public addresses in sixteen different states while the association had gained 101 new life members. And to draw members closer together, there was talk of publishing a periodical.[36]

Accomplishments Past and Present and a New Idea, 1888

Quinton again began the year reporting before the annual BIC conference on January 13. To illustrate the commonalty of all women, she related to the predominantly male gathering the story of one Indian woman who "wanted all the flounces and ruffles on her dress just like her white sisters," and those who surrounded themselves with "little bits of civilization," prompting one Indian husband to declare "oh, Indian women [are] just like other women." The standard of beauty may differ, noted Quinton, but Indian women "are not slow to see it." Thus setting the stage for her association's work, she proudly announced that ten new states, mostly in the South, had entered their work and twenty-one new branches had been formed, seven in the South. There was now a missionary station on the Sioux Reservation near Redbud, another at Fort Hall, Idaho, and a third among the Omahas, the first opened on a reservation. Quinton considered the WNIA's newest undertaking, an idea introduced at Lake Mohonk by Electra Allen Sanderson Dawes, the wife of Senator Dawes and an officer in the Washington, DC, auxiliary. It would sponsor Christian farmers as industrial teachers to the Indians, serving as examples for those living on reservations slated for allotment.[37] Due to a printing error in the WNIA's 1888 annual report, the association provides no record of Quinton's activities for the year; any information we have comes from other sources.

During March the WNIA established its periodical, *The Indian's Friend*, which provided a communication link between the Philadelphia headquarters, auxiliaries, and mission stations. According to Lori Jacobson, this monthly served as a "more consistent public access to the association's platform" and "enhance[d] their engagement in the political arena," with its samplings from numerous publications and annual meeting reports of the WNIA, BIC, IRA, and Lake Mohonk, as well as reports from auxiliaries, statements in regional newspapers about Indian matters, and excerpts from Indian school journals, promoting the sense of a "broad community of interest in Indian affairs." Quinton served as its editor four different times, and at other times wrote many of the articles, thus determining the direction of its contents.[38]

On March 27, Quinton travelled to Washington, DC, to deliver an address before the International Council of Women organized by the National Woman Suffrage Association. Although she was not a suffragette, she would go pretty much anywhere to promote the WNIA message. That day she explained her association's work on behalf of legally oppressed Indian women, who had no voice in the government and no legal control over their children or property. She described "the utter savagery" her association had found in the spring of 1879 when they began their work—including, for example, the 600 Arizona Hualapais who for six months "subsisted on grasshoppers and grass seeds, having only a sand-barren for a reservation, no homes, no property, no clothing even," or the 5,000 Arizona Apache who were "warlike, revengeful, and often stung almost to madness by fraud, falsehood and famine." Then there were the 17,000 Navajo, in New Mexico and Arizona, who although independent and self-supporting were nevertheless living "a wild, Arab sort of civilization." She explained that one lesson the WNIA had learned was that all Indians possessed "the usual human attributes" and were no "worse than others in such circumstances," demonstrating that tribal men were "ready to labor when assured of the products of their toil, the industrial statistics being favorable for those in their situation." WNIA work, represented by thirty-three states and about one hundred societies, had begun to bring change, she claimed. "All now concede that civilization, education, citizenship, and Christianity can alone solve the Indian problem." Because WNIA membership proposed to "labor unremittingly to secure the reign of law and the payment of our national debt to these natives, and the removal from the path of the Indian women" all legal obstacles, she called upon the earnest women among them to join and emancipate the Indian race "from any thralldom, social, civil or political, and to the elevation of woman above all disabilities."[39]

By mid-year, Quinton confided in Herbert Welsh that she was tired. For nine years she had worked "with all [her] *might, & with* no *pause*, & [her] brain & eyes must rest or finish work."[40] Fortuitously, the upcoming June 9–19 meeting in London of the Centenary Conference on Protestant Missions of the World would provide her a much needed respite. Accompanied by Bonney and Boardman, Quinton joined 189 Americans from 58 societies who mingled with 1,579 delegates representing 139 different denominations and societies from ten different countries. Quinton would later share what she had learned in a short presentation before the September Lake Mohonk Conference. After listening to missionary testimonies "from all quarters of the world of wonderful, seemingly impossible things done to meet the needs of God's work" she informed the Mohonk conferees that she now believed the impossible could be done in Indian work.[41]

On November 7, Quinton welcomed seventy-five delegates from fourteen state associations to Philadelphia's Methodist Episcopal Church for the WNIA's annual meeting. In her address, she stressed two points: first, the WNIA's duty to secure legal justice for the Indian, with male reformers leading the work and the women doing their utmost to help, and second, the necessity of taking Indian reform "out of politics," applying civil service rules to Indian affairs. This latter issue she had initially broached during the January 1886 BIC meeting, noting that the WNIA was collaborating with Welsh and the IRA on the issue. She concluded: "What is needed is right, and what is right can be done since God demands it and therefore provides for it."[42] Three years later at Mohonk she would again address the issue when called up by Welsh during his discussion on civil service reform. She explained to the conferees that everywhere she had traveled during her seven-month tour from Florida to California in 1891, she had found "a great desire among Indians for some settled officials, for something permanent, and a feeling that there ought not to be this constant change." She questioned why the office of Indian commissioner could not be permanent. By the time an Indian commissioner had learned his role, a new administration was elected, and reformers had to start all over again reeducating Indian Office officials.[43]

During the annual WNIA meeting, both Quinton and the association received considerable praise from the *Philadelphia Inquirer*—the membership for its "earnest enthusiasm for their work of promoting the social conditions of the Indians," and Quinton for her "earnest appeal for funds to carry on the good work."[44] Her official duties as president completed for the year, following a short rest, Quinton headed to New York City to address the NYCIA. The *New York Times* reported that she gave a short resume of the WNIA's work which now included members in over thirty states. Pushing her new goal of removing Indian affairs from politics, Quinton expressed hope that influence could be brought to bear on President Benjamin Harrison to apply civil service reform rules to the Indian service.[45]

Meetings in 1889 and 1890 and Ute Removal

For the eighteenth annual BIC in January 1889, Quinton served on a three-person committee to present resolutions and topics in discussion during the afternoon session. During her brief presentation, she noted that twenty-seven applications for Indian homes had been made, and the WNIA was currently running three mission stations. The one at the Rosebud Agency, with its newly constructed missionary cottage and chapel, was about to be handed over to Rt. Rev. William Hobart Hare, Episcopal Bishop of South Dakota, missionary to the Sioux, and a member of the WNIA advisory board. The other two were the Bannock and Shoshoni mission station at Fort Hall, Idaho, run by the Connecticut branch, and a mission among the Omaha Indians of Nebraska, served by a WNIA medical missionary and his wife. The WNIA was also proposing new missions for the Kiowa and the Mission Indians of California.[46]

Quinton gave twenty-eight addresses between January 17 and July 8 in four states and organized three new auxiliaries. On July 9 she spoke before the sixth annual meeting of the International Missionary Union in Binghamton, New York, an association of international evangelical missions—the address, a commitment she had made during the Centenary Conference on Protestant Missions in London when she had been appointed to a committee to "secure cooperation amongst the women of the several churches, on missionary lines."[47] Then during August and

September she went on the road again, to attend an Indian council among the Omaha in Nebraska to get their consent for the government to donate reservation land for a WNIA missionary station. She discussed her Omaha visit at Lake Mohonk in October.

On November 6, Quinton attended the annual meeting of the MIA in Boston, where she and Commissioner Thomas Jefferson Morgan both gave addresses. Although Quinton would establish good working relations with a number of commissioners, she had a particularly congenial one with Morgan, both of them being educators. Later, in a December letter to Welsh she wrote: "I have known Gen'l and Mrs. Morgan for twenty years and have the deepest interest and anxiety for his confirmation [as commissioner], & believe in his schemes."[48] Then two weeks later, Morgan joined her at the annual WNIA meeting on November 20 in Newark, New Jersey. Ninety-three delegates representing eight states and Washington, DC, gathered for two days to renew friendships, and as Quinton remarked in her annual address, to learn "what has thus been paid towards the liquidation of our personal debt as citizens of a nation so heavily in arrears materially, educationally and religiously to our native race of Indians." She noted that the additional $5,000 taken in that year would go toward settling part of that debt. Although the association had achieved a lot, more was needed. In her address she called upon the Christian women of the country, "exalted to the heavens in privilege," to bear to "these our brothers and sisters of the native race this word that works out such a life of abundance even here." She inquired, "shall we not lay these dusky hands in Christ's extended, nail-marked palm and say, Know Him and He will show you God's heart?" She then exhorted her members to build "model earthly homes, and teach them how to make these satisfying with pure domestic love, and how to earn and use all needed helps and arts." Earlier in her speech when describing what task was appropriate for the WNIA, she had explained that "first in the order of human life," was the "building of the home, and where all, however humble should be for health of body, mind and spirit."[49]

According to Lori Jacobson, because the WNIA's home building program "focused on Indian home life," it "represented a 'feminine' field of reform that aligned with the WNIA's growing missionary endeavors and satisfied the group's need for distinction from the IRA." It also enabled the WNIA to "reshape its reform work to more closely align with the Protestant domesticity that characterized much of American women's culture in the late nineteenth century."[50]

Between the annual meeting and the end of the year, Quinton gave three addresses in and around Philadelphia and in mid-January 1890 headed for

Washington, DC, to attend the annual BIC conference. General Fisk in his welcoming address reminded members that it had been twenty-one years since the BIC had been organized. "We are old enough to vote now." How ironic that sitting among them were WNIA members, all citizens, who still could not vote. During her appointed time Quinton looked around the room at the various Christian societies represented and said it seemed "as though the machinery [was] now all ready, and all that is needed is to set it in more efficient and active operation." Until then the WNIA was still hard at work. Since the beginning it had founded, directly or indirectly, seventeen different missions among fifteen tribes, and spent that year more than $16,300 ($466,124.47 in 2021), some $5,000 more than the previous year. The WNIA looked forward to the day when they could disband, their task completed—that would happen only when Christian workers were to be found on all reservations.[51]

During 1890 Quinton gave only forty-eight addresses in eight different states and the District of Columbia, burdened by the pressure of legislative work and increased correspondence requiring "from her pen from six to twelve hours daily throughout the summer" as well as the writing of at least 160 articles.[52] One of particular importance was *The Ute Question*, which appeared in the March 20, 1890, issue of the *National Baptist* and was reprinted as a WNIA leaflet. Quinton strongly protested the removal of the nine hundred and fifty Southern Utes from their Colorado reservation to Utah simply because "white neighbors wanted[ed] this more valuable land themselves." This move would simply "shift the evils and burdens complained of by Colorado to the unwilling shoulders of the people of Utah," she complained, wondering if in Christian America "another native tribe of men and women can be despoiled of their rights, robbed of their homes and be driven from good land where self support and civilization with honest effort on the part of Government can be achieved to a mountain desert where civilization and civilized self support are impossible, and where a war of extermination is inevitable?"[53] The same month she wrote Pennsylvania Congressman James Kerr requesting his aid to oppose the removal, calling it an "unjust and unwise measure." By unanimous consent her letter to Kerr was printed in the *Congressional Record*.[54]

In an April article, Quinton explained that the Utes were to be removed to a remote mountainous area in Utah where they could engage in "a safe and easygoing savagery" supposedly without inconveniencing white settlements. But this proposed new home was already occupied by cowboys, Mormons, and some honest settlers who "have announced beforehand their determination to welcome the Utes with hot shot should they be sent hither." She had learned it would be less costly to allow the Indians to remain where they were; the move to Utah would require building a new agency and military post and purchasing the interests of those now living on the proposed reservation. With "no moral reasons for removal, and great moral reasons clearly against it, all just and honorable men would be expected to rally to the support" of Senator Dawes, who, according to Quinton, had declared this new home far worse than represented. She concluded "the best reason for the removal is that there are more votes for it than against it."[55]

This removal was far more complicated than even she was aware. The nearly 1,000 Southern Utes occupied a reservation of slightly over one million acres in southwestern Colorado near Durango, only a third of which if irrigated was useful for farming. Preferring hunting to farming, the Utes had sent a delegation in 1886 to Washington asking to be removed to Utah Territory; their request was turned down, in part because of IRA opposition. Welsh's cardinal rule was that removal and the breakup of reservations should not be done, especially if Indian-held lands afforded housing and self-support. He particularly opposed removal if it merely suited the needs of white settlers. Ute removal had become more public during the earlier January 17, 1889, BIC meeting when Rev. Thomas S. Childs of the Presbyterian board, who had served as secretary of the recent Ute Commission, informed the BIC that the Southern Utes actually wanted to move. Despite proof that his commission had located a far better reservation to which most were willing to go, Childs was unable to convince Painter, Welsh, Quinton, and the BIC that removal was advantageous.[56]

The IRA's anti-removal crusade was extensive and lengthy. It included the publication of two pamphlets by Painter, *Civilization by Removal!: The Southern Utes* (1889) and *Removal of the Southern Utes* (1890), his investigative tour to the old and new reservation, and the mailing of over 20,000 pieces of mail, including personal letters from Welsh, who on February 21, 1892, requested support directly from Quinton. She responded: "This Ute matter makes every drop of one's blood boil with indignation & chill with grief by turns." She continued: "Was anything ever more manifestly wicked & foolish . . . [imprisoning] . . . in perpetual barbarism a thousand souls!" As she had done in the past, she rallied her members, sending out letters to various branches as well as official WNIA leaflets.[57] With her support, Painter and the IRA were able to fend off the Ute removal for another Congressional session.

In early May 1890, Quinton traveled to Hartford to attend the annual meeting of the Women's American Baptist Home Mission Society. She remained in

Philadelphia through all of June and July, working on her correspondence and article writing, and then in mid-August traveled to Lake Mohonk, possibly for a rest at the resort.[58] She returned in early October 1890, joining some 140 guests at the eighth annual conference and was again elected to serve on the Business Committee. She was also chosen as one of seven committee members to present a platform of action at the conference's end, and invited, along with Abbott and Garrett, to prepare resolutions in honor of General Clinton B. Fisk, long time BIC chair and presiding officer of the Mohonk Conference, who had recently died. Over the next three days, members discussed the major Indian issues of the day, from Indian education to legal aid to the Mission Indians. During her morning talk on October 10, she addressed the WNIA's current work, beginning with the forty or fifty Christian homes built by the Home Building and Loan Department. Their California work included the support of a school in the northern part of the state and work in the south among the Mission Indians. They were also trying to buy land in Florida for the Seminoles. "We women have watched the progress of events and of this Conference with deepest interest," she explained, "and we believe this

Promotional photograph showing Mohonk
Mountain House from Sky Top Path, 1893.
Mohonk Mountain House Archives.

is a body called of God to do a great work; and we believe, as General Armstrong once said here, that all that ought to be done can be done." She reminded them that their Indian work can only be accomplished through public sentiment and personal pressure. "Nothing can be done except as it is demanded by Christian citizens." In conclusion, she recommended they all personally work toward the education of the twenty-one thousand Indian children.[59]

Three days later she was on the road again, addressing the Poughkeepsie Indian Association. She made six more addresses, organizing an auxiliary in Springfield, Massachusetts on November 14 before welcoming members to the annual WNIA meeting at the new Old South Church in Boston on November 19. The *Philadelphia Inquirer* reported that the association's receipts for the year totaled $16,501 with expenses being only about half that, and the *Boston Daily Advertiser* concentrated on the public meeting where Quinton read "a most encouraging report," the major points being that Indian citizenship was accomplished, the severalty process was progressing favorably, and nearly $2,000,000 had been appropriated for Indian education. However, "more is needed," Quinton had concluded.[60] She traveled on to New York City to attend the annual meeting of the NYCIA on November 24, giving an account of the work of the various WNIA departments.[61] The next day she organized an auxiliary in Yonkers, followed by more addresses in Philadelphia, New York City, and Newark, New Jersey to finish out the year.[62]

Within a short period of time, Quinton's routine had settled into a predictable pattern, beginning the year with the BIC meeting, the Fall at Lake Mohonk to enjoy the beautiful and peaceful Smiley resort, and the end attending the annual WNIA meeting where she circulated among delegates, renewed friendships, read her lengthy reports, and after becoming president, officiated. The remainder of her year was filled with answering correspondence, writing pamphlets, leaflets, and flyers, organizing auxiliaries or addressing established ones, speaking before various religious and public meetings, and every fourth year or so traveling across the country, scouting out potential sites for new mission stations and visiting existing ones.

Now a dozen years old, the WNIA had succeeded, not only because the leadership had been extraordinary from the beginning, but the women had made a number of very important decisions, including adding many prominent male reformers to the advisory board, forming a corporation for better control, and creating a periodical to tie its membership together. Most important, they had been flexible when necessary. For example, Quinton did not hesitate to change course if need be. In a 1887 issue of the *Christian Union*, she explained the association's move away from exclusive work on behalf of Indian women to a more generalized program of establishing a first-class mission in every tribe to include a night school for adults, domestic art and industrial training, medical and hospital support, and instruction in gardening, farming, and mechanic arts, along with "earnest Christian teaching, on weekends and on Sunday."[63] Two decades later she explained to Mathew Sniffen that although still creating a public sentiment for just Indian legislation, planting Christian missions, and establishing schools where the government was unlikely to build—their work was now to be "constructive, chiefly for the home and family, but always religious, patriotic, and on the line of good citizenship."[64]

By the end of 1890, the WNIA had auxiliaries in most states east of the Mississippi. They had also acquired land from the government for their mission station in Nebraska, and Quinton had rallied members to aid Welsh and the IRA to temporarily halt Southern Ute removal. In the spring of 1891, she would embark upon her most ambitious tour yet, crossing the continent to California to visit the Mission Indians.

5

Quinton's 1891 Cross Country Tour

In her October 1891 letter-report to the WNIA membership published in *The Indian's Friend*, Quinton, who was traveling to California, describes finally escaping the desert: "Its heat and glare had been, it seemed, all that one could well bear, for at times the eyes had to be closed against the blasts as of a furnace, and even the hands shrank from the too heated steel arms of the car seats." She described male train passengers taking "off both coats and vests," often applying "ice water to the head, and face."[1] She, however, did not reveal how she dealt personally with this extreme heat, being more focused on the purpose of the trip. That same year she had written that "Helen Hunt Jackson deservedly stands first in the literary world as connected with modern effort by women for the deliverance of our native American Indians from oppression and injustice, as shameful as have been endured in any civilized land or by any race under the guardianship or power of any civilized government." She had described Jackson's soul as marching on, "still rallying, still inspiring unselfish souls to the cause she died for."[2]

Quinton intended to carry on Jackson's work among the Mission Indians in Southern California and she had begun this journey in Virginia in March. Along the way she organized thirty new auxiliaries; visited established association mission stations and searched for sites for potential new ones; addressed public meetings, various ladies groups, and church meetings; visited government Indian schools and military bases; and attended Indian councils—all the while writing regular accounts of her trip for *The Indian's Friend* and answering correspondence forwarded to each stop.[3] Although the WNIA had already begun work among the Mission Indians of California, this was the first time Quinton would visit their remote villages. Like Jackson, she would be mesmerized, returning to California more times than to any other WNIA missionary field.

Quinton's View of Federal Indian Policy

Quinton began 1891 at the twentieth BIC conference in Washington, DC, on January 8, mere days after the Wounded Knee massacre on the Pine Ridge Reservation. She used part of her allotted time at the conference to compare Christianity to the Ghost Dance religion, which had spread rapidly among various western tribes and ended up playing a role in the massacre.[4] "We have seen the Gospel of our Lord Jesus Christ take savage Indians and barbarous Indian women and convert them in the New Testament sense," she explained, using Dakota physician, Charles Eastman as an example, calling him a savage for fourteen years but now a gentleman of fine education, "an earnest Christian, an active missionary."[5] However, this new religion, the "Messiah craze," was "pathetic," it was "a false religion, a false faith," she concluded. Because reformers had failed them, Indians had adopted it, and now it was essential to get Christian men "among these people who are looking for a Messiah to bring them peace, plenty, and rest from their enemies."[6]

On January 14, Quinton addressed the Brooklyn, New York, auxiliary, blaming the government for the current Indian situation. Americans in their comfortable homes "cannot tell what mental condition is produced in an Indian who is left bare footed on the snow, wrapped in thin muslin sheets and starving," she announced. Such neglect had led them to look for a new Messiah. Concluding that "politics should have no place in Indian affairs," she suggested that if the 15,000,000 Christians in the country demanded such a reform, no "doubt it would be."[7] During the rest of January and early February she gave addresses throughout the state, including one before the Long Island branch of the Woman's Baptist Home Mission Society, characterizing the country's treatment of the Indians as a long "record of cruelty and oppression." The "Messiah craze was a reproach to our name," she declared. "These poor people were kept hedged in without education, without the gospel, . . . only to be victims." Describing the "wrong doing of which history is full," she asked how could "men who are honorable in all their dealings . . . legislate as they had on the Indian question." Her answer: "our legislators doubtless vote[d] for bills without knowing what they contain." Her solutions: the removal of the Indian Office from the Department of the Interior and the appointment of officials who were fit for the job and retained only as long as they remained efficient.[8]

In mid-February Elizabeth Dustin, a special correspondent for the *New York Times* interviewed Quinton, describing her as "one of the most effective speakers of her sex now on the platform." Dustin had learned recently from the wife of an unidentified congressman just how effective Quinton and the WNIA were when the wife, who worked in her husband's office, explained that on one occasion when an Indian bill was pending, over two hundred letters from women across the country arrived in one day's mail.[9]

Quinton's Tours: The Seminoles and Chiricahua Apaches

When Congress adjourned, Quinton set out on a coast-to-coast tour.[10] She and her companion arrived in Richmond, Virginia, during the first week of March to organize for her first visit to the Florida Seminoles. Arriving in Jacksonville on March 7, they set out for Fort Myers, reaching there on the 16th. The Seminole camps that were their final destination were still two hundred miles beyond.[11] Their guide was Francis Asbury Hendry, a former Florida state senator, prominent cattleman, and friend to the Seminoles, whose daughter, Laura Jane Hendry Thompson, her son, and a Miss Emma Clark of Delaware City, Delaware, would join them. Thompson, the telegraph operator at Fort Myers, had "known the Indians for all her life, & [was] most deeply interested in them."[12]

On March 19, the small party headed into Seminole country, spending the first night on beds made of soft palmetto fans, covered with oilcloths and quilts under mosquito netting. Quinton described sleeping "delightfully, soothed by the soft serenade of insects while pond warblers added their bass undertones."[13] The following morning they inspected the 400 acres near Lake Trafford as a potential site for the proposed WNIA Seminole mission. During the following week, they saw eight camps, spending time at four of them, traveling as far as the edge of the Everglades and conferring with the English-speaking leading Seminole men about the prospect of a WNIA mission station for them. Quinton later reported in *The Indian's Friend* the land purchase and intention of building a house, a chapel, and a portable sawmill and acquiring horses and a wagon for the WNIA-sponsored missionaries. Winning, civilizing, and Christianizing "this forgotten remnant of a brave and capable people will be one of deepest interest, and details will be given as fast as prudence permits," she wrote in her April report.[14]

Returning to Fort Myers, Quinton founded a WNIA branch on March 27 and another in Winter Park on March 30. It was not until the July issue of *The Indian's Friend* printed Jacob E. Brecht's June 22 letter that the membership was alerted that he and his wife had arrived at the Florida mission, eager to begin work as WNIA missionaries.[15] Months later, from San Francisco, Quinton wrote

Commissioner Morgan that the sawmill recently provided the Seminoles by the government was en route. Learning from Brecht that a planing mill would provide work and money, she asked Morgan, if it was practical, could he provide one? The following year she informed him that the sawmill was up and running and the WNIA was grateful.[16]

Quinton founded a new association in Jacksonville before moving on into Georgia where she revived and reorganized branches she had founded during her 1887 visit. On April 27 she established the fourth Florida branch in Pensacola, arriving the following day at Mt. Vernon Barracks, Alabama, as the guests of Margaret and Sophie Shepard, who were sponsored by the WNIA's MIA branch to educate the children of the Chiricahua Apache prisoners living there. Quinton complimented their work, describing the small Indian children as trusting the Shepard sisters, running to catch up with them, and "slipping their little brown fingers into the fairer ones, and their wee owners silently accompanying with smile-lighted faces, like happy shadows after sunshine."[17]

The Chiricahua Apaches had been taken prisoner during the 1886 Apache wars. Removed from their San Carlos, Arizona, reservation, they were relocated to the Southeast with Geronimo and other leaders and confined to Fort Pickens, near Pensacola, Florida, while their families went to Fort Marion, Florida. The following year, with IRA support, all were reunited at Mt. Vernon Barracks, Alabama. Quinton had closely followed their plight, lamenting in an August 1890 article that loyal government scouts had been imprisoned along with the militant Apaches, concluding that the Christian men of this country should instruct their representatives to vote and end "this shamefully-delayed justice to its Indian servants and friends."[18]

Disembarking from the train at Mt. Vernon, Quinton witnessed Indian men and women with "beaded bags, canes, whips, bows and arrows, or baskets to sell," most of whom "looked bright and cheery." She was most surprised by Geronimo's "animation and physical vigor," neither "old, sad, nor feeble." Later, she would meet Chato and other loyal army scouts. At sunset, she strolled through the old live oak grounds, entering a number of the old log houses, which, although tidy, were cramped. After visiting the hospital, she walked beyond the schoolhouse—which she later toured, watching the sixty students in action—to the new village on higher ground built around an open plaza, with new two-room plank houses with good floors, windows, open fireplaces, and a quarter-acre garden behind each. Because the 360 Apaches living at Mt. Vernon included only some 60 to 70 men, Quinton ironically described this effort as an "experiment of thus civilizing captive Indian women and children," and an expensive one at that.[19]

On to the Southwest

On May 3 Quinton and her friend boarded a sleeper in San Antonio to cross Texas. Quinton commented on the "wretched hovels of Mexican railroad laborers scattered along the way" revealing "deepest poverty and life at the lowest ebb of comfort and civilization." Arriving in Albuquerque on May 11, they set out for Isleta Pueblo by horse and wagon. High water at the railroad bridge meant the ferry was unable to cross, forcing them to set out on foot, walking a quarter of a mile on the narrow bridge planks. With no transport at the other end, they continued the two miles on to the Presbyterian Mission, visiting with the teachers and students, and later meeting with others in their homes, ending their visit at the nearby Catholic school. Quinton concluded her report with a return to Albuquerque "under a gorgeous sunset."[20]

Quinton had high praise for the Albuquerque Indian School, where young Indian men worked in the shoemaking department, furnishing shoes for the entire school, or the harness shop or the carpentry shop while female students engaged mostly in sewing. She visited the Presbyterian Mission School, half a mile away, and returned to town to address a ladies meeting, organizing the New Mexico Women's Indian Association. On May 12 she continued on to Laguna Pueblo to visit the government school, getting directions to the teacher's home from a young Indian woman who spoke English learned during her two years at Carlisle. "The heart could not but sink to see that despite all the care, labor and love bestowed on her there, she had completely returned to her old life," Quinton wrote, describing the young woman as dressed in "full Indian dress even to the short skirt and solid buckskin bandage which makes the leg from knee to moccasin one straight huge cylinder." She also visited the homes of other returned students, seeing "the old life taken up again" in cramped rooms "where most can barely stand upright, and where moral uprightness also is merely possible." This theme of former students "returning to the blanket" tested Quinton and other reformers, and she made sure that *The Indian's Friend* ran articles on the subject.[21]

She spent a day at Fort Wingate, New Mexico, reporting that fifty-five Navajo men had recently enlisted in the army. Traveling through Gallup in mid-May, she arrived at Fort Defiance, Arizona, the Navajo tribal agency, and remained almost a week. She described the resident Navajos as "bright and capable as those of any tribe," self-supporting, independent, but scattered over a reservation of one hundred square miles, causing her to wonder about a better living arrangement. Although no one thought to ask the Indians what they wanted, her solution would be to settle them in well-watered or easily watered valleys such as the San Juan region, the Chinle Valley, or near Ganado. As they traveled through Indian county, Quinton was continually searching for potential future mission sites. Nevertheless, she also took time to enjoy the splendid scenery, visiting cliff dwellings, or climbing one thousand feet up the mountain to visit Cotton's, a post trader, on the way to the Hopi villages. This trip could easily have been a "life-ending one had not the (wagon) horses been gentle and well-managed," she noted, going into great detail about the flora and fauna en route.[22]

On the way to visit the Keam's Cañon [Keams Canyon] Indian School, a few miles west of Cotton's, Quinton met a party of Navajos, returning from a dance. She described the twenty or so riders as a "cavalcade of barbaric splendor," all decked out in their silvery necklaces, buckles, and bracelets, and wearing bright multi-colored garments and plumes mounted on horses with bridles and other trappings decorated in silver. Her party reached the school after "a never-to-be forgotten acclivitous and declivitous gorge-and-gully-lined fifty miles drive," to visit what she described as "the most skillfully and enthusiastically taught Indian School it has ever been our privilege to visit."[23] Then toiling on foot to the top, Quinton visited the five hundred residents of the three Hopi villages on Second Mesa to view sacred places, watch their snake dances, talk with the women, and visit weavers, potters, and basket makers. Her myopic middle-class viewpoint, allowing little opportunity to see the beauty of the Indian way of life, led her as usual to thoughts of how to change them: "to hasten that new day to them which shall break all bonds, untie strong hands and give to all these immortals their long overdue share of this life as well as of the better and unseen one."[24]

Quinton and her friend then headed for Fort Defiance, where she organized an Indian committee on May 30, and then set out for Gallup to board the train to Holbrook, Arizona. There she was met by Lieutenant Carter P. Johnson, acting agent of the White Mountain Apaches, who drove them in a mule-drawn government ambulance to Fort Apache, over a torturous road that required the travelers to exert all of their "clutching-force" to keep their seats. Quinton described the "continuous panorama of beauty" that spread out in profusion all around them, including "the ledges, scraggy cedars, and cacti and flowers." The trip took two days, and they spent their first night in the home of a Mormon family, where one member instructed them "in the glories" of their faith, only to travel the next day for forty miles over a road rougher than the first. Upon hitting one bump, her unidentified traveling companion, curled up on the back seat to doze, "presto, up she went in an unbroken coil till her top feather touched the roof above." Only her solid mass of luxuriant braids prevented the crushing of her skull as she came down, noted Quinton, who compared the motion of their vehicle to "the rocking of an earthquake, the caressing of a cyclone, and the fanning of a whirlwind combined." From Fort Apache, with its scattered little Indian farms, Quinton set out to visit the Apaches and their "mere brush-arbor" homes, noting "how slow must be all true progress, all social and moral culture without homes better worthy the name" and commenting on how the WNIA Home Building Department could be of valuable assistance here. Watching one old Indian woman carrying a heavy load of cut wood on her shoulders, Quinton informed her membership that "woman's work for woman" was desired here and would surely find much success.[25]

After attending Sunday services in the Army chapel at Fort Apache on June 7, the party headed for San Carlos. On the third day as the "spirited government mules" climbed the summit of 5,600 feet, Quinton made note of the flora along the way, describing "armed cacti [Saguaro] standing twenty to fifty feet tall," and the fragrant blossoms of Acacia trees. Busy answering her correspondence, Quinton informed Welsh that "after four days camping out (under military escort & care we are) nearing San Carlos, Arizona."[26] They arrived at the Agency where it was 125 degrees in the shade. That evening Quinton and her friend were entertained with a bugle and guitar concert. The following day they visited every agency facility, meeting the agent, the teachers, and the Indians, who came in large numbers to learn of the WNIA's work. Quinton had arrived on issue day and witnessed "these 'fierce, savage, cruel Apaches' gathered about the doors and counters where beef, flour, coffee and sugar were being" doled out. She described many as almost naked, some too sick to be present.[27]

From San Carlos, Quinton wrote Commissioner Morgan on an urgent matter. She had just one day before received a letter stating that fifty more students from the government school at San Carlos were to be sent to a Lawrence, Kansas, boarding school at the end of the vacation, and "all the teachers are distressed at the news." Believing that the situation had been misrepresented to him, and based on her week-long stay there, she described the teachers, matrons, and superintendents as excellent. They felt deeply that taking "any more children from here without consent of the parents would be a great blow to this school & to the interest in education." She feared this removal would not only dishearten the teachers but bring upon them "the wrath & grief of all these parents." Earlier another fifty had been taken to Grand Junction, without parental consent, "against their protest, their outcries & those of the children." She suggested a school at San Carlos "*on* the reserve," as well as one among the White Mountain Apache, to educate the children locally.[28]

Running out of space in her report, Quinton briefly mentioned a visit to the Presbyterian Indian Mission School in Tucson on June 21 and a quick stop at Mission San Xavier del Bac. They were unable to visit the Pima and Papago Indians before a day-long trip across the desert in heat that reached 123 degrees.[29] They arrived at Banning, California, on June 22, 1891, and spent the night in a comfortable hotel. A quick trip to San Bernardino followed to execute papers relative to their new Seminole Mission and to collect thirty-five forwarded letters.[30] Included in the Seminole documents was one from J. Emma Clark of New Castle, Delaware, who agreed to turn over eighty acres in Florida, for ten dollars an acre. Quinton telegraphed Commissioner Morgan twice to assure him that the agreement had been sent and later the deed.[31]

Early WNIA Work Among the Mission Indians

Although the WNIA had no mission stations in New Mexico or Arizona yet, as early as 1886 eastern branches had funded work in California on the Round Valley Reservation, in the Coast Range two hundred miles north of San Francisco, turning it over the following year to the Women's Baptist Home Missionary Society of Chicago. Eastern members were also active in Southern California, supporting work that had tentatively begun in the fall of 1888 when the newly formed Atlantic City, New Jersey, association expressed interest in the Cahuilla Indians, raising $200 toward a mission. To encourage support, *The Indian's Friend* had published an article, describing these Indians as desirous of receiving their land in severalty, "anxious to go forward in all right ways."[32]

To elicit government support, in mid-February 1889 Quinton had informed Indian Commissioner John H. Oberly that her association wanted to begin work in the Cahuilla Valley, requesting the Interior department to "resign" the use of the school building as headquarters for this missionary and educational work. He responded that the school was only temporarily suspended, and a new teacher had already been appointed. Furthermore, it was "not deemed good policy to give missionary associations the use of government buildings" for their work, a policy toward the WNIA that would soon change.[33] Modifying her strategy, on March 1, Quinton requested five acres to build a missionary cottage, suggesting that Mission Indian Agent Col. Joseph W. Preston and the agency physician make the

Rev. and Mrs. William H. Weinland and their children,
Elizabeth, Caroline, and Henry in a photograph taken
by N. Harmon of Blairstown, Iowa, about 1889.
William H. Weinland Collection, The Huntington Library, San Marino, California (photCL 39 [365]).

selection. She thanked Oberly on April 12 for the grant of land, promising that her association would "move forward in work at that place as rapidly as practicable."[34]

In early June 1889, even before Rev. William Henry Weinland, newly appointed by the WNIA to work among the Mission Indians, had formally begun his work, Quinton had written him that the commissioner and Interior secretary had granted the WNIA five acres at Cahuilla. He and Agent Preston were to make the selection.[35] Weinland, who had formerly worked in a native mission in Bethel, Alaska, had then transferred to the Moravian Church at Grace Hill, Iowa, for health reasons. When the WNIA affiliate in Bethlehem, Pennsylvania, also expressed interest in the proposed Cahuilla Mission, Quinton had consulted the Provincial Elders' Conference of the Moravian Church, and they had recommended Weinland.[36] He arrived in San Jacinto, Riverside County, on June 19, 1889, accompanied by his wife, Caroline Yost Weinland, and his sister, Sadie.[37] In her earlier letter, Quinton had requested that he keep the cost of their missionary cottage to $500. Three weeks later she admonished him not to build "so small & poorly as to have no comfort," inquiring how much it would cost to build a cottage of three or four rooms, noting she had already raised $700 for other purposes and felt sure that "God will 'supply.'"[38]

Weinland's work and that of others among the Mission Indians carried on at several sites and outlying preaching stations was known as the Ramona Mission, in honor of Helen Hunt Jackson's novel *Ramona*. How this came to be went back to 1881, when Jackson and Quinton had first met and begun corresponding. In late January 1883, Jackson wrote that she was returning to Southern California to put together a report for the Interior department on the best way to provide land for the Mission Indians. She described these industrious people, who had been farming for a hundred years as having "been far more cruelly treated than any other Indians in our land." Months later in July, to her "greatest delight," Jackson informed Quinton that Secretary of the Interior Henry Teller had followed one of her recommendations and hired Anson Brunson and G. Wiley Wells, two Los Angeles lawyers, to serve as U.S. Attorneys for the Mission Indians. (The firm would lay the groundwork that ultimately saved the Mission village of Soboba, later an integral part of the WNIA's work.) At year's end Jackson informed Quinton she was writing an Indian story that she hoped would "reach people who wouldn't read the Century of Dishonor."[39]

The following April, Jackson had informed Quinton that her novel was completed. "I do not dare to think I have written a second Uncle Tom's Cabin," she declared, "but I do think I have written a story which will be a good stroke for the Indians cause."[40] Her poignant presentation of the Mission Indians' plight inspired numerous Indian reformers, including Quinton and Charles C. Painter, the IRA agent. The latter visited Jackson on her deathbed in San Francisco in 1885, promising to take up their cause, and Quinton also hoped that her association could carry on Jackson's legacy. To promote this new missionary field, *The Indian's Friend* began running articles on Mission Indian history in late 1888.[41]

The WNIA had initially planned on beginning its efforts with the Cahuilla village, but the village captain refused to give consent or to grant land for a cottage. "I have no doubt that Catholic influence is behind their opposition," Quinton had written in a July 1889 letter to Weinland. "But we will say nothing about that as we can prove nothing at present."[42] She based her conclusion on the fact that following the May 1888 death of Mrs. N. J. Ticknor, the local teacher, WNIA supporter, and acquaintance of Jackson, the government had replaced her with a Mrs. Thayer, a Catholic from Baltimore. Weinland had agreed with Quinton, accusing Thayer of "underhanded work," causing the Indians to refuse to receive him or grant land for his mission. Like many evangelical Protestant Indian reformers, both Quinton and Weinland were openly anti-Catholic, conveniently forgetting that the Franciscan Order had established missions among these Indians, and therefore, many Indians would be Catholic.[43]

The Cahuilla resistance prompted Agent Preston and Weinland to decide that the small Serrano village of Soboba on the Rancho San Jacinto Viejo in the San Jacinto Valley in present-day Riverside County would be a better mission site. Quinton also thought it best that the Weinlands live in nearby San Jacinto in rented quarters, not on any reservation, and wait "to win the hearts of the people." She immediately applied to Commissioner Morgan, for a tract of land at Soboba.[44] However, since Soboba was not a government reservation, Morgan had no power to grant land to someone else. Therefore, he responded on July 27: "I can see no reason why your Association cannot merely with the consent of the Indians of said village, use the quantity of land desired for the purpose indicated."[45]

In early July 1889, Quinton had informed Herbert Welsh that because the Cahuilla Indians "seemed to be a little loath to grant" them land, the WNIA had decided for the present to work at Soboba. She added that this was a "pleasant providence," since his association had recently helped save the village—a reference to the financial support that Welsh and the IRA had given to attorney Shirley C. Ward, who in 1886 had been appointed Special Assistant United States District Attorney for the California Mission Indians.[46] Four years earlier in 1882 Matthew R. Byrne, a San Bernardino businessman, had purchased seven hundred acres in the northeastern corner of the Rancho San Jacinto Viejo, which included the two-hundred-acre Soboba village. Armed with an eviction order from the Superior Court of San Diego County, he demanded the Indians' removal. In the spring of 1882 Jackson had visited Soboba, and thereafter exposed their vulnerability in her articles and letters to government officials. With the interest she had generated, early efforts of Brunson and

Wells, and IRA financial support, Ward successfully defended the villagers. On January 31, 1888, the California Supreme Court in *Byrne vs. the San Jacinto* (Soboba) *Indians* decided in the Indians' favor on the basis that Mexican land grants had included their right of occupancy.[47]

With Soboba's future secure, in late July 1889 Quinton informed Weinland that she had received "the *formal* 'permit' from the Indian Bureau" to build there with Indian consent, but since they had only had two hundred acres, she thought it best to ask for only an acre or so, just enough for a garden, house, lot, and pasture for a horse and cow.[48] Ultimately, however, the WNIA would decide to build Weinland's cottage in Potrero, a village of 215 residents on the Morongo Reservation, two miles from Banning. Weinland had become acquainted with the potential at Potrero after filling in for Sarah Elizabeth Morris, the government schoolteacher there, who also taught Sunday school. When he learned she was going on a vacation in the summer of 1889, he had offered to take over her Sunday duties.[49] Although this new work required considerable travel after finishing his services at Soboba, for the remainder of the 1889 summer he drove the twenty-some miles to Potrero to conduct a Sunday school and to preach. Once the government secured five acres for the WNIA missionary station, the Weinlands relocated their mission headquarters to Potrero.[50]

In a January 17, 1890, letter giving him permission to spend $500 on the missionary cottage "to make it proper & adequate," Quinton inquired if Weinland thought the Moravian Church would be willing to take over the mission and property. The following month she authorized him to use $250 to build a chapel at Potrero.[51] In mid-February 1890, the Weinlands moved into their two-story redwood home, called the Allegheny Cottage, with a horse stable and buggy shed gifted by the Western Pennsylvania Indian Association at Pittsburgh and Allegheny. On April 20, they dedicated the Potrero chapel, a gift of the Bethlehem, Pennsylvania, branch.[52]

A month after the Moravian Church assumed control at Potrero, Weinland turned over his WNIA-sponsored responsibilities at Soboba to Mrs. William P. Fowler (the former Mary Elizabeth Sheriff). In a February 5, 1890, letter Quinton had informed him she felt sure the association would hire Fowler, inquiring if he thought $400 a year would be sufficient. In late May Quinton reinforced the WNIA's intention to employ her.[53] Fowler formally took charge on June 6, 1890, supported by the NYCIA, and immediately established a Sunday school and sewing classes. In addition, she made house calls, cared for the sick, and held women's meetings, encouraging them to engage in various domestic industries.[54]

Fowler was well acquainted with Soboba. In 1880 she had become the first government teacher among these Mission Indians. She was single and boarded temporarily with Pennsylvania-born Emmaline Jordan at her "little 'mongrel' store-boarding house-post office in San Jacinto," then the valley's only town, riding on horseback the two miles a day to teach in the small adobe school house built by the Indians in 1880 and furnished by the government.[55] Two years later Helen Hunt Jackson had arrived at Soboba, on assignment to write articles on California topics for *The Century Magazine*. "As we went from house to house," Fowler wrote, "I told her of the impending misfortune" of the threatened eviction of the village "and we discussed various ways of trying to help them keep their homes."[56] She had remained at her post until 1885.

Several months after Fowler assumed Weinland's work, the Catholic Church delivered lumber for a new chapel. Finally, on August 2, Rev. P. J. Stockman of San Bernardino applied to Commissioner Morgan for permission to build. On September 5, 1890, Quinton wrote Weinland asking if he thought it best to "*leave* Saboba [*sic*] & go where the Catholics will *not* hinder us. *We* are called to *peace* & there *are* places where we can work without war," she explained. Eleven days later she wrote in despair: "How sad I am that the Catholics are rampant." Then on December 9, she wrote, "I shall perhaps soon go to Washington and *if* so I shall do *all I can* about this Catholic matter you may be assured. Till then I know not what else to say."[57] Once the church building was completed, the WNIA suspended its work, transferring the money to needier missions. Since she lived in nearby San Jacinto, Fowler continued her Sabbath work at Soboba.[58]

Quinton in Southern California

On June 26, 1891, four days after she had arrived in Southern California, an indignant Quinton responded to a June 10 letter from J. N. Patterson, a government auditor, who had turned down her claim for services rendered as a government field matron for lack of proof. The field matron program had been newly created by the Indian Appropriation Act of that year. A matron was to instruct Indian women in food preparation, sewing, laundry work, the care of the sick and of domestic animals, child rearing, and the proper observance of the Sabbath.[59] Quinton suggested to Patterson that he contact Assistant Commissioner Robert V. Belt, who would give him a copy of her oath taken before her appointment. She explained that since March 3, beginning with her arrival among the Seminoles, she had been carrying out her field matron duties, instructing "the women & girls of other tribes en route to this point, as fast as transportation could be provided." She was also considering "the opportunities of the work expected of field matrons and the best methods of perform[ing]" them.[60] This appointment probably originated with Commissioner Morgan who wanted to gauge the effectiveness of this new program. In September 1891, Quinton informed him that she regrettably had to resign her commission although she had found the work "of very deep interest." Among the tribes she had visited, she had learned that "women & girls can be easily taught & influenced, that they can be made ambitious to improve themselves & their homes, & this seems *just* the *time* for this domestic & moral instruction to be given."[61]

Now personally familiar with the field matron program and aware that a WNIA missionary and a matron performed similar tasks, Quinton and the WNIA willingly participated in this government-financed program that proved beneficial to the chronically cash strapped association. Matrons were older single white middle-class women sent to reservations to educate Indian women in various Victorian era domestic tasks as part of the government's assimilationist program. Quinton regularly requested them from the current Indian commissioner for newly proposed mission stations, especially for those in California. At times she even provided the names for those persons she wished to be appointed.[62]

On June 26, Quinton's party was escorted through various Mission Indian villages by Mission Indian Agent Horatio Nelson Rust.[63] They set out by train to Temecula and then by wagon to the village of Cahuilla where on June 27 they met the government schoolteacher, Mrs. Nanie J. Salsberry, described by Quinton as an "earnest Christian teacher" who had won the hearts of her students. Quinton was also pleased with the "the moral tone" of her school and with Miss C. M. Fleming, a young woman who had come to the village as a volunteer. Quinton found the Indians "more civilized and comfortable" than anticipated, describing their captain, Leonicio Lugo, and the other men as possessing "gentle bearing and good manners, glad to hear of our association's work, appreciative of our help to them, and grateful that we proposed still further to aid them on the upward path." Wherever she looked, however, Quinton still saw humble homes of one or two rooms and people in "great need of uplifting, civilizing, industrial and religious teaching."[64]

The party then drove two more miles to the home of an Indian woman named Ramona from whom Quinton purchased a basket. Believing her to be the Ramona of Jackson's novel, Quinton later described her home as a mere cabin "and the life in it was evidently not that of the heroine of the story whose character was of course purposely idealized, though the main incidents of the story were true."[65]

Ramona Lubo poses with an unidentified government schoolteacher and field matron in the Catholic burial grounds at Cahuilla. She was viewed by some as the Ramona of Jackson's novel.
William H. Weinland Collection, The Huntington Library, San Marino, California (photCl 39 [214]).

The woman was in fact Ramona Lubo, widow of Juan Diego, whose murder Jackson had woven into her novel to explain the death of Alessandro, Ramona's fictional husband.[66]

In late June Quinton informed Commissioner Morgan of the good work of both Salsberry and Fleming, requesting that if he appointed the latter as an "industrial teacher" [field matron] for the women and girls, the WNIA would build "a *wee* house & garden" for her. Leonicio Lugo had assured her that his people would grant them land. On August 4, Quinton thanked Morgan for the copy of his letter of instructions to Agent Rust appointing Fleming. This appointment, along with Salsberry's excellent teaching, would meet "the wants of those people very satisfactorily," Quinton wrote, and the WNIA took great pleasure in cooperating with his plans by building a cottage in which Fleming could engage in her industrial work and from which Weinland "at intervals" could give religious instruction and oversee the construction.[67] Finally the long-awaited work among the Cahuilla had begun. It had, however, taken Quinton's presence to do so.

On June 29, Quinton's party arrived at the Cupeño village of Agua Caliente (Warner Hot Springs), after a twenty-mile carriage ride. One of five villages on the Warner Ranch, the village was noted for its sulphur hot springs—an ideal location for a WNIA hospital, Quinton wrote Morgan.[68] She was impressed with Mrs. Josephine Harlan Babbitt, whom she described as "not only teacher, but truest motherly friend, adviser, and moral instructor to her attached Indian friends." Quinton also found the Cupeños "of more aristocratic feeling," possessing "more business ability" than the Cahuillas. Nevertheless, both lacked "sincere and intelligent Christian faith," which would improve them "both morally and materially." The following day after a visit and an address at the school, Quinton described WNIA work before an Indian council called by Agent Rust, reporting later that she had been received with "warm thanks." The next day she attended a school festival sponsored by Babbitt, and at five in the afternoon, with the temperature at 118 degrees, she and her party continued on their journey.[69] The WNIA would ultimately sponsor a medical doctor and support a field matron at Agua Caliente under constrained circumstances.

The 44,000-acre Warner Ranch in northern San Diego County had been named after Jonathan Trumbull Warner, a native of Connecticut, who worked as a fur trapper, clerk, and merchant before becoming a Mexican citizen, receiving a grant of land in 1844 covering most of the San Jose Valley. Gradually between 1870 and 1880 former California governor John Gately Downey had acquired the entire property.[70] When President Rutherford B. Hayes in 1880 rescinded Ulysses S. Grant's 1875 executive order that had created two reservations, including the 1,120-acre reserve on Warner Ranch, Downey decided the timing was right to sell.[71] Despite the presence of dedicated WNIA missionary workers, the next two decades would be difficult for the Warner Ranch Indians, continually living under the threat of removal.

On July 1, 1891, Quinton's party arrived at Pechanga, driving past the new government school where Mrs. Mary J. Platt taught. Several miles up the canyon they met up with her and her students and their parents celebrating an end of the school year picnic. Quinton was impressed by the student's "bright faces, the orderly gentle behavior, [and] the neat and tasteful dress." Just as they gathered to take a commemorative photograph, a messenger arrived with news that the schoolhouse had burned along with all of Platt's belongings. Although lamenting that she would never see the photographs of her husband or children again, Platt "rallied the group and the picture was taken with the Christian leader in the center, as though no disaster had befallen her," wrote Quinton.[72]

When Platt had initially arrived about 1889 to reopen the school, she had found broken windows, a battered door, bullet holes in the blackboard, and a warning

Mary Platt, the government schoolteacher, poses with her students in front of the Pechanga Indian School about 1890. After the school burned, Quinton and the WNIA supported its rebuilding.
C. C. Pierce Collection, The Huntington Library, San Marino, California (photCL Pierce 02427).

that this was no place for a white woman. Undeterred, she had stayed, engaging in temperance work and helping the sick and needy, and teaching their children, earning from Quinton a description as a "faithful and competent Christian teacher." With both Quinton and Rust promising support, the July 1892 issue of *The Indian's Friend* reported her school had been rebuilt.[73]

Leaving Pechanga, the party continued on to the Pala Valley, twenty miles from the San Luis Rey Mission. Once a mission outpost with as many as 1,000 Indians gathering for weekly mass during the 1830s, President Grant had established it as an executive order reservation in 1870; but, public outcry, especially from white squatters living in the valley, had forced him to rescind the order the following year.[74] From Pala they continued through the narrow canyon of the San Luis Rey River described by Quinton as a "dangerous but beautiful drive through three miles of flowers and trees, the wild convolvulus, the snowy large lilies of the stramonium and numberless other radiant blossoms" to the Pauma Ranch. Located near the San Luis Rey River between Rincon and Pala, the ranch, owned by Francis Mora, the third Catholic bishop of Monterey and Los Angeles, had been offered to the government for $31,000 in May 1883. Indian office officials had declined; the price being too high.[75]

Thirteen more miles brought Quinton and her party on July 2 to Rincon and the home of Ora M. Salmons, the government teacher, who Quinton described as exerting a strong influence over the Indians, encouraging them both industrially and morally.[76] After talking to a number of Indian women, Quinton was convinced that "it would be easy to lead them onward in the civilized home-life already begun among them." It was too hot to continue on to La Jolla to visit Flora Glosh's school so they returned to Pala, driving by starlight over the dangerous road where a carriage could easily slip down the steep slope. At Pala, Quinton visited the mission ruins, its graveyard and old church now part of the estate of a Mrs. Veal in whose home they had spent the night. They traveled on to Temecula and caught the train to Colton. Quinton's visit convinced her that it was the WNIA's duty to bring education and "genuine Christianity" to these Mission Indians.[77]

For the rest of July, Quinton held numerous meetings; organized auxiliaries from simple committees to full-fledged Indian Associations in Riverside, Redlands,[78] Banning, Pasadena,[79] Whittier, Pomona, and Los Angeles; and visited the former WNIA missionary site at Potrero, which by unanimous vote of the WNIA Missionary Committee had been transferred to the Missionary Board of the Moravian Church on May 15, 1890.[80] Earlier that month Quinton had informed the Weinlands that the Potrero mission was much loved and it was "a grief to our hearts to part with you and them *officially*. You know that we do *not* part *otherwise*." She had also written Moravian Bishop H. T. Bachman of the Provincial Elders' Conference of the Moravian Church requesting that he appoint Weinland as WNIA counselor and advisor to take on the oversight of all association "new stations and work among the Mission Indians." Weinland eventually became the WNIA traveling missionary.[81]

Northern California WNIA Work

On July 20, 1891, Quinton was in Long Beach where during the closing week of the Long Beach Chautauqua she described the Indians as "industrially, mentally, [and] morally" capable and worthy of citizenship. The Indian question, she concluded, was an educational and missionary issue that should be removed from politics.[82] On July 31, Quinton and her party sailed through the Golden Gate into San Francisco, where during the following month she delivered eighteen addresses, three on August 6, one at a Chinese Mission School, and on August 9 before the gospel temperance meeting in Irving Hall.[83] The following day she addressed three different minister's conferences—Methodist, Baptist, and Congregational.[84] That evening in the parlors of the Occidental Hotel, she organized the Northern California Women's Indian Association. During their second meeting, this auxiliary voted to adopt missionary work on the Hoopa Reservation.[85]

On August 12, 1891, Quinton and her party sailed north to Eureka to investigate conditions on the Hoopa Reservation. She had learned of their dire situation from the corresponding secretary of the California WCTU, Dorcas J. Spencer, who after concluding a talk in Hydesville, Humboldt County, in the summer of 1889, had been approached by Billy Beckwith, a Hupa Indian. He had invited her to accompany him to the reservation to see, among other things, the impact of the presence of Fort Gaston among his people. Spencer later wrote that the officers and enlisted men, fifteen in total, were relieved every three months, bringing "wholly unprincipled men," who were "turned loose to range through the Reservation, to find and debauch the girls, and in every way add to the degradation of these people."[86] A successful WNIA petition drive would lead to the fort's eventual removal and the conversion of its buildings into a government industrial school in 1893.

At Eureka, Quinton joined John Walker, who served as her temporary guide until they met up with Beckwith at Arcata.[87] Together they drove for hours over mountain roads that Quinton described as "hardly more than two feet between our outside wheels and the awful abysses below." Thirty-three miles later they arrived at a place called Brett's where they spent a cool and refreshing night—a compensation for the heat and fleas of the previous night. The following morning they walked a mile over an unfinished wagon road until they were met by men carrying a two-wheeled cart, borrowed at Brett's. This vehicle, narrow enough to travel over the road, took them the final nine miles to Hoopa.[88]

Quinton first paid her respects to Agent Isaac A. Beers, receiving permission to hold a Bible service for the Indians the following day to explain the intentions of the WNIA and to learn personally if they wanted help and instruction. She was convinced there was much to be done, including replacing the soldiers with an Indian police force, establishing a government Indian school, banishing liquor, and introducing Christian instruction. "Nowhere have we seen more marked moral needs," she reported, "nor better prospect of reforms and advancement could the opportunity be supplied."[89]

Returning to Eureka, Quinton founded an Indian association on August 21. Then two days later on Sunday, she gave an address at San Francisco Presbyterian Church, despite having come in that day "dizzy from the sea."[90] The following day she crossed San Francisco Bay, organized an Indian committee in Oakland, and three days later in San Jose appointed an Indian committee. On the 28th Quinton attended the first meeting of the Northern California Women's Indian Association with fifty other women in the First Baptist Church on Eddy Street, where she described her recent Indian visits, including to Hoopa, whose condition, she said, surpassed "any that she had *ever* seen in hopeless degradation." She encouraged this new association to adopt this reservation of some five hundred Indians as their field of work.[91] Leaving her unidentified companion behind, Quinton headed north to Sacramento, establishing an Indian committee on August 30, and the next day arriving at Rancho del Arroyo, Chico, the home of General John Bidwell and his wife, Annie E. K. Bidwell. The couple had met in Washington, DC, while Bidwell was serving as California's congressional representative. Married in 1868, they moved to Chico where Annie Bidwell's humanitarian efforts shifted to working among the small band of Mechoopdas who lived and worked on her husband's estate. Over the years she systematically encouraged them to learn English, adopt western dress and customs, and convert to Christianity, while consoling the sick and injured. Quinton described her work as having brought the Meechoopdas "from barbarism into civilization; from homes which were mere dug-outs, into houses of three rooms" and "from paganism into Christianity." After giving an address in the Indian chapel on the Bidwell estate, Quinton founded an auxiliary in the local Presbyterian Church, with Bidwell, as president. That year Bidwell was listed in the WNIA annual report as the WNIA's western vice president.[92]

From Chico, Quinton boarded a stagecoach that was so full she was forced to sit on top next to the driver for the seventy-mile trip to Prattville, high in the Sierras on the shores of Lake Alamanor. From there she traveled the eighteen miles to Greenville to meet with Charles W. Hall, the WNIA-sponsored teacher, and tour his makeshift school with its thirty-five students, located in Indian Valley, Plumas County. Hall's missionary work dated to the fall of 1889, when Judge Albion Winegar Tourgée had informed Quinton that Hall, a resident of Crescent Mills, had expressed an interest in helping two camps of what the locals called "Digger Indians"—Northern Maidu—near his Indian Valley home. Since Indian students were not entitled to attend public school, Hall had been teaching them for several winters, hoping to build them a formal school. The judge asked Quinton if the WNIA could help.[93]

In late April 1890 Quinton had written Commissioner Morgan, enclosing correspondence between Tourgée and Hall, explaining that she had been writing to Hall for some months and was "satisfied of his earnestness, wish and ability to labor for the Indians near his home." The WNIA was willing to loan him money if the government would pay him $600 annually as a government teacher. Morgan agreed that as soon as the school building was completed, he would ask the Interior secretary for authority to appoint Hall.[94] During the summer of 1890 with the $200 he had borrowed from the WNIA in July, Hall constructed a hewn log cabin with glass windows and a brick chimney. The day school opened on September 23 with twenty-three pupils. The December 1891 issue of *The Indian's Friend* informed readers that Hall had moved to another part of the state, and that Edward N. Ament had assumed the position as head of the Greenville School in mid-October 1891. Under Ament's supervision, it would become a government contract boarding school.[95]

In October 1891, informing Morgan that Hall's total construction costs were $432.14, Quinton respectfully recommended that the government purchase the building for $430 along with the one hundred and sixty acres of land on which it stood. Hall was willing to destroy his filed land papers, leaving the property free and clear for government use. The remainder of her letter dealt with her September 6, 1891, visit to the school, describing its location as good. It could easily accommodate all who were interested in attending. Its influence had already been felt—the home life of many had improved, and "desires for further mental and educational improvement are numerous, not only in this valley, but in others adjoining." After several interviews with Ament, Quinton recommended him heartily.[96] A follow-up letter of February 29, 1892, described Ament as "doing a capital work." The school had an average attendance of thirty-five pupils, who showed great interest, "walking long distances through the snow, thinly clad, to attend even in the severest weather." Florence Ament was assisting her husband, and Quinton asked Morgan if she could be appointed as an assistant teacher. Quinton also requested that the government pay $50 a year to the WNIA for use of the building, reminding him that in a previous letter, he had said the department was willing to pay rent.[97]

From Greenville, Quinton traveled three miles to the home of Mrs. Amelia Martin, Hall's cousin and the wife of an Indian Valley rancher, who had started a Sunday school in the home of Abro Johnson, a Christian Indian. Quinton visited both Martin and Johnson reporting that among the one hundred seventy-five local Indians, thirty-five children had been gathered successfully into Martin's school.[98] The travelers then crossed over the mountains to Chico on September 10 and headed north by train along the narrow valley of the Sacramento River for Oregon. On September 11 Quinton viewed Mount Shasta for the first time, describing its glory as "even greater than anticipated." A few miles south of the Oregon border, at Hornbrook, the engineer put on a second engine to climb the mountain, prompting her to write: "On so wondrous a journey thought takes leave of earth, flits about it and spurns it."[99]

They arrived in Portland on September 14, where Quinton organized an Indian Association in the Presbyterian Church, and three days later organized another in Tacoma, Washington. Returning late to Portland on the 18th, they missed their Columbia River boat and were forced to take the train to Cascade Locks, where they caught another boat, landing at The Dalles and boarding the midnight train for Salt Lake City, where Quinton visited the Mormon Temple, describing it "as a monument to the neglect and un-devotion of American Christians." Openly anti-Catholic, Quinton appeared to be equally scornful of the Mormons. Waxing eloquent on the beautiful scenery as they passed through Colorado, Quinton was "intoxicated with the glories of nature on every hand." In Denver, she organized another branch association, in the Baptist church then boarded the train for the trip through Omaha and on to Chicago. She arrived in New York in time to attend the ninth Lake Mohonk Conference, finally reaching home on October 12. In her ninth letter report, she concluded that from her months of pilgrimage she had learned that "humanity of whatever race, or degree of culture, is bankrupt without Christianity."[100]

Lake Mohonk and After, 1891

Quinton joined the one hundred and sixty-two reformers who gathered at Lake Mohonk on October 7, serving again on the business committee. The Mission Indians were one of the main discussion topics. In January, Congress had finally passed the "Act for the Relief of the Mission Indians in the State of California," which President Benjamin Harrison had signed into law.[101] The legislation was based on recommendations made by Helen Hunt Jackson and Abbot Kinney in their 1883 report for the Interior department on the condition of the Mission Indians. A draft of a bill, along with the Jackson and Kinney report, had first been submitted to Congress in 1884, and although passing the Senate, it failed in the House. It was thereafter submitted annually, with Dawes and Charles C. Painter pushing its final passage.

Albert K. Smiley, host and the leader of the discussion on Mission Indians, inquired of Dawes if Jackson herself had drawn up the original bill and he responded: "Yes, she drew it up herself. She gave it to me." Glad to finally know the bill's origin, Smiley explained that this legislation authorized the creation of a three-man commission to survey and set aside reservation land, and he had been appointed as its chair. IRA agent Painter, and Joseph B. Moore, a Michigan attorney, completed the commission. Smiley explained to the conferees that much of the work had already been done, but Painter was still in California finishing up the commission's work. Smiley personally hoped to "secure a home for all, trying not to pauperize them," but instead make them "valuable citizens of the state [California]."[102]

Kate Foote, president of the WNIA auxiliary in Washington, DC, followed with a short presentation on the Mission Indians.[103] Quinton was next, describing the schools and the government teachers she had met during her recent trip, calling them "teachers, friends and advisers of the pupils," as well as temperance workers—"competent, earnest, and Christian . . . doing their work in a true missionary spirit." She had found the Cahuilla Indians "more civilized and comfortable" than expected, but still with "a great deal of moral instruction" needed. She noted that the ideal location for an Indian hospital was at Agua Caliente with its hot sulphur springs, and there was also a need for a home for the elderly.[104]

Eliphalet Whittlesey, BIC secretary, who had recently visited nine of the houses built by the WNIA Home Building Department, asked Quinton for additional information on this work. Providing some history, she explained that the Alaskan natives as well as the Omahas of Nebraska so far had benefited the most. Repayment was prompt, with few bad debts incurred.[105] Whittlesey's questions were proof that prominent male reformers were becoming aware of the work of Quinton and the WNIA.

On October 27, Quinton spoke before the Baptist Home Mission Union, followed two days later by a talk at the annual meeting of the New Haven Indian Association. On Sunday, November 1, she addressed a gathering in Jamaica Plain, Massachusetts, and the following day in the Old Cambridge Baptist Church she spoke before the annual meeting of the CIA on her recent organizational tour. She had founded this branch of the MIA five years before in the vestry of the First Parish Church with thirty-three women present.[106] The *Cambridge Tribute* reporter, in announcing this annual meeting, remarked that it was some years since Quinton was last heard, "and many who remember her eloquence and enthusiasm will be desirous to hear her now."[107]

On November 4, with nearly every seat in the Boston YMCA lecture hall filled, Quinton addressed the annual meeting of the MIA, which she had organized in 1883, in Boston's Park Street Church, inviting the sixty women present to join in working for "a just, protective and fostering Indian policy."[108] A reporter commented on Quinton's description of her visit to Fort Apache where she found successful Indian farmers selling $20,000 worth of produce to the fort and government in the previous year. In contrast, on ration day among the Apache at San Carlos, she had witnessed extreme poverty as "the sick, the lame, the halt, the blind" waited for their rations. "Things were forbidding to the last degree," Quinton was quoted as saying, defending the Apaches who had been described as the worst Indians when in fact "they are simply more intelligent and have a keener sense of injury when they are wounded."[109]

On November 5 Quinton organized an Indian association in Bridgeport, Connecticut, followed the next day by an address in Brooklyn and another before a large public gathering in Bay Ridge, Long Island. Two weeks later she welcomed WNIA members to their annual meeting at the Christian Church in Allegheny, Pennsylvania. Following a brief respite, she returned to her lecture circuit, making eight addresses in three different states in two weeks.[110]

In between, she answered letters, responding to Commissioner Morgan's December 11 letter regarding a hospital at Agua Caliente. The WNIA, she explained, with his permission and approval, was ready to build one and to support a female physician if his office would grant land near the hot springs so the water could be brought into the building. She also inquired if his office would cover the salary of a field matron. Quinton had someone in mind who could "teach Indian women and girls practically, domestically and morally." The WNIA would provide all other expenses.[111] Quinton could never have imagined the grief this hospital would create for her and the WNIA, part of which was due to Agent Rust, who had also viewed Agua Caliente as the perfect site for a hospital. Encouraged by Commissioner Morgan, he had drawn up plans for the building only to have Morgan turn the project over to Quinton.[112] An angry Rust misrepresented the situation, placing obstacles in Quinton's path. All this conflict notwithstanding, the real reason that a WNIA hospital was never built was Downey's lawsuit against the Warner Ranch Indians for their removal.

The association's chronology, written several years after Quinton's lengthy coast to coast tour, praised her efforts. The trip of thousands of miles had paid for itself in the collections made; and, they had gained thirty-four new branches or committees, seventeen in California alone. Of more importance was that Quinton had "placed the objects of our society before the people, the press and the Christian ministry in the States traversed," noted the author of the chronology.[113]

Quinton had accomplished that and more. Her time in California, especially in the southern part of the state, had opened up new avenues. On a personal level, she was enchanted by the area and went so far as to buy several parcels of land near Perris and Banning and engaged Weinland as a partner in her agricultural endeavors. She also would build a summer home in Perris—Southern California became her special retreat. She returned to the state on official business as often as possible; and, the WNIA founded more mission stations there than in any other state. With the exception of Hoopa, all other California stations were initially operated by the national missionary committee of which Quinton was chair. They were under her direct control, requiring a great deal of correspondence with Indian Office officials, especially with the Mission Indian agent in the case of Southern California as she tried to carry out Jackson's legacy. Quinton would spend much of 1892 dealing with issues that emerged as she pushed the WNIA forward with missionary plans at Cahuilla and Agua Caliente.

6

California Mission Stations at a Critical Juncture, 1892

During 1892 Quinton focused on the WNIA's missionary work at Agua Caliente and Cahuilla where Commissioner Morgan appointed the women she had recommended as field matrons and medical missionary. The Greenville school also was growing, requiring her continual attention. Fortunately, she and Morgan respected one another; most often Quinton got what she requested. That, however, was not the case with Mission Agent Rust; still smarting over his hospital at Agua Caliente, he thwarted her every move.

Compared to her hectic schedule the previous year, Quinton's activities in 1892 were unremarkable. She delivered only 55 addresses, as opposed to the previous year's 110, and founded only three Indian committees. This slowdown was due in part to the increased volume of correspondence necessary to meet the WNIA's enlarged legislative and missionary program,[1] and her personal business arrangement with Rev. William Henry Weinland. Quinton directed her association's efforts on behalf of the Colorado Utes, successfully working with Welsh to prevent their removal to worthless lands in Utah.[2] She also oversaw the association's new missionary efforts among the Hopis at Keams Canyon, Arizona.

BIC Meeting and Addresses

Although she traveled less than in the previous year, Quinton still maintained a rigorous schedule. On January 4 she addressed a Ladies Union meeting in Philadelphia, and the following day spoke before an Indian association in Morristown, New Jersey, before heading to Washington, DC, to present the WNIA's missionary work of the past year at the twenty-first annual BIC conference on January 7. The association now had workers in forty states, operating among fifteen tribes continuously and with another fifteen on a temporary basis. She was particularly pleased that this year reflected "a perfect revolution in educational matters." Indian education had become a part of her association's work nearly ten years earlier on October 3, 1882, when the executive committee had revised their constitution to reflect this new goal. She stressed that all education should be in English, provided by the government, and with reformers pushing "to the utmost" to achieve this goal. Concluding her remarks, she gave another nod to the application of Civil Service rules to the Indian service.[3]

During the question-and-answer part of the meeting, BIC president Merrill E. Gates, called on Quinton for clarification of various items. Each time she responded, Commissioner Morgan interrupted, explaining that he had already addressed that particular issue. Although no doubt annoying, these interruptions reflected that Morgan was clearly focused on Quinton's concerns, and Quinton did not seem to mind the interruptions. She had begun her remarks with her recent tour, describing the whisky traffic among the Seminoles as "a source of vast evil" slowing down WNIA work, and describing the Hopi as "a quiet, industrious people." She found quite "touching" the many illustrations of the Apache at Fort Apache, whom she found willing to work even though the wives of the officers had told her that they were not. She witnessed one Indian woman walking a long distance with a load of hay on her back, who, after receiving her money, immediately paid off her debt to the trader and bought a horse to work next year's crop. Morgan interrupted to explain that a new day school had been opened at Fort Apache, to which Quinton expressed "gladness." She noted that "the visit that went most to [her] heart was among the San Carlos Apaches," where on annuity day she saw "such a collection of human wretchedness [she had] never seen in one picture." Through interpreters she had learned they wanted their children educated in a reservation day school; Morgan responded that he was sending their children to Haskell in Kansas and Genoa in Nebraska, respectively, until the government could build them a school. The Apache had also asked for police courts, not wanting their agent to serve as arbiter, to which Morgan explained that the agent had been relieved and the new agent had agreed to establish Indian courts.[4]

Quinton's presentation was witnessed by Caroline H. Dall, reformer and essayist, who was reporting on the proceedings for the *Cambridge Tribune*. Describing Quinton as "no longer young" but with delightful energy and spirit, Dall praised both the "admirable report" of her recent trip and her visits to government schools. "The confidence she [Quinton] inspires in the natives is a rich reward," continued

Dall, who challenged women to take up her crusade. "Oh! Women, idle in your comfortable homes, listlessly preparing for the insane asylum, . . . can you not see the redemption offered to you in noble work? Can you not realize that one such meeting as this is worth a dozen 'Suffrage Conventions?'"[5]

Leaving Washington, DC, briefly, Quinton spoke in Brooklyn at the Marcy Avenue Baptist Church but returned on January 15 to address the Washington, auxiliary. While there, she took the opportunity to get letters from members of the House and Senate Indian committees to support the IRA in its continual struggle to convince Congress to provide generously for Indian education in its annual Indian Appropriation Bill.[6] To aid WNIA auxiliaries on "how best to do their legislative work," in 1888 the association had founded a Committee on Indian Legislation, headed by Kate Foote, president of the Washington, auxiliary, who according to Wanken was not only "politically astute," but possessed a "much broader understanding of legislative affairs than most in her organization." Thus she was "able to apprise her sister reformers of which legislation suited their philosophy." Foote corresponded with the influential Herbert Welsh of the IRA, wrote articles for *The Indian's Friend*, and published several WNIA pamphlets on what she thought was needed. Then in 1891, to further assist Foote, the WNIA introduced the short-lived Committee on Legislative Work to advise auxiliaries on how to push forward legislation she recommended. It lasted only three years. Then when Foote married in 1895, she relinquished the chairmanship of the original Committee on Indian Legislation. She was never replaced.[7]

Quinton's next three addresses were in Philadelphia, followed in mid-February by one at the Indian association in New York City. The same day she informed Welsh that the WNIA was doing all it could, "& in many ways, & on many lines, for this Ute case, as well as for Approp'ns." She agreed to use "every nerve & muscle" on behalf of the latter, explaining that the WNIA had its legislative committee hard at work, although she included no specifics. A week later Quinton wrote she had done everything she could, working up to midnight daily. "Am worn out & must stop, for at least a few days." In her judgment, however, the Appropriation Bill would pass; it did in early March with only minimal reductions.[8]

January also saw Quinton dealing with the property she had purchased the previous year in California. In a letter to Weinland on the 1st, she questioned him about the deed for the five acres in Banning. It incorrectly listed her residence as San Francisco not Philadelphia and had the wrong county for Banning. Besides managing documents, in her deal with Weinland, he had agreed to clear the property, plant it in sultana grapes, and maintain the plantings until, at some point, he would buy an acre and a half at her cost.[9]

Seminole Mission and the Greenville School

Quinton remained close to home during March 1892, leaving only twice to address an Indian association in Yonkers and a gathering in New York City. Her correspondence, however, never ended. Late in the month, she informed Morgan that because their missionaries among the Florida Seminoles, Dr. Brecht and his wife, were sharing a small house with another family and were in the "greatest discomfort," he and another man had built temporary housing for them, using lumber not otherwise needed. Quinton explained that this structure had been constructed on association-owned land in Florida, not on the adjacent government-owned land, and she assured the commissioner that the WNIA would pay for its removal when the buildings were completed.[10]

The following month she made additional requests on behalf of the WNIA Seminole work. The government-owned land would provide a better site for buildings, and the association tract, a far larger piece, was better for farming if the Indians chose to settle there. Quinton inquired if the government overseer would plow the land for Indian use, giving them the waste lumber from the government sawmill to build homes, especially if the wood came from logs on association land. She agreed to pay for the milling and the sawing. She also asked if logs from association land could be sawed in the government mill, with some of the waste given to neighboring poor whites. They were good and respectable people, "& it will be helping to the Indians to have those in that vicinity settled in decent houses," she concluded.[11]

Late in March, Quinton asked Morgan to appoint Florence Ament as an assistant to Ament's husband, Edward, at the Greenville [CA] Indian Industrial School.[12] Under Ament's stewardship, Greenville had become so successful that parents from miles around were asking to have their children boarded there, she noted. At the end of 1892, Quinton asked him if the Indian Office could make an appropriation for boarding some of these students. He responded on January 4, 1893, requesting additional information. She forwarded his letter to Ament and explained to Morgan that Ament was willing to lodge and board the students in his own home if need be. Ament responded to Morgan on January 21, that he had learned from Quinton that it would be possible to establish a boarding school to accommodate one hundred students if forty acres adjacent to the current schoolhouse lot could be deeded to the government in a clear title. He and

In this 1894 photograph, Edward Ament, his wife Florence, and their daughter Edna, pose with students from the Greenville Indian Industrial Boarding School. The school was a particular favorite of Quinton, who visited often.
Indian Valley Museum, Taylorsville, California.

A. G. Swan, a local farmer, and J. R. Murray, the local postmaster, were willing to sign such a pledge.[13]

In early February 1893, forwarding the pledge to deed the forty acres, Quinton informed Morgan that some of the young male students had "walked three miles through snow in severe cold with their feet tied up in barley sacks, having no shoes, in order not to lose a day." In the meantime, Ament was willing to buy a house and add to his own in order to board some fifteen to twenty pupils if the government would pay $15 a month per student.[14] Reminding Morgan's successor, Daniel M. Browning, that her association initially had funded the schoolhouse, in early November 1893 she wrote that they had raised money to build a dormitory to house thirty to forty Indian students, and she was now applying for the government subsidy per student. Then in a follow-up letter of December 8, 1893, she offered the government, "free of expense," the fully furnished dormitory in return for the usual school rations. In accepting the offer, Browning wrote Ament requesting he submit a cost estimate.[15] Ultimately becoming a government contract school, Greenville received regular funding per boarded student.[16]

The efforts among the Seminole and at Greenville illustrate how effective Quinton was at managing her association's relationship with the federal government.

It was a relationship that required patience and perseverance, for the wheels of government tended to move slowly. It also required constant attention and understanding of details on the ground. It may seem odd now that a high-level government official was dealing with issues as small as the purchase of a house, but Quinton's own command of these details certainly made such attention more likely. She was a steady force through several administrations, and her attention to detail and continual correspondence ensured that things did not get lost in the transitions. Her experience at Agua Caliente, on the other hand, would show that even with all of these qualities in play, the WNIA's efforts were sometimes utterly confounded, in this case by personal conflict, miscommunication, and, it seems, an unwillingness to listen to the Indian people themselves when their views differed from hers.

The Agua Caliente Hospital

The WNIA success at Greenville would not be replicated at Agua Caliente, where despite heroic efforts, the association-sponsored hospital never became a reality. Early on Quinton had realized that building a hospital was going to be a bumpy ride. The problem was not the concept of the WNIA sponsoring a hospital, which they had done at numerous other locations; rather, it was the site. Having corresponded with Commissioner Morgan about the hospital at the end of 1891, Quinton wrote him in early January 1892 that it seemed that neither the government nor the WNIA could obtain a legal right to build at Agua Caliente. She suggested that if the Indians understood and wanted to have their hospital, they might set land aside. "May we try this experiment *with your approval*," she inquired. At month's end, in response to his letter, she wrote that her association was still waiting to hear from Josephine Babbitt, the schoolteacher, as to whether or not the Indians had accepted their offer of a hospital. As soon as they made their decision, the WNIA would construct a cottage for the physician and government field matron. The hospital would soon follow with buildings constructed with Indian consent to "*be their property*, upon *their pledge to us*, as an association, that we may *use* the same, for their help, in all respects as if the buildings were our own."[17]

In late February, Quinton informed Morgan that she had heard from Babbitt that the Indians were pleased about the hospital but hesitant to do anything because Agent Rust had instructed them not to make a formal agreement without his written approval. Since Morgan approved, she asked him to write the Indians and Rust. He complied, giving Rust authorization in an April 26 letter.[18] Quinton also wrote directly to Rust, who responded two weeks later that he would prepare an agreement, forward it to Mrs. Babbitt, and inform the village captain to have the Indians give their consent and set aside the land. Shortly thereafter, on May 6, Rust informed Morgan that although Babbitt had used her influence, the Indians had declined to sign because they were pleased with the present physician and did not need a hospital. He wrote, "I judge that they will not consent unless ordered and if ordered they will accept it and I judge will not be offended."[19]

Earlier, on April 4, 1892, Quinton had explained to Weinland that Morgan, Charles C. Painter, and A. K. Smiley all approved of their plan to build and then give the structure to the Indians. However, Quinton was adamant that "the hospital *touch* the Hot Springs so as to have a free supply of hot water." But this was also a move to protect Indian rights to their springs. According to Quinton, Rust "did *not* want the Indians to have *any* hold on the Springs," and therefore he wanted the association to "build *a distance away*." Quinton implored Weinland to look over all the pros and cons, and not "let Rust's plans to take advantage of the Indians be successful if you can help it!"[20]

On April 10 Quinton traveled to Rhode Island to give a Sunday evening address at the Union Congregational Church, attended by more than 1,000 people.[21] On the following day she wrote Weinland a lengthy letter expressing the hope that he would not fall into Rust's trap, "for all his arguments are specious & fallacious." The agent was determined that the hospital should be built a distance from the hot springs. If that were the case, Quinton saw no reason for even building it. During her visit the previous year, Rust had deplored the mere idea "of these splendid springs in the hands of such savages!" She encouraged Weinland to look carefully for a building site and report back. She warned that, "If we do *not* build at the hot springs then some white men will get the springs, sooner or later."[22] On April 21 she complained that Rust was playing "sharp" with her, claiming he was helping when in fact he was writing to Morgan "in such a way as to *prevent*" him from approving their plans. She concluded with a note of thanks for his planting all five acres of her land: "May we be prosperous in it & you be enabled to buy when & as you desire."[23]

Negotiations concerning the hospital consumed much of Quinton's summer. Rust had ramped up his opposition, prompting her to write Weinland in mid-May that the agent "*pretends* to approve & yet so writes as to make them afraid to consent." She wanted Weinland to inform the Indians that the government could not and would not build a hospital—only the WNIA was able to do so. She already had collected $900 for the building, sending along a rough diagram of the missionary cottage and hospital with an open piazza between. To ensure sufficient ventilation, she recommended large windows opening from both top and bottom. There were three bathrooms, one for men, one for women, and the third for the WNIA-sponsored missionary and government field matron. An acre would suffice for the buildings, to include "a stable roof to well protect horse & buggy in rains & a little out house," and a small vegetable garden. "Our being there for *their* good alone will keep out *selfish* men," she declared. "Poor souls! How they are ground & robbed of favors even by the machinations of the selfish & compassionless!" She concluded, "if H. H. [Helen Hunt Jackson] were alive she would say, 'be *sure* & let the Ass'n build the hospital.'" Less than a week later Quinton reported that Rust claimed that according to Kate Foote, the Catholics opposed the hospital. Quinton disagreed, continuing to blame Rust. "He *ought* to be exposed," she wrote. However, she deferred to Weinland's judgment, hoping to "circumvent his [Rust's] machinations."[24]

On May 23, Quinton wrote Rust that she had just received copies of his correspondence with the Indian Office for the WNIA Missionary Committee to consult, and after reading it, begged him to use the persuasion he referred to in his letter of May 6 "to induce the Indians to give their formal consent and agreement to the pledge we sent them to sign." The money was ready and two women had been selected—a physician and a field matron. Then turning to flattery, she wrote: "Your name as a friend to our work, and your expressions, often made in public, and quoted by us in print as those of our friend and helper, naturally make all feel that you *will* favor this project." She asked that Rust visit the village, using his persuasive powers and his official influence to get the desired consent and "such success will gratify all here and in Washington."[25] A week later, she informed Weinland that she had written Rust, and as soon as Morgan returned to Washington, she would also ask him to write the agent to make him "see that for his own interest he'd better help us on the hospital."[26]

In mid-July Quinton traveled to Washington to confer with Morgan and with Josephine Babbitt, who had come from California to help facilitate the building of the hospital. During their discussion, the subject of renting a house for the proposed physician and field matron was raised, prompting Quinton to write Weinland: "We all think that to *rent* is good, if Indians are *cordial*."[27] A week later, re-emphasizing that the WNIA would never build a hospital without the Indians' consent, Quinton's distrust of Rust became even more blatant, calling his excuses for not going to Agua Caliente, even after Morgan had asked him to do so, as "*so puerile*." Rust had openly revealed his opposition to her, and to

Dr. W. E. Ferrebee, the agency physician, "and told it in effect to Mrs. Babbitt now just before she came north." Quinton accused Rust of possessing "*no principle* of right action, & will betray any trust if *he* is not at head of all." The WNIA could not lean on him as he "serves *self & not Indians.*"[28]

Quinton's dream of a hospital was severely threatened when Downey and the Merchants' Exchange Bank of San Francisco filed in the Superior Court of San Diego County to remove the residents of the five villages from Warner Ranch in August 1892. There were two suits, *John G. Downey vs. Alejandro Barker, et al.*, against the residents of Agua Caliente and Puerta la Cruz, with Barker heading the list of eighty-six village defendants, and *John G. Downey v. José Quevas, et al.* against Mataguay, San Jose, and La Puerta, with Quevas heading the list of sixty-two defendants. Although Quinton had been working on hospital details for months, WNIA membership only learned in the August 1892 issue of *The Indian's Friend* that a local official [Rust] had failed to add his written consent to the "most cordial approval of" the government, thus preventing its building that summer. Now they learned that ex-governor Downey "will at once begin suit for the ejectment of these Indians." Because of these actions, Quinton and the association had decided temporarily that it was "clearly best not to expend" their funds in building the hospital. The article ended with: "RIGHT is still on THE THRONE, the sun rises on the darkest night, and faith is ever justified. God's delay is safety, and we need not fear."[29]

Despite the pending lawsuit, Quinton moved forward, informing Weinland in late September that she intended to inquire of the Missionary Committee if renting housing was viable, and if so, how much the association could afford. She had also requested that the IRA take up the Indians' case, and its new president, Philip Garrett, had replied favorably. She would also bring the subject up at the next Mohonk Conference. On October 1, without her knowledge, Rust had rented a two-room cottage on a weekly basis in Agua Caliente for the two women. Quinton immediately viewed the arrangement as too risky. On October 3, she wrote Weinland that a failure to pay weekly would be "ground for turning us out." Rust had put "himself again between us & our work with the Indians," she bitterly declared, his ways were as "specious" as ever.[30] In a second letter to Weinland dated October 3, Quinton, having just received his September 28 letter, explained she had just sent a letter off to Washington requesting that Rust instead allow the Indians to rent directly to Mrs. Babbitt or their missionaries. The WNIA could not send money to the agent, Quinton remarked, otherwise the association should "best drop the project till the suit is settled."[31]

Josephine H. Babbitt poses with her students before the government Indian school at Agua Caliente village (Warner Hot Springs) on Warner Ranch. She became a strong supporter of Quinton's efforts on the Indian's behalf. *Horatio N. Rust Collection, The Huntington Library, San Marino, California (photCL 7 [12]).*

On the same day, Quinton had also written to Babbitt describing the situation as insecure, having "not a *particle* of faith in Maj. R's sincerity." Even more appalling, Quinton had been informed by C. M. Fleming, field matron at Cahuilla, that when she was away from the WNIA cottage, Rust had "spent the night in it with a woman of questionable character." Then in late October Quinton informed Weinland that Indian Commissioner Morgan would not permit the WNIA to rent from Rust.[32]

To make matters worse, a number of Quinton's letters to Agua Caliente had gone astray, prompting her on November 23 to inform Babbitt that she was rerouting her letters through Washington for forwarding. Filling Babbitt in on lost information, Quinton wrote that Morgan would not let the WNIA take a cottage in Agua Caliente weekly from Rust "under the circumstances." Therefore she asked if Babbitt would be willing to rent it in her name, accepting the weekly receipt. "We have waited in the greatest suspense for many months," she noted, "and the doctor and her friend have held on far longer in faith and hope than I thought possible." Quinton appended an addition to this letter after receiving news from Weinland that Rust had demanded back payment to September 1 for the house he had leased. Calling the payment of back rent a wise move and a way to acquire the lease from Rust, Weinland had agreed, although Quinton viewed it a fraud to demand rent for a building the association had not even been aware of, let alone occupied.[33] Weinland's move paved the way for the missionary work at Agua Caliente to proceed without the agent's involvement.

Learning from Weinland's November 22 telegram that Indian consent to proceed with the hospital had finally been granted, Quinton informed Morgan that since the WNIA was now renting directly from the Indians, the Missionary Committee had employed Dr. Rebecca C. Hallowell as their medical missionary, asking him to appoint the doctor's friend, Julia M. French of San Francisco, as a government field matron.[34] "We are prepared to build a hospital when the land question is settled," she wrote, "& with your protection & aid, hope to do a good work for the Indians."[35] Quinton telegraphed Weinland, following up with a letter for him to begin making house repairs. He was to telegraph as soon as they were completed so Dr. Hallowell could set out. Quinton had also asked if he could meet both Hallowell and French and drive them to Agua Caliente.[36]

Agua Caliente was not the only Mission village to receive a new field matron. Quinton had learned from Weinland that Fleming, the matron at Cahuilla, had resigned because of ill health. Fortunately, Quinton knew a woman doctor she thought could take her place and admonished Weinland to keep the key of the WNIA cottage: "It is ours, & *not* Gov't's, or Maj. R's, & so it is under your care as our Sup't." Her acquaintance, Dr. Anna Hayward Johnson, a practicing physician from Orange, New Jersey; a graduate of Vassar and the Woman's Medical College of Pennsylvania; and a former Hampton teacher, was appointed by the commissioner.[37]

Summer Meetings and the Hopis

Despite juggling the complicated negotiations at Agua Caliente, Quinton continued her other activities. On May 8, she addressed a union meeting of five churches in Syracuse. Two days later she spoke before the Syracuse Indian Association, at a union meeting in Hamilton, New York; and later in Yonkers at a young people's association. On May 19, she attended the Hampton Indian school commencement, writing in *The Indian's Friend*: "there is something on such occasions which appeals to the best and highest in every human breast." But this was different, for "there was a pathos and appeal never before here present—" a reference to

General Samuel Chapman Armstrong, the school's founder, whose stroke had prevented him from addressing the large gathering. The accolades reminded her of the tenderness of a final farewell to active service. Everyone seemed to sense it, she remarked, making the occasion "morally superb."[38]

Quinton spoke in Richmond, Virginia, on May 20, and the next day addressed the Washington auxiliary, giving "a stirring account of her journey of eight months through the Southern and Western states" and of the branch associations she had organized. She was followed by Dr. Susan La Flesche Picotte, the WNIA's medical missionary among the Omahas, who addressed the issue of increased alcoholism among her people, especially following Nebraska's passage of a bill permitting liquor sales to Indians. An *Indian's Friend* article noted that the Washington branch had completed their pledge of $100 towards building a cottage for the resident physician in Agua Caliente.[39]

In addition to supervising WNIA missionary work in Southern California, Quinton was also overseeing new missionary efforts among the Hopis at Keams Canyon, Arizona. In early September she wrote Morgan explaining the WNIA had a plan to "*hire*, at first, a part of a large & good adobe house there, from a good & friendly & more intelligent Indian family" as a residence for their new doctor and the government field matron. Having visited the site the previous year, Quinton knew this field was untouched, and that the school doctor was too distant to accomplish what she was proposing. The WNIA-sponsored physician would visit Indian homes and the tribe but not the government school, so Morgan should fear no conflict. Quinton sought his approval, with the missionary cottage and perhaps a small hospital coming later. She was already consulting with the wife of Ralph P. Collins, superintendent at Keams Canyon school.[40]

With encouragement from Collins, a government promise for protection from the more nomadic Navajos, and help in purchasing building supplies, some Hopi had agreed to move from their lofty multi-storied communal mesa homes to the plains below, building homes closer to their fields and pastures, to live in what white reformers perceived was a more "civilized" manner. In the July 1892 issue of *The Indian's Friend*, Collins had reported that twenty-two homes were done but in need of furnishing, and already WNIA members from Allegheny, Pennsylvania, and Newark, New Jersey, had begun sending barrels of home furnishings. In January 1893 the Missionary Committee reported the number of completed houses had more than tripled.[41]

Quinton also spent much of the fall and early winter negotiating another arrangement with Weinland to manage her personal property in Perris. On

September 21 she asked if the Moravian governing board could put someone else in his place at Potrero, would he be willing to move to Perris where his children could go to school. He could continue his WNIA missionary work from there and serve as an agent for her and three of her acquaintances, clearing, planting, and cultivating their lands at $100 each. She also inquired if he would buy five acres from her at Perris, at $50 an acre, on credit for three or four years. He could plant figs, guavas, grapes, or oranges. She also suggested that he could pay for two of her Banning acres. They could share expenses. Her stepson, George H. Quinton, would be moving to California to manage her property, she explained.[42] Although confirming a week later that George would not be going to California yet, she was still considering putting up a shell of a two- or three-room house but not finishing the inside. She inquired if Weinland might think about living in it until she needed it.[43] In late October she was still negotiating on behalf of the three other individuals. Then in mid-November she complained to Weinland that her Perris land had been planted before the piped water was ready, and she had lost hundreds of vines. At year's end, Weinland decided to remain in Banning, and on January 3 of the following year she offered to sell him her five acres there.[44]

A Return to Lake Mohonk

Quinton resumed her schedule of addresses in September, giving a dozen and organizing three Indian committees in Maine. In mid-October, the annual Mohonk Conference offered her a bit of relaxation as she mingled with other Indian reformers and Commissioner Morgan. Smiley welcomed attendees on October 12, 1892, including Judge Joseph B. Moore, who had served with Smiley and Painter on the Mission Indian Commission, and delivered an address on the Mission Indians.[45]

When it was Quinton's turn to report, she addressed the obligation of churches to educate Indian students, claiming that "the Christian tide is so strongly set to-day on this Indian question that there is no danger of its going backward." She had witnessed the same "tide" in the Keams Canyon government school, which she described as Christian "by the presence of Christian teachers." She praised their teaching of patriotism, instilling piety and the Christian idea, concluding that religion would have a place even if the churches were no longer in control of Indian education. She emphasized that the key to funding education was to ensure that Congress appropriated sufficient money, remarking that "if all the friends of the Indians who are here would make it a duty, when they return home, to speak of this to those who lead public opinion, we should have money enough."[46]

The conferees also listened to a report of the Lake Mohonk Committee on Legal Assistance to the Mission Indians. At the conclusion, members voted on authorizing an appeal for $2,500 to support this work.[47] This committee had been formed at the 1886 conference following what the *New York Herald* had described as Mrs. Osia Jane Joslyn Hiles's "thrilling narrative of the pitiful condition of affairs in Southern California." Hiles, a well-to-do Milwaukee widow, was a member of the Wisconsin Indian Association, a WNIA auxiliary.[48] When she offered to contribute $5,000 to pay the Mission Indians' legal bills, thirteen others joined her and the Lake Mohonk Legal Assistance Committee was born.[49] To further the work on behalf of the Mission Indians, members also agreed that the IRA's work be enlarged and broadened, delegating Charles C. Painter to investigate and make inquiries on which Mission cases should be pursued and to locate a first-class attorney to prosecute them.[50] Painter would choose Frank D. Lewis, of Pomona, who was appointed by the Indian Office as a special attorney for the Mission Indians.[51]

Lewis, in attendance at Mohonk, then described the complicated Indian land claims, prior removals, and current villages threatened, especially those on the Warner Ranch.[52] He addressed the recent action against the village of Agua Caliente, with its estimated two hundred residents living on 1,200 acres and the adjoining villages with their two hundred acres.[53] Because this work was onerous, he needed assistance. Lewis then urged Conference members to consider employing Shirley C. Ward, who had saved the Soboba village. The conference voted to do so.[54]

In early April, she accused Lewis of wanting the hospital built half a mile away instead of at the hot springs, and like Rust, helping white men to acquire the springs. Then two weeks before the Conference, she wrote Weinland accusing both men of expecting Downey to win his suit. "I fear *both* are bought off!" she exclaimed. To Babbitt, she expressed much the same sentiment, claiming that Lewis and Rust expected the Indians at Agua Caliente to be ejected.[55] Eager to accuse him, Quinton had failed to recognize any of his beneficial work on behalf of the very village in which she wanted to build her hospital.

At Mohonk, Quinton took the opportunity to confer with Morgan about hiring Dr. Anna Johnson as the field matron at Cahuilla. He agreed that if there was money available, he would appoint her. Several weeks later, after hearing from Johnson that Morgan had offered her a position in either Kansas or Arizona, Quinton, mildly chiding the commissioner, wrote: "there is some forgetfulness, I think, for we built our cottage at Coahuilla [*sic*] for this work." The WNIA would be "grieved to lose Dr. Johnson as she is a woman to elevate the whole tribe & to move them in many ways." Quinton explained that Johnson would not only do medical work but "*in spirit*, [would be] our helper too, & we will aid her work for the Indians." If Morgan was low on funds, Quinton offered $20 a month from the WNIA, if the government picked up the remaining $40 a month.[56] In the end, Johnson received her appointment to Cahuilla.

Between her attendance at Lake Mohonk and the annual WNIA convention Quinton gave four addresses. Then on December 7 and 8, 1892, she welcomed 110 WNIA delegates from nine states to the Clinton Avenue Congregational Church in Brooklyn. *The Indian's Friend* reported that during the mass public meeting on Wednesday evening, Commissioner Morgan gave a "forcible and eloquent speech" on "What Next for the Indian." Two Carlisle Indian students followed, one giving an address on immediate citizenship for Indians. "The whole Convention glowed with earnest thought, and showed the reality and steadiness of purpose, which with an unwavering sense of obligation and faith in God, have united and hold the women of the Association to their sacred work."[57] Ten days later, Quinton gave her final address of the year at the Woman's Medical College of Pennsylvania in Philadelphia.

Although Quinton's addresses in 1892 were fewer and her travels less extensive than in the previous year, her correspondence had become more burdensome as she dealt with California stations among the Mission Indians and an increasingly recalcitrant Mission Indian agent. The problems that had begun in 1892 in Agua Caliente and minimally in Cahuilla would worsen in the following year.

7

Continued Issues at Agua Caliente and Cahuilla, 1893

During 1893, in addition to giving more public addresses than in the previous year, Quinton organized five new associations and committees, and, at the invitation of the Brooklyn auxiliary, visited their Montana mission in June. However, one of the highlights for both Quinton and her association was their participation, along with fifty other national women's societies, in the six-month-long Columbian Exposition in Chicago. Beginning in May, the WNIA's presence in the exposition's Woman's Building enabled the association to hand out literature to the many thousands of visitors and for Quinton to give ten of her sixty-seven public addresses to a totally new and enlarged audience.

In between these addresses, Quinton spent much of the summer and fall corresponding with Rev. William Henry Weinland as well as Mission Agent Horatio N. Rust and Indian Commissioner Thomas Jefferson Morgan to calm down controversies that arose in two of the association's California missions, one raised by Agent Rust at Cahuilla over the WNIA cottage and others created by over-zealous WNIA workers at both Cahuilla and Agua Caliente—issues that dragged on through the administrations of Commissioner Morgan and his replacement, Daniel M. Browning, and agent Rust and his successor, Francisco Estudillo.[1]

Quinton's official year began with an address before a public meeting at the Presbyterian Church in Wilmington, Delaware on January 10, 1893, one of just under seventy that year. That number was dictated by the lack of funds to hire clerical services while she was on the road; it was amazing the WNIA even survived the year. Early in 1893 the Philadelphia and Reading Railroad went into receivership, followed by a wild stock market response and a string of other railroad failures. Five hundred banks and sixteen thousand businesses declared bankruptcy. Although the country would remain in the grip of the Panic until 1897, loyal WNIA supporters continued sending in dues. Over twenty new honorary members pledged $50 ($1,461.19 in 2021 dollars) and over thirty new life members contributed $10. The Maine auxiliary with a membership of slightly over two hundred raised $547.81. Total receipts for the year were $10,366.71 ($299,746.51 in 2021 dollars) with a total carry over balance bringing cash on hand to $16,300.06 ($471,320.98 in 2021 dollars). The only reference in WNIA literature to the trying economic times was a reference to the lack of money "for clerical services at home" which "forces the conviction that the whole subject of our financial resources should receive immediate and earnest attention from this body"—with no follow up.[2]

The BIC Meeting and Indian Education

Two days after her Wilmington speech, Quinton attended the annual BIC meeting in Washington, DC. Her presentation addressed schools and the work of the Christian teachers she had met, expressing no fear "about the future of Government education among the Indians." It had "advanced to such a point in educational matters that it can not recede," she concluded. All the missionary boards in attendance ran contract schools and thus received government reimbursement, so education was crucial to all. The discussion became even more earnest once it turned to compulsory education, which Congress had decreed in 1890.[3]

The previous year Commissioner Morgan had presented his plan for a national system of Indian schools before the Mohonk Conference. Among his suggestions had been compulsory education. Although he had clearly stated that it was the responsibility of the federal government to provide Indian education, he also stressed the urgent need "of consecrated missionary work and liberal expenditure of money on the part of individuals and religious organizations in behalf of these people."[4] As much as their finances allowed, Quinton and the WNIA were heeding Morgan's request.

Quinton personally favored compulsory education, downplaying the use of force as "more an alarm in imagination than in reality;" necessary in no more than one in a hundred cases, referring specifically to Keams Canyon school and the village of Oraibi's refusal to send their children. In that case soldiers were dispatched, and "in the early morning the cannon, which had been placed during the night, spoke, and a cloud of smoke rolled up," and "the Indians looked on with amazement, then got together, had a hasty conference, and came down and capitulated in a body."[5] Summarizing the BIC meeting, *The Indian's Friend* concluded that "the greater wrong would be to suffer new generations of Indians to grow up in savagery," and therefore agreed that if needed, force should be applied.[6] Before adjourning, the BIC resolved to appoint a committee to convey to incoming President Cleveland the necessity of appointing an Indian commissioner who would "carry on the Indian Office in the spirit and along the lines herein suggested"—the issue of removing the politics from Indian affairs was a BIC goal as well as a long time personal goal for Quinton, who was one of fifteen appointed to the committee.[7] Already in Washington, she stayed behind to address a session of that city's auxiliary.[8]

A Problem at Cahuilla

To further the WNIA's work among the Cahuillas, on January 11, Quinton requested from Morgan a grant of five acres or less "for educational & missionary purposes," to include the WNIA missionary cottage, recently built and now occupied by Dr. Anna Johnson, the field matron he had recently appointed. Quinton reminded Morgan that their cottage had been located "per" his permission by the WNIA missionary superintendent, Reverend Weinland, with Indian consent. Four days later she informed Weinland that the association did not need five acres, only enough for a small pasture and space for their missionary to raise fruit trees and vegetables, especially "if they object, as they once did"—a reference to her 1889 request to Commissioner Oberly that the village captain had refused. Weinland wrote Rust on January 23, respectfully requesting to meet him at Cahuilla at his earliest convenience, explaining he was representing the WNIA in locating the acreage in question.[9]

A week later Quinton learned from Weinland, who had just returned from a visit to Cahuilla, that Rust had made a contract with the Indians to rent land with an adobe house on it, repair the house, move the WNIA cottage to that land, and hand over all improvements to the Indians at the end of five years. Quinton informed Commissioner Morgan that her association had no prior knowledge of this arrangement, and Rust had "not the slightest authority" to deal with the WNIA cottage. In addition, she had learned that Rust had forbidden Johnson from occupying the WNIA missionary cottage. She requested Morgan protect the cottage "from this unauthorized plan" and direct Johnson to do her work. Quinton described Rust's actions to Weinland as "the greatest imprudence & dishonesty I've ever heard of I think, of *any* Agent." She could not believe that he had dared to give away their cottage and forbid a government appointee from carrying out her work.[10]

The following month, Rust began complaining that the WNIA's Cahuilla cottage had been "built without his knowledge or consent." On February 4, 1893, Quinton assured Morgan that it had been built with the government's permission and the consent of the Indians on a site selected by Weinland and C. M. Fleming. "Major Rust *did know* of this location and *made no objection* or protest about it, then or after the cottage was built," she wrote. "Never till some time after the house was done & occupied," did she hear "a growl about the location" from him. To defend her position, she included detailed facts on its placement and a diagram of the school lot, schoolhouse and yard, and their cottage, which located outside the school fence, was separated from teacher Nanie J. Salsberry's living quarters (attached to the school) by twelve feet, leaving space for a playground on three sides of the school.[11]

Quinton explained that its placement had been agreed upon by Leonicio Lugo, the village captain at the time; Salsberry; and Fleming, Johnson's predecessor. In fact, Lugo had indicated that the "correct place" was to the west of the schoolhouse where it now stood. For security reasons both Salsberry and Johnson, like Fleming, had preferred living near one another, being the only two white women in the village. More important, the current location was the only available one near the school because of the presence of large rocks. Although Rust had been ill at the time of site selection, he later met in Banning with Weinland, who explained its placement and Rust offered no protest. Rust, Quinton concluded, only wanted "the whole affair into his hands." The WNIA would never do that because agents, Rust included, were either too busy or too far away. Instead Weinland as WNIA superintendent of missions was totally in charge. She trusted the cottage need not be disturbed.[12]

The previous month Quinton had asked Weinland to send her anything he had in writing about permission granted them for the cottage's placement. She could not remember if she had been given verbal consent and then reported it to him. Several days later she again implored him to search for either her letters or Morgan's. "I was on the wing all that time & did not reach home till Oct.," she explained, "& I think I sent the letters to you." She feared that without such proof, after Morgan left office, the cottage would have to be moved, as Rust was currently threatening. If only the Southern California Indian Association (SCIA) would purchase it from the national Missionary Committee, Quinton noted. They could have it for $200 with four years to pay. "I am crushed with cares & worries & work now & I shall have to leave all & go out & beg that money if we have to move the house."[13]

Major Horatio Nelson Rust as photographed by Crandall & Dewey of Pasadena. During his tenure as Mission Indian agent, he and Quinton tangled on several issues. *William H. Weinland Collection, The Huntington Library, San Marino, California (photCL 39 [203]).*

Johnson had apparently innocently initiated this latest controversy because she was displeased with the land upon which her cottage stood. It had no water, making it impossible to pasture her horse and a cow, which she deemed essential for her own use and to provide milk for the old and sick. She saw her role as a field matron to keep a model home inside and outside, with chickens, fruit, flowers, and vegetables, presenting a "neat and civilized look to the home which is an inspiration to all beholders." Therefore, without Quinton's knowledge, and with Rust's help, Johnson had rented land with available water to, among other tasks, teach the Indians to garden.[14]

Rust believed he was simply aiding Johnson in her quest. On February 20 he wrote Morgan that she had accompanied him to Cahuilla on January 2; together they had examined the WNIA missionary cottage which he described as a "very cheap affair of two rooms unfit for any Teacher to occupy." When she informed him that the cottage was to be moved, they located, to the west of the school, an appropriate site of four to five acres with an adobe house on it. According to Rust's hand drawn map, the land contained both warm and cold springs. In "the name of some Riverside Lady," he made an agreement with the Indian owner "that the Ladies Association" (a reference probably to the Riverside branch of the Southern California Indian Association) could have the lot with the adobe house for five years at $24 annually. Rust, who presumed he "had done all parties concerned a favor," denied forbidding Johnson from occupying the cottage or suggesting he would move it. "I did nothing more than stated above and tried hard to please the lady by helping her in every way I could to begin her work," he wrote Morgan. In his draft copy, he described Quinton's accusations as "a *base falsehood,* while in his actual letter he wrote: There "*is no truth in Mrs. Quinton's statement* to the contrary and if I were to remain as Agent I should heartily wish she would keep out of the state for I know she has only made trouble from the day she began what she calls her work in So. California."[15]

Commissioner Morgan had become a personal sounding boarding for Quinton and Rust, who both denied they had said or acted as the other claimed. It is impossible to know the truth. Although Rust's letters exist, there are none from Weinland, and only positive excerpts from Johnson's reprinted in *The Indian's Friend.* On February 14, Quinton informed Weinland both that Rust claimed he never forbade Johnson from the cottage's use and that Johnson claimed he had. Quinton's animus toward the agent was growing, and she had "no fear of a bully, or of a man who has no conscience," describing Rust as hating her "because he has not been able to make me do his way & over awe me." She also complained that no one could make contracts without WNIA consent, for they had no discretionary money. And she was so "burdened to exhaustion often already," that she could not go out and raise additional funds. Beginning to accept the idea that the cottage may have to be relocated, Quinton recognized that since Johnson was not fearful, maybe there was no need for its location near the school. Claiming that Johnson's ideas matched her own, Quinton described the field matron as a "Dr., sister, nurse, teacher, gardener, & all, to the Indians." In fact, Quinton seemed pleased that Johnson had acted on her own.[16]

Not until mid-April did Quinton confide to Weinland that Johnson had bought "the new lot & its old adobe for $60." Quinton had then written the Indian Office asking them to "set apart" that five acres selected by Rust "for education and missionary purposes," and inquired if the government would be willing to buy the WNIA missionary cottage for Salsberry's residence. In an early April letter to Acting Commissioner Robert V. Belt, Quinton explained she had seen for herself how cramped and uncomfortable the schoolteacher's quarters were. If the government agreed to purchase the cottage, saving them the expense of moving it, the WNIA would repair and enlarge the adobe home on the requested lot. Then, Johnson would still be living on WNIA premises but in the improved adobe house with new rooms and no rent to the government for several years. If officials did not agree, Quinton informed Weinland the association would give it to the SCIA if they moved and repaired it.[17]

WNIA members were kept in the dark about this controversy, informed in the February 1893 issue of *The Indian's Friend* only that everything was going smoothly at Cahuilla and at Agua Caliente. Johnson had arrived on January 20, taking "up her work with enthusiasm, courage, and hope," and Weinland was busy superintending the repairs on the rented house at Agua Caliente, at which WNIA-sponsored physician Dr. Rebecca C. Hallowell and field matron Julia M. French had arrived on January 17. This work at Agua Caliente was described as "an enterprise which calls for much heart, much prayer, labor, and material aid, all of which are pledged with the free-will offerings of many."[18] Hallowell's medical missionary duties were underwritten that January by the over three hundred members in NYCIA branches at Harlem, Yonkers, Poughkeepsie, Kingston, and Hopewell Junction, which had suspended their support at Soboba in 1891 because of the presence of a Catholic church in the village.[19]

In his early February article, Weinland continued in the same positive vein, extending a welcome to the three women as "valuable co-workers in behalf of the Mission Indians." He was most pleased with Johnson's appointment, as were the Indians, happy to have a physician in their midst, ending their seventy-five-mile trip to the Colton Agency for medical treatment from the government physician. Weinland was pleased for a different reason. He was convinced that the Indians' constitution and the peculiar line of diseases to which they were subject called for "special study and investigation," believing medicines affected them differently than the rest of the population, and he liked the idea of a resident doctor. To acquaint the membership with Johnson's work, the March issue of *The Indian's Friend's* included an extract from her most recent letter, describing the current village captain, Gabriel Costo, as "indefatigable in his assistance"; the former captain, Leonicio Lugo, as supportive; and Dr. Wainwright "in every way most kind." Johnson reported that on her first Sunday, sixteen Indians had come to her Christian service; twenty-seven the following Sunday; and that on one day, she had ridden thirteen miles, calling on eight patients, giving medicine to twelve who came to her, and food to three very old and five very sick Indians. The April issue reported that during her first five weeks, she had "a record of 322 medical calls made, or received, for medicine or advice about sickness."[20] There was no hint of any problems with Agent Rust.

WNIA Missionary Work at Agua Caliente

In one of his articles in *The Moravian,* Weinland explained that Hallowell and French were at Agua Caliente to establish a hospital, a project long in the planning stage. "It is our earnest prayer that as time passes, this small hospital may grow and develop into a very useful institution," he informed his readers. The greatest obstacle was Downey's lawsuit. The ex-governor claimed the springs as part of his property, although "the Indians have lived there in undisputed possession for a century or more." Because many white people suffering from rheumatism had found relief in the medicinal waters of their hot springs, the Indians had built neat bathhouses, and rented their adobe homes to summer visitors, reaping them "a rich harvest." Downey in the hopes of reaping an even bigger harvest had hired some of the best lawyers, noted Weinland, who concluded "May our just God overrule for justice and truth" and help Frank D. Lewis and Shirley Ward in the Indian's defense.[21]

The March issue of *The Indian's Friend* included extracts from Hallowell's January 19 letter, describing a rainy trip from Temecula in style in Jacob Bergman's covered carriage instead of in an open one-seat buckboard. Hallowell and French had spent the night in the home of Bergman's son, where they were met by Weinland, who escorted them to Agua Caliente. Because the carpenter had not finished the windows in their cottage, the two women spent the night with Babbitt. In her first report, Hallowell wrote that these windows were "a boon," allowing the sun light to stream in. She appreciated the cottage floors and described the presence of unbleached muslin "tacked across the ceiling to hide the tule roof and to keep the dust from falling," as a nice addition. Finishing her colorful description of her new home, Hallowell made a statement that caused Quinton to cringe. "It has been supposed that we turn one of our two rooms into a hospital at once," she had written, pondering how the one or two surgical cases could be nursed, fed, and bathed while she and French lived, cooked, and slept in the other room. "For such work I think we must have more room, more comforts, more help, and more means."[22]

Quinton was concerned with the idea of the two women sharing their tiny-two room home with male patients. Dr. Wainwright had initially written for approval to allow Hallowell to take in a surgical case or two, and Quinton had agreed, only if the physician was willing. Reminding Weinland that this current problem existed because the WNIA could not get land to build their hospital, Quinton had followed his suggestion, modifying her original plan. The plan now was to let Hallowell treat the Indians in their own homes, win them over, and then after the lawsuit was settled, build the hospital. In the meantime, if Hallowell was willing to take in the sick and care for them, the WNIA would supply her with cots and beds and a tent as needed, where she "*could* have a patient in it & just begin that, as a bud, to let the people see how nice it would be." Quinton, however, cautioned that since Hallowell had "lived handsomely, & is used to comforts, we must not *require* of her what she did *not engage* to do," and Wainwright had to understand that the WNIA work was "wholly private." He could only consult. No agent could take on any case. "We have had enough of mixture with Maj. R.[ust] though we have kept clear of any relations with him." In conclusion, she hoped that Weinland could get "Maj. R. to be fair & sweet & do his best to save us trouble." Two weeks later, summarizing her previous letter, Quinton reminded Weinland that the donors had raised money to build a permanent hospital, not a temporary one. "And it would be wrong, dishonest in us to require Dr. H. to take a work so onerous & which she did not go out to do." To her dismay, Quinton had recently learned from Hallowell that the Indians at Agua Caliente really did not want a hospital, "nor to have other Indians come" to their village.[23]

A Change of Administration in Washington

Dealing with the distant California mission stations through letters was challenging enough, but now Quinton faced problems closer to home. Grover Cleveland's return to the White House in 1892 meant a change in the Indian Office personnel, significantly in Morgan, who was not only a friend but one with whom she had a good working relationship.[24] Cleveland, who assumed the presidency on March 4, 1893, had chosen Daniel M. Browning as Indian commissioner and Hoke Smith as Interior secretary. Both men were unknown to Quinton, and she would have to educate them on the work of the WNIA. Less than a month after his appointment, she wrote Smith to congratulate him, enclosing letters from three government teachers working among the Mission Indians. Having learned that Rust had also resigned, the teachers had asked Quinton to present their petitions and personal letters to the secretary requesting Weinland's appointment as Mission agent. Quinton also enclosed a petition representing a number of Indians as well as the WNIA's endorsement of Weinland, describing him as "a man of very quiet demeanor," with executive ability, integrity, and a devotion to the Indians. Since their work was "domestic, industrial, medical, moral and religious," she believed his appointment "would be the best possible aid" to her association.[25] On March 18, N. J. Salsberry, Ora M. Salmons, and Dr. Johnson also sent letters to Smith.[26]

Three days earlier, Weinland had written Smith requesting he be appointed as Mission agent, explaining he had lived among these Indians for the past four years and would do "honest work" on their behalf. Although Francisco Estudillo was already the official appointee, Quinton continued to encourage Weinland.[27] On April 13 she wrote she had interviewed Smith and several senators in the hope of preventing Estudillo's appointment from being confirmed. "Shall remit no exertion, & have many helpers in Wash'n," she confided. "The Lord speed the right." Two days later Quinton wrote she had heard from Senator James K. Jones, a Democrat from Arkansas and current chairman of the Senate Indian Committee. If they could provide proof that Estudillo was "an intemperate man, or otherwise unfitted," his committee would not confirm. She had already requested they delay until such testimony could be found. She asked Weinland to get someone from San Jacinto to write Jones a letter, cautioning him that because he was requesting the position, he could not write such a letter. "Do all you can, please, & so will I to prevent this confirmation," she concluded.[28]

On April 16 Quinton wrote that the morning paper declared all nominations but one from Delaware had been confirmed. She still did not want to believe that Estudillo was the new Mission agent until she was obliged to; she had sent fresh letters to Washington the previous day. "If he *is* in we must be all the more diligent & watchful & alert for our poor Indians," she declared. Although half ill, she explained that she had to speak to a large gathering that evening at the Presbyterian Church. Ten days later she was still holding out hope, planning on personally seeing Secretary Smith. "But I think the case can yet be saved," she noted, "we'll see." As late as May 2 she was still hopeful, not necessarily to get Weinland into the position but that the San Jacinto letters would at least encourage the government to abolish the agency, "& then all, as *citizens,* will be free of the agent at least![29] The idea of ending the agency continued to be a suggestion for the improvement of current Indian affairs.

Although Quinton was unable to secure an appointment for Weinland, she did ensure that his children could continue to attend the Potrero Indian day school. On May 8 she wrote Browning, Morgan's successor, regarding a new policy that prohibited the few white children living at Potrero from attending the school. Explaining that Weinland was the pastor at the little church there and that he was "a benediction and civilizer among the Indians," she saw no harm in his children and the other white students who lived in the village attending, viewing it as a "positive advantage to the little Indians to have these well brought up little white children among them." She carefully explained that the WNIA's relations with the government's Indian educational work had "been most cordial, and we trust that these mutually helpful relations may continue without interruption." On May 19, Quinton informed Weinland that she had heard from Acting Commissioner Frank C. Armstrong, granting permission for Weinland's children to attend with the understanding that white students would "not occupy the time & attention of the teacher to the disadvantage of the Indian pupils."[30] Quinton again had proved her mettle with a new administration.

Conflict at Cahuilla

To ensure the continuation of their work at Cahuilla, on June 2 Quinton wrote to educate Browning on her association's work, explaining that they had erected a missionary cottage in the village and that from there Dr. Johnson, the government field matron, was engaged in "most excellent & practical work." With few details, Quinton wrote that Johnson had rented a five-acre parcel with both water and grass available, not far from their cottage, a lot which Rust "thought the best one for our work." The father of the current owner had died on the premises, "making it of less value in his eyes," and Johnson had bought out the son's tribal rights, paying him $60, to hold it for the WNIA. Quinton, therefore, requested that Browning direct attorney Frank Lewis to set apart this acreage to the WNIA. From Quinton's perspective, the fact that Johnson had purchased the "possessory right" of the Indian owner meant in reality the Indians had given their consent. Although there was some opposition from the more conservative village members, who Quinton complained always resisted progress, she assured Browning that the progressive element wanted the WNIA work to proceed.[31]

Two weeks later Quinton was still fuming over Rust's promise months previously to give away WNIA property, describing the action as "highway robbery!" She had just returned home from Washington after consulting with officials. "Bonnet not yet off," she wrote Weinland. "Had not a moment there to write." She had been assured by the Indian Office that "the order has gone to Maj. R. to locate our five acres so as to include the cottage where it is," Estudillo not having yet assumed charge. She again urged Weinland to hunt up the original letters written between her and Morgan locating the cottage. She only hoped it was not on the school lot.[32]

In mid-July Agent Estudillo informed Browning that he had not as yet visited Cahuilla as per his instructions. At present he was more interested in the situation

Warner Hot Springs (Agua Caliente) village street scene in 1900. Considered a potential site for a hospital, Quinton and Rust struggled over whether the WNIA or the government should receive credit for its founding.
C. C. Pierce Collection, The Huntington Library, San Marino, California (photCL Pierce 01721).

at Warner Ranch. Instead, the Cahuilla captain and several others had visited him at the agency in Colton. Since they had no desire to give away the land in question, Estudillo requested that Browning withhold any actions until he made his visit and filed a report; he finally visited on July 26.[33] Two weeks earlier Quinton had written Browning, enclosing Thomas Kirker's surveyor's note and a formal application from WNIA for the Cahuilla land. Indian consent had been obtained, she noted, and her association had received the best reports of Johnson's work. Although some of the non-progressive elements were opposed, she understood that Estudillo "distinctly approved our work & said that he should help us, & I trust that this is true." In her conclusion, she requested a brief interview with Browning during her next Washington visit.[34]

On July 28, Estudillo informed Browning that he had met at the Cahuilla school with a large group of Indians. Dr. Johnson had also been in attendance. The Indians had given him a petition signed by thirty-six men, of whom sixteen were part of the twenty-five who had signed Johnson's original petition, requesting the land for the WNIA. In front of Johnson, the sixteen publicly denied that they knew the true nature of what they had signed, believing it was a simple statement allowing her the right to live in their village. Protesting vigorously against granting the land, they accused the field matron of deceiving them. More important, this land in question contained all the valuable warm springs, used in common. Estudillo had explained to Johnson "every word that was spoken by the Indians." Forced to listen to their charges, the agent assured Browning that the matron's feelings "were sorely tried." Despite her egregious actions and the Indian's demand of her removal, Estudillo assured Browning he had ordered them to treat Johnson with respect, advising patience. For the present, he recommended that the department not grant the land, adding that Quinton's comment that he would aid in securing the grant was incorrect. He assured Browning that he had only one "object in view—& that is the best interests of the Indians."[35]

Earlier, on July 25, Estudillo had informed Quinton of his visit, explaining much of what he later wrote Browning, assuring her that he had done all he could to alleviate Johnson's "distressed feelings." He blamed the surveyor for including the springs, letting Quinton off the hook: "I am sure you do not wish to take all the valuable water that the Indians have besides their best land," he wrote. In recommending Johnson's removal, he noted that "no matter what she did now, her accomplishments would be nothing" and suggested the matter be dropped and renewed at a later time on a different piece of land.[36] Having heard from both Estudillo and Johnson, on August 5 Quinton informed Weinland that "all *looked ended* for us" at Cahuilla. Nevertheless, ever the optimist, Quinton had gone to Washington to confer with Browning the previous Thursday, receiving assurances that he would stand by the WNIA. Johnson would not be turned out. In the meantime, Quinton had informed Johnson that her work would continue. Quinton had also asked Weinland to assure Estudillo that the association did not want the springs, only sufficient water use for the lot. She would write the agent "a pleasant letter" asking him to wait and listen to both sides.[37]

During the first week of August, Quinton wrote Estudillo, saying his letter of July 25 had brought her "real sorrow." Cordially thanking him for his kindness to Johnson, she assured the new agent that she was also personally interested in these Indians' welfare and had been ever since her friend Helen Hunt Jackson had acquainted her with their needs. Explaining that the timing of his visit had been unfortunate because there had been a full delegation of conservative Indians and only a small number of the more progressive villagers, she tried to impress upon him how important Johnson's work was. She not only gave out rations, but "*voluntarily*" added her medical services. Furthermore, unbiased observers praised Johnson's earnestness and devotion. Quinton was convinced that had all the Indians been present, the outcome would have been different. Although not giving an outright apology, she admitted she had made some mistakes, especially in calling for a survey without his approval and naming Johnson in the agreement, when the WNIA was solely responsible for the government application. Although Johnson had rented the land without the WNIA's knowledge, they would not have objected, for the move had helped both her and the Indian owner. Quinton also assured Estudillo that had she known the land included all the water, she would not have approved it. Putting her best foot forward, she wrote: "I cannot but think that with your kindness, fairness, & courtesy, & with your *power* as Agent, you can find a way out of all these difficulties." She then begged him to aid them "to the best of [his] ability as a patriot & as a Christian man."[38]

Estudillo did not view his visit as "unfortunate," assuring Quinton that eight out of ten Indians wanted the field matron removed. He had "correctly and truly" informed Johnson of everything the Indians had said and vice versa, and if she said otherwise, then that confirmed his belief that she had deceived them. "I assure you I am prepared to believe that she has made other misrepresentations," he asserted. Although absolving Quinton of the water issue, he assumed Johnson and the surveyor had known. At present, there was no way he would consent to a gift of this tract but if Quinton was willing to let the matter rest, he would search for a suitable location. He assured her that he had "no feeling other than sympathy" for Johnson.[39]

Quinton cordially pointed out to Estudillo that he had misunderstood certain points in her previous letter. By her use of "unfortunate," she meant only that the progressive Indians were not present. Based on fourteen years of experience, she knew they tended to have "hope for the future," and it was with this group that Johnson had the most influence. Quinton's association sought only "to lift the tribe into a better civilization and into practical *right living* in *every* way," and "the progressive spirits are the ones to do most towards this." She believed that this opposition was new and temporary and his "protection & *moral support* [would] *right* the matter." She requested that he consult with Weinland on the claim that Johnson had deceived the Indians. Because the WNIA had been trying to get this land gift settled for years, Quinton was certain the Indians understood exactly what Johnson was doing. Also, Weinland had assured her that the tract involved did not include the major water supply nor, did the Indians use its hot springs. The

WNIA only wanted land to build a "little model home "and to have pasture for a pony and cow. In conclusion, the press, Congress, and the government endorsed the work of the WNIA and that of their branches in forty different states. "Our motives are as well known as our work," she assured Estudillo.[40]

Not until mid-August did Quinton receive official notice from Browning that the land grant was not forthcoming. He quoted extensively from Estudillo's July 28 letter, explaining that without Indian consent, the Indian Office could not grant the land. On August 17 Quinton revealed the contents of Browning's letter to Weinland, informing him she had re-filed with the Indian Office for the land, hoping the progressive villagers who had supported Johnson would sign a petition asking for her retention.[41] On the same day she also sent a long letter to Browning embellishing the arguments she had used with Estudillo. She complained that the agent had not gotten the feeling of "the *whole* village," and now some of the very Indians who under "a *new* and *unfriendly* influence" had asked for Johnson's removal had since then expressed to Johnson "regret and *shame* for their words that day." Furthermore, Weinland had assured her that the Indians' main source of water was not on the tract in question, explaining, "they might as well protest against this selection on the ground of there being *a tree* growing on it." Laying it on a bit thick, she concluded that on behalf of the WNIA, "an association of Christian women. . . . we *do* ask the privilege of continuing labor in a village where our work has been hitherto so welcome."[42]

In September, Estudillo informed Browning that he had returned to Cahuilla, requesting the presence of the Indians and Johnson. Out of the thirty-one that had gathered, ten had signed the original agreement and stood by their initial decision. And because the remaining Indians continued to oppose the donation, Estudillo had no reason to change his recommendation. He had since learned that only twenty-two had signed the original land grant, not twenty-five, and three of them were school children under seventeen. He had no idea how many more children were among the original signers. "I did this that the lady may not be able to say that I in anyway ruled out her voters." He cautioned Browning that if Johnson did not get along with the Indians it would require his "constant attention at that one reservation," seeing "no end to trouble and annoyance." However, he had no fears that the Indians would do anything to her, describing them as "law abiding people harmless, and industrious."[43]

Quinton asked Commissioner Browning, in a November letter, to prevent Johnson's removal, having learned from Estudillo, Weinland, and Johnson herself that there was increased effort to do so. She informed the commissioner that she would come to Washington, DC, to confer with him in early December and could no doubt prove to him "the gross misrepresentation & injustice of the whole affair." Because the WNIA annual meeting was to be held in Washington for the first time that year, Quinton would have time to confer with both he and Secretary Smith. Busy with the meeting and the BIC conference in mid-December, Quinton answered Weinland's latest letter on December 23, describing her visits to the Indian Office as "most encouraging," leading her to believe that Johnson would not be turned out. Even if she were removed by the government, the WNIA would appoint her as their missionary. "We must not let go of what has been gained in that agency by all our work," she concluded.[44]

A New Issue at Agua Caliente

In addition to defusing the situation at Cahuilla, Quinton had to come to the defense of Dr. Rebecca Hallowell and Julia French at Agua Caliente—both controversies time consuming and requiring extensive correspondence. On August 22, Quinton informed Browning that during a recent visit to the village, Estudillo had learned that an Indian boy had stolen French's watch. The Indians were angry about this, blaming the women for inviting the children into their home, and demanded that they leave. Although Estudillo had promised his protection, Hallowell and French telegraphed Quinton: "Ordered out. Send protection. Indians deny Agent's power." Quinton immediately asked Browning to telegraph the agent and the interpreter to protect the women. He did so two days later. Quinton was convinced that this was a plan to drive the Protestants out, "for threats of this sort have from time to time come to us," explaining that these problems in Cahuilla and Agua Caliente were "wholly new in our work."[45] This was true; in no other state did the WNIA face opposition from Indian agents. But then the WNIA had far more stations in California, and only there did the Catholic Church have a role in missionizing the Indians.

On August 29 Estudillo informed Quinton that he had received a telegram from Washington five days before, asking for the facts behind a reported disturbance and the need to protect French and Hallowell. Because French had written him the same day with no mention of any disturbance, he had reported back that there was no foundation to the report. Although he had been sick and unable to visit the village, he had "no fears of any trouble whatsoever."[46] Quinton, fearing the worst, on September 4 enclosed a copy of Estudillo's letter, informing Browning that in her August 14 letter Hallowell had explained that the Indians had ordered them to leave the village within thirty days. (Hallowell had also informed Estudillo that she was not afraid because she lived in WNIA housing under a contract.) Although agreeing to protect them, the agent had still recommended they leave. Meanwhile, the village captain had forbidden the children to take instruction from French. However, the ever-hopeful Quinton had described the situation to Browning as "an incited caprice that will pass over."[47]

On September 6 Quinton informed Estudillo that there was "considerable 'foundation' for the report" of a disturbance, for the Indians, after holding two councils, had demanded the women leave. Appealing to his ego, she wrote that she, Hallowell, and French fully understood that he had the "power as Agent to protect them." The whole thing would blow over once the Indians felt his disapproval and came to realize his "sincere support of the government matron and of our Christian worker, two women of highest character, culture, position, and devotion to their work."[48] However, Quinton was beginning to have second thoughts about building a hospital at Agua Caliente, writing in late October, "all these late developments & childish turn arounds of the Indians, & their bondage to priests will *always* antagonize, & spoil our influence if they *can,* while there are agencies at least."[49]

The World's Columbian Exposition

In between dealing with the California stations, Quinton had continued her addresses before union meetings, drawing room gatherings, and clubs, an average of seven a month until April, when she gave twice as many. She also had organized three new associations.[50] However, much of her time in mid-May and later in September was focused on the World's Congress of Representative Women held in conjunction with the World's Columbian Exposition in Chicago, commemorating the 400th anniversary of Columbus's landing in the New World. The *New York Times* alerted its readers to the nineteen different congresses meeting between May and October, noting that the one most women would be interested in was the Memorial Congress meeting on May 15, dealing with "Woman's Progress." From all over the globe, distinguished women in positions of leadership in such fields as philanthropy, social reform, education, the law, the arts, industry, and literature descended upon Chicago. The *Times* described it as "a wonderful gathering of brainy women and a most impressive one, as showing their progress in the latter half of this century." Quinton was among the long list of attendees.[51] Quinton, when available, or her temporary private secretary, Miss Clarabel Gilman, secretary of the Jamaica Plain auxiliary of the MIA, sat at Desk 39 of the Woman's Building handing out WNIA pamphlets and other WNIA literature.[52]

The Columbian Exposition featured exhibitions of various Indian schools, as well as an exhibit of past and present homes and various industries.[53] Quinton gave seven addresses during the Congress in May and several more each in August and September, asking during one talk: "in the latest floodtide of the world's philanthropy and Christian work are women seen and felt?" Her response was: "Let the overwhelming statistics of the last thirty years give the answer."[54]

Weinland Moves On

Quinton was also facing the eventuality of Weinland's "official relations" with the WNIA terminating. The July issue of *The Indian's Friend* announced just such a situation since his "personal ministry" at the Potrero church and his other work had grown, requiring all of his "time and strength." He was to be succeeded by his former assistant, Edward Helmich, who came highly recommended by the Missionary Board of the Moravian Church. However, correspondence between Quinton and Weinland revealed the real reason was a lack of money. In mid-April she had written: "we want you just as before, *if* we can raise the salary," explaining that WNIA's presence at the Exposition had been costly and therefore they could only afford one salary. She wondered if by chance the Moravian Board could pay Helmich so Weinland could continue as before. "And now *which* shall it be?" she asked. "You or he?" Presumably by late April, Weinland had decided that he would be the one to leave because Quinton in her letter did not mention his salary, only how to raise $500 for Helmich, who would have the same duties.[55]

Quinton had come to depend on Weinland's wise counsel as supervisor and manager of her California properties. She would have been loath to have asked Helmich to do the same. She had little confidence in him, whereas both Hallowell and French described Helmich as doing "faithful work," and "most kind and helpful in our small needs." Practical and knowledgeable about carpentry tools, he had put up a coffee mill for them and plugged up a rat hole.[56] These traits did not impress Quinton, who needed a strong presence to defend WNIA work. Although in a mid-July letter to Browning, she had said she knew "only good of him" and described Helmich as coming highly recommended, to Weinland the following month she had agreed that he was "hopeless," adding that he had "*not* the *tact requisite* for *that* field." She was bitter because he had not stood up against the Catholics, having said to her that they "had all the power" and "nothing more could be done at present." She only hoped that the Moravians would put him somewhere else. In early September Quinton was still displeased, claiming Helmich had less education than she had originally thought and possessed little business knowledge. Also, his health was not up to such rigorous travel as the job required. She continued to try and figure out how to get Weinland back with a higher salary, explaining she could do so when the Seminole Mission was finally turned over. Then in an October 31 letter, with no explanation, she wrote that Helmich had left California and was now in Bethlehem, Pennsylvania. He never returned, and Quinton finally had the money to reemploy Weinland.[57]

Piegan Tour

Busy with the expo and dealing with the California stations, Quinton had time for only one tour during 1893. In late June she was invited by the WNIA-sponsored missionaries of the Brooklyn Women's Indian Association's mission among the Montana Piegan to attend the government Indian school's exhibition and join in their July 4 celebration. This station was a state mission supported entirely by Brooklyn women and their Bay Ridge branch.[58] The work had initially begun in June 1885 when an unnamed physician offered her services to the WNIA Missionary Committee. The government gave their approval the following month, and the New Haven Women's Indian Association offered their support, but it never got off the ground. Then in the fall of 1889, Brooklyn women were asked by the national missionary committee to reestablish the work and assume the responsibility. Although they had gathered the funds, not until the fall of 1892 did Dr. Daniel Dorchester, the Superintendent of Indian Schools, at their request, visit the reservation and accept possession from the government of one hundred and sixty acres, a mile from the agency, for missionary work. Then the Brooklyn association sponsored Rev. E. S. Dutcher and his wife Mary B. Dutcher, employees of the Methodist Episcopal Board. The missionaries and their two small children arrived on April 1, 1893, temporarily living in the government school until they were able to move into their own cabin, which Dutcher enlarged himself with Indian help and funds from Brooklyn. The following summer he also built a chapel. Money for furniture, horses, wagons, and farm implements was provided by the Bay Ridge branch. This fully equipped mission, costing the WNIA some $4,000 ($115,657.33 in 2021 dollars), would be handed over to the Methodist Episcopal Missionary Society by the Brooklyn auxiliary on August 1, 1894.[59]

Leaving Chicago late on June 28, 1893, Quinton and at least one unidentified companion, traveled nearly 1,600 miles by train, arriving on July first at Kipp, Blackfoot Station, Teton County, Montana. Since Reverend Dutcher had not received their telegram, there was no one to escort them the eight miles to the

Brooklyn Mission or the extra mile to the Blackfeet Agency boarding school where they were to be entertained. Quinton was forced to walk around the small community with its little station, some Great Northern Railway shops, a post office within a store, and a small café in search of a ride, finally explaining: "a former collector of customs, for we were near the Canadian border, courteously proffered the services of his horses and buggy and himself generously drove the editorial 'us' over the grassy sea to the mission and school." They found Dutcher busily remodeling his home. Only Quinton could make the small cabin, two horses, grass, sky, and snow-covered Rocky Mountains sound like a grand place.[60]

After an initial greeting by the Dutchers, Quinton and her companion traveled on to the school, where at teatime they were cordially welcomed by school superintendent, W. H. Matson, the teachers and students, and Blackfeet Agent George W. Steell. In her letter-report, Quinton described the Piegan Indians as "bright, alert, cheerful-looking Indians," and their children as "healthy, happy, and to be doing capitally well especially in English speaking." Initially Steell had been forced to bring in the Indian police to reinforce his order to the parents to send their children to the government school. By the time of Quinton's visit, however, the parents were well pleased with the school. Part of their dissatisfaction may have been its original location. According to Matson, the school had been removed from its "unfavorable agency surroundings" and rebuilt at a "judicially selected" site on Willow Creek. Like all government boarding schools, it was expected to be agriculturally self-sustaining, which in the Montana winters was difficult. Although it had a successful dairy, raising chickens had proved difficult because of the large number of dogs present in the Indian camp.[61]

Quinton attended the morning Sunday school on July 4. Duly impressed, she wrote: "We have never seen any children more obedient to orders or more prompt in marking time." As the day progressed, Quinton observed more and more tents beginning to appear on the prairie, evidence that the Piegans were gathering for the upcoming celebration. She described the excitement of these colorful Indian tents, with bright streamers and shouting children on agile Indian ponies "careening" around on the prairie as proud parents watched. The only shadow on this happy scene was a broken arm, sustained when the daughter of the chief tumbled off her pony. Because the agency doctor was twenty-two miles away, it took a full day before she had her arm cast.[62]

The children's July 4 presentations, mostly patriotic in nature, were followed by short speeches by Quinton, Dutcher, and Steell, ending with a holiday dinner provided by the government, followed by fireworks. Leaving the school on July 5, Quinton paid a short visit to the Dutcher's log cabin, describing it as "cheery," filled with homemade furniture. A tour of the agency headquarters followed. The next day she was driven out several miles to visit some Indian homes, concluding that much work still needed to be done. Quinton ended her report expressing pleasure in having seen "'the image of God' in these men and women, of having felt their capabilities as well as their needs."[63] Unfortunately her rosy description included no useful information on the actual work being carried out at the mission station by the Brooklyn auxiliary.

Lake Mohonk

Quinton delivered seven addresses at the World's Congress after Montana and before heading to the annual Lake Mohonk Conference on October 11. There she spoke about her visit to the Piegan Reservation where "Christly principles" had taken hold and begun to mold the Indians. She found expressive faces and genuine feeling among these people, who had "already made remarkable progress, and are eager to go forward." She called their school a "capital" one and described the July 4 celebration "an inspiration and a joy" and Agent Steell as an "honest, sensible, and practical man." Lamenting that after serving three years, he had been replaced because of a change of administration in Washington, DC. She described him as a good agent, overcoming the Indians' fears and prejudices, winning their confidence and abolishing alcohol. Fortunately, the new agent, Captain L. W. Cook, was also well spoken of.[64] During her second, shorter presentation, Quinton announced that the WNIA mission among the Florida Seminole had been transferred to the care of Bishop William Crane Gray of the Protestant Episcopal Church of Southern Florida, and a mission among the Hopi in Arizona had been opened by the New Jersey auxiliary.[65]

Between her Mohonk appearance and her welcome to WNIA delegates at the annual meeting in Washington, DC, Quinton gave seven addresses. On December 5, Kate Foote, president of the Washington auxiliary, welcomed WNIA members to her city, which according to the annual report was "gleaming from White House to Capitol in the first showy ermine of the season, and glorious under a brilliant sunset." The opening reception was held at the Corcoran Art Gallery, and later delegates visited the Capitol, the House and Senate Chambers, and the White House, where they were welcomed by President and Mrs. Cleveland.[66] Ten days later in her presentation at the annual BIC conference Quinton described this latest WNIA meeting as one of the best ever. "It was enthusiastic, harmonious, and its spiritual tone was more earnest and tender than ever."[67] The annual report had made no mention of any hardships during this, the first year of the Panic of 1893.

On December 15, 1893, Merrill E. Gates, president of the BIC, welcomed Quinton and other members of various religious societies to the annual BIC conference. A brief history of the conference revealed to attendees that most of the current government's Indian policies had originated during such meetings. The Board, in fact, had drafted the very first bill on severalty. During Quinton's presentation she described the initial WNIA work as demanding the maintenance of treaty provisions before they moved on to severalty and citizenship. Now familiar with BIC history, she exclaimed: "Our society popularized the ideas which we now find that the Indian board then had, though we did not know it till now." Her remark prompted *The Indian's Friend* to report that this "proves that the modern reform in Indian affairs was divinely ordained," with different reform groups working separately and without knowledge of the work of others, arriving at the same ends.[68]

During the BIC meeting, the issue of extending civil service rules to more Indian Office officials was once again brought up, with Quinton adding her comments and strongly supporting the idea. Ironically, she had ended 1893 determined to keep Indian issues apolitical, but she had been forced to play her own political cards to salvage the missionary work in two of her association's California stations. Not only had she bombarded the Indian commissioner and interior secretary with letters but had personally visited them in their offices to encourage them to do her bidding. With her long years at the helm of the WNIA, Quinton had gained her share of political allies, but she must have looked back fondly to the missed opportunity of having one of her own as Mission Indian agent. None of the extreme measures she had been forced to undertake would have been necessary had Weinland been named to replace Rust. Now she was dealing with Rust's replacement. Nevertheless, for the present, she had won, and all three WNIA-sponsored workers remained at their posts; Helmich had left, and Weinland was back as WNIA superintendent.

Quinton could count many successes during 1893, including the WNIA's attendance at the Columbian Exposition, fifteen missionary cottages, chapels, and schoolhouses built during the year, and her many addresses spreading the word of the association's work before widely diverse groups. But the real coup was the presence of Commissioner Daniel M. Browning at the annual meeting. He had praised the WNIA, giving his assurance that his office would promptly aid their efforts. During his presentation, he emphasized "the co-operative work of [the] Government and the Association," testifying to the "wide usefulness of the" association.[69] His address received a hearty applause. Again, through her visits, letters, and actions, Quinton had won over a newly appointed commissioner. During the remainder of Browning's tenure, she would turn to him often for support.

8

Missionary Work and Meetings, 1894–1895

The drama and intrigue at Agua Caliente and Cahuilla finally over, Quinton remained close to home in 1894, venturing only as far as Kentucky and Ohio for addresses, founding five Indian committees, and continuing her support for Civil Service rules to be applied to the Indian service. In 1895 she toured for five months, writing in *The Indian's Friend:* "presto change has been the order of the day since March 5th when the city of brotherly love with a tempestuous play of wild winds among its domes and steeples, streets and alleys, was left behind," concluding that "it was a good time to seek milder air and a sunnier clime, and the season made farewells easier." She was headed for Helen Hunt Jackson country, to revisit her beloved Mission Indian villages and renew acquaintances with Weinland and the WNIA-sponsored workers she had so ably defended.[1] Until then, she kept in touch with Weinland regarding her California property, and these letters offer a glimpse into the issues facing women absentee landowners at the time.

Her California Property

In an early January 1894 letter to Weinland, Quinton complained that she was still agonizing over her California agricultural pursuits on her Perris Valley property. She had offered her stepson George land if he worked for her for three years; he moved to Perris in late March. She inquired of Weinland if she should plant oranges and peaches there instead of in Banning, or whether to sell some land, or keep it and plant more. She was hoping to find a market for at least some of her grapes in Philadelphia. In this letter it is also clear some of the other things that weighed upon her. She explained she was pressed day and night with no let up, not only because the new administration required "much extra care," but because she received so many letters begging her "to help right gross wrongs" for which she could not say no. And now she was needed to go out and hunt up advertisements to support the association's monthly publication.[2]

In mid-February Quinton learned that some of her Perris lots were advertised for sale as the water taxes had not been paid. Some lots were even listed in her stepson's name, prompting her to write Weinland: "He has not a foot of land. I hold deeds for all." From the beginning a Mr. Hall had handled her affairs, and although she was current in sending him money for taxes, he had apparently not paid them. She had been telegraphing and writing, hoping that her lands were safe. She again asked Weinland to act as her agent. He could live in Perris, use her house, and send his children to a regular school. In a late March letter, she was still furious with Hall, informing Weinland that she had treated the man with the utmost kindness, even giving him twenty acres. As her "not very courageous" stepson was due to arrive in California soon, she told Weinland it would give her great comfort if he could befriend George.[3]

By summer Quinton was dealing with a water crisis on her Perris property and contemplating moving her house to another location. In late May she had informed Weinland that George had learned that nearly all her land was below the water pipeline and thought an artesian well might be needed. Noting that had she known this, she would never have built there, she also mentioned that he was lonely and needed work. Months later she told Weinland that if she sold, it would be her land in Banning, for her Perris lots might be desirable for town lots. She reminded Weinland that she had only bought at Banning to help him and wondered if they would have a grape crop this year to turn into raisins. Still later she asked him to send her a small paper box of raisins to see if she could sell them in Philadelphia. In a postscript she explained that she had broken up her Philadelphia house, stored her furniture, and moved to Merchantville, New Jersey. Then in mid-November, she wrote that after being shut up with a bad cold, she had finally been able to go to Philadelphia to see a grocer. Soon after she wrote again with the local prices she had been quoted, noting that they preferred Greek raisins. To make any money she would have to sell only to large hotels and schools but had no time this year to start investigating the matter; she asked that he do his best for her, and next season she would work on the idea of selling raisins.[4]

Civil Service Reform

Despite concern over her California agricultural efforts, Quinton remained focused on WNIA reform efforts. In early January 1894, she informed Weinland that she was "on a new tack" with her December appointment to the BIC business committee, promoting legislation to get "agents out of politics." This policy change rested on President Cleveland, who, she opined to Weinland, "*could* cure all the evils if he *would*, & we must try & press it." Then four days later she updated Welsh on the matter and reported that she had spoken to General Eliphalet Whittlesey, secretary of the BIC, Theodore Roosevelt and others, who explained that getting a law placing agents under civil service might not happen. Ever the optimist, she believed she would simply have to put so much pressure on Cleveland that he would be glad to say: "I will appoint no agents who have not the endorsement of the civil service committee." He could "be made to say that cordially," she concluded.[5]

The application of Civil Service rules to the personnel of the Indian Office had been an abstract ideal to Quinton until her trip to the Blackfeet Reservation, where she met Agent George W. Steell. Bothered by his removal after a three-year successful tenure simply because of an administrative change in Washington, she informed Welsh in late October 1893 that she had not only written President Cleveland to find support for Steell, but also two Georgia friends who were intimates of Interior Secretary Hoke Smith. Steell's case was a perfect example of how poorly the present system worked. He was not only an exemplary agent, but Quinton had also learned that both the Indians and the local white population wanted him retained. She believed if competent people were appointed and not removed every four years, the whole issue of the so-called Indian problem would be settled. "We women are very much interested in it;" she exclaimed, and "we think both administrations are just as naughty as they can be."[6]

During the December 15, 1893, BIC meeting Quinton had discussed her association's current work, concluding with a description of their recently adopted resolutions, one calling for the extension of civil service classification to include agents, special agents, and inspectors—of particular interest because of Steell's removal. Her comments were in keeping with the afternoon session at which Theodore Roosevelt addressed the case for a merit system. Roosevelt, who had been a U.S. Civil Service Commissioner from 1889 until 1895, explained that one of the first things he had done to extend civil service reform to some parts of the Indian service was to get several Indians appointed to teaching positions.[7]

The BIC's resolutions in 1893 included one calling for the extension of civil service rules to agency clerks, assistant teachers, carpenters, engineers, and farmers. In addition, a second resolution urged the president to adopt a "fitness and merit" test for Indian agents and the passage of legislation "removing their appointment entirely from the arena of politics." Quinton commented: "Let us make it our business to see that the Congressmen are awakened." "God is alive and on the throne," she declared. "I do bespeak for all friends of the Indian the most earnest work in carrying out that part of the resolution especially asking Congress to take the matter out of politics," she concluded.[8] A little over a week later, she informed Weinland that she had again been appointed to the BIC's business committee, and they would soon be asking for congressional legislation ordering that agents be appointed for their "*fitness & kept* in, till *unfit*, & I believe we shall get that," she confided. It was now the time "for radical work & I'm doing all I can for it & driving work day & night."[9]

Quinton's first opportunity to promote her new agenda came during the regular monthly meeting of the NYCIA on January 15, 1894, when the members adopted resolutions favoring the expansion of civil service to include agents, special agents, and inspectors. Her point was obvious; all past Indian work was "simply like pouring water into a sieve" since agents hardly had time to become acquainted with the tribe they represented when they were removed.[10]

California Mission Stations

Although focused on civil service reform, Quinton was also concerned about the WNIA industrial school at Greenville. In a January 26 letter to Commissioner Browning, she explained that Edward Ament's earlier estimate of operating expenses had been insufficient, and she was requesting the government provide a total of $90 per capita for ten months of the year. Browning responded, explaining that since contracts had already been made, it was too late to change. Although disappointed, Quinton thanked him, asking if the government could at least provide one hot meal a day to the day students, all from distant poor homes. Its "*very hard to draw the line in the face of a hungry child*," especially when those privileged with hot meals lived at the school, sharing its shelter and comfort, she wrote. If his department would grant "this one more boon, I think we shall not ask further help."[11]

In early March, writing that her earlier promise for no more requests for assistance was "rash," Quinton asked for a twice a week visit by a physician to the school's thirty-two students. In the future the WNIA hoped to sponsor a lady doctor. On March 9, thanking Browning for providing the mid-day meal, she inquired if there was a government appropriation for "the old, poor and helpless among the Mission Indians." She noted that at Cahuilla there were eight or ten old women, unable to work, who needed and had asked for rations. Could he instruct Estudillo to furnish them?[12]

Quinton learned that the school's food contractor, who had just died, had been providing the WNIA with supplies at $7.50 per capita per month; she could find no one willing to match his price. In June, she asked Acting Indian Commissioner Frank C. Armstrong for an increase to $9 for the next year's contract. In return the WNIA would furnish a seamstress once a week each month as well as such items as wood, candles, soap, brooms, and "good substantial food." Quinton concluded that Greenville was progressing, with a total of eighty pupils enrolled with "a steady attendance of nearly all," and the WNIA was extremely pleased with Ament's management.[13] Ament's July 1, 1894, school report was as positive as Quinton's. Explaining that the WNIA had purchased the 140 acres on which the schoolhouse stood and built a dormitory with dining room, kitchen, and a separate building with a washroom, bathrooms, and storeroom, he attested to an improvement in the advancement of some of his pupils since the new facility had opened on January 1, 1894. He thanked "the generous and untiring efforts" of the WNIA and the "willingness which the Indian Office has shown to help this school."[14]

In late August, Quinton thanked Browning for the monthly increase. To better position her next argument, she explained that the Aments, with only the help of a cook and an occasional assistant, were bearing the entire labor of running the school on a salary that had been set when they were running a day school of forty students and was "probably the lowest in the whole Indian service for the work done." She respectfully asked the Indian Office to raise the salary, concluding that the WNIA hoped to soon add a wing to their dormitory and possibly employ a lady doctor.[15]

Also during the summer, Quinton had received encouraging news about Cahuilla. On May 31 she wrote Weinland that Estudillo "was becoming very suave to us all, as he finds that he cannot upset us in Washington." Recently the agent even "*cheerfully* promised Dr. Johnson that he would ask leave to build the bath house for the school girls, which she has before asked and he would not listen." Quinton described the agent as converted to Johnson "at least *outside*, and I think will find it to his interest to co-operate, or take the risk of losing his own head." She relayed the disappointing news that Johnson might have to leave because of her mother's health. Johnson did leave, and her replacement, Anna J. Ritter, arrived in February 1895.[16] Two months earlier, Johnson had sent a letter to the *Riverside Press & Horticulturist* reporting on her Cahuilla work, soliciting help to make them self-supporting. The hand-mill she had purchased for the women to grind their acorns, wheat, and corn had given them more time to make baskets. She had already sold over $200 worth and hoped "to sell quail for the men this winter," creating a market in San Jacinto. The women, who faithfully attended her weekly sewing class and her Sunday morning service were "quiet and reverential," understanding the simple lessons she was teaching. She asked readers to educate public opinion, send orders for baskets and quail, and help support their Christmas festivities with a tree for the children and material for the women's sewing class.[17]

In late July, Quinton inquired of Weinland if there were any change in Cahuilla and Agua Caliente, reporting that from her end "all seems to be peaceful & progress certainly has been made at both."[18] This tranquility was due in part to Weinland's return as WNIA superintendent. His reappointment date is unknown but his missionary reports in *The Indian's Friend* began to appear in February 1894, reflecting monthly visits to the two villages, conferences with WNIA workers, and temperance lectures. He visited Soboba several times and was invited to preach at Palm Springs, describing this as the time "for sowing seed though mentally many are sluggish and spiritually deadened by formalism and ignorance." In the March issue he reported conducting his usual morning service at Potrero and traveling on to Palm Springs to preach and then visit some nearby Indian homes.[19]

Addresses and Meetings, 1894–1895

In mid-February 1894, Welsh inquired if Quinton would attend the upcoming commencement at Carlisle Indian School. She had already informed Capt. Richard Henry Pratt, the school's founder, that she would, if possible.[20] Carlisle celebrated its fifteenth anniversary with an athletic exhibition, a cadet parade, and speeches and music. Although Quinton's published schedule did not reflect her attendance, her lengthy report describing the event in the April issue of *The Indian's Friend* proved she had joined the fifteen hundred people attending, who included such dignitaries as Commissioner Browning, Senator Henry Teller, General Eliphalet Whittlesey, and Charles C. Painter.[21]

The following month Quinton gave six addresses, including one before a large group at the Brooklyn Indian Association's annual lunch at the Pouch mansion, the proceeds to go towards missionary work among Montana's Piegan Indians.[22] She next spoke in Lancaster, Pennsylvania, Morristown, New Jersey, and Newark where she gave two addresses. Home for a couple of days, she wrote, tongue in cheek, about her "rapid flight across the Alleghenies and over the scarcely budding levels of the Keystone State" to attend a meeting of the Pittsburgh Indian

Association in the YMCA Hall on April 11. Her next stop was Louisville, Kentucky on the fifteenth, followed the next day by another before a Union Ladies meeting. In Henderson, Kentucky, she attended a reception at the elegant home of branch president Mrs. Robert Soaper, and a meeting of the Indian association on the following day. Both this WNIA auxiliary and the one in Louisville were supporting work among the Seminoles. Dayton, Ohio, was the next stop where on April 23 Quinton founded an Indian committee. During these meetings she described a kinship forming that outlasted "all merely worldly ties and which has in its promise of a union continued when all things of this life shall have ended."[23] On April 29, 1894, speaking before the NYCIA in New York City, she was quoted as saying that "the Indian problem [had] long since ceased to be an Indian problem. It was a political one."[24]

From May to August, Quinton gave seventeen addresses at a variety of venues. In late September she returned to Homer, where she discussed her association's Indian work before a large group of Methodists, Congregationalists, and Baptists at her former church.[25] On October 10, she attended the twelfth annual Lake Mohonk Conference. "Never were so many notables present or was there so great pressure for opportunity to speak," she wrote. There was a "constant rain of notes and requests from friends who desired to hear some especially interesting or well known speaker."[26] One was Nancy Cornelius, an Oneida woman from Hartford who was sponsored by the Connecticut Indian Association—the first Indian woman ever to train as a nurse. At least three of the speakers were prominent WNIA members, including Louise Hoppock, president of the Redlands Indian Association (RIA), who brought Indian basketry and pottery to display.[27]

When it was her appointed time, Quinton explained that the WNIA's Seminole mission station, begun in June 1891, had been transferred for $1 to the care of Bishop William Crane Gray of the Protestant Episcopal Church of Southern Florida in December 1893.[28] This work had proceeded very slowly because the Seminoles were "more timid and distrustful than any tribe" she had ever known. Then after noting their work among the Montana Piegans, she stressed that the intent of the WNIA was "to do pioneer work and establish missions in otherwise unproved Indian tribes." Her goal was for every tribe to "have a good mission before the year 1900 strikes." She concluded her article in *The Indian's Friend* with praise for the year's conference, calling it the best of all because "of its glow, high moral sentiment and distinguished personnel."[29]

Ten days later she was in Rhode Island to establish another Indian committee, followed by six other addresses. On November 26, she shared the podium with

Chauncey M. Depew, a lawyer and executive of the New York Central Railroad to address a large meeting of the NYCIA, described as "crowded with fashionable folk." While Depew addressed the deserving qualities of the Indians and their mistreatment at the hands of white men, Quinton enthusiastically spoke on WNIA successes, relating several anecdotes of interest "about the needy and down-trodden condition of the Indians." *The Indian's Friend* noted that Depew "paid a graceful and grateful tribute to the memory of H. H. [Helen Hunt] . . . and congratulated the Association upon its work."[30]

In early December 1894, Quinton officiated at the annual WNIA meeting in New Haven, hosted by the New Haven Indian Association. Sara T. Kinney, president of the Connecticut Indian Association, presented her with a gavel carved from Hartford's famous Charter Oak. Again, Quinton was unanimously elected to serve as president of the national association for the following year.[31] The *New York Times* reported one hundred and fifty delegates from forty states attended, while the *Bangor Daily Whig & Courier* announced that there was a delegate from Bangor and four from the Portland, Maine, branch, whose membership supported missionary work among the Nebraska Omahas, Florida Seminoles, and Indian Territory Shawnees. The reporter listed several prominent members of the WNIA executive board whose names were "a guarantee for the power and excellence of the work, which the society propose, viz. to rouse public opinion and influence the government to take adequate measures for converting the Indians into American citizens." Included were Mrs. Clinton B. Fisk of New York, whose husband, a distinguished Civil War general, had endowed Fisk University and served as BIC president from 1881 until his death in 1890; Elizabeth Eliot Lyman Bullard, president of the MIA and whose brother, Charles William Eliot, was Harvard's long-time president; and Mrs. Lyman Abbott of Brooklyn, whose husband was a lawyer, Congregational minister, and editor of the *Christian Union*. Fisk and Bullard were both in attendance. The Bangor paper also reported that the WNIA had a Washington, DC, correspondent, who watched "legislation on Indian affairs and communicates quickly with branches in any Congressional district in the United States."[32]

Quinton resumed her regular traveling schedule on January 8, 1895, addressing a public meeting in Moorestown, New Jersey, before attending the annual BIC meeting on January 16 in Washington, DC. President Gates convened with the sad news that the Indian reform arena had lost two prominent members, IRA officers Charles C. Painter and James E. Rhoads. Describing them as guarding "the interests of the Indians here in Washington at many threatened points," Gates expressed a special sadness in Painter's death because he "held the threads of these different lines of work in his hands," and "no one has yet been able to gather up all the lines of effort." Quinton read a formal resolution, concluding "we shall ever be inspired by the memory of their courage, fidelity, high patriotism, and consecrated Christian character."[33] Quinton later described the meeting to Welsh as "of unusual interest," although all were saddened by the death of Rhoads and Painter. "How shocking the suddenness was, not for their sakes, but for ours," asking "who can take Prof. Painter's place? It will be most difficult certainly to fill it after his able and devoted work."[34]

During her regular address at the BIC, Quinton noted: "It would be unnatural for me to say a word on Indian work without making reference to our society." Describing the WNIA's recent convention as one of the largest and best ever, with Indian workers "full of spirit and interest," she remarked that Greenville was now a boarding school and that the WNIA was working among the Hopi in Arizona, one of thirty-five different mission stations they had founded during the last eleven years.[35] Reports concluded, among their resolutions, the BIC pledged to support Interior Secretary Hoke Smith in his declared purpose "to develop a competent, permanent, non-partisan Indian service." Then on January 17 Quinton and the other members of the BIC business and resolutions committee hand carried the BIC's resolutions to President Cleveland.[36] Philip Garrett reported that his committee was kindly received by the president and Smith, and as evidence of their acceptance of conference demands, the Interior department had already submitted the names of all proposed agents for their consideration. Quinton was particularly pleased when Smith reappointed Major Steell as Piegan Agent. The March issue of *The Indian's Friend* described this action as "an admirable illustration" of Secretary Smith permitting "no political considerations to prevent putting the right man in the right place over Indians."[37]

Quinton resumed her scheduled calendar in early February, making five addresses that month, including before the nonsectarian National Council of Women of the United States, which opened its three-day session on February 18. Established in 1888 by prominent women's rights leaders, the council campaigned for reform on various social issues. Quinton, as a delegate from a fraternal organization, was allotted five minutes on a day devoted to the influence of women in religion. Prominent women representing every conceivable organization in the United States and Canada were in attendance, including such groups as the

National League for Colored Women, the Eastern Stars, the WCTU, and the International Order of Kings Daughters and Sons.[38]

A Western Tour and a New Desert Mission

On March 5, 1895, Quinton traveled from Philadelphia to Chicago for some association business before boarding the train to Los Angeles for an extended tour to California and the northwest.[39] On March 12, she arrived at Val Verde Station, close to her Perris Valley home, some twenty-five miles from Redlands where Albert K. Smiley and his wife now resided.[40] On March 15, her address before the RIA was anticipated by "An Interested Worker," who hoped it would be well attended "and rouse deep interest among our citizens, whose efforts toward the establishment of good government for all are so well known." The *Los Angeles Times* reported the meeting was well-attended, presided over by Louise Hoppock, auxiliary president, with speakers arranged on a stage draped in several Indian blankets with Indian baskets and bowls scattered around. Quinton was joined by Dr. Anna Johnson, Edgar A. Allen, superintendent of the Perris Indian School, two of his students, and Albert K. Smiley. Allen spoke first, addressing the issue of the "evil practice of the Government in appointing cheap politicians as Indian agents." His students followed with "short but creditable speeches." Johnson then described her work at Cahuilla, exhibiting a rabbit skin robe, cut so that fur appeared on both sides. Quinton's "exceedingly interesting" address described the WNIA's eleven years of Indian work. Smiley, the last to speak, expressed great pleasure that "women of culture were taking hold of this work."[41]

On April 2, Quinton, joined by Weinland, Smiley, and Hoppock, set out on a two-week carriage trip, stopping first at Perris Indian School. Established in 1892, it was the first off-reservation boarding school in California educating students from age five to the early twenties in both agricultural and domestic science.[42] As they traveled through Mission villages, Quinton in her typical rosy prose described the colorful floral-filled drive to Temecula, past the fine old ruins at Pala, past the Pauma Ranch, until they arrived at the government school at Rincon, where they were the guests of Ora Salmons. They saw evidence of her excellent teaching and positive effects of the Dawes allotments with Quinton describing one young woman who had cleared, fenced, and worked her ten acres, even making her own adobe bricks. On the 4th they climbed the steep mountain to La Jolla to visit Flora Golsh, who had taught at that school for nine years. Ascending Palomar Mountain to 6,000 feet, they had a hot meal and sat before a blazing fire at Bailey's, commenting that it was much too cold for camping.[43] Eight hours of down-climbing brought the party to Warner Ranch and Agua Caliente, where they were greeted by Hallowell and French, the first a WNIA-sponsored missionary and the other a government field matron, and Babbitt, the schoolteacher, and spent the night. Quinton stayed in the WNIA cottage, describing its two rooms as a "pleasant surprise with its snugness, taste, and many homemade conveniences and adornments." The party then called upon Indian residents, visited the school, bathed in the hot springs, participated in the Sunday service in the schoolhouse to listen to Weinland's sermon, and finally joined with almost the entire village to attend the marriage ceremony of Celsa and Pedro Apapish. Quinton described the ceremony as beautiful, impressing all.[44]

On Monday, April 8, the travelers headed to Foster, where they caught the train to San Diego to visit a few sights and collect and dispatch their mail, returning to Foster to resume their carriage ride to Mesa Grande, climbing ten miles of steep road, for a visit to the government day school. Their next stop was Cahuilla, over a lengthy stretch of road that alternated between mountains and deserts. Quinton described the flora display along the way as either the loveliest of flowers or the driest of vegetable, including cactus sage or greasewood. They arrived on April 12, finding the teacher, Nanie Salsberry, "as faithful, beloved, and successful as ever" and meeting Anna Ritter, Dr. Johnson's replacement. No time for house calls, Quinton and her party conferred with the Indians at the school and inspected Salsberry's new accommodations and the addition to the WNIA cottage. Pleased with the village progress, Quinton did recommend that the missionary cottage be whitewashed to match the schoolhouse and that outbuildings be constructed, for which Smiley immediately contributed $10. The July issue of *The Indian's Friend* reported the completed construction of a shelter for the pony, carriage, and hay and a new storeroom, all freshly whitewashed, making "the cottage visible from afar, perched as it is on its hill-top beside the Government school house," all glittering "in its new dress of white."[45]

They next headed for Hemet, which Quinton described as a "promising boom town," with its beautiful valleys and a brilliant climate. On Saturday they arrived at Banning, and on Easter Sunday, April 14, attended Weinland's service at the little Moravian Indian church at Potrero, four miles away. On the way, Quinton described a small tidy farm, with "a painted, red roofed cottage nesting under ornamental and fruit trees, and a pretty green hedge before it," thrilled to discover that it had been built through a loan from the WNIA home building program. Ever optimistic, she described her excursion as delightful, gaining facts and inspirations to share with auxiliaries and to include in her addresses.[46]

On Monday, the 15th, Quinton and her party set out to investigate a potential WNIA station among the Desert Cahuilla at Martínez (on today's Torres-Martínez Indian Reservation)—the Indians having requested a resident missionary.[47] From Banning they traveled east on the Southern Pacific through Cabazon, Palm Springs, Indio, finally detraining at Walters, some eighteen miles from the Salton Sea, where they were met by Weinland's interpreter, John Morongo,[48] and a local government schoolteacher, who escorted them in two wagons deeper into the desert for another five miles to meet with more than fifty Indians, dressed in their best clothing, who had gathered at the council house of their small village. When invited to speak, Quinton asked what they wanted in the way of a church. Their response: a mission like the one at Potrero. Although grateful for Weinland's monthly visit, they wanted their children brought up in a society under the influence of a permanent missionary family. Explaining that her association had as many stations as they could sustain, Quinton suggested that if the Moravian board would supply a missionary and his salary, the WNIA would build a cottage and a chapel for them. In the meantime, Weinland recommended the Indians petition the government for an artesian well and Quinton agreed to carry it to Washington.[49]

That evening, with few accommodations available, the group was scattered throughout the village, with Quinton assigned to the council house, a tidy large room with an earthen floor, four glass windows, and a new bedstead with coiled springs. For company, she was assigned two young Indian girls who slept on the floor. Quinton described "their whispers and laughter making merry," putting her to sleep.[50] The Desert Mission now a priority, Quinton appealed to her membership, generating a $300 gift from a New York woman for a missionary cottage and the promise from the Brooklyn auxiliary and its Bay Ridge branch to provide the missionary's salary. Only the missionary's appointment by the Moravian board remained. The April 1896 issue of *The Indian's Friend* reported the government had already made an appropriation to have water piped to Torres, an Indian village to the northwest of Martínez.[51]

Between March and her return to Philadelphia in late September, Quinton addressed forty-six different audiences, thirty-four in California alone, the remainder on the way home. For example, on April 19 she spoke before the Indian association in Riverside, then set off to Claremont to organize an association. On April 25 she addressed a union meeting in Pasadena. Writing Weinland that evening, she provided a partial itinerary, explaining she had returned to her Val Verde home between the Riverside and Claremont addresses and had reorganized the Pasadena auxiliary. She and Louise Hoppock were off to Los Angeles the following day, with a return on April 27.[52]

On May 6 Quinton addressed the RIA and three days later in Cahuilla delivered another address at the Indian school. On May 12 she attended a Sunday service at Agua Caliente and the following Sunday a service at the Perris School, returning to her Perris Valley home to catch up on some of her correspondence, including a telegram from the association's treasurer that the Indian Office was inquiring if the WNIA wanted to renew their contract for the Greenville School or place it "wholly under the care of Government." On May 21 she informed Commissioner Browning that the WNIA preferred to continue to rent its school and property for the next three years but proposed to sell all their "floating property," such as furniture, stock, vehicles, and implements now. They wanted the Aments to remain and to receive a salary increase. "Their devotion of time, strength, & *means* to the school, has been very great, & they should be compensated as to relieve the great strain upon them in these matters." She also informed Browning that Ament had not received the agreed-to contract funding for the forty-one boarding students going back months, forcing him, for the first time, to use his own money to pay the bill. He was now "in great need of money." She also corresponded about Greenville with William H. Hailmann, superintendent of Indian schools, having conferred with him in Washington when last there. On May 30 she set out for Riverside to address the local Indian association.[53]

Leaving Southern California, Quinton headed north, spending the first week and a half in San Jose as the guest of Mrs. [Charlotte] T. Ellard Beans, the wife of a prominent Santa Clara Valley banker, president and manager of the Bank of San Jose. While there Quinton made six addresses, one before the state normal school and another before the local Indian association. Founded in 1891 by Quinton as an Indian committee, they had reorganized on July 23, 1894, as the San Jose Indian Association prompting her to describe them as "full of good works and zeal wisely directed."[54]

From San Jose Quinton headed to San Francisco where beginning on June 11 she gave an address every day for the next four days.[55] Then on Sunday, June 16 she spent a pleasant day, including a drive through the city's Golden Gate Park with Mrs. E. A. Weaver, General Armstrong's sister.[56] On June 19 at the city's Calvary Presbyterian Church, Quinton spoke during the weekly prayer service, describing the Indian as progressing morally and industrially. She received strong praise for her "warm sympathy and sincere admiration" for the Indians.[57]

Children and adults pose in front of the earlier version of the Greenville Indian Industrial Boarding School, part of which later burned.
Indian Valley Museum, Taylorsville, California.

The next day, she set out for a ten-day visit to the Greenville Indian Industrial School following a very circuitous route, first to Sacramento and then by train over the Sierras through forty miles of snow sheds to Reno, arriving late at night. A short train ride the following day to Beckwourth, California, ended in a stage ride bouncing over the forty-two miles to Quincy where she spent the night before driving the final twenty-three miles to the school. On Saturday she stepped out into the 98-degree heat with "phenomenally robust" mosquitoes standing "poised on wing tip ready and longing to snatch the first kiss" to be greeted by Edward and Florence Ament and faced with a waiting packet of letters, all requiring immediate attention. That day she informed Interior Secretary Smith of her arrival, explaining that although she was aware that Commissioner Browning had signed the payment orders, the funds for subsistence of the boarding children at Greenville still had not been paid. From the beginning of the school year the previous September, the amount due was nearly $2,500. School would have been suspended had it not been for the kindness of a local merchant who supplied the food on credit, and Ament who had advanced the money.[58] That Sunday, Quinton saw for the first time the new Jamaica Plain dormitory and attended a church service in the schoolhouse, meeting with bright-eyed students and shaking hands with the "welcoming fathers and mothers," speaking to "all of God's goodness to them and to us."[59]

For the next week she visited Indian homes, finding much that could be improved, and viewed classes that reflected "the intelligent and faithful work" of the Aments and Harriett Newell, a school assistant whose work was funded by the San Jose branch.[60] Quinton was particularly impressed with the unusual talent she discovered in the students' drawing and composition work. To keep local Indians informed on issues relative to their wellbeing, she appointed three of them to serve with Ament as a Committee of Consultation.[61] On June 29 she met at length with Supervisor William M. Moss, the government assessor; together they made a complete inventory of the school's floating property, prompting Quinton the next day to inform Weinland that there was now "much talking & planning in transferring this school."[62]

To Browning, Quinton, optimistic as ever, described the work at the school "*as well & faithfully done*," the "*health of the children* [as] *being excellent*," and "*the ignorant fears, distrust & superstitions of the parents* [as] *greatly diminished*." Because more local Indian residents were asking to have their children admitted, the WNIA, to ensure the facility continued to meet these goals, had decided to finally place it under government care. Therefore, Quinton proposed either to rent or lease their acreage and buildings to the government and sell all floating property for $200 annually, enclosing a list of all items from furniture to pillows, or sell everything for $2,000. She also recommended the government purchase the adjoining farm of 272 acres to use as a school farm. With the available timber on the property and a portable sawmill and the school farm, the school could be self-supporting, providing jobs for local resident Indians. On July 5 she sent a follow up letter to Browning explaining that the WNIA had spent more money than they were requesting. Furthermore, the government had not paid rent for the last few years even though it was officially a government contract school, and the Aments had supplied books, slates, pencils and "given themselves to the work with a devotion" she had never seen excelled.[63]

Following a thorough inspection, Moss reported to Browning that although the school was "the most crude and primitive" he had ever visited, it had "a good effect and the Indians [were] very kindly disposed towards it." He praised the good ladies for what they had done and agreed with Quinton that it had grown beyond her association's ability to run it. Noting the $200 a year rent was not unreasonable, he enclosed an itemized list of personal property, the first value placed by Quinton and the second by him, recommending the government accept his appraisal and his recommendation that the proposal to sell was the best choice. Thousands of acres of government land adjoined the WNIA's forty acres on the north, with one particularly good location for building an entirely new plant. There was abundant water, with rights belonging to Ament's father, who had agreed to deed it to the government. The land and water rights alone were worth $2,000. Because of the inferior construction of the buildings, Moss thought that Quinton would accept $1,600 but cautioned that the full amount was not unreasonable. The one caveat was a danger of fire, for the stove pipes passed through the ceiling without chimneys. He advised against buying the neighboring dairy ranch, recommending instead they continue to buy milk and start up a blacksmith or a carpentry shop. The idea of a sawmill, as Quinton suggested, could provide employment. He recommended that Ament remain with $800 annual salary and his wife as a matron with $400. There should also be a cook, a laundress, and a seamstress, at $400 each, and two additional teachers.[64]

On July 3, Quinton took a last look at her beloved school, describing the buildings as plain and without polish "but the main good sought by them has been attained, and for all else we can wait." Then accompanied by Supervisor Moss, who was on his way to visit Northern California Indian day schools, leaving the group at Prattville, Quinton and the Aments started on their seventy-mile drive down the mountains to Chico, where Quinton was met by John and Annie Bidwell, who had invited her to attend the July fourth celebration on their estate. Although heavy rains forced the festivities to be held the following day, Quinton was impressed with the well managed procession, decorations, music and speeches, describing the day as "a bright and happy one," ending in games and foot races.[65]

On July 8 Quinton set out for Portland, enjoying the majestic Mt. Shasta en route arriving on July 10 for a three-day stay. On the twelfth she addressed a drawing room meeting in the home of Caroline Elliott Ladd, chair of the local WNIA auxiliary and widow of William S. Ladd, a prominent philanthropist, businessman, and banker, gaining pledges to support the WNIA missionary work among Chief Lot's band of Lower Spokane Indians. Leaving Portland, Quinton traveled to Tacoma on July 14, giving an evening address in the Congregational Church. That Monday she reorganized the Indian Committee she had formed in 1891 into an association, with Mrs. A. B. Bull assuming its chairmanship.[66] On July 16, she headed for the WNIA's Spokane Mission, disembarking at Davenport where she was greeted by Captain John W. Bubb, agent at the Colville Agency, who escorted her the twenty-four miles to his home at Fort Spokane to spend a pleasant evening with his family and the officers and their wives. On July 19 she visited the Indian agency and Chief Lot's settlement, Wellpinit,[67] where at dusk she met with Helen W. Clark, the Presbyterian missionary, in front of her WNIA-built log schoolhouse and living quarters. "None who knows such work as hers, and the busy days needed for its support, can doubt that we met as sisters in the most tender and blessed toil that earth can know," wrote Quinton. She was concerned about Clark's isolation due to the seasonal closure of the school three weeks previously, which had prompted Indian families to move to their small farms, leaving Clark alone with her dog. Clark expressed no concern for her own safety.[68]

Agent Bubb was enthusiastic about Clark's educational work, describing her as "an indefatigable worker" and her school as making more rapid progress than any of the others. He reported that the log schoolhouse, located near Chief Lot's church on the eastern end of the reservation, had opened its doors about January 1, 1895, with an average attendance of forty-nine. Lot and his followers were so pleased with the school that a number of adults attended, with Lot visiting daily to observe what was going on, giving Bubb the impression that he was taking lessons.[69]

WNIA members had learned from Clark's letters that she had moved in on December 18, doing much of the interior plastering before opening the school in early January with twenty-five students, including two adult men and their wives. In the May issue she reported fifty-five students, including eight married men and four married women. The school room held only forty comfortably, therefore Clark had described the rest as "corded up in the corner, of course, book in mouth and slate on back to acquire learning by inhalation and absorption!" She also described her welcome by Chief Lot and his followers, explaining that her job had been easy because they were already familiar with Christian teachings. Before moving to their current reservation, a Father Ells had brought them to "the knowledge of the truth, and all speak gratefully and reverently of him and his work," she had explained. This Father Ells was in fact Rev. Cushing Eells,[70] a Congregational minister who, along with Elkanah Walker, had been appointed as missionaries by the American Board of Commissioners for Foreign Missions to Oregon in 1838.[71] They had worked for nearly a decade among the Spokane Indians at Tshimakain Valley (Walker's Prairie), twenty-five miles northwest of Spokane.[72] However, Clark explained that in 1880 Rev. George L. Deffenbaugh, a missionary among the Nez Perce, had established a Presbyterian Church at Lot's camp, and now Lot and his followers were Presbyterians. After Deffenbaugh

Chief Lot dressed in a hooded coat and holding a pipe sits in a wheeled desk chair as he poses for a portrait probably taken by Clair Hunt in Wellpinit about 1900. Lot was chief of the Lower Spokanes.
Chappie Dunning Collection, Northwest Museum of Arts & Culture/Eastern Washington State Historical Society, Spokane, Washington (L95-39.18).

left, Lot became dissatisfied with his replacement, an educated Nez Perce, and requested a white preacher. Helen Clark had been sent.[73]

Quinton's interest in the Spokane Indians dated back to the autumn of 1891 when she had read in the *New York Tribune* Chief Lot's speech requesting a school for his people. Her initial appeal to the membership had been unsuccessful, as all auxiliaries were pledged to other work. Finally in July 1894, members of the Rhode

Island Women's Indian Association at Providence expressed an interest. In late October they formally adopted the work as a state mission, with auxiliaries in Providence and Newport providing the missionary's salary. The government had previously granted five acres for missionary and educational purposes, with the land selected in the village center by Agent Bubb, Chief Lot, and Helen Clark.[74]

The day after Quinton arrived at the reservation, Chief Lot and his family drove from their little farm to the school to greet her. He spoke no English and the interpreter was sick, forcing Quinton to lament how helpless she felt, with "a world of facts that we sorely coveted, and yet all were sealed to us." She learned from Agent Bubb that Lot had set up his winter home across from the school, filling it with children unrelated to him, enabling them to walk to school but also so he could attend with slate in hand. On Sunday, July 21, Quinton attended a church service in the native language, a dialect of the Interior Salish, followed by an hour of Sunday singing. After an interpreter had been located, she addressed the gathering, and for the remainder of the day discussed plans to enlarge the schoolhouse and build a woodshed. Then on Tuesday, she and Clark took the day off for an outing, although a thirty-five-mile drive in the dust and 102-degree heat could hardly be viewed as restful. Wednesday evening Bubb and his wife hosted a reception, and the following day Quinton set out for Davenport and from there to Spokane by train, then on to Helena, Montana.[75] Too tired to visit the Piegan Mission, Quinton turned homeward, stopping in Bismarck, North Dakota, to address a ladies' conference. She had been on the road for five months, covering more than 9,000 miles. From Chicago on August 6, she informed Weinland that she would be in Philadelphia in a day or two and was "oh so glad being just worn out!" She intended to go off and rest somewhere or "break down."[76]

Lake Mohonk and a Return to Speaking Engagements

After her western tour, Quinton headed for Clifton Springs, New York, to enjoy the mineral springs, writing on August 19 that she had come for the cure.[77] Once back on the circuit, she delivered seven addresses during September, mostly in private parlors. On October 5 she informed Weinland that she had spent two days in Washington, DC, conferring with Commissioner Browning and Secretary Smith, who had been most cordial, approving her suggestions. "I feel sure that changes will come, & important ones," she noted. "You will be glad to know that the Secretary is greatly interested in presenting at the Mohonk Conference a new plan by which to take the Indian out of politics," she wrote. "It is to get a new act of Congress placing the Indian under a Commission of three; one Republican, one Democrat, and an army officer," reemphasizing that Smith was going to present this plan at Mohonk, she concluded "I hope we can all work for it and put it though."[78] Although Smith was unable to attend, he later revealed his plan "for securing permanence of service in Indian Affairs." The WNIA, during their December 1895 annual meeting, resolved to petition Congress on behalf of his proposal separating "the Indian service from the mutations of politics."[79]

On October 9 Quinton joined the one hundred and forty conference guests at Smiley's Lake Mohonk resort. She was again elected to the committee on business and resolutions. Her account of the WNIA's work was brief, describing it as "in one sense educational." She had found changes in California since her last visit four years earlier—new homes, small well-tilled farms under fence, trees planted, new glass windows in houses, plank floors instead of earth, improved government schools, and a mill for grinding acorns. Her visit to the Spokane mission "was a joyful one." But she was most moved by her visit to the Desert Cahuilla. "The glaring sand, the parching heat, the absence of all that to us makes life pleasant, presented a scene of poverty and need I had not before met," she exclaimed. She hoped to open a mission among them, one of thirty tribes still without "the gospel in this Christian land."[80]

For the remainder of October and all of November, she delivered eleven addresses, including one at the Pioneer's Reunion, held on November 12, where she and three thousand "pioneer women workers" met at the metropolitan Opera House in New York City to celebrate the eightieth birthday of suffragette Elizabeth Cady Stanton, described as still "full of brightness and humor showing a mind still clear and vigorous." Former WNIA president Mary Lowe Dickinson managed the proceedings, which included speeches by the president of Bryn Mawr College, Clara Barton of the Red Cross, Susan B. Anthony, and Quinton on "Women in Work for Indians," prompting the comment in *The Indian's Friend* that "there was an embarrassment of riches and the closing hour was a late one."[81]

Twelve days later Quinton presided over the seventh annual meeting of the NYCIA,[82] and on December 4 welcomed delegates from seven different states to the Grace Temple in Philadelphia for the WNIA's annual meeting to, among other activities, listen to presentations from prominent male reformers including Philadelphia lawyer Philip C. Garrett, a member of the IRA executive board and of the BIC, who addressed the topic of law for the Indians. He was joined by Quinton's pastor, Rev. George Dana Boardman; Rev. H. L. Wayland, author of the WNIA's first petition to Congress; and Herbert Welsh, executive secretary of the IRA.[83] Quinton said the conference "passed off delightfully. All was harmony, love, and enthusiasm."[84] Added to the ending of another successful WNIA annual meeting was the fact that Weinland had finally answered her entreaties and sent in his belated missionary report detailing his Sunday school and morning and evening services at Potrero, his preaching visits to Cahuilla and Agua Caliente, and his two visits to the Desert Cahuilla at Martínez.[85]

Quinton had spent much of 1894 and 1895 dealing with the WNIA's work in California or her own properties there. Fortunately, things at least had quieted down at Cahuilla and Agua Caliente. More important, she had begun to build a solid working relationship with Commissioner Browning, getting much of what she requested for the eleven active missions operated by the association. In 1895 she had returned to California, spending ten days at her beloved Greenville school, paving the way for its sale, with a quick visit to WNIA workers among the Mission Indians and establishing the WNIA's last California mission among the Desert Cahuilla at Martínez. At the end of the tour, she visited the WNIA Mission station among the Spokane for the first time. But for the foreseeable future she would be focused on moving the new desert station forward and dealing with the aftermath of a destructive fire at Greenville in 1897.[86]

9

1896 to 1899, and California Bound

During the last four years of the nineteenth century, Quinton kept up a steady pace, some years giving fewer addresses, but continuing her routine of beginning the year attending the BIC in Washington and ending at Lake Mohonk and the association's annual meeting. She would oversee new missionary work among the Hupa and the work among the Desert Cahuilla, continually fussing over the slowness of the latter. There would be setbacks going forward, such as a destructive dormitory fire at Greenville before the sale was completed and the loss of the Warner Ranch court case in California. The usual changes that accompanied a new administration would require Quinton to again learn the strengths and weakness of new Indian Office personnel. After establishing good relations with Commissioner Browning, she would have to start all over again with the incoming commissioner, William A. Jones, and a new Mission Indian agent, Lucius A. Wright. Fortunately, relations with Wright would never be as contentious as they had been with the previous two agents. Growing old in the job and tiring more quickly, she made plans to relax in her Perris Valley home during 1896 but was unable to do so until 1898, squeezing in a visit along the way to the MIA station among the Hualapai of Arizona and the Navajo, both for the first time.

The BIC and the Teller Bill

The continued economic hard times during 1896 kept Quinton close to Philadelphia. The WNIA's sole organizer, she still inspired audiences, giving fifty-one addresses, and organizing seven new branches.[1] On January 10, 1896, she spoke before the New Century Club in Philadelphia[2] and five days later joined representatives from missionary boards and Indian associations at the twenty-fifth annual BIC conference in Washington, DC. Former Commissioner Thomas

Jefferson Morgan, now secretary of the American Baptist Home Mission Society, led off the reports. Quinton briefly described her association's eleven current missions, beginning with Dr. and Mrs. Jacob E. Brecht's work among the Florida Seminoles, still in the preparatory stage, "removing obstacles, gaining a solid basis for permanent work."[3] She singled out the medical work of Dr. Hallowell, although describing all the work among the Mission Indians as purifying and elevating the "moral tone of the people." The Greenville School, the "beloved child of many prayers and much labor," had been "transferred to the management, control, and entire support of the Government," while the association still engaged in missionary work there. The rest of the WNIA-sponsored stations were run by auxiliaries—Maine worked among the Absentee Shawnees of Indian Territory, and New Jersey among the Hopis of Arizona. The MIA-sponsored day school among the Hualapai of Arizona had been transferred to the government while Connecticut was still supporting a mission school and a farmer among the Bannocks and Shoshonis of Idaho; and finally, Rhode Island had just opened its mission among the Spokane Indians. All were breathing "prophesies for future enlargement and success," she concluded.[4]

During the afternoon session, attendees discussed the Teller Bill, loosely based on Interior Secretary Hoke Smith's earlier recommendation but put forth by Colorado Senator Henry M. Teller. The legislation proposed to remove Indian affairs from partisan politics by abolishing the position of Indian commissioner and his assistant, replacing them with a three-person commission—two civilians, one from each political party to hold the office for four years, and an officer of the regular Army.[5] Unable to attend, Smith had asked IRA member Francis E. Leupp, to open the discussion.[6] He explained that Teller's bill differed in "important particulars" from Smith's proposal, especially excluding a provision for the agent's tenure to be based on faithful discharge of duties. Quinton, displeased that the bill did not "empower the commission to select the agents," declared that it failed to "take the Indian service out of politics. It simply divided the position between the two parties." She and her association objected because every four years new members would be appointed, "reinaugurating the spoils system at the very fountain head of the Indian service."[7] At one point, Caroline Dall spoke up, recommending a bill embodying Smith's suggestions instead of requiring the friends of the Indians to be content with compromise legislation. Quinton responded immediately: "We do compromise when we have to; this bill, however, is not a compromise." The head of the Indian Bureau needed more power, not a division of power, she noted, concluding that the time had come to go boldly to Congress and demand a better bill. "This is not framed so as to get the Indian service out of politics, for it leaves the appointing power just where it is now."[8]

Conference members moved that their business committee submit a draft and appoint a committee to confer with the Indian Office, Senator Teller, and the proper committees in the House and Senate as "to the points to be secured in a new law." The motion was adopted unanimously; Quinton and Garrett were appointed to serve, with Dr. Abbott as committee chair. Then during his few comments, Garrett reported the kindly reception the previous year's committee had received, evidence of which was this current discussion. He further cautioned that this newly proposed commission must be nonpartisan with an indefinite tenure and with the sole power to appoint all agents. In its final platform, the BIC approved Smith's plan, recommending a modification of Teller's bill along the lines of the secretary's original proposal.[9] Not until early January 1897 was a revised bill introduced by James S. Sherman, chairman of the House Committee on Indian Affairs.[10] It never became law.

The Hoopa Station

Her BIC duties over, Quinton resumed her speaking engagements, making seven addresses in and around New York, including one on January 22, 1896, before the Brooklyn Indian Association where she described the work that had been accomplished and the proposed new mission among the Desert Cahuillas.[11] Returning to Philadelphia, she responded to Browning's January 20 letter, expressing pleasure that he found no obstacle to the government purchase of the Greenville School, hoping the sale would be completed soon, noting that the WNIA needed the funds to open up new fields.[12]

One of these new fields was the Hoopa Reservation in northern California. Six years earlier Mrs. Dorcas J. Spencer, corresponding secretary of the California WCTU, had alerted the membership to the conditions on the reservation, prompting Quinton to visit during her 1891 tour. Other than an association-wide petition drive that had resulted in the removal of Fort Gaston, nothing else was undertaken until the San Jose Indian Association reorganized and member Emma Hapgood Denton moved to the Hoopa Valley in late August 1895 as the kindergarten teacher in the government boarding school. She expanded her work to include a Sunday school and song service on Sunday evenings, sending reports to Cornelia Taber, corresponding secretary of the San Jose auxiliary.[13] In mid-January 1896 Denton consulted with Hoopa Agent William E. Dougherty about bringing in a trained missionary, explaining that her association had already selected San Jose resident Rev. Lyman Paul Armstrong. Taber, in turn, informed Quinton that the San Francisco and San Jose associations had already pledged the first year of Armstrong's salary, requesting her to bring this matter before Commissioner Browning. In a January letter to Browning, Quinton reminded him that during her last visit she had mentioned the efforts of California workers to bring a missionary to Hoopa. Now that "the way seems open, the agent seems to favor it, and a capital man has been found for the field," she was requesting his approval, inquiring if there were any vacant government buildings to be used for temporary housing. If not, could the government grant the WNIA an acre of land upon which to build a cottage?[14]

When Browning did not respond, Quinton wrote again in early March, requesting a speedy reply, reiterating that "*the* work needs to begin *at once*." The WNIA had long sought someone of Armstrong's qualification and were fearful of losing him. A short notice in the May issue of *The Indian's Friend* reported that Armstrong had sailed from San Francisco for Hoopa on March 26.[15] Several months later Quinton reassured Browning that the San Jose women in charge of the Hoopa work were responsible and practical. The previous November Nellie Blessing Eyster, president of the San Francisco auxiliary, had requested a large grant of land to establish an industrial farm at Hoopa where a resident missionary would live. Dougherty had declared her proposal "wholly impracticable," urging Browning to reject it. Quinton assured Browning that Eyster's request was a blunder. Eyster had little to do with the work at Hoopa except to gather the missionary's salary. The San Jose Association would instead supervise the work and build the cottage, placing it "outside the *school*." With that clarification, Quinton requested a half-acre of land. If not possible, then she asked to buy an acre or half acre. In conclusion, she wrote that she was "trusting that no friction will arise, & that Mr. Armstrong's work may be wholly wise & greatly helpful to the Indians."[16]

There was no real friction only a slight glitch with housing. The half-acre that Dougherty and Armstrong had ended up selecting under Browning's orders had no trees for building, thus Quinton was forced to ask Browning for the use of the old government schoolhouse, currently used as a carpenter's shop and in good shape, to move onto their lot. The large 24 x 48-foot building provided ample living quarters, an assembly room, and two rooms upstairs for teaching adults.[17] Agent Dougherty readily agreed, personally assisting in its removal and offering to cut any timber at the agency sawmill without charge. Supported by a gift of $600 from philanthropist Phoebe Apperson Hearst, the structure was renovated and work was well under way by the following spring.[18] After all of this, Armstrong stepped down. He was replaced by Pliny Earle Goddard and his wife Alice, who had come highly recommended by Philadelphia Quakers.[19]

The Desert Mission

While the Hoopa station was progressing, Quinton remained focused on the Martínez station, explaining to Weinland that in three of her last ten addresses in February she had spoken before Moravian congregations in Pennsylvania, appealing on behalf of this work. "Greatly interested," these congregations were busy collecting funds for an artesian well, Quinton explained. She had also conferred with Rev. E. T. Kluge, who had already chosen an excellent man and his wife as missionaries, although they were unavailable for the next two months.[20]

The next step was the cottage. Quinton, having personally endured California's summer heat, suggested a double roof with twenty inches of air space in between; large windows; adobe walls; an open passage with no walls between the little kitchen and the bedroom; and a large living room with a large lounge for Weinland's use when visiting.[21] Months later she implored Weinland not to let the "house be roasting by being all small rooms," requesting a copy of the plans. After reviewing them, she suggested another window for the sitting room and windows on each side of the fireplace, agreeing to find the money for the upgrades.[22]

Then to her dismay, Quinton, learning in late February 1896 from Weinland that Anna Ritter, Dr. Johnson's replacement at Cahuilla, would be leaving her post to study medicine, inquired if he knew a good Moravian woman to take her place. She did not inform Browning of Ritter's plans for several months, and when she did, she suggested a Miss Alberta Hartzell of Redlands on a strong recommendation from Louise Hoppock.[23] Browning, unable at that time to appoint a new field matron, instead transferred Mrs. C. C. Moses from a school in Wisconsin.[24]

March was equally busy for Quinton with nine addresses primarily in New England. She returned home to find several letters from Weinland and his missionary report, which she described as a "boon." In April she gave seven addresses, traveling between Philadelphia, New York City, Buffalo, and Newark, ending the month with a talk before the Friends' (Quaker) yearly meeting. In late May, Quinton traveled to Washington, DC, to confer with officials, informing Weinland in early June that she had met not only with Browning but with a Mr. [Charles F.] Larrabee, whom she described as "chief of land and water division," in an effort to ensure adequate water for the new desert station. Because the Torres reservation was so large—some 20,000 acres—she had requested ten acres at Martínez, later deciding that five acres would do.[25] Two days later she sent a follow up letter to Browning, referencing the earlier petition she had presented him from the Indians at Martínez requesting an artesian well and asking that the water supply the government had recently given to the Indians at Torres be extended to Martínez. He responded on June 17 that in April he had recommended to Agent Estudillo to solicit bids to do the work. When the paperwork was not returned to the Indian Office, Browning had directed the agent to expedite the matter.[26] In the meantime, Quinton's request for ten acres slowly moved through the process with William H. Sims, acting secretary of the Interior, informing Browning on June 20 that Estudillo had been granted authority to set apart, with Indian consent, a plot not to exceed ten acres of unclaimed land.[27] Despite continued changes of administration, Quinton had proven persuasive enough with new officials to generally get her requests granted.

That spring the Indian Office extended Civil Service rules over additional positions in the Indian Service, including field matrons, which for Quinton meant that she no longer had any power over appointments. In early June she informed Weinland of this change, emphasizing the need to encourage Ritter to remain as long as possible. On the positive side, Quinton reported that the SCIA had agreed to take over responsibility for the Cahuilla station.[28] She could now devote more time to the sale of the Greenville school, which had been dragging on for months. She had reduced the price from $2,000 to $1,500 in a June 27 letter to Browning, although explaining their improvements alone amounted to more than $1,400. A month later she sent an abstract of title, informing him that Ament, acting on their behalf, had accepted the offer, although she still thought it too low.[29]

In desperate need of a rest, in May Quinton spent several weeks at Clifton Springs, New York, known for its mineral springs. In a late June letter to Weinland, she described herself as "*so* worn & tired. *Must* see a Dr. & rest & build up." For the next several weeks she stayed at Dr. Strong's Sanitarium in Saratoga Springs, New York, with its mineral baths and massages.[30] The Philadelphia summer heat also took its toll. She hoped to go to the seashore for a few days, accompanied by a trunk full of work. She needed to have her eyes treated and work done on her teeth and to "put into a dry dock for general repairs." So overworked, she often thought of resigning, but asked Weinland not to mention that fact. On the positive side, Josephine Babbitt had come for a visit, and the association had almost $500 for building a house, stable, and fencing at Martínez.[31]

Quinton spent much of September coordinating the proposed Desert Mission with Reverend Kluge in Pennsylvania and Weinland in California. Although the Moravian Board had agreed to dig a well and were recommending the missionary,

Quinton informed Weinland that she had stressed to Kluge that until a formal transfer of the mission was made, it was still under WNIA control, and that Weinland, as WNIA superintendent, was still in charge, working with the agent to set the land aside and supervising the carpenter building the cottage. Only when it was completed would the transfer be made to the Moravian Church. On the tenth, she wrote Weinland that although the government had assured her of water for the site, she was pleased that the Moravian Board had agreed to pay for the well and for the chapel. Concerned about the intense desert heat, Quinton stressed, "We *don't want* a 'poor little tucked up' cottage on that *hot reservation*." The rooms "should be decently comfortable." By this time, they knew that Rev. David J. Woosley and his wife had been selected as the missionaries.[32]

While Quinton worked on getting a well and a decent cottage, Weinland, accompanied by his interpreter, John Morongo, and Woosley, met with Agent Estudillo. On September 6 they proceeded by "burro express" to Martínez where

Moravian minister David J. Woosley and his wife and child pose in a donkey-drawn wagon in front of the WNIA constructed missionary cottage in Martínez about 1900. The cottage's double-roofed construction was intended to provide some protection from the intense desert heat.
William H. Weinland Collection, The Huntington Library, San Marino, California (photCL 39 [172]).

the agent explained to the Indians that both he and the Indian Office approved of this project. Following Woosley's introduction, the Indians were invited to speak, a number expressing their appreciation for the mission. An agreement was drawn up, and each Indian "touched the tip of the penholder" to his name. In the meantime, Weinland and Woosley had chosen a site for the cottage and chapel, some five hundred feet north of the government school.[33] Quinton, who had earlier reviewed the cottage plans, informed Weinland on September 28: "My heart is jubilant over the outlook of that work."[34] In December she heard from the Woosleys, who had already given their first Sunday school service on November 15, dedicating the chapel in December.[35]

Lake Mohonk and the Annual WNIA Meeting

After weeks of mineral baths and references to exhaustion, Quinton looked forward to a long rest in her California home. She had packed her furniture and books and sent them to George in Val Verde.[36] Scheduled to be at Lake Mohonk on October 14, she squeezed in a talk before the Indian association in Kingston, New York, on the twelfth. Chosen once again to serve on the Mohonk business committee, Quinton was joined by Anna L. Dawes, the senator's daughter. Among the attendees was Mary Louise Eldridge, who spoke on her Navajo work funded by the Massachusetts auxiliary. This was Quinton's first opportunity to meet with Eldridge; the next would be on her visit to the Navajo reservation during her 1898 tour.[37] During her presentation, Quinton reminded those present that the primary object of the WNIA's 1881 petition (recommending land in severalty, education, and citizenship) had been to destroy the reservation system by individualizing property ownership. It was now the reformer's responsibility to help the Indian cease being an Indian so "that he may become wholly a man."[38]

The conference over, Quinton wrote Weinland that she was searching for a boarding house and working on the November issue of *The Indian's Friend* and the program for the upcoming annual convention. Four days later she noted she had located new lodgings a block from her previous place.[39] Following her Mohonk attendance, Quinton had returned to her circuit, giving several addresses before heading to New England for two weeks, addressing the annual meetings of the New Haven and Hartford branches, and then presiding over the WNIA annual meeting on December 9 and 10, 1896, in New York City. Reelected as president, she expressed her gratitude and officiated over another successful gathering, including the Thursday evening public meeting which was a delight, "and all present seemed as much to enjoy it, as many glowing testimonies then and later proved."[40] She finished out the month with three public addresses in Delaware.

Letters to Weinland reflected her frustration at continually postponing her California visit. She decided to wait until after the December convention and the printing of the annual report, which would take all of January. She hoped to set out February 1 and stay for several months. Mid-March 1897 came and went, and she had not yet left. Her California home was nearly done, and she hoped to see it in May. A month later with her annual printing completed, she was still tying up loose ends. "Unless I can go before the great heat comes, I'll hardly dare to go at all," she concluded. [41] It would not be until June 1898 that she actually left.

The Greenville School and a Change of Administration

Quinton's 1897 calendar was uncharacteristically short, with few addresses from April through September, although she did establish two new Indian committees and the Elizabeth Haddon Indian Association in Haddonfield, New Jersey.[42] At the end of the year she went into the hospital for an unexplained surgery, which may account for her inactivity during those months. However, her year began on a positive note. On January 6 she informed Reverend Weinland that the Desert Mission had "gone forward without delays or back-sets."[43]

Two weeks later she attended the annual BIC meeting, again serving on the business committee. Her yearly missionary report was brief. Much of the missionary work was under the direction of state auxiliaries with "cheering progress," she explained. The newest station in the California desert under the Brooklyn and Bay Ridge branches had opened "very promisingly,"[44] although she had learned from Kluge that the government had not yet found water, forcing Quinton and Weinland to decide to have a well dug and buy a gasoline engine and pump. In a February 17 letter to Weinland, she agreed to ask Kluge's Moravian Board and auxiliaries for $150 each toward the cost. The following month she assured Weinland that the WNIA Board had promised to raise $180, and the Brooklyn ladies thought they could also raise money. With these assurances, Quinton telegraphed him on March 9 to go ahead and buy the engine.[45]

She was also still dealing with the sale of the Greenville School. Negotiations had been lengthy. Not until September 7, 1896, had Ament sent Quinton the property and water deed that his mother, Sarah Ament, had signed on July 22. Quinton immediately forwarded them to Browning, who on September 29 returned them, requesting changes. In her response on October 1, Quinton agreed to follow his instructions, hoping that the "law's delay" may be as brief as possible. Finally, on December 23, 1896, having complied with all of his recommendations, she sent the deed and other pertinent papers, "trusting that the sale may now speedily be concluded."[46]

On January 30, 1897, Browning sent Ament a letter with additional instructions, which Ament followed, sending it on to Quinton, who after signing, forwarded the paperwork back to Browning. Hearing nothing, she wrote him on March 25, only to learn that five days earlier there had been a school fire.[47] "My soul goes down into the depth over the burned dormitory," she responded immediately. Ever optimistic, she wrote it "should not make a great difference in the price," for the land and water were more valuable, explaining that getting the money would "vastly lighten [her] load of *over* work & care which [was] nearly killing [her]." She concluded, that "for two years nearly we have been seeking to effect or complete this sale & my courage is at a low ebb."[48]

The day before the fire Quinton had given an address at an Indian association meeting in Brooklyn and another one in New York City on March 28, returning to Philadelphia the following day.[49] Quinton learned the details from letters that awaited her return, enabling her to inform Browning that none of the fifty-three students were hurt. The boys had bravely "worked like experienced firemen" to save everything they could. She hoped the government would put up a temporary dormitory, or even better, "a *good* one." Currently the boys were living in the new chapel, while the girls and their teachers were in the laundry and schoolhouse.[50] She had learned from the Aments that the fire had originated in the cook's upstairs bedroom. Although nothing could be saved in the girls' dormitory, all the bedding in the boys' dormitory, the furniture in the sitting room, and everything in the children's kitchen had been saved. Browning telegraphed the Aments to make whatever arrangements they could for the children, asking for their recommendations. In the meantime, lessons continued in cramped quarters.[51]

On April 9 Quinton learned from Browning that a special investigative agent had ruled the fire "purely accident"; the sale could proceed. Initially the government had agreed to pay $1,200. Browning now suggested $600, enclosing the old deed, requesting a new one and an affidavit. On April 12, Quinton returned the paperwork. On April 30, 1897, Acting Commissioner Thomas P. Smith authorized the payment, and on May 22, informing him the money had arrived, Quinton recommended that when rebuilt, the dormitory be large enough to hold one hundred students. "*It can easily be filled*," she informed him, "many are already begging admission."[52] Concerned that the government would not rebuild, Quinton wrote

Commissioner Jones on July 1, assuring him that Ament was an able and faithful man. In the meantime, on June 26, James J. Anderson, Supervising Instructor of Indian Schools, strongly recommended rebuilding for one hundred students, news that Smith informed Quinton of on July 6. Two days later she assured him she was pleased with Anderson's favorable report, writing again on July 14 that she was also glad the building would hold one hundred students, notifying the membership of the news in the August issue.[53]

If the fire were not enough of a headache, Quinton had faced yet another change of administration when William McKinley took over as president in March 1897, forcing her once again to reeducate Indian Office officials of the importance of the WNIA's work. During the February 27 meeting of the WNIA Executive Board, she described a call upon the president-elect at his Canton, Ohio, home in January, recalling the "cordial and very pleasant manner in which he received her and of her belief that he will do first that which is *just*, and afterward that which is expedient."[54] In April she traveled twice to the capital, once early in the month to speak on behalf of retaining Dr. William H. Hailmann as superintendent of Indian schools. McKinley ignored Quinton and Hailmann's other supporters, instead appointing Estelle Reel.[55] At month's end Quinton met with the new Commissioner, William A. Jones, who she characterized as "good, true, honest, & will do well I think." She had also tried twice in late April to visit with the incoming Interior secretary, Cornelius N. Bliss, finding him out both times. She informed Weinland she would try again before returning home. Although her opinion of Bliss was not recorded, *The Indian's Friend* described him as possessing an ability and integrity in the business world, "and with these qualities brought to bear on the problems and responsibilities of his new office, we may hope for much."[56]

Quinton was most concerned with the position of Mission agent. Unable to meet with Secretary Bliss, she wrote McKinley on May 31 charging incoming agent Dr. Lucius A. Wright "with all sorts of iniquities, including drunkenness," but never revealed her sources. Her letter had been referred to Bliss, who assured her that after a thorough investigation, he was satisfied that she had been misinformed. Wright's commission would be issued immediately. Bliss had written Herbert Welsh on July 1, mentioning Quinton's accusation and suggesting that he "caution the good lady to be more careful in her statements." Wright had been recommended by Senator George W. McBride of Oregon, who according to Bliss was always mindful of his recommendations. Furthermore, Bliss had received unqualified denials of Quinton's charges from twenty leading citizens from Southern California.[57] In the meantime, Quinton had written Weinland requesting he send signed statements of five or six citizens of San Jacinto relevant to Wright's drinking so she could keep her "position in the confidence of the Pres." On July 3, she described Wright's assuming the position of agent as "a burning shame," concluding that if he drank again, she hoped Weinland "would be able to testify to it, to me, by *citizens signatures* so I *can use* them."[58]

The Warner Ranch Lawsuit

Quinton's official itinerary reflected only two public addresses in New Jersey in May and none in June. On the first of June, having returned from Washington the previous evening, she wrote Matthew Sniffen, Welsh's assistant, enclosing a letter dated May 24 from Rebecca Hallowell, the WNIA's medical missionary at Agua Caliente. Hallowell explained that Babbitt, the local schoolteacher, had been informed by a reliable source that the Indians at Agua Caliente were "dissolute, quarrelsome and unworthy of any further care from the Indian Rights Association." Hallowell feared that if this accusation went unchallenged, the Mohonk Conference would refuse to continue its "financial aid in carrying on the trial." Having lived and worked there for four years, she described the residents as "sober, industrious and law-abiding," busily working their well-cultivated fields. "We think they do remarkable well, and we are often surprised at their continued courage and patience," she had concluded. To Sniffen, Quinton also described the Indians as "doing wonderfully well considering that their hands and hopes are so tied." She informed him that this issue would be addressed in the July issue of *The Indian's Friend*.[59]

Quinton and Hallowell were referring to Indian reaction to the lawsuit brought by former Governor Downey in the Superior Court of San Diego on July 27, 1892, to dispossess the residents of the five Warner ranch villages. When the initial suit only covered two villages, a second one had been filed and the two cases combined for trial, which had begun in June 1893 with Shirley C. Ward and Frank D. Lewis defending the Indians. The suits slowly moved through the lower courts with delays, partially due to Downey's death in 1894 and the substitution of his nephew J. Downey Harvey as plaintiff.[60] When Judge George Puterbaugh disqualified himself because of a conflict of interest, the case was transferred to another department of the superior court with Judge W. L. Pierce presiding. Pierce finally submitted his ruling against the villages on December 29, 1896, just before he retired. Meanwhile, WNIA missionary activities at Agua Caliente had continued with members and missionary workers unaware of this December decision until the February issue of *The Indian's Friend* described the case as one that "should thrill every honest heart with indignation." Quinton concluded that "an effort will be made to secure a reversal of the decision."[61]

That effort was immediate. Denied a request for a new trial on April 24, 1897, Ward and Lewis, supported by Lake Mohonk and the IRA, which furnished the $6,100 indemnity bond, appealed to the California State Supreme Court to protect the Indians from the eviction scheduled for July 15, 1897. On June 19 Ward informed Welsh that he considered "the chance of success upon appeal" to be "most excellent."[62] *The Indian's Friend* described the case as important, trusting that as in the Soboba case, "complete success may crown its generous labors."[63] The situation had been specifically difficult for the Agua Caliente villagers, although Lewis and Ward were confident, believing that "both morally and legally the Indians own the lands on which they are now living."[64]

Burdened by work and worry over Warner Ranch, on June 29, along with two trunks full of papers, letters and work, Quinton headed to Homer, New York, for two months of "pure air & quiet."[65] On July 3 she informed Weinland that she needed to lighten her "load of care" and wanted the Moravian Board to take over the Desert Mission. Growing increasingly frustrated with Kluge, she informed Weinland two months later that she hoped his Board would take the mission by October. However, not until November 19, 1897, was the station finally turned over.[66]

By this time, Quinton had dealt with the incoming administration long enough to conclude that it was "a corrupt, greedy, political shame! God help us, & the Indians as well as the whites." She wrote, "after all the hungry white men are placed," maybe later on they could "induce the President to give *some* thoughts to Indian interests." She provided no proof for such an accusation, which seemed odd considering her high praise of the Indian commissioner in an earlier letter. Her frustration spread to her plans to go to California. She had given up; it was too late "to plunge into the heat there." Maybe next winter. That same week she wrote Sniffen twice, congratulating Welsh upon providing the indemnity bond. "That is a splendid deed," she wrote, "May it save their homes to those people." In a second letter she expressed delight that the friends of the Indians were responding with contributions for the appeal of the Warner Ranch Indians. Although her published itinerary showed only one address in July in

Homer and one in September in Binghamton, New York, where she organized an Indian Committee, she did not find the peace and quiet hoped for, describing her summer to Weinland in a late September letter as very busy, "*no* pause of work & *not one day* of rest or vacation yet."[67]

Lake Mohonk and Annual Meeting, 1897

On October 13, 1897, Quinton joined some two hundred other reformers for the fifteenth annual Lake Mohonk Conference to discuss among other topics, the fate of the Mission Indians. Their first speaker was Joshua W. Davis whose interest dated back eleven years to when he and his wife had accompanied Charles C. Painter on an investigative trip to Southern California. When the Mohonk Conference established their Committee for the Legal Defense of the Mission Indians, Davis had been appointed its chairman. However, the seriousness of this new crisis at Warner Ranch had prompted the Mohonk committee to turn to the IRA and Welsh, who secured a $4,000 appropriation from the IRA and with a friend came up with the remaining monies from their own pockets. Davis moved that the defense of the Mission Indians be transferred to the IRA. The conference concurred.[68]

Quinton, for the first time, addressed the abolition of certain agencies, listing nearly a dozen that she claimed officials agreed could be spared, with superintendents of the government boarding schools supporting the Indians in their transition. The Mission Indian Agency was on the list. This "political childhood" of the Indians needed to be ended, she exclaimed, "the sooner they can get on their own feet and look after their own affairs the better." She recommended that the conference prepare a resolution reducing the number of agencies in a "gradual and rational way," but, for whatever reason, her suggestion was not included in their final resolutions. She then briefly addressed the WNIA's current eleven missions and their assistance to seventy different tribes to date, totaling between $15,000 and $28,000 annually and supporting the construction of a dozen missionary cottages and half dozen chapels.[69]

For the first time in her presidency, Quinton did not officiate at the annual WNIA December meeting, having undergone an unidentified surgery on the first of the month. Although the doctor declared the operation a success with complete recovery, Quinton described being in the "valley of the shadow" for days," finally sitting up for a few minutes on December 10. She convalesced in Merchantville, New Jersey. "Cant exert myself safely *yet*," she informed Weinland on December

18, hoping to see him before spring. Her first public address of 1898 was not until February 21 before the NYCIA.[70]

Quinton Tours Again

Finally in March 1898 Quinton was sufficiently recovered to set out for California, informing Weinland that she had arrived on the 12th, and inquiring if he knew where she could buy olive trees to replace the lemon and orange trees that had died. The day after she arrived, students at nearby Perris Indian School, first the all-boy brass band and then the eighteen-member girls' mandolin and guitar band, entertained her "with a full matinee of spirited music well executed."[71] In a late May letter she informed *The Indian's Friend* that she had been in Redlands, visiting Hoppock and Smiley, the latter having presented the city with a $50,000 public library surrounded by sixteen acres on April 29. On May 2 Quinton joined a dozen other guests in an excursion planned by Hoppock, picnic lunch included, to drive eighteen miles from Redlands to Perris Indian School in two carriages. Perris School, now nearly doubled in size under the capable and efficient care of Superintendent Harwood Hall, was "a happy body of youth and children working from love, and under good and sanitary influences, physically and morally."[72] On June 3 she gave two addresses in San Jose and on Sunday, June 5 spoke before the Los Gatos Presbyterian Church, organizing an Indian committee. The following day she addressed the Pastors' Union of San Jose, and two days later was in Oakland speaking at the First Congregational Church.[73] In early August she learned from Weinland that he would be moving permanently to Banning into a new home. His successor at Potrero finally had been appointed.[74] Two weeks later she informed him that Babbitt had visited with news that the Indians at Agua Caliente wanted Dr. Hallowell and Miss French to leave. "Both have been imprudent lately," noted Quinton with no explanation. Hallowell's sons had long "begged her to come home," so Quinton thought she might be persuaded to do so by year's end. Then in late August Quinton made preparations to visit the MIA's Arizona mission station among the Hualapai.[75]

Described as among "the poorest of the poor tribes," the seven hundred Hualapais had become an MIA project in mid-1894 when the auxiliary sent Frances S. Calfee to occupy their rented house in Hackberry in the Hualapai Valley. She had previously worked among the Hopis. Calfee had started a school in June with seventeen children, providing them a noon meal, but Mary E. Dewey, MIA's corresponding secretary, wanted more for the Indians. Therefore, she had appeared before the 1894 Lake Mohonk Conference to appeal for support. Dewey described the Hualapais as living in a "state of uttermost poverty and degradation," but wanting more for their children. "For us to refuse people who ask simply for education is as if, with bread in our hands, we should deny it to starving men." Receiving continued support from the MIA and wider recognition from Lake Mohonk, by 1897 some Hualapais were living in houses, planting small gardens, and educating more of their children.[76] When Calfee was appointed as a government field matron, the MIA was upset about losing her as their missionary but saw the value of a salary saved, and made major improvements and purchased the Hope Ranch five miles north of Hackberry with the goal of establishing a boarding school. During her September 1898 visit, Quinton described the Sunday school as "a bright one," and the day school as full of "good work" and "happy pupils," receiving a "well-prepared, orderly lunch" at noon. Addressing the October 1898 Mohonk Conference, Quinton described cheerful Indians with the "old-time sadness of expression" gone from many faces.[77]

Leaving the Hualapai Sunday school behind, Quinton traveled to the Navajo Reservation to visit the association's newest mission opened in March of that year at Two Gray Hills in the San Juan valley of New Mexico, with Massachusetts women again providing much of the funding.[78] Escorted by Mary Louise Eldridge, the WNIA's superintendent of Navajo work, and accompanied by Hausteen, a Navajo man riding alongside on horseback, Quinton set out on September 7 for the first leg of the journey, camping at sunset after a drive of twenty-five miles. Eldridge set up camp, built a blazing fire, groomed and fed her two horses and her guests, then with her trusty pistol beneath her pillow to ward off bears and mountain lions, encouraged them to settle down for the night. Quinton did not expand on these conditions, but one must wonder what was going through her mind as a city woman enduring primitive conditions. At one point when one of the horses spooked, Quinton made a "precipitate exit, preferring to walk awhile." The next day, driving up and down steep trails, past Navajo hogans with cheery greetings extended, they arrived before sunset at the J. L. Crozer Cottage,[79] after traveling thirty-five miles to meet the new WNIA missionary, Henrietta G. Cole.[80]

Formerly in charge of the infirmary at Williams College in Massachusetts, Cole had begun dispensing medicine, dressing wounds, and making home visits to sick Navajo women immediately upon arriving. Describing the two-room mission cottage as comfortable but inadequate for the work that she was doing, Quinton recommended it be enlarged to include a hospital ward. Quinton also visited a group of three hundred Navajos, who influenced by Eldridge, had set up a system of irrigation and built log houses and fences.[81]

Lake Mohonk and WNIA Meeting, 1898

Quinton returned in time to attend the Mohonk Conference in mid-October and be reelected to serve on the business committee. During her report, although briefly mentioning the Mission Indians and her visit to the Hualapai, she devoted most of her time to her Navajo visit. She portrayed Eldridge as "devoted and brave," not hesitating to camp alone with only the protection of a blazing fire and her trusty revolver. Quinton was most impressed with her latest project, enabling the Navajos to irrigate their wheat crop.[82]

This conference, however, had a more urgent tone than usual, first, because of the recent removal of Dr. William H. Hailmann, Superintendent of Indian Schools. Despite his splendid record and appeals for his retention, Hailmann was a victim of transition to the incoming McKinley administration. Quinton, to no avail, had written letters and conferred with officials on his behalf. The second issue was a recent uprising among the Pillager band of Chippewa Indians in Minnesota, a topic addressed at length by both Rev. J. A. Gilfillan, who had worked among them for years, and the IRA's Washington, DC, agent, Samuel M. Brosius. The BIC later characterized this incident as caused by "abuses and frauds in the management, or mismanagement, of their timber lands, and in harsh, if not unjust, treatment in connection with the prosecutions for a whisky sales to Indians."[83] At the end of the conference, attendees resolved to establish a committee of seven to, among other duties, look into the causes of this unrest and present them before Congress, the president, and the press.[84] Fortunately the incoming administration under President McKinley rightly viewed this "miniature rebellion" as worthy of exercising executive clemency. According to the *Philadelphia Press* and the *New York Times* numerous witnesses testified that the trouble was "caused by the brutal rapacity" of officials who were allowed to resign.[85]

The conference over, Quinton gave four addresses in November before officiating at the WNIA annual meeting December 7–8 in Portland, Maine, where she was reelected unanimously. Days before on November 26 and 27, the city had suffered a severe storm: the steamer *Portland* on its way from Boston sank with a loss of all on board, and wrecked vessels and damaged shoreline properties stretched from Cape Cod to Portland. Hundreds had died. Despite this tragedy, the meetings were larger than usual and the many references made to the storm "attested to the sincere sympathy of the visiting delegates." The first page of the

WNIA annual report read: "though the shadow of a great disaster was over the whole city and the pall of a great sorrow rested upon many of its homes, the greetings given were warm, the welcome real."[86]

During her presidential address Quinton referred to the recent 1898 Spanish American War as a lesson for Indian reformers, encouraging Christian women to demand of their congressmen "a decimal portion of the gold so freely given" for the freedom of the Cuban people to achieve a similar freedom for the "reservation-imprisoned, hand-tied spirit-crushed red men and women" of America. She concluded it was the duty of American women to aid "home-born Indian countrymen" gain "the freedom, protection, and opportunity so freely and generously given by our nation to foreign missions."[87]

Usually in January Quinton would attend the BIC meeting with representatives of missionary societies. However, the federal government had recently phased out funding for religious contract schools, the primary purpose for the meeting and therefore these meetings were no longer held.[88] Instead during January 1899, she gave eight addresses before various Indian associations and churches.[89] During the early part of the year she limited her talks to New York State, enabling her to spend six months in Rochester to be near a sickly elderly aunt and to put several issues of *The Indian's Friend* together, having served since 1896 as its sole editor.[90]

From Rochester in late May, she informed the new Interior secretary, Ethan Allen Hitchcock, of the WNIA's history of work among the Mission Indians, work that had begun in June 1889 when the association secured five acres at Potrero, hiring the Weinlands, then turning the station over to the Moravian Church the following June. In September 1896 the association had established their station at Martínez, turning it over to the Moravians on November 19, 1897, having built a cottage and chapel at both sites. Now she was requesting a formal transfer of these properties to the governing board of the Moravian Church, securing to it "all rights and privileges possible under the regulations of the department." On June 17, Acting Commissioner A. C. Tonner informed Lucius A. Wright, Agent for the Mission Tule River Agency, of her request and that he was to "formally reserve these two tracts of land" to the Moravian Church and make a record of such transfer in agency files.[91]

The following month, Quinton complained to Rev. Paul de Schweinitz, secretary and treasurer of the Moravian Board, that Weinland's reports for *The Indian's Friend* no longer included "points to catch or waken interest." Although Weinland was no longer affiliated with the WNIA, he still provided articles for the association's monthly periodical. De Schweinitz immediately recommended to

Weinland that he find "incidents" to "fire the zeal" of Quinton's members, using his "fertile imagination" to dress up his work experiences "in an appropriate garb." Shortly thereafter, Weinland wrote an appealing history of Southern California Indians for an unidentified illustrated Los Angeles newspaper that *The Indian's Friend* reprinted, describing the article as so excellent that "we cannot forbear reproducing it" for the benefit of our readers.[92]

Lake Mohonk and WNIA Meeting, 1899

In late August, with her aunt fully recovered, Quinton headed to New England to give a series of addresses, informing Weinland on the 24th that she was "very near to broken down," concluding her "strain has been so long and of so many kinds."[93] Fortunately much of her responsibilities as chair of the national Missionary Department had been reduced as most WNIA missionary stations were now supported by state associations, and the Southern California missions had either been turned over to a California auxiliary or the Moravian Board. However, Quinton still remained the sole organizer and the face of the association. She gave six addresses in September and October before heading to the seventeenth Mohonk Conference. In his personal invitation to her, Smiley suggested she come early before the opening of the sessions on October 12. Enclosing a train timetable, he recommended buying a ticket as far as New Paltz, where his carriage would meet her.[94]

During her short address, Quinton listed the current stations, nine of which were under the care of larger auxiliaries. She announced that their Seminole work had encouraged the state of Florida to set aside a large parcel of land for Indian use, and that the NYCIA had built a hospital among the Navajos at Jewett, New Mexico.[95] And, in honor of her husband, Mary S. Crozer had funded the purchase of forty acres and the construction of the schoolhouse at their newest station, the Helen R. Foote School and Mission in Fall River Mills, Shasta County, California.[96] Had there been more time, Quinton would have gladly related "touching stories of workers just from their fields," she concluded.[97]

An article in *The Indian's Friend* described the conference as "a dwelling place of delight" with its bright skies, "unrivalled autumnal colors," and earnest speakers who gratefully recognized the great progress made under the present administration, welcoming Commissioner Jones with warm applause following his admirable address.[98] In an October 18 letter, Quinton characterized the meeting as "earnest & spicy," possibly a reference to the first order of business, the report of the seven-member committee appointed the previous year to look into the "defects and abuses of Indian administration." To reach their goal of removing the

Lake Mohonk Conference of Friends of the Indians attendees
on the east porch of Mohonk Mountain House, 1899.
Note the large number of women in attendance.
Mohonk Mountain House Archives.

Indian Office from politics, the committee had presented four recommendations, adopted unanimously: 1) Abolishing Indian agencies as rapidly as possible, placing the Indians under the care of the superintendent of the agency school; 2) ending the distribution of rations and annuities; 3) placing the position of Indian agent on the classified Civil Service list; and 4) increasing the power of the Indian commissioner "so that he may no longer be held responsible for that which he cannot control."[99] Unfortunately their efforts failed to bring about any of these recommendations.

Following Lake Mohonk, Quinton returned to her lecture circuit and putting the November issue together. She described her situation as living out of her bonnet "& on the spur ever since."[100] She opened the annual WNIA meeting on December 6, 1899, in the Association Hall in Trenton, New Jersey. The *Trenton Daily Gazette* described it as "one of the largest and most prominent gatherings of women that has ever come together in this state." Almost sixty delegates assembled, all from the northeast, and the number increased greatly during the open public meeting to listen to Commissioner Jones speak "with delightful frankness, clearness and effect of the present Indian situation." He praised the WNIA, describing its work "as reaching the home, the family life, and individual character, and thus doing what the government does not and cannot do."[101] Quinton had again succeeded in gaining the trust of an Indian commissioner.

In her rousing address, with numerous references to current international events, Quinton described "the faint dawn of an age of righteousness" as "overspreading the earth," bringing with it the disappearance of many wrongs. Freedom, law, and education were now decreed by the current Indian policy. Although the WNIA had worked directly or indirectly with forty-seven tribes and tribal remnants, there were still some 15,000 Indian youths without schools, 65,000 Indian men without "safe, sure homes, and means to live," and some 200,000 without the benefit of Christianity. Because partisan politics and inferior qualifications still controlled appointments, WNIA work was not yet done, she concluded.[102]

By now, Quinton had been engaged in Indian reform for almost a quarter of a century. Cofounder and sole organizer, she had spread the message of the WNIA from coast to coast and had overseen numerous mission stations as chair of the national committee. The country was changing and about to enter a new century, but the work that Quinton and the WNIA had set out to do—that of establishing pioneer school and missionary work among the sixty-eight tribes listed in Commissioner Price's 1882 report as having no resident missionary—was not yet completed.

During the last four years of the 1890s, Quinton had had numerous successes. She had continued to establish new branches while spreading the message of WNIA work during her numerous addresses. She had supervised missionary efforts on the Hoopa Reservation, been in on the ground floor of a new desert mission in California, and successfully sold the Greenville School, despite the devastating fire. She had once more survived a change in Indian Office personnel, willing incoming officials to grant her wishes. But complete civil service reform had not yet been achieved nor had any agencies been closed. She had, however, returned for another long visit to her beloved California. But her strength was beginning to wane, she was about to reach seventy. The next two years were sad ones; Mary Lucinda Bonney, longtime friend and cofounder would die in 1900 and the following year the Warner Ranch Indians would lose their case in the U.S. Supreme Court.

10

The Dawn of a New Century, 1900–1902

The first years of the new century saw changes and tragedies, including the death of Mary Lucinda Bonney and the forced removal of the villagers at Agua Caliente and the other four villages on the Warner Ranch. In 1902, Quinton returned to California, and eleven years after her first visit to Agua Caliente, commiserated with the Cupeños as they grieved the pending loss of their home. She also visited the two WNIA mission stations at Martínez and Yuma. Despite all the problems in California, including a very personal attack upon her character by Southern California reformer, Charles Fletcher Lummis, Quinton and her association never wavered in their support of the Mission Indians, aided by new members including Constance Goddard DuBois and Osia Jane Joslyn Hiles, as they stepped in to fill the void left by the death of Helen Hunt Jackson.

Addresses and Lake Mohonk, 1900

Quinton's official year began with her January 11, 1900, address before the Philadelphia Indian Association, the first of fifty-two in twelve different states. By summer, writing from St. Ignace, Michigan, she informed Smiley she had been "on the wing" for months, having come to Michigan, where the weather was never too warm, to get caught up with her correspondence and editorials for *The Indian's Friend*.[1] Five days later on July 19 she received a telegram that longtime friend and mentor, Mary Lucinda Bonney, was gravely ill, having fallen and broken a hip. Quinton rushed to Hamilton, New York, to sit by her bedside until she died on July 24.[2]

Quinton remained in Hamilton until mid-August when she returned to her scheduled addresses, giving five before heading off to the Lake Mohonk Conference, which opened on Wednesday, October 17. She had responded to Smiley's invitation with: "God bless it & you its hosts & head. And may the enlarged topic, the Depressed Races, have able, earnest & fruitful discussion," a reference to the recent addition to the conference of discussions on the inhabitants of Puerto Rico, Hawaii, and the Philippines.[3] Before leaving for New Paltz, Quinton had informed Commissioner Jones that she had learned that Edward Ament was resigning as superintendent of the Greenville School. His health had been "*greatly* impaired by the care and toil of his ten years of leadership," she explained, hoping he could be relieved immediately and allowed to return when his health was restored. Describing him as "a most conscientious, efficient, and faithful Supt. and teacher," Quinton concluded that Ament deserved "all the favor and kindness that can be shown him." Because the school was "especially dear," she implored Jones to make sure he appointed a man of "*real* Christian character." The commissioner agreed to reinstate Ament when his health improved.[4]

Quinton called the work of her fellow Mohonk reformers "practical, educative, [and] uplifting," the movement on behalf of the Indians as having "a divine purpose." She concluded that "all such races can be and are to be brought up to the stature of Christian manhood." She claimed that "any evils which belonged to the childhood of the Indian service have ceased to exist," due to God and the friends of the Indians, who agreed with one another about the ultimate goals of citizenship, compulsory education, and the end of the Indians as a dependent race. The WNIA had already engaged in work on behalf of forty-seven tribes or remnants, building them forty-one buildings, including missionary cottages, chapels, and schoolhouses, even constructing a hospital on the Navajo Reservation the prior year.[5]

The conference over, Quinton addressed a parlor meeting at Lake Mohonk and then gave eight addresses before presiding from December 9 through 12, 1900, over the twenty-first anniversary of the WNIA's founding in the large newly constructed First Baptist Church of Philadelphia.[6] She concluded it was only fitting to have the anniversary meeting in the very church where the "first step of the movement commemorated was taken" by one of their own.[7] The accomplishments of their two decades of missionary work were bittersweet in light of Bonney's memorial. Those unable to attend sent written remembrances to be read. At the end of the proceedings, Quinton described "an intimate friendship of more than twenty-five years" and "a long comradeship, as close as sacred, in Christian service."[8]

The Mission Indians

Her presidential obligations completed, Quinton finished the year giving three more addresses in December before resuming her schedule on January 24, 1901, speaking before the Baptist Home Mission Union. Almost seventy, she would deliver only half as many addresses in 1901 as the previous year, staying close to home; the reduced schedule allowed for more editorials and a concentration on the Mission Indians. In *The Indian's Friend*, she quoted from an article by Rt. Rev. Joseph H. Johnson, who five years earlier had become the Bishop of the Los Angeles Diocese of the Episcopal Church. Accompanied by Rev. H. B. Restarick of St. Paul's Episcopal Cathedral, the bishop had recently returned from a ten-day reservation tour of Mission villages presenting a portrayal of wretchedness and misery.[9] He had also recently endorsed Wright's reappointment as agent. A troubled Quinton headed for Washington the first week of February to confer with Commissioner Jones and California Senator Thomas R. Bard about Agent Wright. Unfortunately, she left no record of the discussion. She had already forwarded Weinland's January 17 letter criticizing Wright to Merrill E. Gates, BIC secretary. In returning the letter, Gates wrote her on February 11 that not only had Bishop Johnson endorsed Wright but Smiley had also sent a strong letter on his behalf.[10] Two days later she urged Weinland to go to Los Angeles and meet with the bishop; the WNIA would pay his fare. A week later she again encouraged him to go, especially now that the Rev. Johnson's "statements offset" his own.[11] Other than a veiled mention of his drinking, Quinton nowhere explained her strong disdain for Wright or named her sources—it could simply have been her great desire to have Weinland in the position.

In late February a slightly perturbed Bishop Johnson wrote Quinton that he was afraid she had the wrong impression about his stance on the Indian question. When he was interviewed by the *Los Angeles Times*, he had not been interested in agency matters and merely repeated that agents Wright and Estudillo had been "pleasantly spoken of by certain persons upon the reservation." Learning more, he was beginning to feel that Wright might not be right for the job. He had informed Washington officials, suggesting instead a San Diego individual, although in actuality much preferring an army officer. The interview with Weinland had gone well; the bishop found the cleric to be "a very excellent sort of man," who means well; however, there was an impression abroad that he was "not always as wise and judicious as he might be." Although providing no evidence, he assured Quinton that he really knew nothing of that and was trying to avoid controversy.[12]

On March 2, pleased that the meeting with the bishop had gone well, Quinton informed Weinland that she had "renewed hope" they would soon have good news. Two weeks later, a saddened Quinton wrote that politicians had "pelted" California Senator Thomas R. Bard with letters in favor of Wright; Bard had yielded, reappointing that "wicked agent;" she had no idea what to do next. She would, however, write Weinland "as *any* new light comes on the case." Months later she called Wright's reappointment "*One* of the darkest transactions we have had to complain of, *if* so, in all these late years." She was, however, pleased to learn that Rev. David J. Woosley had begun work among the Yuma Indians and hoped for a good result.[13]

At the end of March, Quinton offered to sell Commissioner Jones the WNIA's missionary cottage at Cahuilla for $200 to be used for schoolwork. Located adjacent to the school on the five acres the government had granted them on March 20, 1889, the cottage had cost $500 including later improvements. Learning from Weinland that it and its repairs had cost less, she lowered the price to $100.[14] While Quinton was transferring WNIA stations that served the Mission Indians, she was also spending more paper and ink on their plight, writing her own articles and printing those by Constance Goddard DuBois, who praised Quinton and her association for preparing the way for Indian self-support.[15]

President of the Waterbury, Connecticut, auxiliary, a WNIA affiliate, DuBois was a novelist and ethnographer who spent summers from 1897 to 1907 with her sister and husband in Chula Vista, in San Diego County buying native-made baskets, encouraging a native lace industry, and gathering information on Luiseño and Diegueño mythology, and religion. During the winter she wrote and lectured, bringing the Indians' precarious situation to a wider audience. She had toured the more remote Mission reservations in San Diego County, gathering information for a novel. Titled *A Soul in Bronze: A Novel of Southern California*, it was serially published in 1898 in *The Land of Sunshine: The Magazine of California and the West*, Southern California's most prominent magazine. In 1900 DuBois also wrote an exposé on the Indians' extreme destitution, which was republished by the IRA.[16] Quinton, reflecting her proprietary attitude toward the Mission Indians and not having met DuBois yet, described the author to Weinland as "high church" sentimental with "a *romantic* admiration for the Jesuit fathers, & likes [agents] *Estudillo, Wright* etc!!" Concluding that DuBois "*apparently* feels *she* is about to be best friend those Indians have!" Quinton inquired if Weinland had met her yet.[17] Following an exchange of letters between the two women, unfortunately lost, Quinton came to support DuBois and her efforts on behalf of the Mission Indians.

Adding to DuBois' articles, Quinton also printed a lengthy report by Charles L. Partridge that was far more positive than that of Bishop Johnson. Partridge, a resident of Redlands, accompanied by his sister, Henrietta, secretary of the RIA;

Mrs. Charles Meigs, an RIA member; and Reverend Weinland, had toured eight of the thirty-three Mission reservations for five days in mid-April. Of the two hundred families, numbering 1,000 Indians, Partridge found only three who he could call truly destitute. At month's end, he addressed an RIA meeting at the same time that Ella Morongo, Captain John's daughter, read extracts of letters written by local Indian children describing their home lives in a positive manner.[18]

The disparity between the reports by Bishop Johnson and Partridge, which some feared might hamper the reform movement, was exacerbated in May when Louise Hoppock, president of the Southern California Association, gave an informal talk before the NYCIA. Her report, like Partridge's, was more uplifting, explaining that many of the Indians were indignant over the negative representation of their situation.[19] Quinton, although displeased with dissention, defended Hoppock in a July editorial because her opinion was based on experience and observation. This deepening rift forced Quinton to write another editorial, explaining that although there was "deep poverty,—some of it culpable," with much suffering "from inescapable poverty" among some Mission Indians, there were also progressive Indians who were finding work and supporting their families. However, this disparity did not alter the government's obligation to provide land and water for all Southern California Indians who had been evicted from their lands. In the August issue, she also included letters from two Indian youths, presenting a positive view, reflecting plenty to eat and money for necessities, as well as a letter from Hoppock regretting that her statements had been misunderstood as she had never intended to hinder "any relief that might be gained for the needy."[20]

Quinton had been closely following the ins and outs of the Warner Ranch lawsuit. Although in January 1899 the New York City auxiliary had transferred their medical missionary work in Agua Caliente to the Moravian Church, Quinton and her membership remained interested in the Indians' well-being because former missionaries, Weinland and Woosley, remained at their posts, and Babbitt still taught at the government school. A backlog had meant that the case was not heard by the California Supreme Court until April 19, 1899. Several new justices had been added since the Soboba trial, resulting in a less sympathetic court. In a four to three split decision on October 4, 1899, the Court found against the Indians, and an application for a rehearing had been turned down. The growing notoriety of the Warner case, however, had prompted the U.S. Attorney General's Office to appeal to the U. S. Supreme Court.[21] In March 1901, Shirley C. Ward pleaded the case before the Court. The previous month Brosius had informed Weinland that

Ward had been in Washington for weeks preparing. His confidence had been so strong, Brosius wrote, that "I have sort of imbibed his belief in ultimate success."[22]

On May 13, 1901, the U.S. Supreme Court upheld the previous decision of the California Supreme Court. Despite the clarity of their case and their diligent research, Ward and Lewis had only delayed the inevitable. After nearly thirty years of threats, intimidation, and lawsuits the Warner Ranch Indians had lost their homes. In a June 3 letter, Quinton expressed dismay: "It is awful that Agua Cal. is wrenched from those Indians!" The following month she wrote Weinland that she was "heart sick over the fate of the poor Indians." The situation was an outrage, everyone "helpless together in the case." She had written the Indian Office to retain Mrs. Babbitt, hoping she would remain with them wherever they ended up. Quinton also was sad to report that the government had declined to buy the association's cottage at Cahuilla. "So we shall get nothing from that source, to my great regret."[23] On a positive note, Commissioner Jones, in an undated letter, reprinted in *The Indian's Friend*, assured Quinton that his office was "carefully considering the question as to what should be done for the relief of the Mission Indians." Because they would in all likelihood be forced to give up their lands, the government would provide other lands and give support during removal. In the meantime, the attorney general had made arrangements for them to remain until the next session of Congress, to harvest crops and get ready for removal.[24]

The WNIA membership did not learn of the court decision until Quinton's July editorial. Quoting from a "private letter from a devoted friend of theirs," Quinton recited "the sorrows and moans of the people thus rendered homeless and, for the present at least, helpless." She concluded that the Indians at least had Babbitt (the likely author of the private letter) to lean on. Her presence would "soothe, reconcile and help them to adjust themselves to whatever is inevitable."[25] Quinton had also recently learned that DuBois was "greatly disturbed" by Hoppock's earlier comments, believing that "such testimony had ruined the plans which she [DuBois] and her friends had at the time." In a letter marked "All confidential, very," Quinton explained that because DuBois was president of an auxiliary, her dislike of Hoppock, whom Quinton described as more "sensible & practical," was quite complicated. Although beginning to see DuBois as an "able, & a *literary* worker," Quinton was still disturbed by the lack of harmony within the WNIA. Quinton, most of all, wanted for the friends of the Mission Indians to simply "*agree* upon *some* plan, and then push it." She concluded, "It needs *all* the forces for success," in a letter postmarked St. Ignace, Michigan, where she remained through August because it was cool there.[26]

On August 11, Quinton informed Weinland that she now believed that Dubois had "a *good heart, & means* to be right in all," and "*cares* for *our* cooperation, & I want her to have it." A week later she wrote she had learned that DuBois intended to purchase the San Ysabel Ranch for $30,000 if the government did not buy a home for the Mission Indians. She would turn the hotel on San Ysabel into a school for Mission Indian teachers and open a mission at the village of Mesa Grande. Quinton saw no harm in the women undertaking such a plan as the Moravian Board could not cover the entire field. "All is friendly with Miss Du B. *now*," wrote Quinton, publishing another one of DuBois' articles, this one recommending the purchase of a large tract of land upon which the Warner Ranch Indians and others from "more destitute reservations" could be settled.[27] No reference, however, was made to the San Ysabel Ranch purchase. Also, DuBois, who had originally supported allotment, was now suggesting that the process be postponed for the Mission-Tule agency until Congress found a new home for the Warner Ranch Indians.[28]

While focusing much of her attention on the Warner Ranch case, Quinton was forced to turn down a potential new station for California due to a lack of funds. Earlier in May, Hoppock had enclosed a letter from Weinland and Henrietta Partridge asking Quinton's opinion about taking on additional work at the Mission village of Rincon. On June 3 Quinton informed Weinland that it was impossible. The WNIA had worked longer in California than in any other field, and it was now the responsibility of the Moravian Board, which should also provide his salary the next year. The Southern California auxiliary can do no more, she declared. "This is my *earnest request* at present," she wrote, "and I will confide to you that unless relief comes for my over-burdened hands I must lay down *all* my work." The following month, she expressed great sadness in being unable to support his work. "There ought to be funds enough to do all that is in your hands, and to send a worker also to Rincon."[29] She wrote Weinland again on August 20, delighted to learn that he had found a way to carry out his work in Rincon. Hoppock and her association, in an undisclosed plan, had managed an arrangement to assist Reverend Woosley in a move from Walters on the Colorado desert to Rincon, where according to the records of the RIA, he would "be able to reach several reservations now untouched by evangelical work."[30]

The Seminoles and Lake Mohonk

During the late summer and fall of 1901 Quinton turned her attention again to the Florida Seminoles, where the WNIA in 1891 had opened a station. On August 9, in response to her June 12, 1901, letter, Acting Commissioner A. C. Tonner informed her that the federal government had bought 23,061 acres for the Seminoles at a cost of $13,353.52. He also explained that previously, on May 29, 1899, the Florida state legislature had reserved thirty-six townships, or about eight hundred thousand acres, for Indian use.[31] In an editorial, Quinton clarified that there was, however, a catch: the federal government had to buy out the rights of the railroads, corporations, and large landowners and patent the land to the State of Florida so that the entire tract could be permanently secured for Indian homes. Since most of the land was already deeded to others, this present action was essentially useless, Quinton concluded.[32]

Months later J. E. Brecht, former WNIA missionary, informed Quinton that he had actually purchased 12,000 out of the 23,061 acres, with Inspector Andrew J. Duncan buying the rest. This information prompted Quinton in her October editorial to proudly note that "thus more than half of the land now actually secured to these Indians was gained as the direct result of the work of our Association."[33] However, the railroads, large landed interests, and other corporations were fighting against this dedication of land to Indian use, exerting influence in the Senate to prevent the passage of any legislation setting aside land. Therefore, Brecht wrote on September 4, the "land matters for Seminoles, is rather, precarious"; they "are crowded on every side-any amount of whisky is being hauled to them in the last four years," he concluded.[34]

On September 12, Quinton thanked Smiley for inviting her to attend his annual "feast of Tabernacles" on his mountain top, noting she would try and get there early to speak to him about the Mission Indians. Since April she had been hard at work, with seven addresses that month and her usual heavy editorial work and correspondence. In late May she had again spent some time at the Clifton Springs Sanitarium. Finally on October 16, she and a hundred other conferees assembled at Lake Mohonk to be welcomed by Smiley who declared that it was best that the Indian question no longer monopolize the entire conference. During her address Quinton again expressed a desire to see the reservation system ended with unnecessary ones immediately abolished, land divided by allotment, genuine citizenship to all, and Indian funds paid out to individuals. She assured conferees that Christian women were "interested in the evangelization of all these peoples named in this Conference," to be attained by a combined effort of all Christian workers. On Friday morning Constance Goddard DuBois described her several-hundred-mile wagon camping trip to visit the remote Mission Indian villages, explaining she had a business scheme to help them and was ready to give Congress the proposition but included no details. Quinton summarized all for *The Indian's Friend.*[35]

In November, Quinton addressed the nineteenth annual meeting of the NYCIA,[36] and officiated at the annual WNIA meeting in December. She had hoped to make this her last year as president, informing the nominating committee she was "extremely desirous of retiring." However, the advisory board had dissuaded her, explaining "her judgment and experience" were still needed. During her presidential address, she reminded members that twenty-three years ago when the association was started, Indians "were starving prisoners in a wilderness picketed with border dangers of many kinds," with no assured homes, often "driven at the bayonet's point to unfriendly rigorous regions, a spectacle of torturing conditions or of cruel neglect." Now more than twenty-seven thousand out of the thirty-four thousand Indian youths were attending the more than 251 government Indian schools. Three and a half million acres now supported fifty-five thousand Indian allottees, and seventy thousand Indians were citizens. She asked if it was "pure sentimentalism" or an "optimistic dream" that had pushed the WNIA into the forefront of demanding severalty, law, and citizenship for the Indians in their third petition. No, this work had been achieved with Divine help, she assured them.[37]

On December 26, 1901, Quinton invited first lady Mrs. Theodore Roosevelt to become an honorary vice president of the association, a long-standing tradition. Four days later Mrs. Roosevelt accepted.[38]

A New Year and Off to California

Changes were afoot for the upcoming year. For an unexplained reason, the WNIA formally changed its name to the National Indian Association (NIA), prompting Quinton to explain to Weinland that all branches and auxiliaries could now let men join "if they wish" but there was no requirement to do so. She hoped this change would bring in much needed help. She had also been reelected unanimously, explaining that "no suitable woman who could command her time could be found."[39] Also beginning with the February 1902 issue, Marie E. Ives of New Haven, chairman of the Young People's Department, would take over as editor of *The Indians' Friend*, relieving Quinton of this task, although she continued to write her many articles and remained, still, the association's primary speaker.[40]

Quinton gave three addresses in January and then on February 15 attended a reception in her honor hosted by the Washington auxiliary, described in the *Washington Post* as a "delightful affair." She was called upon to give "a word of cheer, encouragement and advice." From there, she spent ten days in a Daughters of the American Revolution Congress in Washington, DC, representing the Regent of Independence Hall chapter of Philadelphia, and afterwards, tended to official business with the Indian office, explaining to Weinland that she planned on speaking to the commissioner on several matters.[41]

Then, with luggage packed and proofs off to the printers, she and an unknown companion started "through the cold and slush for the land of sunshine and flowers." One night in Charlotte, another in Atlanta, a week in Alabama and they arrived "in the balmy summer of heart and hair in the midst of peach blooms in New Orleans, queen of the Gulf." Following a reception by the New Orleans Indian Association and an address before the Indian meeting with more than 250 "earnest" women in attendance, she headed west, first to the Yuma Indians, whose work the Louisiana branches had agreed to support and where Weinland had been preaching monthly for more than a year.[42] This new station at Fort Yuma Indian Boarding School—in Imperial County, California, across the Colorado River from Yuma, Arizona—was supported by various auxiliaries and supervised by the WNIA Missionary Committee that Quinton still chaired.

It had taken Quinton considerable time to pull together enough resources to establish this work, needing to first wait until several existing mission stations had been transferred. After conferring with members of the Bethlehem, Pennsylvania, auxiliary and two members of the Moravian Board, in late January she had been told that they could do little more than support a once a month preaching session for Weinland at the school because it had a Catholic superintendent. Quinton promised her support through funding from the Redlands Indian Association and the Bethlehem and Allentown auxiliaries. Eventually she hoped to fund a permanent worker and to build a cottage, freeing Weinland for his other work. However, he had to promise to send in a report after every visit to enable her to "keep up the interest in any *other* way than by this *living link*."[43] Although displeased with sharing a mission with the Catholics, on February 3, Quinton informed Weinland she would still visit the new Yuma station on her way to California. A week later, she asked him to alert School Superintendent John S. Spear of her upcoming visit.[44]

Quinton traveled by train across Texas and New Mexico before checking into the comfortable Southern Pacific Hotel at Yuma, Arizona, posting a batch of letters and telephoning her safe arrival. School Superintendent Spear drove her across the Colorado River to the California side to visit the Indian boarding school where she met and dined with the teachers. Weinland arrived the following day and toured her around. Quinton was appalled at the Indian housing she saw, especially the fine dust everywhere that made cleanliness impossible.[45] Weinland, true to his word, returned to the Yumas on April 30, remaining until May 3, visiting Indian homes and giving two illustrated sermons, dutifully sending Quinton his report afterward.[46]

Once in California, Quinton informed Commissioner Jones of her March visit to Fort Yuma. Thanking him for his letters of introduction, she described her stay as "full of interest." The school was "going on well under" Spear, who she described as genuinely earnest in helping the Indians. Commissioner Jones could read an account of her visit in the May issue of *The Indian's Friend*. She also brought him up to date on the Greenville School, expressing severe disappointment about the new management, describing the lowering of the moral tone since the Aments had left. "Our hearts ache over that our dear school," she concluded.[47]

Accompanied by Weinland and an unidentified companion, Quinton next set out for the Desert Mission to meet Rev. Robert Staveley, the new missionary at Martínez, and to confer with the Indians in council on March 19. They complained bitterly about local whites who were encroaching upon their lands, stealing their horses and cattle. One Indian had already lost six horses, and another, eight burros. Quinton later wrote that she had spent five hours in the council "and oh, the pathos of it all," agreeing at the end to take to Commissioner Jones their requests for eight more wells, a land survey, and wire fencing to protect their livestock.[48]

During the second half of April Quinton spoke before an art history club and an Indian association in San Jose, followed by two addresses in San Francisco before joining the Weinlands on May 5 at Hemet to drive the sixty miles to the Cupeño Indian village of Agua Caliente, at the request of Josephine Babbitt.[49] They arrived on May 6 to a village that had changed markedly since Quinton's first visit in 1891. "Now in the many homes new lights gleamed from the windows on the hillside, in the vale, and the new schoolhouse with its comfortable living rooms alight gave us Mrs. Babbitt's warm welcome," she wrote. However, a profound sadness permeated the village. All convened in a council at the schoolhouse where the Indians declared emphatically that this was their longtime home, informing Quinton they wanted to send a delegation to President Roosevelt to tell him what was in their hearts and to convince Congress to buy it for them. Initially she advised against this because the highest court in the land had made its decision. But after listening and seeing their aggrieved faces, she believed that even if they failed, they would have the satisfaction of knowing they had done everything to save their village. During a second meeting, the Cupeños chose two delegates. Quinton and her group then headed for Banning, spending Sunday attending Weinland's service at the former WNIA chapel in Potrero.[50]

Moravian Missionary chapel in Potrero originally constructed by the WNIA on the Morongo Indian Reservation for Rev. Weinland.
William H. Weinland Collection, The Huntington Library, San Marino, California (photCL 39 [095]).

Meanwhile, from Philadelphia *The Indian's Friend* continued to cover the situation at Warner Ranch, recommending the federal government purchase the ranch.[51] Indian Office officials had tried, but the price was prohibitive, therefore, in late November 1901, the Office had sent an Interior department inspector to confer with Agent Wright. They spent a week in December examining potential sites, settling on the Monserrate Ranch between Bonsall and Fallbrook, where insufficient water resulted in the idea being dropped. Even the Cupeños had complained to Quinton about this choice in their council with her. Furthermore, her attendance at this council drew her into a heated controversy with Charles Fletcher Lummis, founder in 1901 of the Sequoya League, a West Coast-based reform organization, and editor of *Land of Sunshine* magazine (later renamed *Out West*).[52]

The Warner Ranch case would be the League's first big cause. Using his friendship with President Roosevelt, Lummis secured the creation on May 28, 1902, of the Warner Ranch Indian Commission, to serve without compensation to select a new home for all of the Warner Ranch Indians. Lummis, Partridge, and Russell C. Allen, manager of the Sweetwater Fruit Company in northern San Diego County, and a classmate of Roosevelt's, were appointed. During a month-long investigation, they inspected 107 ranches, finally settling on the Pala Valley, in San Diego County, in October 1902.[53]

Quinton Provokes Lummis

Lummis viewed Quinton's visit to Agua Caliente as interfering with his authority as a member of the Warner Ranch Indian Commission. He accused her in a May 23 letter of telling untruths that would only cause "greater distress and suffering," begging her to "be judicious and friendly to the Indians" and not give the Indians ideas "which in the present state of the case may be disastrous to them." If he thought a delegation to Washington would aid their cause, he would have accompanied them. Anyone with common sense knew that the president and Congress could not reverse a Supreme Court decision.[54] That same day Lummis had also written Babbitt inquiring about Quinton, this woman who was "stirring up unrest and trouble down there and turning the Indians against the only friends who are able to do anything for them?"[55] He had asked the same question of Agent Wright, who mistakenly identified Quinton as head of the Indian Rights Association and described Babbitt as her "right bower in this county," also as belonging to the same association.[56]

On the same day that Lummis had written Quinton, the *Los Angeles Times* published an article describing her as "a wild-brained person" who had started a crusade to upset the almost perfected plans of the Indian commission. Instead of believing in these commissioners, who served without compensation, the Indians had turned to this "gobernadora" (she-governor), "this delirious woman in their last despair because she tells them just what they want to believe." Although Lummis had tried to gain the Indians' trust, it was easier for them "to believe this woman, who claims to be greater than the Supreme Court, and that the men who are to move them are wicked." The *Times* pulled out all the stops, describing her as a "female false pretender." Immediately realizing the article was "misleading in every way, and false from 'start to finish,'" Babbitt wrote Lummis on May 25.[57]

Meanwhile, Quinton protested to Weinland, taking exception to certain criticisms, especially being called "wild brained." She was "a patriot & Christian," she wrote, "a descendant of Gov. Bradford of the Mayflower, the Adamses of Mass., etc. & several cyclopedias [had] sketches" of her. She hardly was an "obscure" bystander, having been general secretary and president of the NIA for twenty-three years, visiting every state and territory except two on the association's behalf. She described herself as "modest & *not* ostentatious," as "a peacemaker by nature" and

Author, editor, and reformer Charles Fletcher Lummis at his desk. He and Quinton clashed over what he saw as her interference at Agua Caliente (Warner Hot Springs).
Braun Research Library Collection, Autry Museum, Los Angles, California (P.32603).

not one to "take on airs" or arrogate powers. Of more importance, by the time she had arrived at Agua Caliente, the Indians had already made up their minds to send a delegation.[58] Weinland immediately came to her defense, explaining he had been present during the visit in question, and the information reported was incorrect. In response, *The Times* criticized him as not "conversant with the facts of the case."[59]

Even Commissioner Jones had read an extract of the article, writing Quinton on June 5 that although he was displeased with its content, he assured her that he did not credit her, as the news items claimed, of "endeavoring to lead the Indians to hold back from cooperation with the Commission which has been appointed to select another home for them." Although he did understand "their pitiful longing to remain in their old home," it was unwise to permit their coming to Washington with Babbitt to plead their cause. It was quite hopeless. He explained that the Indian Office had secured the appointment of the committee from Congress "with great difficulty," and that it was the Indians' only hope for the future.[60] Then Rust jumped into the fray, sending in his opinion. Noting his "old arch enemy" [Quinton] had "bobbed up again as a mischief-maker among the Warner ranch Indians," he complained that she had dismissed his offer of help and taken over his idea "of a long-promised hospital" at Agua Caliente, sending her own physician and sponsoring a government field matron who were poorly equipped and unqualified. He also bitterly complained about her "pitiful failure" at Cahuilla.[61]

Quinton, undeterred by the Lummis attack or that of the *Times*, read a paper on Indian education before the all-day semi-annual meeting of the Pasadena Women's Missionary Union on May 27. According to a *Times* article, following her reading, she had explained and defended her actions at Agua Caliente. The Cupeños were "old friends of hers," she had said, and although informing them that "such a journey would be time wasted and money thrown away," if they thought it their duty, "then they might go." Although she had "not put the idea in their heads," she had "given them some advice as to what men might make the trip, as best representing the Indians." Then later in a letter in *The Indian's Friend*, she described this meeting as memorable because of the presence of several foreign missionaries and a fine library.[62]

Returning to her California home on June 3 she found Lummis's May 23 letter, which Babbitt had forwarded. Quinton composed a response, enclosing it with a seven-page handwritten explanation and informing Lummis she was committing it to his care to be sent to the *Times*, hoping it would be printed. She explained she had been working without pause for twenty-three years on behalf of the Indians, and "no soul can rejoice more over any good you can achieve for the Cupenos," hoping that "the way may open for a conference" with him on the subject. She concluded that Rust's article was "as false as brutal & needs no reply, as it condemned itself."[63]

During the end of July, in Los Angeles for a week, she did meet up with Lummis, convincing him that she was devoted to the Indian cause. He was forced to admit in the *Times* that her motives "which appeared so insurrectionary at the time, were misunderstood," concluding that he would be "sorry to have the head of a national organization, as she is, discredited without cause."[64]

During August, Quinton continued her addresses, traveling back and forth to San Francisco several times, speaking before the Calvary Presbyterian Church on August 31 to a "large and appreciative congregation" and the following day held a conference in the parlors of the Occidental Hotel. On September 3 she gave an address before the Century Club of California, a private women's club founded in 1888.[65] Several days later she was at Rancho Chico visiting Annie Bidwell. A widow since 1900, Bidwell was solely responsible for the Mechoopda Indians who lived on the estate. Quinton had written sometime in late August about a possible visit, receiving a gracious letter from Bidwell on July 31. "I am very anxious for the pleasure of communion with you, my dear friend," she wrote. "You can inspire our dusky friends and comfort them. So come to us, I beg."[66] Leaving Bidwell on September 7, Quinton passed through Redding, enduring stifling heat that reached 104 degrees in the shade, a railway climb around the base of Mt. Shasta, and finally a stage ride to reach the association's Helen R. Foote Memorial School.[67]

After several days, and an address before the Presbyterian Church of Fall River, she took the train to Portland on September 18, giving addresses both there and in Tacoma, Washington. On September 26 from Portland, she wrote Smiley, thanking him for her invitation to Mohonk. The same day she boarded the sleeper to Boise and Cheyenne where she had speaking obligations; a landslide and a wrecked freight train prevented her from meeting either. On October 6 she finally reached Chicago, finding fifty letters waiting to be answered.[68] A week later she again wrote Smiley requesting a warm room above the ground floor because as her wheels of "pilgrimage moved on to Dakota" she had picked up a hoarse cold which was proving to be an "obstreperous member to manage."[69]

Lake Mohonk, and the Annual Meeting

On October 22, Quinton joined other invited guests at the twentieth Mohonk Conference as Smiley greeted them, expressing pleasure in seeing "a company of men and women together who are trying to lift up the dependent races." During her appointed time, Quinton described her visit to the Yumas, suggesting that since they dealt with continual dust during the summer and mud in the spring, it would be best to move them from their deep basin to higher ground. At Martínez she had found real progress, although they still lacked legal protection and needed "help in civilizing work." Because of their small number, she suggested they should be moved from the desert to join the rest of their tribe near Banning, even though she was aware of their strong love for their desert home. She had found them faithful to their church duties and appreciative of what was being done for them.

Her visit to Warner Ranch and the Cupeño village of Agua Caliente had been difficult. "I have seen many pathetic Indian situations but that one was harder to endure than most of them." She firmly believed that the Indian question would end only when the reservation system was overturned, Indians made citizens, and their children educated in public school. The editor of *The Indian's Friend* praised her for packing into her ten-minute address "a vast amount of information, and doing it vividly and gracefully."[70]

December 9–12, 1902, Quinton presided over the twenty-third annual meeting of the NIA. It had generated sufficient press coverage that Quinton's youngest brother, Rev. George Wakefield Stone, who lived in Santa Cruz, California, wrote that he was glad it had gone off so well. "It must have been quite an affair to have attracted so much attention from the press," he concluded. Stone, the field secretary of the American Unitarian Association for the Pacific States Department, had just resigned from his ministry and was looking for a new church in Sacramento and Stockton, working both places at the same time. He cautioned his sister not to taken on any new work. "It is not right for you to have so much *detail*," he wrote.[71]

The first two years of the new century had seen the death of Bonney, the final decision in the Warner Ranch Indian case, and other substantive changes. Men could now join the WNIA, now the National Indian Association, and its Philadelphia headquarters would soon be moved to New York City. Through all these changes, Quinton had continued to organize, deliver addresses, spread the NIA's message, and visit association stations. Some burdens had been lifted from her shoulders with the appointment of a permanent editor for *The Indian's Friend*. In the next couple of years she would be relieved of the presidency but remain the powerful chairman of the missionary department for a few years more, receiving all the missionaries' letters, summarizing them for her articles, and visiting stations, namely Martínez in the California desert and Weinlands' work among the Yumans. As honorary president she would remain the visible face of the association.

11

Quinton's Final Years

In 1903 Quinton tried to retire but the association brought her back again when her successor stepped down. But at the end of the 1905 annual meeting, she formally gave up the presidency, becoming Honorary President. Still the public face of the NIA, she continued her addresses and remained the chair of the Missionary Committee, corresponding with the few remaining association-sponsored missionaries, summarizing their letters for her articles. Then in 1909 John W. Clark assumed her role as chair of the committee, further reducing Quinton's direct involvement with the NIA, although some missionaries continued to correspond with her.

A Focus on Former Mission Stations

Heeding advice from her brother George, Quinton gave fewer addresses in 1903, the first on January 19 before the NYCIA, followed by a parlor meeting in Philadelphia, and one before the Morristown, New Jersey Indian Association. In February she gave one address, in Wilmington, Delaware. Late in the month George wrote that he had moved to Redlands to revive an old church.[1] On March 3, she gave three addresses, one on the twenty-first anniversary of the Washington, DC, auxiliary, which she had founded.[2] Mid-month, Ella Boardman, her pastor's wife, wrote thanking her for sending the NIA leaflets she had requested and complimenting her great Indian work. Boardman had just come from a visit with Annie Bidwell, who had said "such loving, appreciative things" about Quinton's work that Boardman felt obligated to pass the information on. "Work in itself is such a sustaining power," Boardman noted. "An active mind shut into a helpless or inadequate body seems the hardest trial. One can bear any amount of pain, if one can keep on at work."[3]

At the end of April Quinton learned from Rt. Rev. William Crane Gray, Missionary Bishop of the Protestant Episcopal Church of Southern Florida, of his recent tour and impromptu religious service there. The bishop, who had taken over the WNIA's Seminole work in December 1893, explained that although Florida had set aside land for the Seminoles "so far as the State has ownership and authority," every sixteenth section was still school land and railroads had a claim on a part of it. In addition, "wealthy Roaches from Chicago had bought more than 2000 acres" and were having the land cleared for orange groves; others were buying thousands of acres valued for cypress timber. If Indian-held land was not protected soon, he feared they would be pushed into the gulf. The only solution was a congressional appropriation to Florida for an outright purchase; thus, he was turning to Quinton and the NIA for support. Quinton, quoting from his letter, asked members to urge Congress to purchase the lands from these corporate interests.[4] Continually receiving requests for support, even from former stations long turned over to other societies, Quinton did her best to support them.

Quinton, however, was very much still focused on the association's work in California, informing Commissioner Jones on April 28, 1903, that the wells on the Torres reservation were a success. It was his intention "to drill as many wells as possible, or at least a sufficient number to furnish all the water necessary for these poor people." She had also learned from Weinland that on his way to the Yumas, he had stopped at both Martínez and Torres. The wells at section eight near Martínez were not as successful as hoped, he noted. However, drilling was proceeding on section sixteen, which had recently been added to the reservation by Senate Bill 5212. The eight wells at neighboring Torres were providing good water, and he described fields of barley, corn, beans, peas, melons, pumpkins, sweet potatoes, and tomatoes as well as pasture for their horses. "You have so long worked to get water for them," he informed her, "that the sight of water flowing freely on their land would truly be a good eye-salve."[5]

For the rest of the summer, Quinton remained busy writing and addressing meetings.[6] In a June article she informed readers that former missionary, Mrs. Henrietta G. Cole, her health restored, was now working among the Navajo at Chinle, Arizona—the NIA's fourth mission among the Navajos.[7] In July Quinton gave four addresses in upstate New York including organizing an Indian association in Cortland and later one in Homer in August. Then she made a quick trip to Maine to address a WCTU meeting, trying to arrange a visit with her brother Seymour.[8]

In her July article she included an appeal from Rev. W. H. Gill, a missionary of the American Sunday School Union, on behalf of the 1,000 Mohave-Apaches (Yavapai) living on the Old Fort McDowell military reservation on the Verde

River in Arizona. Decades earlier these Indians had left their waterless Gila River reservation to move to the Verde River, the home of their ancestors, with a promise from General George Crook that if they served as army scouts during the Apache wars they would be allowed to remain. Gill had written Quinton in March 1903, explaining that last spring these Indians, who had for three years been living "in miserable brush tepees on the barren hills," petitioned President Roosevelt requesting the northern part of the reservation be allotted. Roosevelt had issued an executive order, and on January 14, 1904, the Philadelphia auxiliary would undertake their work with Mary K. Gill as field matron. In subsequent articles, Quinton reported that Gill had begun a dairy industry and was encouraging the raising of poultry and basketmaking among the women. By November Gill had added several more Jersey heifers and was planning on selling butter to purchase additional cows. She was also raising bees.[9]

While Quinton and the NIA were focusing on stations in other parts of the country, the drama at their former station at Warner Ranch ended. In the August 1903 issue, Quinton wrote: the anxiety "felt and expressed in many quarters" was largely dispelled as the Cupeños and others were removed to Pala under the "admirable management" of Special Inspector James E. Jenkins with the "valuable and efficient moral support" of Josephine Babbitt, and others. She was left to wonder if the government would keep its promises to build houses and provide water "to render the shoe-deep sand about them fertile." The December issue reported that fences had been built, ditches dug, and some plowing had been completed.[10]

About the same time, Quinton learned that a Catholic priest had visited Martínez, asking to build a church there. The Indians had rejected his proposal because they had the Moravian Church. Undeterred, the priest made the same request at Torres and was rejected but then offered one Indian a new home and a second, some money. Weinland explained that a petition to Commissioner Jones was prepared with "*the majority of the Indians of the entire desert*" signing. On August 21 Weinland received a letter from the village captain at Martínez that land was being cleared at the eastern end of the village, and adobe bricks were being made for a new church. During Weinland's most recent visit, the Indians had informed him that if a church were built, it should be at Alimo Bonita where most of the Catholic Indians lived. The village captain asked him to seek assistance from Commissioner Jones, hence, Weinland had written Quinton for support.[11]

A week later, Weinland informed Quinton that while the Woosleys were visiting in the East, he had been put in charge at Martínez and Potrero, and some older

Indians had assured him that if a Catholic church were built, they would remain faithful to the old Moravian church. The village captain, backed by Agent Wright, had actually ordered the work stopped, and then Wright had asked the Indian Office what action he should take. Samuel M. Brosius, the IRA Washington agent, immediately filed a petition protesting the location of the proposed Catholic Church, leaving Weinland to assume it would be located elsewhere. The Indians had also expressed thanks to Quinton for water. During his last visit Wright had told them that he, not Quinton and Weinland, was responsible for the wells; but, the Indians, Weinland noted, knew better. In conclusion, he and his wife expressed sadness for Quinton's retirement, describing her as "the life of the association."[12]

With the coming of fall, Quinton's thoughts turned to the October Lake Mohonk conference. Her address was brief, noting among other things that the NIA "had the job of giving Christian teaching to fifty tribes and separate parts of tribes, and there have been some wonderful stories in connection with that work." Having remained close to home during the year, she had no personal experiences to relate, noting only the work of an Alaskan missionary associated with the building of over a dozen cottages through the Home Building and Loan Department. Now they live in comfort whereas before they had one room, an earthen floor, no furniture and thirty or forty people of both sexes who "lived without sanitation or morals!" To Quinton, the "crowning joy" of all of her association's work was that of their mission stations, noting in conclusion that there were still some thirty tribes "who need the blessed evangel of God's love."[13]

Major Changes Ahead

At the conclusion of the December 1903 NIA annual meeting, Quinton stepped down after seventeen years as president. Soon, the association headquarters would be moved to New York City, but with no reason for this given in NIA literature.[14] Mrs. Thomas Kimber, chair of the nominating committee, reluctantly accepted Quinton's resignation. In explaining that members had come to depend on her "superior knowledge and executive ability," she described Quinton's "withdrawal from the office" as giving them the feeling they had been orphaned "at a loss what step to take next."[15] The incoming president was Helen Edith Ainsworth Wakeman, who for fifteen years had been engaged in Christian work on New York's East Side.[16] The membership was assured that the ship was safe. Quinton would remain on as vice president, a reserve pilot steering the association "from rocks and shoals." Among those who praised Quinton's long presidency was Estelle Reel, Superintendent of Indian Schools, who described her as a good general who had led them to many victories. Mary Dewey, longtime secretary of the MIA, wrote that Wakeman would be shaking in her shoes "if she did not know that she could rely on [Quinton's] large knowledge & sincere good will."[17]

Quinton remained the face of the NIA, its only organizer, president of the NIA corporation, a director, and chair of the national missionary department, still receiving letters from current and former missionaries, which provided a constant source of material for her monthly articles.[18] Although no longer president, she still made forty addresses in 1904. For the first three months she traveled only as far as New York City. The last three weeks in April she visited government officials in Washington, DC, concluding with an address before the Washington auxiliary on April 30 and at the Memorial Chapel the following day. The remainder of May she gave six addresses and only one in June before informing Weinland on July 15 that she was heading for Homer for five weeks.[19] During September she gave five addresses before setting out for the Mohonk Conference in mid-October. One of the more critical subjects discussed by the 150 attendees that year was a plea for the landless Indians of Northern California, with an address on the subject by Brosius, expanded on by Quinton during her short address. She praised the work of the Northern California Indian Association (NCIA), a San Jose affiliate actively working on the Indians' behalf, especially spearheading the movement to get congressional monies to buy land for homeless California tribes.[20]

Quinton spent November in New England addressing various auxiliaries before presiding over the December 8, 1904, NIA annual meeting in Helen Wakeman's absence. Wakeman had declined to continue as president in 1905, so the nominating committee had timidly approached Quinton about returning to the role. Initially declining, she later agreed to serve another year.[21] The following day she wrote Commissioner Jones, expressing her regret about his decision to retire, informing him that the day before, the NIA had addressed their vote of thanks "for the many aids given to [their] work" during his administration. She also thanked him for the "able, efficient, conscientious and constant service [he] had rendered all these years for the civilization, elevation and prosperity of the Indians of our country." Having learned that Francis Ellington Leupp, an IRA member, was his replacement, she was reassured that the work Jones had started would continue.[22] Jones responded on December 31, thanking her and her association for their "kind consideration of" his efforts.[23] The third week of December Quinton had sent the association's resolutions and memorials to President Roosevelt, praying for his support for "the land-destitute Northern California Indians, the water-robbed Pimas, the schoolless youth of Indian Territory, and the continuance of the educational work of the Indians of Indian Territory."[24]

Quinton, now seventy-two, and back at the helm of the NIA, presented thirty-eight addresses but stuck close to home, and spent parts of July and August in Homer. In mid-year she took over the secretary's column, "From the National Headquarters," but continued to write her monthly missionary reports. In a new column on legislation, she highlighted specific topics including the recent use of Indian trust funds to support sectarian contract schools, written because an amendment prohibiting such activity had been recently removed from the current Indian Appropriation Act. She cited $55,620 belonging to several Sioux bands being promised to Catholic schools, asking her membership to write their legislators to propose a bill distributing trust funds pro rata to tribal members, making sure that if such funds were earmarked for education, Indian consent was given.[25]

With her latest missionary effort on her mind, in the March 1905 issue of *The Indian's Friend* Quinton described the work done at the Yuma mission by the new field matron, Mrs. Grace Lea. A former children's hospital nurse, Mrs. Lea and her husband, Rev. Frank T. Lea, who had also studied medicine, had served for four years as missionaries in Africa. It had taken Quinton more than a year to make the Leas' missionary work in Yuma a reality. In late January 1904 Commissioner Jones had approved of a field matron cottage, in February, John S. Spear, superintendent of the government school, was authorized to construct it, and in September the Leas, funded by various Massachusetts auxiliaries, had arrived at Yuma. To ensure a permanent missionary presence, on December 3 Quinton had requested a plot of land from the government. On February 17, 1905, Acting Commissioner Charles F. Larabee informed her that the acting secretary of the Interior on February 11 had requested that Spear, with Indian consent, set aside a tract not exceeding four acres for NIA use.[26] In a later report, Quinton described the missionaries' first three months at Yuma during which they had handled 130 medical cases and been visited by more than three hundred Indians, many of whom stayed to use Mrs. Lea's sewing machine.[27]

In May Quinton traveled to New England to address the annual meeting of the Women's American Baptist Home Mission Society, which earlier had taken over the responsibility of two NIA mission stations: Two Gray Hills and the Second Mesa Hopi Mission. In her June article, "From the National Headquarters," Quinton praised these same New England workers, especially the Jamaica Plain group for their work among the Yuma.[28] During June she made four addresses, and late in the month addressed the July meeting of the National Education

Association, held in conjunction with the Department of Indian Education in Ocean Grove, New Jersey. The railroad had granted special rates to encourage attendees to listen to Commissioner Leupp, Estelle Reel, and Quinton. Afterwards she addressed the joint Cortland, New York, and Homer Indian associations' annual meeting, which she ended up chairing.[29] Because she was in the vicinity of Homer so often on speaking tours, in September she purchased a house and lot there on Clinton Street.[30]

That same month, she featured the activities of a new missionary in Northern California, Rev. G. J. Wentzell, with whom she had been corresponding for over a year. Currently in charge of three local churches, he and his wife were "highly esteemed by the Indians," noted Quinton, and were now holding meetings every other Sunday at the NIA's Greenville chapel. Extremely busy, when on February 5, 1904, he finally answered her letter of December 16, 1903, he claimed he was the "only preacher within a radius of 25 miles," reporting he had made a thorough canvass of Indian camps located in two of the valleys, describing the residents as "exceedingly dirty and very unhealthy," plagued with drunkenness. He was, however, gaining their confidence, helping them to write letters and welcoming their children to school. Although providing about the same amount of service for the Greenville church, which paid him $300, he complained to Quinton that the NIA, which had hired him in August, had paid him only $100 for doing twice as much as his predecessor.[31] In a letter the following May, he described driving over 769 miles, making 320 calls, performing eight Christian burials, and holding regular services in the chapel. The previous winter had been easier on the Indians with less snow and fewer deaths due to contagious diseases, possibly because many had built "new bark-houses which [were] much cleaner than the old ones." He had recently encouraged a number of local Indians to clean up their cemetery, about a mile from the chapel, and "now this little burying ground looks as neat as any in the valley, as far as cleanliness [was] concerned."[32]

Although in her September 1905 article, Quinton presented Wentzell's work in a positive light, she was disturbed by the contents of his August 10 letter, which had reached her in Homer. He again complained of his salary, using the term "back salary." In her August 23 letter, she explained he had no back salary. The NIA's elected missionaries were "engaged in regular, specific, full business form, and to *them* we *pledge* a *salary*." To other association workers the help is "tentative, informal and continues only while the pledged conditions continued." He had come to their attention as the pastor of a church, having already accepted their "meager salary" without applying to the NIA for help, therefore taking "the *risk* of having *only* their [church] compensation." She explained that he was already working among the Indians, writing to her that he intended to continue, not requesting financial help initially, merely assuming the NIA would help him as they had his successor. "With that *supposition* we had *nothing whatever to do*," she explained. To raise money from donors, she had to explain the work they were paying for. "As a *practical* man you sure would not 'pay' for work of which you had not positive knowledge." Yes, she agreed the NIA had encouraged his work, but in turn he did not reciprocate by giving her "*proper information to awaken interest.*" Instead, he had threatened to sow discord about their work, had called into question the honesty of her dealings with him, and threatened to close the chapel, which, she explained, he could not do. The land upon which it was built belonged to the NIA, and the custodian had the key, which could only be used by those the association approved of. In conclusion, she believed he intended no wrong, not even a discourtesy, as he was "being absorbed and busy in" his work. Her letter reflected the keen executive skills which had served her well for decades as president and chair of the missionary department.[33]

Months later, as an explanation of the misunderstanding, Quinton informed Emma L. Trubody, whose husband had been the industrial teacher at Greenville, that Wentzell had not written her for nine months and therefore she thought he had left the field. His failure to correspond had stopped her efforts to raise funds, and she had not been able to send the donation of $100.[34] His name never appeared again in NIA literature.

On September 9, 1905, Quinton thanked Smiley for her Lake Mohonk invitation, writing that "no doubt it will be delightful & profitable as ever." The conference opened on October 18, and during her five minutes she addressed the general need to Christianize the Indians without mentioning any current mission stations.[35] A month later she presided over the twenty-sixth annual convention of the NIA in New York City. When the nominating committee called upon her to stand for re-nomination, she declined, as "her health absolutely require[d] rest and relief from official care." She did, however, accept the title of Honorary President. Then appealing for the continued enlargement of the NIA's work, she welcomed Rev. William Brewster Humphrey, the first man to serve as president.[36] He served only one year, replaced by Sybil Carter, founder of the Sybil Carter Lace Association, who decades before had taught her first lace-making class to Ojibway women at Minnesota's White Earth Reservation. Another change was the hiring of John W. Clark, a Christian worker and lawyer from England, who was soon serving as both corresponding and general secretary, jobs Quinton had held from the association's beginning.[37]

Johnson Missionary Work at Greenville Chapel

Although no longer president, Quinton remained the public face of the NIA, delivering twenty-four addresses in 1906, corresponding with the Indian Office, and writing her articles on NIA-sponsored missionaries. The most active were Rev. W. H. Gill and his wife Mary among the Apache-Mohaves, and Rev. Frank T. Lea and his wife Grace among the Yumas.[38] However, with the recent departure of Rev. Wentzell, Quinton was still looking for another minister to resume preaching at NIA's chapel at Greenville. But she also wanted to sell the land and its chapel, which had been financed in 1897 by the Jamaica Plain auxiliary of the Massachusetts Indian Association.[39] With that combined goal in mind, in early March 1906 she wrote Commissioner Leupp that an opportunity had just opened up for her association to "secure a good missionary and his wife for work there," and she was renewing her query about a possible government purchase of the land and chapel. "Now, if Government could purchase the lot and Chapel and add one or two living rooms it seems to me that it would be an admirable plan for your office to employ a field matron & we employ her husband as our missionary,"[40] she wrote.

Quinton had Rev. John M. Johnson and his wife Cora I. Johnson in mind. The previous month Johnson had introduced himself as a thirty-four-year-old man with a wife and two children and eight years of ministerial work. Currently he was the appointed pastor of the Methodist Episcopal Church in Greenville and had been preaching at the Greenville Indian Industrial School since September 1, 1905. He had been informed by Dr. Wimberley, the school superintendent, and Mr. and Mrs. Trubody that Quinton was "thinking of employing a regular missionary to work among the Indians" and was writing to learn "what kind of a proposition" she was prepared to make. Calling the Indians "religiously inclined," he believed "a great work can be done among them."[41]

Although Quinton had a plan mapped out to accomplish both objectives for the NIA, Commissioner Leupp quickly complicated matters when in late March, he suggested that Emma L. Trubody would be a good field matron, prompting Quinton to respond that her qualifications were impeccable but did not think she would accept because of her husband's illness. Nevertheless, Quinton wrote Trubody.[42] She and her husband, Charles, had been employed at the Greenville school since 1895, he as the industrial teacher, and she as the kindergarten teacher. However, currently

Charles was living in San Francisco. To further expedite matters, Quinton wrote both Acting Commissioner Larrabee and Johnson on March 27 suggesting to the latter that he could become the NIA missionary at $300 and his wife a part-time field matron at $300. However, since there were no living rooms at the chapel, they would have to find rooms to rent.[43] Larrabee responded that Cora Johnson could start immediately with an additional $10 a month towards rent, or Trubody could be appointed by the government at $720 a year.[44]

On April 12 Quinton informed Johnson that Trubody had first claim based on ten years in government service and would not have to take the required Civil Service test. Furthermore, the Indian Office had already offered the position to her. Quinton's suggestion was that Trubody continue in her current position and Cora Johnson take the exam and become field matron, that way the NIA would gain "three good workers for and among all those Indians." She explained, "it seems to me therefore that you two and Mrs. Trubody must decide which is to have the new office." The Johnsons, completely willing to withdraw, visited Trubody, learning that she had already written Quinton to not consider her for the position.[45] The conflict resolved, on April 18 Larrabee appointed Cora Johnson as a part-time field matron for $300 plus $5 a month toward rent, with the option of becoming full time once she passed the examination. Quinton thanked him days later, informing Johnson of the agreement, and that he would be paid $300 a month as the NIA missionary. In her April article, Quinton proudly announced the upcoming opening of the old Greenville mission with a new NIA-sponsored missionary and a government field matron.[46]

With new positions settled, on April 17 Quinton addressed a packed parlor meeting in Germantown, Pennsylvania, organizing an Indian committee. The following day she spoke before another parlor meeting of the Philadelphia Indian Association with members voting to use their treasury for the Apache-Mohave mission.[47] At month's end she sent letters to John D. Rockefeller, founder of Standard Oil, and his wife, Laura Spelman Rockefeller, educator and philanthropist. "It is rather a dangerous experiment to be as generous and helpful as you so kindly have been to me personally for many years," she wrote him on April 23, "lest one should come again with an open palm." As the major money raiser for the NIA, she needed $1,000 "to make safe for some time several interests of the association." The following day she wrote Mrs. Rockefeller, who had earlier invited her to call. Quinton not only wanted to see her for "general principles," but to share with her some facts of the NIA work. Quinton called by the home twice, only to find Mrs. Rockefeller at their summer home. When Mrs. Rockefeller expressed her regret that

Quinton had retired, Quinton explained she was still in charge of the missionary work which was "the apple of [her] eye" and "the centre of [her] heart for which [she had] worked with all [her] strength for twenty-seven years." Although now she needed to rest, she had interests she was unable to leave behind, explaining that a dear friend had been providing her $200 a year for her own expenses but she had died a few weeks previous. With no one to take her place, Mrs. Rockefeller's gift would "be of more than usual value and joy." She concluded, "May I hope that I can still keep your hand as for so many years?"[48] The outcome is unknown.

In mid-May, instead of calling a formal meeting of the national Missionary Committee, Quinton, explaining this was a "crowded season of the year" for her, sent a formal letter to each member, addressing current missions. The first was the Mohave-Apache station where Quinton had gotten a partial government salary of $300 for Mrs. Gill as a part-time field matron. With the new stone church about to be completed, she recommended the work be turned over to the Presbyterian Board, already in control of most of the Indian mission work in Arizona. The cottage at the Yuma mission was finally completed and able missionaries were doing well with the cooperation of the new government school superintendent Ira C. Deaver. Quinton was in the process of finding a suitable society to take it over. The third mission was the reopening of their former work at Greenville. Rev. John M. Johnson had recently resigned his pastorate in Greenville and was disposed to "remain on the field for our work," she explained. If the committee could raise his salary "I think we can secure a wise, important and permanent Christian worker for the Indians of the five valleys centering at Greenville." She asked that they vote not only on selling the chapel and the lot but raising the funds to employ Johnson. A week later she informed Leupp that the Missionary Committee had agreed to sell.[49]

Having anticipated the outcome of the Missionary Committee vote, on May 8 Quinton had sent Larrabee a copy of the association's deed to the 2.13 acres upon which the Greenville chapel stood. It had been signed by Sarah Ament on July 19, 1897. Larrabee responded on May 16, asking her price, explaining the matter would be "given further consideration." Six days later Quinton informed Commissioner Leupp that the Missionary Department had voted to offer the chapel and lot, located near the school, for $500. Should the government agree to the purchase before January 1, 1907, the association would donate the chapel bell and the organ.[50]

During the same period Quinton received a mid-May report from Johnson. They were now living in their rented cottage and had already been invited to an Indian picnic and had preached one service. In another letter, he wrote they had sent for the civil service examination papers and had already driven two hundred miles on the reservation, making over thirty house calls. Not until May 22 was Quinton able to inform Johnson that the Missionary Committee had voted to engage him as their missionary and that the association would be offering to sell the chapel and property to the government. She requested that he write monthly "for the present of letters help zeal greatly and you can write wholly frankly to me on all points."[51] Quinton informed the membership in her July column that their favorite old mission had reopened on May 1 with the Indian Office providing the Johnsons with a cottage, conveyance, sewing machine, and cooking stove. Then in October she quoted from Cora Johnson's most recent letter, praising the industry of the Indians, noting they had employed Indian girls in their own home, finding "no white worker [had] pleased [her] better."[52]

Having solved the complicated matter at the association's Greenville Chapel, Quinton began to look forward to the fall season and to Lake Mohonk. On September 14, responding to Smiley's invitation, she joined reformers including Commissioner Leupp, who *The Indian's Friend* had recently described as "universally acknowledged as the best informed man on Indian affairs" ever to be appointed to the position. Quinton kept her comments brief, mentioning only their "model Christian settlement" in Alaska,[53] The conference over, she returned to her addresses before attending the annual NIA meeting where she presented her missionary report, highlighting the Apache-Mohave station, Greenville, and the Yuma mission.[54]

The new year 1907 found Quinton busy with her monthly articles, informing the membership in the January issue of *The Indian's Friend* that Reverend Johnson had driven 590 miles among the camps, ridden horseback where there were no roads and walked 90 miles to call on the sick. In another letter, he had written Quinton that he had traveled over 800 miles and that the student population at Greenville was increasing. Mrs. Gill at the Apache-Mohave mission had reported to Quinton that she had expanded her dairy, and that her turkey and bee raising enterprises were ongoing, and she was encouraging the Indians to plant a winter garden.[55]

A Return to California

Early in January 1907 Weinland had written to Quinton that he had left his Banning home and returned to his former cottage, resuming care of the Potrero Indian Church. She expressed pleasure that he was again in charge. "But you really have the care of that work, and, of course, your presence in it makes all much more sure."[56] In March she asked if he could put her up for a night or two on her way

Missionary cottage at Potrero, on the Morongo Indian Reservation. Built by the WNIA initially for Rev. Weinland, it was soon turned over to the Moravian Church.
William H. Weinland Collection, The Huntington Library, San Marino, California (photCL 39 [108]).

to her California home if she went by the southern route on the Southern Pacific line. She had stayed longer than expected in Homer, giving addresses before the Baptist Homer Mission Society there as well as the Indian associations in Cortland and Homer. Her departure delayed, it would be too hot and unsafe for her heart on the southern route, so instead she took the Union Pacific through Chicago, Omaha, and Salt Lake City informing Weinland she had arrived in Perris, on June 5, having addressed a minister's meeting in Los Angeles beforehand.[57] Later in the month, waxing poetic, she wrote how thrilled she was to see the glorious mountains, her orange groves, and hear the "scores of song birds."[58] Quinton would remain in Southern California until May 1909, missing the Mohonk Conference and the annual association meeting for two years in a row, although diligently sending in her missionary reports and articles.

From a Jamaica Plain Association report, the membership learned that she had spent a good part of the summer of 1907 searching for a new missionary field and communicating with Indian Office officials.[59] It had been providential that she had taken the more northern route, for it enabled her to stop in Nevada to look over sites for a potential new station.[60] She ultimately chose the Walker River Paiutes at Schurz, Nevada, concluding that since they had already received their allotments in 1906, their location near a lake should make their self-support easy. Rev. and Mrs. William H. Gill, who had visited with her in Long Beach for two days en route from their former Arizona station, would begin this new work on October 2, 1907.[61]

In a mid-July 1907 letter to Weinland, Quinton wrote that she had received an invitation from the NYCIA to attend the second Zayante Conference at Mount Hermon, California, beginning on July 17. "I am not well enough," she informed him. "The great heat, with the long years of work & wear make it impossible for me safely to take the journey & the fatigues of the conference." She needed absolute rest and no extra strain.[62] The first Zayante Conference, attended by prominent clerics, university professors, reformers, and a small group of Indians, had been called to direct attention to the plight of California's Indian population. During this second conference, Indian delegates would present a petition to the president and Congress requesting land for homes; protection from liquor traffic, education, physicians, and legal protection.[63]

During the second week of August, Quinton gave two addresses in Long Beach and a third before the Mission Society of the First Methodist Episcopal Church in Los Angeles. Then on September 5 she spoke at the Asbury Methodist Episcopal Church in Los Angeles. Two days earlier, from Long Beach, she had written Smiley thanking him for his invitation to "the happy Indian Conference on 'his heavenly hills," but it looked like she may be kept all winter in California and would miss the "delightful Assembly." She also had "the joy of finding our *new* mission station at *Walker River*, Nevada," and only a couple of days ago had seen the new missionaries, the Gills, off to this field among the Paiutes, their former mission station having been turned over to the Presbyterian Board. On October 10, still at the Windermere in Long Beach, she informed him she was selling her "ranch" and could not leave yet. However, Sybil Carter, the new NIA president, would be at Lake Mohonk "& a tongue for the cause we all together serve." Then on October 25 Quinton addressed a convention of twenty-six churches in Los Angeles and on November 8, 1907, attended an all-day Woman's Mission Union meeting, addressing "Work Among the American Indians."[64]

During 1908 Quinton remained busy, giving a dozen addresses in Southern California. The first was on April 28 during an Indian Conference in Riverside which she described as "catching the spirit of the quarter-century old Indian Conference at Lake Mohonk." Hosted by Frank Augustus Miller, proprietor of the Glenwood Mission Inn, some fifty to sixty Indians attended as well as 150 delegates, including NIA members from the northern and southern California auxiliaries, Charles Fletcher Lummis, Albert K. Smiley, and Stanford president David Starr Jordan, who served as conference chair and whose wife was one of several Northern California Indian Association (NCIA) vice presidents. Other attendees included college presidents, ministers, and prominent citizens, who according to Quinton "made earnest appeals for landholdings to make homes possible" for California Indians—a long-time goal of the NCIA.[65] The association's president, Mary Haven Edwards; corresponding secretary, Cornelia Taber; and general secretary, C. E. Kelsey had in 1903 launched a successful petition drive, securing a congressional appropriation of $10,000 for an investigation that Kelsey conducted. His comprehensive report resulted in a congressional appropriation in 1906 of $100,000, followed later by another $50,000, for land purchases.[66]

In early August, Quinton addressed the Third Zayante Conference, describing the gathering as "fine & much fruit is expected,"[67] rejoicing in visits with old friends Annie Bidwell and Mrs. Dorcas J. Spencer. Pleased to meet the eleven Indian delegates, Quinton remarked on Kelsey's paper on Indian education, Taber's sketch of the NCIA, Bidwell's narratives of her Indian work, and the spicy talk by Clara D. True, Superintendent of the Malki Indian Agency on the Morongo Reservation. Quinton noted that True had made a raid on bootleggers on the San Manuel Reservation near San Bernardino. Other speakers included field matrons, teachers, and missionaries, whose collective motivation was "to secure justice for Indians, to remove disabilities from them and to open their path to elevation, progress, [and] prosperity." Quinton concluded that the conference was "one of unsectarian, radically Christian workers breathing true Christian patriotism with love for and service for the highest interests of our aboriginal fellow citizens."[68] This conference and the earlier one at Riverside had enabled Quinton to mingle with Indian reformers much as she would have at Lake Mohonk or an annual NIA meeting.

From June 4 to December 3 Quinton gave a dozen addresses before such diverse groups as the WCTU, the Federation of Women's Clubs, and mission unions, all in Long Beach, which appeared to serve as her temporary headquarters from the summer of 1908 to the following summer, moving several times within the city, she explained to Weinland in a February 1909 letter that she was currently living in a rooming hotel.[69] Her temporary quarters did not interfere with her ability to maintain an ongoing correspondence with NIA missionaries, especially the Gills at the new Nevada Mission among the Paiutes and the Johnsons at Greenville, enabling her to glean interesting items for her progress reports in *The Indian's Friend*.[70] However, with the arrival of fall and she still in California, on September 4, 1908, Quinton had to again decline Smiley's invitation to the Lake Mohonk Conference. The following month she thanked him for inviting the NIA's secretary John W. Clark, describing him as a "noble & able man—was a lawyer nine years in England before coming to America—has been prominent in Christian work here for years." His attendance was crucial because NIA president Sybil Carter had died suddenly on August 28.[71] Also unable to attend the December 11, 1908, NIA annual meeting, Quinton sent in her list of those who had died during the year and her annual missionary report, which was read by Clark and printed as a separate pamphlet.[72]

A short notice in *The Indian's Friend* of April 1909 described her affiliating with the Plymouth Congregational Church of Long Beach.[73] Then a couple of months later, she and twenty-five members of the Gaviota Chapter of the Daughters of the American Revolution celebrated at the home of a prominent Long Beach member, giving speeches, toasts, and "the will to serve native land in highest realms which made the day delightful, memorable."[74]

From 1909 forward, it is difficult to follow Quinton's activities because her itinerary no longer appeared in the association's annual report. Occasionally she would include some reference to her activities in her monthly missionary articles but most of the time they dealt only with association missionary work. In a January 1909 article, she described the NIA's first missionary work in Oregon among the Klamath, giving a bit of personal information. The previous January, while still in California, she had inquired of Horace G. Wilson, the superintendent of the Klamath Indian School, if he would be willing to allow the NIA to open an Indian mission on his reservation, which served as the home of the Klamath, Modoc, and Piute. If so, she asked that he request land from the government to enable the NIA to build a missionary cottage. She enclosed a NIA leaflet on their Alaska work to serve as an example of the association's capabilities.[75] In the past she would have simply visited the agent herself, but instead she sent Rev. F. T. Lea in September 1908 in her place. Following a thorough investigation, he chose Yainax, a sub-agency some forty miles east of the Klamath agency as the station site. Mr. and Mrs. H. W. Peffley, missionaries from St. Louis, were chosen to begin work in late October 1908.[76] Citing details from their first month's report, Quinton informed the membership that because of the size of the reservation and the scattered populations, Mrs. Peffley had already traveled some 220 miles by wagon over rough roads during her first thirteen days as the government field matron.[77]

Quinton's Declining Role

Sometime in August 1909 Quinton returned to Homer, which alternated with Syracuse as her home for much of the remainder of her long life. On October 5, 1909, she declined Smiley's annual invitation to attend Lake Mohonk, claiming she was "still too worn and weary to take even the short journey from here to your mountain of delights." She blamed "the fatigues of the past year, the long hot summer journey and other fatigues make a quiet autumn and winter here, in the quiet flat [in Homer] which I have taken, imperative."[78] She also did not attend the NIA's December meeting, although the annual report described her busy year, writing letters on their behalf to missionaries and government officials, her addresses and articles, and her organization of a new SCIA branch in Pasadena. Her burden of chairing the Department of Missions had been passed on to John W. Clark in September.[79] In the May 1910 issue of *The Indian's Friend*, Clark in a short note about Quinton described her as well and although no longer active in any official capacity, "as deeply interested as ever in its work, and still finds time to do much efficient service for the cause so dear to her." The October issue printed her latest article encouraging NIA workers to again return to their summons to become responsible stewards, "truth-telling" to others both formally or informally, using their "tongue and pen as to injustice" and beginning their crusade anew. She described the NIA methods as "simple, practical, [and] successful."[80]

For decades she had ended each busy year with an attendance at Smiley's Lake Mohonk Conference and the association's annual NIA meeting. Now as the years went by, she was often forced to turn down her Mohonk invitation. On September 3, 1910, writing from Syracuse, she thanked Smiley for her invitation, hoping to attend. The following month she explained she had a bad cold and it looked as if she would miss the conference. "This is almost unbearable to me, but if it is on that divine list of what is 'best' I must bond to it," she concluded.[81] She did, however, attend the December NIA annual meeting, preparing and reading the year's necrology. *The Indian's Friend* reported with pleasure her presence after an absence of three years.[82]

Quinton did attend the 1911 Lake Mohonk Conference, all the more appreciative in accepting Smiley's invitation because she had been absent for four years from what she called that "Assembly of the saints" and its noble work.[83] Upon returning home to Syracuse, she wrote Smiley that she was still magically at Mohonk "soaring in soul over its inspiring mountains & valleys, hearing its delightful speeches, meeting its choice souls, breathing its life-full air, physically & spiritually."[84] Although she was not at the December annual NIA meeting, the assemblage paid her a tribute, recognizing her continued support from her upstate home, especially the aid for their work "with her pen, as strength permits." She had prepared the necrology of the year, which was read by another.[85] She would, however, attend the thirty-third annual meeting of the NIA in December 1912.[86] In January 1913 she hit the lecture circuit again, giving an address on the NIA's Indian work before the Independence Hall Chapter of the Daughters of the American Revolution in Philadelphia.[87]

The 1913 Mohonk Conference was a difficult one for the reformers, for Albert K. Smiley had died on December 2, 1912. His half-brother Daniel Smiley sent out that year's invitations; receiving hers caused Quinton to tear up "for the past & joy for the present, in the memory of those gone." The month before, Quinton had moved back to Syracuse from Homer to spend the winter with her brother Seymour, who got sick shortly thereafter, forcing Quinton to stay home. She wrote Daniel: "It is to me a bereavement to miss your assembly ever sacred to me for so many reasons!"[88] She also sent a short letter to be read before the annual NIA meeting, noting she would miss the happy greetings, hearing various department reports but most regrettable was "the failing to hear the convictions of members regarding our future duty, their hopes of success in expressed obedience to these convictions, the outlining of plans for and methods of finding means to serve the needs of yet other tribes of our native Americans."[89] In 1914 she attended both the thirty-second Lake Mohonk Conference in mid-October and the NIA meeting, presiding over the nominating committee's report and writing and presenting the necrology for the year.[90]

During the 1915 season, "Providence permitting," Quinton hoped to attend the Mohonk conference, informing Daniel Smiley that she was staying at the Ontio resort in Unadilla, New York, under the proprietorship of Albert A. LeRoy. She called it a "charming place, a loving imitation of the dear old queen Mohonk." In mid-October, expressing disappointment and sorrow, she informed Smiley that she was not well and could not "risk the fatigues of that most interesting occasion with its coveted reunions & fellowship." She did, however, write up Ella Covell Boardman's obituary for *The Indian's Friend*.[91] The following year Quinton again thanked Smiley for her invitation, intending to go. As the conference neared, she requested a room with a little heat because she had a heavy cold. The day before the conference she cancelled because of a cold rain.[92] World War I resulted in the conference's postponement, but Quinton was able to attend the annual NIA

Detail of a photograph taken at the 1914 Lake Mohonk Conference of Friends of the Indian. Daniel Smiley (#98), proprietor of Mohonk Mountain House, stands beside Amelia Stone Quinton (#97).
Mohonk Mountain House Archives.

meeting in 1916 and 1917.[93] The following year she permanently moved to Ridgefield Park, New Jersey.

She wrote at least one more article for *The Indian's Friend's* January 1918 issue in which she declared that the New Year had brought with it "new summons, commands and promises" and challenged the membership to open a new mission station.[94] Then months later in April, she joined Rev. William Henry Weinland at the NYCIA meeting to listen to his account of his first work among the Mission

Indians. She followed with a short address, describing his "unbounded faith and constant courage." She also attended the 1918 and 1919 NIA annual meetings,[95] as well as the one on December 2, 1920, giving a brief address, with a plea for Indian citizenship as a matter of justice. Now eighty-eight, she attended the forty-second meeting of the NIA on December 1, 1921, addressing the gathering, praising their constancy and faithfulness, and urging that they move "forward until all the blind on that white field and other and large fields come to the source of all light and strength."[96]

Over these later years, occasionally the local newspapers provided information on Quinton's activities. In early May 1910 the Homer paper had reported that she had taken rooms in the home of Erastus Jones on Cayuga Street. Then in June she participated in activities associated with Cortland Normal School (formerly Cortland Academy), giving a talk on "The Olden Days." The following month a personal note in the *Cortland Standard* described her as leaving for a two-week trip to Spafford Inn at Skaneateles Lake.[97] During 1911, Quinton lived in Syracuse, spending the summer in Homer, temporarily occupying an acquaintance's apartment. She returned to Syracuse in early October 1911.[98] The following year she again returned to Homer for the summer, making a quick trip to Syracuse in August because of the death of Seymour's wife.[99] In October she was back to the Homer/Cortland area where she gave a talk on "Work Among the Indians" before the Sennighly Literary Club.[100] In the fall of 1914 she purchased a house on South Main Street opposite the Baptist Church with the intent of repairing it for a summer residence; but she sold it the following March. In September she returned to Syracuse to spend the winter with Seymour, with the intention of attending Lake Mohonk in October, which she did not due to his illness.[101] After her move to New Jersey no local papers contain anything about her prior to her death.

On June 23, 1926, Amelia Stone Quinton, almost ninety-three, died of a cerebral hemorrhage in her New Jersey home. She was buried in Glenwood Cemetery in Homer, New York.[102] Seymour had set up a trust fund for her which at the time of her death amounted to about $9,500. Her estate went to the Protestant Episcopal Church and the Episcopal Diocese of Central New York, the Church of Domestic and Foreign Missions Society, the Church Pension Fund, and St. Paul's Church of Syracuse.[103]

Conclusion

There is no doubt that Amelia Stone Quinton was a woman possessed of great energy and stamina, as well as tremendous organizational and diplomatic skills, and charisma, and a concern for others that usually rose far above any for herself. To have year after year inspired women across the country to form associations, raise money, and accomplish goals, while at the same time forging effective working relationships with men, who held the political power, convincing them to do what she wanted most of the time, suggests an uncommon person. In today's world she would undoubtedly have held a high-ranking position in business or the non-profit world. At the same time, Quinton was a real person; she had her prejudices and people she did not like. One suspects she might have been termed pushy or bossy when she felt she had to accomplish something. While she kept no known personal journal, the many letters she wrote in service to her WNIA work reveal a person who was observant of both people and her surroundings. Her descriptions of the land were often lyrical, possibly reverting to her school days writing poetry. And she saw a great deal in her travels, holding no apparent fear of long rides on narrow bumpy roads; walking in mud; sleeping under mosquito netting in a primitive tent or wrapped in buffalo robes under a wagon; or being at any one of the many remote locations she visited.

During the formative years of the WNIA Amelia Stone Quinton was so closely intertwined with the association that one could not have existed without the other. She shaped it through her public addresses and voluminous writing, her organizing skills, and her founding of missionary stations. Although the association continued for another quarter of a century beyond her death, it was still essentially the same association she had created, with the same goals. During the fiftieth anniversary on December 7, 1929, a "special jubilee number" of *The Indian's Friend* printed a report on its fifty-fourth Indian mission at Turtle Mountain,

North Dakota. Quinton would have been pleased, having once described missionary work to Mrs. Rockefeller as the "apple of her eye" and the "center of her heart." Among the 150 guests present at this golden anniversary luncheon was Matthew Sniffen, longtime member of the IRA who noted he had visited every station, finding "excellent work done by efficient and devoted missionaries"—a testimony to the long standing affiliation forged between Quinton and Welsh, founders and secretaries of their respective associations.[1] The NIA survived the Great Depression, founding a new station at Yerington, Nevada, in 1933.[2] Finally on April 18, 1951, at the seventy-second annual meeting at the Allerton Hotel in New York City, NIA president Mrs. Arthur F. Adams called the meeting to order and the twenty-three members present voted to disband. Assents were mailed to current members.[3] It can be said that the association had finally reached its originally hoped-for obsolescence.

To understand Quinton's legacy and what she accomplished, one only has to look at the association's 1881 constitution. Adopted when Quinton, Bonney, and their followers were still calling themselves the Indian Treaty-Keeping and Protective Association, the constitution identified the association's primary object as to "awaken a Christian public sentiment which shall move our Government to just dealing with the Indian tribes among us." To achieve this object, the association intended to circulate the association's literature to the public and memorials (petitions) to Congress; hold "popular meetings," and send articles to local newspapers "to promote the growth of right sentiment concerning our national and so our individual duty to Indians."[4] Their revised constitution, adopted on October 27, 1883, added the "abolition of the reservation-system," a common-school education, and "educational or mission work, or both, for and among Indians to hasten as much as is in our power their civilization, christianization and enfranchisement."[5]

Under Quinton's guidance, the goals that she and her association had actual control over were slowly accomplished one by one. During 1886 alone the WNIA membership had grown to include eighty-three branches, and members had sent sixty-five petitions to Congress and circulated 49,000 pieces of association literature.[6] Throughout the year, Quinton gave numerous addresses to a wide variety of public and private audiences, and about every fourth year she took an extended tour, establishing more auxiliaries and mission stations along her route. As the face of the WNIA, each time she gave an address Quinton was awakening a Christian public to the inequities faced by the country's Indian population. During the eighth annual Lake Mohonk Conference on October

10, 1890, she received ample praise from Merrill E. Gates, the presiding official of the conference, when he said, "I have seen Mrs. Quinton come from the train after a long and exhausting journey, hasten at once to a little hall half-filled with persons who doubted whether the Indians were worth doing anything for, and inspire and lead them on to good work for the coming year."[7]

In each annual report Quinton gave detailed information on the work of the various WNIA departments, all accomplished under her guiding hand. At the beginning of every year before the Board of Indian Commissioners and at the end of the year at Lake Mohonk, she described her association's ever-growing accomplishments, singling out, for example, homes built by the Home Building department, or legislation passed, or mission stations funded and handed over to a missionary society to care for. She had concluded in one pamphlet that reformers had reached an interesting period of their Indian work: "We now see the Indian question in the concrete, and the case is one of life, worthy life for Indians, or ones of death by slow and torturing degrees of lost manhood, degradation, sin and despair."[8]

In an 1893 article, Quinton explained that the work of a WNIA missionary included teaching an Indian to keep an orderly home, prepare meals, and care for the sick. The Indians were expected to learn domestic skills and arts and become self-supporting, and above all, to learn the truths of the gospel and be converted to practical Christianity. This was only part of the pioneering work that Quinton and the WNIA undertook in all of their mission stations. WNIA-sponsored missionaries aided by government field matrons made house visits, ran day schools and Sunday schools, and gave temperance instruction and religious teaching. At the time of the publication of her article, the WNIA had already founded twenty-five mission stations, directly or indirectly, transferring them to the care of various Protestant churches.[9] A decade later in her presidential address, Quinton explained that the WNIA had planted "thirty-six missions in eleven years, built homes by loan funds for scores of Indians, reaching with the direct influences of civilization hundreds of Indians." (By 1908, the association, with Quinton directing the work, had established about fifty-three mission stations.) She explained they had also "stirred the interest and gained the help of young people in many States; gave libraries to Indian schools, and reading matter to individual Indians."[10]

One of Quinton's personal goals was to take the Indian out of politics, a goal expressed initially in 1886. Although this was not in the purview of the WNIA, it was accomplished to some extent by the extension of Civil Service rules over Indian Office employees, legislation that Quinton and Welsh worked together to support. In the same speech she also identified education as a goal, explaining that by 1888, the WNIA had added fourteen more Indian missions in which education was emphasized.[11]

Goals beyond the direct control of Quinton and the WNIA were also achieved, such as the ending of the reservation system and extension of citizenship for those tribes that came under the provisions of the Dawes legislation. Quinton and her association had lobbied on its behalf. Citizenship had come with allotment, but for those tribes whose reservations were not allotted, citizenship came for them and all Indians in 1924 by an act of Congress, two years before Quinton's death. Therefore, during her lifetime, she was able to see most of the goals that she and her membership had worked to achieve.

The organization that Quinton had helped create was a powerful network of upper-and middle-class friends, a unique hybrid organization, religious and political, missionary and reform-minded. It was women-based with strong male participation and advice throughout. While its male counterparts strove to turn Indian men into Christian farmers, WNIA members evangelized Indian women, teaching them Anglo ways to keep house, prepare meals, sew clothing, and approximate the "true womanhood" ideal, adapted to reservation conditions. It began as a variation of a women's missionary circle and ended up the same way. It reaffirmed its missionary origins by establishing mission stations across the country, creating a niche for itself in the process, but remained committed to its original purpose of political petitioning and public opinion work, seeking to change federal Indian policy. Reflecting its members' cultural world view and the assimilationist program of the government's Indian policy, state branches, individually or cooperatively, financed reservation irrigation projects, missionaries, and physicians; built missionary cottages, chapels, and hospitals; supported government field matrons and teachers; built schools and Indian homes, and provided funding for the post-secondary education of Indian students. Later, the association added the promotion of common and industrial school education, civil rights for the Indians, and allotment. In the process not only did Indians benefit materially but association members acquired organizational skills and a sense of accomplishment.

However much today's perspective may be at odds with the ideas of assimilation and severalty, any failure to address them leaves us poorer in understanding and in possibilities for change. Even this focused examination of Quinton and her role in the Indian reform movement makes clear that the reasons nineteenth-century people supported assimilation and severalty were often diametrically opposed. Quinton and others in the reform movement thought that this offered Indians the most hope for land ownership, citizenship, and other rights all people should have. Other non-Indians were really only motivated by self-interest, wanting simply to get and keep the best land for their own use and that of others of their social class. And there were Indians, such as Henry Roe Cloud, who supported assimilation, while other Indians were vehemently opposed to it; sometimes their reasons reflected differing personal analyses of the world around them and what might provide the best future.

Quinton and, by default, the WNIA reflect the discontinuity that underlay views of Indians by non-Indians. Quinton was driven by strong internal religious and moral beliefs. As Lori Jacobson suggests, "[Quinton's] choice to focus on America's indigenous people was motivated by the sense that the people with power in America were failing to live up to their obligations, to the nation's obligations. Quinton's desire to make positive change through her moral influence (in addition to her prodigious organizational and leadership skills) were a perfect match to America's "Indian problem" which was perceived by reformers to be first of all a moral failing."[12] In at least one situation, Quinton was forceful in her objections to children being removed from their parents to attend school. And in regard to the Ute removal, she wrote how the "matter makes every drop of one's blood boil with indignation & chill with grief by turns." And she also spoke of the need for "liquidation of our personal debt as citizens of a nation so heavily in arrears materially, educationally and religiously to our native race of Indians."[13] But this fundamental belief in fair treatment for and the humanity of Indians is still set against the idea that Indians needed someone to step in and bring them Christian religion; institutional schooling; and new ideas of farming, housekeeping, cooking, and caring for the sick. These were well-intentioned actions that in retrospect often failed to address Indian needs from an Indian perspective.

The ideas that motivated Quinton are ideas fully of her time. As we noted at the outset, American society during Quinton's time was dominated by evangelical, revivalist Protestant Christianity, which molded much of its citizenry. Middle- and upper-class women like Quinton were constrained by society's expectation that they achieve "true womanhood," meaning they were pious, pure, submissive, and domestic, with their home viewed as their "proper sphere." Yet, "real women" were motivated to fulfil their role as moral guardians by joining reform movements and seeking charity and missionary work outside their homes. Many females and males believed that the Christian religion had the power to transform Native Americans into "civilized" citizens and were inspired to form associations to try to achieve this goal. Quinton remained focused on this goal all her life. She and the group were not drawn in to other issues such as suffrage and there is nothing in any records found so far that might satisfy curiosity as to why. But I believe she needs to be understood for who she was and all that she accomplished, and the more broadly we envision her within her time, the more she can be appreciated.

My hope is that this biography will place her on par with the leadership of the Woman's Christian Temperance Union and the General Federation of Women's Clubs, where she deservedly belongs; and, that other scholars will engage in additional research in the multiple facets of her work, and especially expand the knowledge on the WNIA as an expression of women's activism and its role in adding Indian women to the Indian reform movement's assimilationist ideal.

Notes

Abbreviations

Annual Report	*Annual Report of the National Indian Association*
ASQ	Amelia Stone Quinton
BIC	Board of Indian Commissioners
IRA	Indian Rights Association
ITKPA	Records of the Indian Treaty-Keeping and Protective Association, Dec. 1880.
LMC	Lake Mohonk Conference
LR	Letters Received (for National Archives)
LS	Letters Sent
NA	National Archives
NIA	National Indian Association
RG	Record Group
SC	Special Case
WHW	William Henry Weinland
WNIA	National Indian Association and Women's National Indian Association

Introduction

1. "Mrs. Amelia Stone Quinton," *New York Times*, June 25, 1926, 21; Mrs. J. B. Dickinson, *Address of the President of the WNIA* (Philadelphia, November 17, 1885), 2.
2. WNIA, "Constitution," *Annual Meeting and Report of the WNIA, October 27, 1883* (Philadelphia, 1883), 19.
3. National Indian Association (NIA), "Mrs. Amelia Stone Quinton," *Indian's Friend*, July 1926, 6; see also NIA, *Forty-Seventh Annual Report of the NIA* (hereafter cited as *Annual Report*) (New York, December 1926), 27–28.

4. "Who Have Been the Consistent Friends?," *Quarterly Journal of the Society of American Indians* 2 (January–March 1914), 85.
5. NIA, "An Indian Tribute to Mrs. Quinton," *Indian's Friend*, January 1930, 7. In 1920 the federal government granted the WNIA eighty acres for this missionary station upon which they built a mission house and chapel. The station was transferred to the board of American Missions of the United Lutheran Church in America in October 1928, see NIA, "The Rocky Boy Mission," *Indian's Friend*, May 20, 1920, 6.
6. Margaret Jacobs, *White Mother to a Dark Race: Settler Colonialism, Maternalism, and the Removal of Indigenous Children in the American West and Australia, 1880–1940* (Lincoln: University of Nebraska Press, 2009), 97. The other two were anthropologist Alice Fletcher and Estelle Reel, superintendent of Indian education from 1898 to 1910.
7. Valerie Sherer Mathes, "WNIA Missionary Stations," *Gender, Race and Power in the Indian Reform Movement: Revisiting the History of the WNIA*, ed. Valerie Sherer Mathes (Albuquerque: University of New Mexico Press, 2020), 227–41.
8. NIA, "The Address of the President," *Annual Report, December 1901* (Philadelphia: George Dukes, 1901), 14; see also, Helen M. Wanken, "Woman's Sphere and Indian Reform: The Women's National Indian Association, 1879–1901" (PhD diss., Marquette University, 1981), 345–46, https://epublications.marquette.edu/dissertations/AAI8203780/.
9. NIA, "Address of the President," *Annual Report, December 1908* (New York, 1908), 26.
10. Francis Paul Prucha, *The Great Father: The United States Government and the American Indians* (Lincoln: University of Nebraska Press, 1986), 263–64.
11. Francis Paul Prucha, "Indian Policy Reform and American Protestantism, 1880–1900," *Indian Policy in the United States* (Lincoln: University of Nebraska Press, 1981), 230–31.
12. William G. McLoughlin, ed., *The American Evangelicals, 1800–1900: An Anthology* (New York: Harper and Row, 1968), 1.
13. Barbara Welter, "The Cult of True Womanhood, 1820–1860," in *Dimity Convictions: The American Woman in the Nineteenth Century* (Athens: Ohio University Press, 1976), 21. Linda K. Kerber in "Separate Spheres, Female Worlds, Woman's Place: The Rhetoric of Women's History," *Journal of American History* 75 (June 1988), explains that "sphere" is a trope used by historians to describe "women's part in American culture" (10). See also, Mary P. Ryan, "American Society and the Cult of Domesticity, 1830–1860" (PhD diss., University of California at Santa Barbara, 1971); and Nancy F. Cott, *The Bonds of Womanhood: "Woman's Sphere" in New England, 1780–1835* (New Haven, CT: Yale University Press, 1977). Jacobs, *White Mother to a Dark Race*, 88–93, calls this American maternalism. See also Louis Michele Newman, "The 'Indian Problem' as a 'Woman Question,'" in *White Women's Rights: The Racial Origins of Feminism in the United States* (New York: Oxford University Press, 1999), 116–31.
14. Helen M. Bannan, "'True Womanhood' and Indian Assimilation," *Selected Proceedings of the Third Annual Conference on Minority Studies*, vol. 2, ed. George E. Carter and James R. Parker (La Crosse: Institute for Minority Studies, University of Wisconsin, 1976), 187.

15. J. F. Stearns, *Female Influence, and the True Christian Mode of Its Exercise: A Discourse Delivered in the First Presbyterian Church in Newburyport, July 30, 1837* (Newburyport, MA: John G. Tilton, 1837), 10–11.

Chapter 1

1. "Homer Village," *The Family Magazine or Monthly Abstract of General Knowledge, 1837* (Cincinnati: Eli Taylor, 1837), 324; see also *A Gazetteer of the State of New York* (Albany: C. Van Benthuysen, 1843), 133, for Homer's 1840 population; *A Gazetteer of the State of New York* (Albany: John Disturnell, 1842), 204–5; and John W. Barber and Henry Howe, *Historical Collections of the State of New York* (New York: S. Tuttle, 1842), 124–25. See J. H. French, *Gazetteer of the State of New York* (Syracuse: R. Pearsall Smith, 1860), 252–53; and "Homer," *Gazetteer and Business Directory of Cortland County, New York for 1869* (Syracuse: Journal Office, 1869), 85–91.
2. "In Memoriam," *Homer Republican*, January 31, 1884, for quotes. "A Catalogue of Marriages confirmed by Elder Alfred Bennet [*sic*]," Kellogg Memorial Research Library, Cortland County Historical Society, Cortland, New York.
3. For Seymour Henry Stone, born July 27, 1831, see *Register of the Empire State Society of the Sons of the American Revolution* (Empire State Society, 1899), 312; for Quinton, see Frances E. Willard and Mary A. Livermore, eds., *A Woman of the Century: Fourteen Hundred-seventy Biographical Sketches Accompanied by Portraits of Leading American Women in All Walks of Life* (Buffalo, NY: Charles Wells Moulton, 1893), 592, and Mrs. John A. Logan, *The Part Taken by Women in American History* (Wilmington, DE: Perry-Nalle, 1912), 407; for Lucius Bennett Stone, born October 15, 1835, see Thomas McAdory Owen, *History of Alabama and Dictionary of Alabama Biography*, vol. 4 (Chicago: S. J. Clark, 1921), 1629; and for George W. Stone, born February 29, 1840, see *Homer Republican*, June 13, 1895.
4. "In Memoriam," *Homer Republican*.
5. Mary's occupation was listed as "keeping house." See 1850, 1860, 1870, and 1880 Censuses of the United States; 1855, New York State Census; retrieved from Ancestry .com. Federal censuses are also available at www.census.gov.
6. "In Memoriam," *Homer Republican*.
7. *Cortland Academy: Twenty-Seventh Annual Catalogue for the Year Ending July 8, 1846* (Printed by R. A. Reed), back cover, 13.
8. Mrs. A. C. Swanson, "A Centennial Tea-Bell, 1876," *Centennial Temperance Volume: A Memorial of the International Temperance Conference held in Philadelphia, June, 1876* (New York: National Temperance Society and Publication House, 1877), 394–95; and Mrs. Amelia Swanson Quinton (1885), "A Spring Song," *Woman in Sacred Song: A Library of Hymns, Religious Poems and Sacred Music by Woman*, comp. and ed. Eva Munson Smith (Oakland, CA: Arthur E. Whitney, 1888), 872 (second poem). She read one of her compositions during the July exercises, see *Order of Exercises at the Thirtieth Anniversary of Cortland Academy*, Tuesday, July 3, 1849.

9. *Cortland Academy: Twenty-Seventh Annual Catalogue and Catalogue of the Officers and Students of Cortland Academy, for the Academic Year 1849–50* (Homer, NY: Rufus A. Reed, 1850), 19; and "Cortland Academy," *Gazetteer and Business Directory of Cortland County*, 86.
10. "In Memoriam," *Homer Republican.*
11. "Minutes, Memberships, Homer Baptist Church Book," courtesy Kellogg Memorial Library.
12. Willard and Livermore, *A Woman of the Century*, 592–94.
13. Marriage certification, Morgan County Archives, Madison, Georgia.
14. Lucian Lamar Knight, *Georgia's Landmarks, Memorials and Legends*, vol. 2 (Atlanta: Byrd Printing, 1914), 1885.

    Amelia Stone Quinton (hereafter referred to as ASQ) left no details of life in Madison. For a contemporary account by another Northern evangelical Christian who moved to the South to teach, see Dolly Lunt Burge, *The Diary of Dolly Lunt Burge, 1848–1879*, ed. Christine Jacobson Carter (Athens: University of Georgia Press, 1997). Although they apparently never met, their life experiences would have been similar as they lived in Madison around the same time. Burge, a Methodist, was sixteen years older.
15. Morgan County Historical Society, "Morgan County," *Morgan County, Georgia Heritage 1807–1997* (Marceline, MO: Walsworth, 1997), 1.
16. Curtis D. Johnson, *Islands of Holiness: Rural Religion in Upstate New York, 1790–1860* (Ithaca, NY: Cornell University Press, 1989), 119–20, 126.
17. "Board of Trustees," *Georgia Female College* (Madison: Published for the Georgia Female College, 1850), 2; "Trustees," *Catalogue of Georgia Female College, 1855–56* (Printed by Benj. G. Liddon, 1856), 4; Knight, *Georgia's Landmarks*, 884; and B. D. Ragsdale, "Georgia Female College–Madison," *Madisonian*, January 27, 1933. All courtesy of the Morgan County Archives.
18. For Frank, see John W. Burney, "Memoirs of John Swanson," *Weekly Madisonian*, April 26, 1895, 1, and for his parents and siblings, see "John Swanson Pioneer, 1779–1847," and "The John Swanson Family Pioneer," *Morgan County, Georgia Heritage 1807–1997* (Marceline, MO: Walsworth, 1997), 239, courtesy of the Morgan County Archives.
19. "1811 Tax Digest," 24; "1838 Tax Digest," 24; and "1842 Tax Digest," 30 in *Morgan County, Georgia Tax Digest Entries*, Morgan County Archives. See also "John Swanson Pioneer, 1779–1847," *Morgan County, Georgia Heritage*, 239. Two Antioch Baptist Church Membership Rolls from 1809–1843 list one black male slave with a Swanson surname and four female slaves, courtesy of the Morgan County Archives.
20. *Southern Miscellany and Upper Georgia Whig* (Atlanta, Georgia), December 4, 1847, 4.
21. Morgan County Archives, "Inventory & Appraisement of the Estate of John Swanson, deceased," *Court of Ordinary, November Term 1847*, Books 12 and 13—a handwritten account of every item, its value, and its recipient, as well as sale of his property, price, and purchaser. See also *Inferior Court Minutes*, 1834–1851, and *The Ancestry and*

Descendants of Frank Marion Swanson, vol. 1, comp. Marion Swanson Wattenbarger, 1997, 106–8, in Family Files #88, Swanson, Morgan County Archives.

22. For inheritance, see *The Ancestry and Descendants of Frank Marion Swanson*, 106; for slave and acreage see "1849 Tax Digest," 140, "1858 Tax Digest," 272, *Morgan County, Georgia Tax Digest Entries*, Morgan County Archives. In 1858 he was paying taxes on $300 in household goods, and $700 for "all other property."
23. Jesse Harrison Campbell, "James F. Swanson," *Georgia Baptists: Historical and Biographical* (Macon, GA: J. W. Burke, 1874), 466, 467, 469. For hotel, see "Some History of the stores on the east side of Jefferson Street, from Main Street to First Street," House Files, no. 97, Morgan County Archives. Fears & Swanson ads, "Not Going to Atlanta," "New Goods," and "Swanson, Jett & Co.," *Madison Family Visitor*, January 5, 1856, 3; September 6, 1856, 4; and November 1, 1856, 3. For pianos, see *Madison Family Visitor*, March 15, 1856, 2.
24. Campbell, "James F. Swanson," 467–68. See also "The John Swanson Family Pioneer," *Morgan County, Georgia Heritage 1807–1997*, 240.
25. Southern Baptists called for stronger denominational unity, leading in 1845 to the formation of the Southern Baptist Convention.
26. Campbell, "James F. Swanson," 469; and "Apalachee Baptist Church," *Morgan County, Georgia Heritage, 1807–1997*, 12.
27. Campbell only referenced New York, it is unknown if he meant Homer or New York City. According to Willard and Livermore, *A Woman of the Century*, 593, it was "the enervating climate" of the South that resulted in "a period of invalidism" sending ASQ to an undisclosed destination.
28. Campbell, "James F. Swanson," 467, 468, 469. He also preached at Augusta's First Baptist Church.
29. Campbell, "James F. Swanson," 469, 471.
30. Campbell, "James F. Swanson," 471–73. The will was probated December 6, contents unknown. See also, *The Ancestry and Descendants of Frank Marion Swanson*, 62.
31. Owen, "Lucius Bennett Stone," *History of Alabama and Dictionary of Alabama Biography*, 1629, and Thomas M. Owen, comp., "Lucius Bennett Stone," *Alabama Official and Statistical Register, 1903* (Montgomery, AL: Brown Printing Company, 1903), 48; "George W.[hitefield] Stone," *Homer Republican*, June 13, 1895; and "Seymour Henry Stone," *Register of the Empire State Society of the Sons of the American Revolution*, 312.

    After the war, Lucius worked in merchandising, mining, and farming and served as a Georgia state senator from 1900 to 1903. George abandoned the law and went into business, becoming vice president and superintendent of the Delaware Mutual Life Insurance Company, serving as a national bank examiner from 1889 to 1895. In 1898, he was ordained a Unitarian minister, see "George W. Stone," *Homer Republican*, June 13, 1895. The biography included with his papers at the Andover-Harvard Theological Library, Harvard Divinity School, Cambridge, has him a captain in the First Volunteer Corps, Cortland County, not with the Twelfth New York Volunteers. Seymour moved to Syracuse at fourteen, apprenticed in the silver shop of B. R. Norton & Company, eventually buying it with a partner. He is listed as a jeweler in the 1870 census. A vestryman in St. Paul's Episcopal Church, he was a long-time member of the Scottish Rite of Freemasonry, see *1920 Proceedings of the Fifty-First Council of Deliberation of the Bodies of the Ancient Accepted Scottish Rite of Free Masonry . . . in the State of New York* (Printed by Order of the Council of Deliberation, 1920), 25, 97.

Chapter 2

1. Willard and Livermore, *A Woman of the Century*, 593; *The Sailors' Magazine and Seamen's Friend for the Year Ending December, 1873*, vol. 45 (New York: American Seamen's Friend Society, 1873), 217; and *Cortland County Republican*, January 15, 1874.
2. *Temperance Society of the Town of Homer, Minutes, 1841–1842*, 10, #6252, Temperance Society of Homer Records, Division of Rare and Manuscript Collections, Carl A. Kroch Library, Cornell University, Ithaca, NY. According to Johnson, *Islands of Holiness*, by 1825 Cortland County had twenty-two distilleries, and as consumption increased, members of evangelical churches "were at the heart of the county's early temperance movement," 115–19, esp. 117.
3. Anne Firor Scott, "Women, Religion, and Social Change in the South, 1830–1930," in *Making the Invisible Woman Visible* (Urbana: University of Illinois Press, 1984), 199.
4. "Women's State Temperance Union," *Buffalo Evening Courier & Republic*, May 26, 1876, 1, notes a Mrs. A. C. Swanson from Brooklyn in attendance.
5. Mrs. Annie Wittenmyer, *History of the Woman's Temperance Crusade* (Philadelphia: Published at the Office of the Christian Woman, 1878), 544–56; Mrs. Swanson is listed on 552 under "officers and earnest workers." See also *Third Annual Report of the Brooklyn Temperance Union* (New York: N. Tibbals & Son, 1877) 7–11; and *Centennial Temperance Volume*, 693–94.
6. *Centennial Temperance Volume*, 380, 407, 693; chapter 1, note 8 above; and *Third Annual Report of the Brooklyn Temperance Union*, 2.
7. Church notices, *Brooklyn Eagle*, January 20, 1877, 3.
8. Lori D. Ginzberg, *Women and the Work of Benevolence: Morality, Politics, and Class in the Nineteenth-Century United States* (New Haven, CT: Yale University Press, 1990), 1. She makes no mention of female Indian reformers; however, WNIA missionary stations would fit the criteria of training programs and shelters.
9. WNIA, "The Address of the President," *Annual Report of the WNIA, December 1892* (Lancaster: Examiner Publishing House, 1892), 10.
10. Ginzberg, *Women and the Work of Benevolence*, 12, 14.
11. *Cortland County Democrat*, March 8, 1878.
12. *The Bi-Centennial Celebration of the First Baptist Church of the City of Philadelphia*, 107–19, 209 (Boardman, who served from 1864 to 1894), 391 (founding of the circle), and 122–23, 330 (WNIA). For Mrs. Boardman's organizing, see ASQ, "Care of the Indian," *Woman's Work in America*, ed. Annie Nathan Meyer (New York: Henry Holt, 1891), 377.

13. *The Bi-Centennial Celebration of the First Baptist Church*, 123–24. Francis Paul Prucha, *American Indian Policy in the Formative Years: The Indian Trade and Intercourse Acts, 1790–1834* (Lincoln: University of Nebraska Press, 1970), writes that trade was "the most important source of legitimate contact between Indians and whites, and from earliest colonial days it had been of great economic and political significance" (66); for the 1818 memorial see 71.
14. Francis Paul Prucha, ed., *Documents of United States Indian Policy*, 2nd ed. (Lincoln: University of Nebraska Press, 1990), 33.
15. Ginzberg, *Women and the Work of Benevolence*, 37.
16. Ingalls served two years at the Nevada Paiute Agency before taking over the Union Agency in Indian Territory (Five Civilized Tribes). During 1872 and 1873, he had served on a special commission with Major J. W. Powell, visiting the Indians of Idaho, Utah, Nevada, Arizona, and Southeastern California and taking a census of Indians on the Pacific coast. For Ingalls' second report at the Paiute Agency see *Annual Report of the Commissioner of Indian Affairs (CIA) to the Secretary of the Interior (SI), 1874* (Washington, DC: Government Printing Office, 1874), 282–84. For the Union agency see "Testimony Taken Before the Committee of Indian Affairs," House of Representatives, 44th Congress, 1st sess., Misc. Doc. #167, in *Index of the Miscellaneous Documents of the House of Representatives for the First Session of the Forty-Fourth Congress* (Washington, DC: Government Printing Office, 1876), 52.
17. Women's Baptist Home Mission Society, *The Women's Baptist Home Mission Society, 1877 to 1882: Minutes of Annual and Special Meetings, and Annual Reports of Corresponding Secretary During the First Five Years* (Chicago: R. R. Donnelley, 1883), 1. See also "Women's Baptist Home Mission Society: Its History," *National Baptist*, May 17, 1877, 1.
18. The ABHMS was founded in 1831 in New York to raise money for missionary work in North America.
19. *The Women's Baptist Home Mission Society, 1877 to 1882*, 1, 2–3, 26–27. The resolution referenced an apocryphal 1831–32 treaty giving Indian Territory in fee simple. This same treaty is also mentioned in "The Indians," *National Baptist*, May 29, 1879, 6; and "Women's Baptist Home Mission Society, Chicago," *National Baptist*, June 5, 1879, 5.
20. *The Women's Baptist Home Mission Society, 1877 to 1882*, 28; for background, see "The Rev. Dr. H. L. Wayland Dead," *New York Times*, November 8, 1898, 3.
21. *Baptist Home Missions in North America, 1832–1882* (New York: Baptist Home Mission Rooms, 1883), 519, 520–23.
22. "Special Meeting," *The Women's Baptist Home Mission Society, 1877 to 1882*, 5.
23. "Women's Baptist Home Mission Union of Philadelphia and Vicinity," *National Baptist*, December 4, 1879, 5.
24. *The Women's Baptist Home Mission Society, 1877 to 1882*, 3, 5–7.
25. ASQ, "The Women's Baptist Home Mission Society," *National Baptist*, January 22, 1880, 5.
26. ASQ, "Women's Home Mission Society," *National Baptist*, June 10, 1880, 5.

27. John M. Rhea, *A Field of Their Own: Women and American Indian History, 1830–1941* (Norman: University of Oklahoma Press, 2016), 40, notes that between 1878 and 1879 the Philadelphia branch raised $922.90 for their Indian Territory work. For Committee formation see *Records of the Indian Treaty-Keeping and Protective Association* [ITKPA] *from Dec. 1880*, [handwritten by ASQ], box 1, folder 1, Women's National Indian Association Papers, collection no. 9237, Division of Rare and Manuscript Collections, Carl A. Kroch Library, Cornell University, Ithaca, NY (hereafter cited as ITKPA, WNIA Papers, Cornell), preface, 1–2, 3–5.
28. ASQ, "A Misapprehension Corrected," *National Baptist*, November 18, 1880, 5.
29. ASQ, "The Women's Indian Association," in *The Gospel in All Lands*, ed. Eugene R. Smith (New York: Missionary Society of the Methodist Episcopal Church, December 1887), 539.

Chapter 3

1. ASQ, "Care of the Indian," 373, 388.
2. WNIA, "The Work of our General Secretary," *Fourth Annual Report* (Philadelphia: Press of Grant & Faires, 1884), 27. Wanken writes in "Woman's Sphere and Indian Reform" that ASQ was "the real power behind the movement" (20), and that she was "lord of the expedient and a sharp operator" (27).
3. John M. Rhea, "From Indian Territory to Philadelphia: A Critical Reexamination of the Origins and Early History of the Women's National Indian Association, 1877–1881," in Mathes, *Gender, Race, and Power in the Indian Reform Movement*, 27–54.
4. "A Sketch of the Life of Mrs. Mary L. Bonney Rambaut given by herself to her friend Mrs. Amelia S. Quinton," September 1894, American Baptist Historical Society Archives Center, Mercer University, Atlanta, Georgia. According to "A Brief Historical Sketch," 21, Bonney furnished the money while ASQ worked "as God opened the way," *Records of the ITKPA*, WNIA Papers, Cornell.

   For a comprehensive history, see Wanken, "Woman's Sphere and Indian Reform." See also, Helen Marie Bannan, "Reformers and the 'Indian Problem,' 1878–1887 and 1922–1934," (PhD diss., Syracuse University, 1973), 91–96; Gregory Coyne Thompson, "The Origins and Implementation of the American Indian Reform Movement, 1867–1912," (PhD diss., University of Utah, 1981), 31–42, 158–71, 195–98; Sara Northrop Romeyn, "Building a Political Empire: The Early Women's National Indian Association, 1875–1885," 140–80 in "A Sentimental Empire: White Women's Responses to Native American Policy, 1824–1894," (PhD diss., George Washington University, 2003); Lori L. Jacobson, "The Women's National Indian Association and the Erotics of Reform," in "Agencies and Associations: Women Write Indian Reform in Nineteenth-Century America," (PhD diss., State University of New York-Buffalo, 2007); and Jane E. Simonsen, *Making Home Work: Domesticity and Native American Assimilation in the American West, 1860–1919* (Chapel Hill: University of North Carolina Press), 73–75.

5. "A Disgrace to the Nation," *New York Times*, January 8, 1878, 1; for Barnes see "Reports of Agents in Nevada," *Annual Report of the CIA to the SI, 1875* (Washington: Government Printing Office, 1875), 336–37.
6. S. S. Cutting, "The American Home Mission Society," *National Baptist*, March 14, 1878, 5.
7. ASQ, "Care of the Indian," 377, and WNIA, "A Historical Sketch," *Indian's Friend*, October 1896, 2. Fifty-eight years later, NIA executive board member Georgia M. Penfield wrote "Reasons Which Led to the Forming of the National Indian Association" for the March 1937 *Indian's Friend*, 2–4.
8. During the World's Missionary convention in London in 1888, Bonney was married to her former pastor, Thomas Rambaut, by George Dana Boardman, her current pastor, see Valerie Sherer Mathes, "Mary Lucinda Bonney and Amelia Stone Quinton, Founders of the Women's National Indian Association," *American Baptist Quarterly* (Winter 2009), 421–40.
9. First quote, see WNIA, "Constitution of the WNIA," *Annual Meeting and Report of the WNIA, October 27, 1883* (Philadelphia, 1883), 19; and Mary P. Ryan, *Womanhood in America: From Colonial Times to the Present* (New York: New Viewpoints, 1979), 88.
10. Susan Zaeske, *Signatures of Citizenship: Petitioning, Antislavery, and Women's Political Identity* (Chapel Hill: University of North Carolina Press, 2003), 3.
11. Alisee Portnoy, *Their Right to Speak: Women's Activism in the Indian and Slave Debates* (Cambridge, MA: Harvard University Press, 2005), 49. See "Catharine Beecher: Circular Addressed to Benevolent ladies of the U. States," in *The Cherokee Removal: A Brief History with Documents*, ed. Theda Perdue and Michael D. Green (Boston: Bedford/St. Martin's, 2005), 113–14. For non-Beecher petitions see Romeyn, "Petitioning for a Sentimental Empire: Anti-Removal Efforts, 1828–1840," in "A Sentimental Empire," 56–90; and Mary Hershberger, "Mobilizing Women, Anticipating Abolition: The Struggle Against Indian Removal in the 1830s," *Journal of American History* 86, no. 1 (June 1999): 15–40.
12. ASQ, *Earnest Work Needed*, pamphlet, Historical Society of Pennsylvania, Philadelphia, Pennsylvania, https://digitallibrary.hsp.org/index.php/Detail/objects/13718. On January 14, 1880, ASQ attended the first union anniversary of the WBHMS and the WABHMS in New York City, addressing the subject of an Indian Memorial and petition, see *The Women's Baptist Home Mission Society*, 7.
13. For first quote, see "Memorial Letter, Accompanying the Indian Petition of 1881," in ASQ, "Care of the Indian," 380; see also, NIA, "The Memorial Letter of 1881," *Indian's Friend*, July 1908, 6. For final quote, see *Earnest Work Needed*.
14. Quinton at the time was employed by the WBHMS to visit churches in and around Philadelphia and Eastern Pennsylvania and organize branches of the society. See "Third Annual Report," *The Women's Baptist Home Mission Society, 1877 to 1882*, 42.
15. For presentation, see U.S. Congress, House, vol. 10, part 2, 46th Cong., 2nd sess., February 20, 1880, *Congressional Record*, 1044; WNIA, *Annual Meeting and Report of the WNIA, October 27, 1883*, 6; and ASQ, "Care of the Indian," 378, and "Justice"

National Baptist, February 19, 1880, 5, for text. On the top of the copy of *An Earnest Petition Needed* in the Historical Society of Pennsylvania ASQ had written: "The first leaflet of the Woman's Ind. Assc'n circulated in the summer of 1879 with the first petition of the assoc'n & before any organization was effected indeed."

16. "Women's Home Mission Union," *National Baptist*, February 26, 1880, 5. For ASQ's April 15 reading of a paper on the Indian Question, see "Women's Home Mission Union," *National Baptist*, April 22, 1880, 4; for her attendance on May 27 at the third annual meeting of the WBHMS in Saratoga, New York where she was appointed Secretary *pro tem*., see *The Women's Baptist Home Mission Society, 1877 to 1882*, 7; and for her address on Women's Work, "all aglow with the spirit of missions," see "Women's Home Mission Union," *National Baptist*, October 14, 1880, 5.
17. "Minutes for the Central Indian Committee of Dec. 11, Dec. 31, 1880, and Jan. 20, 1881," 3–9, *Records of the ITKPA*, WNIA Papers, Cornell. Denominations were Baptists, Episcopalians, Presbyterians, Quakers, and Methodist-Episcopalians. See also WNIA, "A Historical Sketch," *Indian's Friend*, October 1896, 2, 11; and ASQ, "A Grand Example," December 23, 1880, 5, and ASQ, "Broken Covenants," December 30, 1880, 5, *National Baptist*.
18. ASQ, "Care of the Indian," 379–81.
19. "Minutes of the March 17, 1881, Meeting," 11, *Records of the ITKPA*, WNIA Papers, Cornell; and U.S. Congress, Senate, "Senator Dawes Presents Petition," 46th Cong. 3rd sess., January 27, 1881, *Congressional Record*, 953–54.
20. Helen Jackson (H. H.) *A Century of Dishonor: A Sketch of the United States Government's Dealings with Some of the Indian Tribes* (Boston: Roberts Brothers, 1888), 31.
21. "A Historical Sketch," *Indian's Friend*, 11; and Valerie Sherer Mathes, "Helen Hunt Jackson, Amelia Stone Quinton, and the Mission Indians of California," *Southern California Quarterly* 96, no. 2 (Summer 2014), 172–205.
22. Jackson to ASQ, January 27, 1880, box 64, Collection 100, Special Collections, UCLA Library, Charles E. Young Research Library, University of California at Los Angeles, reprinted in *The Indian Reform Letters of Helen Hunt Jackson, 1879–1885*, ed. Valerie Sherer Mathes (Norman: University of Oklahoma Press, 1998), 88; and Jackson to ASQ, December 18, 1880, and January 12, 1881, Helen Hunt Jackson, 1830–1885, BANC MSS 99/279 cz, Bancroft Library, University of California, Berkeley, CA.
23. ASQ to Dawes, March 12 and April 2, 1881, Henry Laurens Dawes Papers, Manuscript Division, Library of Congress, Washington, DC (hereafter cited as Dawes Papers).
24. "Minutes of the March 17 Meeting,"10–14, *Records of the ITKPA*, WNIA Papers, Cornell. See also "The Chronology of Our Organization," *Indian's Friend*, February 1897, 2. On May 24, 1881, ASQ attended the 4th annual meeting of the WBHMS in Indianapolis addressing "the needs of the Indian women," raising them "to a consciousness of what they may become," see *The Women's Baptist Home Mission Society, 1877 to 1882*, 9–15, ASQ on 9, 11, 13.
25. "Minutes of the Fifth Meeting, June 3, 1881," 15–17, 18–20, *Records of the ITKPA*, WNIA Papers, Cornell.

26. *Annual Report of the Association for the Advancement of Women, for 1881* (Boston: Cochrane & Sampson, 1882), 8, 9.
27. "Minutes of the Fifth Meeting, June 3, 1881," 25–26, 29, 32–33, 34–36, *Records of the ITKPA*, WNIA Papers, Cornell. For auxiliaries see also WNIA, "Our Association's Chronology: Number Three," *Indian's Friend*, March 1897, 2.
28. Originally a recommendation of the Boston Committee, see "Final Recommendations," *The Indian Question. Report of the Committee Appointed by Hon. John D. Long* (Boston: Frank Wood, 1880), 25. The Dawes legislation of 1887 raised the twenty to twenty-five years.
29. ASQ, "Care of the Indian," 382–83, 387. See also WNIA, "Our Association's Chronology," *Indian's Friend*, April 1897, 2.
30. Bannan in "True Womanhood," 190, writes that although they wrapped this petition in "embroidery and ribbons and presented their appeal as 'the plea of all womanhood,'" they had in fact stepped "far outside their customary sphere." Romeyn in "A Sentimental Empire," notes that the WNIA's petitions were typeset and widely distributed by their petition committee whereas the 1830s women's Indian petitions were locally based, handwritten, with less than one hundred signatures,154; for the 1882 petition, see 157–62.
31. ASQ, *A Retrospect and Its Lessons* (WNIA: Annual Address, Dec. 6th, 1894), reprinted as WNIA, *The Providential Beginnings* (WNIA; ca. 1906). Long was a major figure in the Boston Indian Committee.
32. See Sarah Whitmer Foster and John T. Foster Jr., "Historical Notes and Documents: "Harriet Ward Foote Hawley: Civil War Journalist," *Florida Historical Quarterly* 83, no. 4 (Spring 2005): 448–67; and Maria Huntington, *Harriet Ward Foote Hawley* (BiblioLife, LLC, 1923 reproduction).
33. For text see U.S. Congress, Senate, vol. 13, part 2, 47th Cong., 1st sess., February 21, 1882, *Congressional Record*, 1326–30; reprinted as *Proceedings on the Occasion of the Presentation of the Petition of the Women's National Indian Association, by Hon. H. L. Dawes of Massachusetts in the Senate of the United States, February 21, 1882* (Washington, DC: 1882), 1–12.
34. WNIA, "Our Association's Chronology: Number Four," *Indian's Friend*, April 1897, 12.
35. "Ninth Meeting, March 16, 1882," 36–37, *Records of the ITKPA*, WNIA Papers, Cornell; see also "Our Association's Chronology: Number Four," 12.
36. For the latter item, see "The Aborigines. Meeting of the Indian Treaty Keeping and Protective Association," *Philadelphia Inquirer*, March 23, 1882, 2. For another of her articles, see ASQ, "The Indians Again," *Southwestern Christian Advocate*, June 1, 1882, 1.
37. "Tenth Meeting, May 17, 1882," 40–43, *Records of the ITKPA*, WNIA Papers, Cornell. See also WNIA, *Annual Meeting and Report of the WNIA, October 27, 1883*, 6–8.
38. *The Women's Baptist Home Mission Society, 1877 to 1882*, 15–22.

39. "Eleventh Meeting, October 3, 1882," 46, 47, 54–57, quote on 54, *Records of the ITKPA*, WNIA Papers, Cornell; see also WNIA, "Constitution of the National Indian Association," *Fourth Annual Report* (Philadelphia: Grant & Faires, 1884), 57.
40. "12th Meeting, November 21, 1882," 61, 65, *Records of the ITKPA*, WNIA Papers, Cornell.
41. "13th Meeting, December 19, 1882," 66, *Records of the ITKPA*, WNIA Papers, Cornell. Carlisle was founded in 1879 by Richard Henry Pratt, who served as its long-time superintendent. See "Women to Aid the Indians," *New York Times*, December 6, 1882, 2. Melissa Phelps Dodge's husband, a one-term congressman and part owner of Phelps, Dodge, & Company, was a member of the first BIC.
42. See Valerie Sherer Mathes, *Charles C. Painter: The Life of an Indian Reform Advocate* (Norman: University of Oklahoma Press, 2020).
43. WNIA, *Annual Meeting and Report, 1883*, 16, 19–22; see also WNIA, "Our Association's Chronology: Number Six," *Indian's Friend*, June 1897, 11–12. For Welsh's WNIA support, see "Indians. An Eloquent Plea for the Rights of the Red Men. Personal Experience of Herbert Welsh, Esq." *Brooklyn Eagle*, March 1, 1883, 2.
44. WNIA, "Report of the Missionary Committee," *Fourth Annual Report*, 32; and Mrs. J. B. Dickinson, *Address of the President of the WNIA* (Philadelphia: November 17, 1885), 9.
45. IRA, *The Third Annual Report* (Philadelphia: Office of the IRA, 1886), 13, reported the two associations were "working in perfect harmony, and each helps to secure the better accomplishment of the other's work." See also NIA, "The Indian Associations," *Indian's Friend*, October 1903, 2, 10.
46. WNIA, "Report of the Missionary Committee," *Fourth Annual Report*, 32, reprinted as WNIA, *Missionary Work of the WNIA* (Philadelphia: 1884).
47. Mrs. Amelia S. Quinton, "Women's Work for Indians," *The National Exposition Souvenir: What America Owes to Women*, ed. Lydia Hoyt Farmer (Chicago: Charles Wells Moulton, 1893), 301, 303.
48. Wanken, "Woman's Sphere and Indian Reform," 255–57, 262. Her chapters on California Missions, 300–339, and the Seminole Mission, 277–99, reflect a "less flattering side of the WNIA; anti-Catholic campaigns, paranoia, witch hunts, and a particularly uncomplimentary picture" of ASQ emerges, 276. By 1920 the association had expanded their work to fifty-two tribes, for list see NIA, "The Work of the National Indian Association," *Indian's Friend*, September 1920, 6.
49. For resolution, see WNIA, "Our Association's Chronology: Number Seven," *Indian's Friend*, July 1897, 2; WNIA, "What Our Missionary Work Will Be," *Annual Meeting and Report, 1883*, 10–13; Massachusetts Indian Association (MIA), *Annual Report of the MIA, January 1884* (Boston: Frank Wood Printer, 1884), 12; WNIA, "Report of the Recording Secretary," *Fourth Annual Report*, 24–25; and Wanken, "Woman's Sphere and Indian Reform," 262–69.
50. See Valerie Sherer Mathes, "WNIA Missionary Stations," in *The Women's National Indian Association: A History* (hereafter *The WNIA: A History*), ed. Valerie Sherer Mathes (Albuquerque: University of New Mexico Press, 2015), 301–11.

51. WNIA, "Report of the Missionary Committee," *Fourth Annual Report*, 33 [reprinted as *Missionary Work of the WNIA, 1884*]; WNIA, "Our Associations' Chronology: Number Eight," *Indian's Friend*, August 1897, 2. See also WNIA, *Missionary Work of the WNIA and Letters of Missionaries* (Philadelphia: November 17, 1885), 3–12. Initially this work was to have begun among the Navajo but the resignation of their agent forced a change in plans. ASQ sent news of their mission work to other magazines, see for example Rev. I. E. Graeff, "Friends in Need are Friends Indeed," *The Guardian: A Monthly Magazine for Young Men and Women Sunday Schools and Families*," June 1885, 168.
52. For committee work see Wanken, "Woman's Sphere and Indian Reform." For more on home building, see Sara N. Romeyn, "Building a Domestic Empire: The WNIA's Home Building Program, 1880–1895," in "A Sentimental Empire,"181–219; Simonsen, *Making Home Work*, 71–96; and Carol Anne Chase Lastowka, "At Home and Industriously Employed: The Women's National Indian Association," (master's thesis, University of Arizona, 1994).
53. WNIA, "Our Association's Chronology: Number Five," *Indian's Friend*, May,1897, 2.
54. WNIA, *Annual Meeting and Report of the WNIA, October 27, 1883*, 8; and WNIA, *Official Pamphlet of the NIA [sic], with Suggestions and Facts for Its Helpers* (Philadelphia: November 1882), 5; ASQ, *Suggestions to Friends of the WNIA*, 4; WNIA, *How to Organize an Indian Association* (Philadelphia: 1888); and "The Indian: By Mrs. Amelia Stone Quinton, President of the Women's National Indian Association," in *The Literature of Philanthropy*, ed. Frances Goodale (New York, NY: Harper & Brothers, 1893), 119, 120.
55. For participants, see "National Educational Topics," *New York Times*, August 1, 1883, 8.
56. For 1882, see "Editor's Note," *Christian Educators in Council: Sixty Addresses by American Educators*, 6. See also Morris S. Daniels, *The Story of Ocean Grove: Related in the Year of its Golden Jubilee* (New York: Methodist Book Concern, 1919), 250.
57. "Table of Contents," *Christian Educators in Council*, 3–4.
58. ASQ, *The Mohonk Indian Conference* (Philadelphia: WNIA Leaflet, 1885), 4. See Mathes, *Charles C. Painter*, 31, 62.
59. ASQ, "Woman's Work in Solving the Indian Problem," *Christian Educators in Council*, 103, 104. See "Discussing Education," *New York Times*, August 12, 1883, 2; and "National Education. Meeting of the Delegates at Ocean Grove, N. J.," *Brooklyn Eagle*, August 12, 1883, 8.
60. ASQ, "Woman's Work in Solving the Indian Problem," 104, 105.
61. WNIA, "The Work of our General Secretary," *Fourth Annual Report*, 27–30; and *A Few Facts Concerning the Condition of Indians* (Philadelphia, 1884), partly reproduced in "Some Infamous Facts Tensely Told," *Council Fire and Arbitrator*, June 1883, 89–90.
62. *Brooklyn Eagle*, April 3, 1884, 3, for a notice of her address; "Friends of the Indians. Ladies Who Are Interested in a Practical Work of Civilization," *New York Herald*, April 8, 1884; "Friends of the Red Men," *New York Times*, April 9, 1884, 3; and

"Sympathy for the Red Men. The Work of the New-York Indian Association," *New York Times*, November 14, 1884, 8. For complete itinerary, see WNIA, "The Work of Our General Secretary," *Fourth Annual Report*, 27–30.

63. WNIA, "Our Association's Chronology. Number Eight," *Indian's Friend*, August 1897, 2.
64. WNIA, "Our Association's Chronology. Number Nine," *Indian's Friend*, September 1897, 2; and WNIA, *Fourth Annual Report*, 27–30.
65. Valerie Sherer Mathes, "Iron Eyes' Daughters: Susette and Susan LaFlesche, Nineteenth-Century Reformers," in *By Grit & Grace: Eleven Women Who Shaped the American West*, ed. Glenda Riley and Richard W. Etulain (Golden, CO: Fulcrum Publishing, 1997), 135–52.
66. WNIA, "Our Association's Chronology. Number Ten," *Indian's Friend*, October 1897, 2.
67. WNIA, "Our Association's Chronology: Number Eleven: Our First Mission Field," *Indian's Friend*, November 1897, 2.
68. WNIA, *Fourth Annual Report*, 37. Ultimately the Women's Methodist Episcopal Board of the West assumed control of the Ponca, Otoe, and Pawnee sites; for chronology of her trip, see 30.
69. "The Work of the New-York Indian Association," *New York Times*, November 14, 1884, 8.
70. WNIA, *Fourth Annual Report*, 53–55. "Women's National Indian Association," *Southwestern Christian Advocate*, February 5, 1885, described this meeting based on the report sent them by ASQ. The institute, founded in 1866 for the sons of Episcopalian soldiers who died during the Civil War, was reopened during the 1880s to educate young Indians. For an interesting report see BIC, "Report of E. Whittlesey. The Lincoln Institution," *Twenty-Second Annual Report, 1890* (Washington, DC: Government Printing Office, 1891), 1.
71. WNIA, "The President's Address," *Fourth Annual Report*, 8.
72. WNIA, "Advisory Board," *Annual Report of the WNIA, November 30, 1887* (Philadelphia: Royal Printing Company, 1887), 6; and WNIA, "Advisory Board," *Annual Report of the WNIA, November 1888* (Philadelphia: J. F. Dickson, 1888), 6.
73. ASQ, *Suggestions to Friends of the Women's National Indian* Association (Philadelphia: 1884), 3.
74. Mrs. A. S. Quinton, "A small Request to Pastors," *Southwestern Christian Advocate* (New Orleans), February 16, 1882.
75. WNIA, "Advisory Board," *Annual Report, November 30, 1887*, and WNIA, "Advisory Board, *Annual Report, November 1890* (Philadelphia: J. A. Wilbour, 1890), 6.
76. Founded in 1869 during the administration of President U.S. Grant, according to Robert H. Keller, Jr. *American Protestantism and United States Indian Policy, 1869–82* (Lincoln: University of Nebraska Press, 1983), 18, the BIC was "a group of wealthy, independent citizens armed with authority equal to that of the secretary of the interior to oversee and correct abuses in that department and its Indian Office." See also Prucha, *Documents of United States Indian Policy*, 126–27.

77. Larry E. Burgess, "The Lake Mohonk Conferences on the Indian, 1883–1916," (PhD diss., Claremont, 1972), 70, 73; and Larry E. Burgess, "What is a Woman Worth?" in Mathes, *The WNIA: A History*, 1–22.
78. The founding was inspired by Welsh and Henry Pancoast's investigative tour of the Great Sioux Reservation; see Herbert Welsh, *Four Weeks Among Some of the Sioux Tribes of Dakota and Nebraska, Together with a Brief Consideration of the Indian Problem* (Germantown, Philadelphia: Horace F. McCann, Steam-Power Printer, 1882), and Henry S. Pancoast, *Impressions of the Sioux Tribes in 1882, with Some First Principles in the Indian Question* (Philadelphia: Franklin Printing House, 1883).
79. William T. Hagan, *The Indian Rights Association: The Herbert Welsh Years, 1882–1904* (Tucson: University of Arizona Press, 1985) (hereafter cited as *The IRA*), 11–19; and IRA, "The Object of the Association," *The Fourth Annual Report of the Executive Committee of the IRA* (Philadelphia: Office of the IRA, 1887), 3–4.
80. Hagan, *The IRA*, 25. In 1888, the IRA had 28 branches, over half "moribund," 48. By 1885 the WNIA had 56 branches in 27 states, see Quinton, "Care of the Indian," 385.
81. Hagan, *The IRA*, 23, 256.
82. During the 1877 removal of the entire tribe from their Nebraska reservation to the Indian Territory, many died, including Standing Bear's son. The chief, his wife and a small party of followers returned to Nebraska to bury the boy and were arrested. Tibbles, who believed Indians had legal rights under the Fourteenth Amendment, hired lawyers who successfully argued their case in *Standing Bear v. Crook*. See Thomas Henry Tibbles, *Buckskin & Blanket Days: Memoirs of a Friend of the Indian* (Lincoln: University of Nebraska Press, 1969), 199; Thomas Henry Tibbles, *The Ponca Chiefs: An Account of the Trial of Standing Bear* (Lincoln: University of Nebraska Press, 1972); Valerie Sherer Mathes and Richard Lowitt, *The Standing Bear Controversy: Prelude to Indian Reform* (Urbana: University of Illinois Press, 2003), and Valerie Sherer Mathes, "Boston, the Boston Indian Citizenship Committee, and the Poncas," *Massachusetts Historical Review* 14 (2012), 119–48.
83. Had the Poncas been Massachusetts residents, they would have become citizens in 1869 with the passage of legislation that declared Indians and people of color citizens of the Commonwealth, see Ana Marie Plane and Gregory Button, "The Massachusetts Indian Enfranchisement Act: Ethnic Contest in Historical Context, 1849–1869," *Ethnohistory* 40, no. 4 (Autumn 1993), 587–618.
84. For Longfellow, see Mathes, "The Banner Association: Twenty-Five Years in Massachusetts," in *The WNIA: A History*, 155–56, 165; and Valerie Sherer Mathes, *Helen Hunt Jackson and her Indian Reform Legacy* (Austin: University of Texas Press, 1990), 21–37.

Chapter 4

1. Wanken, "Woman's Sphere and Indian Reform," 53.
2. BIC, "Journal of the Fourteenth Annual Conference with Representatives of Missionary Boards and Indian Rights Associations," *Sixteenth Annual Report of the BIC, 1884* (Washington, DC: Government Printing Office, 1885), 54.

3. WNIA, *Annual Report, November 17, 1885* (Philadelphia, 1885), 11–12, 14–16. See *Southern Workman*, March 1885, 26; and "The Women's National Indian Association," *Lend A Hand: A Journal of Organized Philanthropy*, vol. 1, 1886 (Boston: Lend A Hand Publishing Company, 1886), 58–59.
4. See, for example, "National Indian Association. Organization of an Auxiliary in Cincinnati," *Cincinnati Commercial Tribune*, March 9, 1885, 4.
5. Valerie Sherer Mathes, "Baptist Missionary Work at Round Valley, California," *American Baptist Quarterly* (Fall 2010), 172–86; and Mathes, "The Women's National Indian Association Comes to Round Valley," in *Divinely Guided: The California Work of the Women's National Indian Association* (Lubbock: University of Texas Press, 2012), 51–77; see also WNIA, "The Round Valley Mission," *The WNIA Report of Missionary Work, November 1885 to November 1886* (Philadelphia: Royal Printing Company, [1886]) 6–9, 11–23.

   On November 4, Acting Commissioner A. B. Upshaw wrote ASQ that her request for missionaries to Round Valley had been forwarded to Agent Theodore F. Willsey, see Upshaw to ASQ, November 10, 1885, and Upshaw to Willsey, November 10, 1885, Letters Sent (LS), Education Division, vol. 2, LB-pages 177–79, Record Group 75, Bureau of Indian Affairs, National Archives, Washington, DC (hereafter cited as RG 75, BIA, NA).
6. ASQ, *The Mohonk Indian Conference* for her reflections on the meeting. Her personal invitations are in the Quaker Collection, Haverford College, Haverford, Pennsylvania. See also Cathleen D. Cahill, "'Noble Women not a Few:' The Lake Mohonk Conferences," in Mathes, *The WNIA: A History*, 213–39.
7. The wife of William Winslow Crannell, Elizabeth was a nationally known anti-suffragist, organizing and becoming president of the Albany Association Against Woman Suffrage in 1892. She edited the *Anti-Suffragist* from 1908 to 1912. See "Mrs. Crannell's Burial," *New York Times*, November 2, 1936, 21; and Valerie Sherer Mathes, "New York Women and Indian Reform," *New York History* (Winter/Spring 2013), 95–96.
8. Lake Mohonk Conference (hereafter cited as LMC), "Woman's Work for the Indian," *Proceedings of the Third Annual Meeting* (Philadelphia: Sherman & Co., 1886), 46–48.
9. LMC, "A Special Committee," *Proceedings of the Third Annual Meeting*, 72; for this meeting, see WNIA, "Meetings Addressed [by ASQ]," *Annual Report, November 17, 1885*, 16.
10. ASQ was unanimously appointed by the executive board as chair of the Missionary Committee in December 1885, see WNIA, *Report of Mission Work, November 1885 to November 1886*, 5. For attendance see "Helping the Red Man," *North American* (Philadelphia), November 18, 1885, 1; and "Hope for Red Men," *Philadelphia Inquirer*, November 18, 1885. For Fletcher see Joan Mark, *A Stranger in Her Native Land: Alice Fletcher and the American Indians* (Lincoln: University of Nebraska Press, 1988). To reach a wider audience, ASQ wrote "The Women's National Indian Association," *Southern Workman*, December 1885, 122.

11. "To Help the Red Men. Speeches Before the Indian Rights Convention at New-Haven," *New York Times*, November 21, 1885, 1.
12. Henry Ward Beecher, "Sympathy for the Indian. Plymouth Church will Contribute to the Women's Association," *New York Times*, December 19, 1885, 3. His sister, Harriet Beecher Stowe, was a vice president of the Connecticut Indian Association, and his granddaughter, Annie Beecher Scoville, was chair of the WNIA's Home Building and Loan Department.
13. The Niobrara League, a branch of the Woman's Auxiliary to the Board of Missions of the Episcopal Church, was engaged in missionary work among Indians. See "Civilizing the Indian. The Annual Meeting of the Massachusetts Indian Association—an Earnest Address," *Boston Daily Advertiser*, January 22, 1886, 6.
14. WNIA, "Meetings Addressed," *Annual Report, November 1886* (Philadelphia: Royal Printing Company, 1886), 14.
15. ASQ to Atkins, June 17, 1886, Letters Received (LR) #162234–1886, RG 75, BIA, NA. See also Gregory C. Thompson, "John D. C. Atkins, 1885–88," *The Commissioners of Indian Affairs, 1824–1977*, ed. Robert M. Kvasnicka and Herman J. Viola (Lincoln: University of Nebraska Press, 1979), 181–88. During the October 9, 1886, meeting, ASQ reported that the WNIA Round Valley mission had two Sunday schools, two sewing schools, women's meetings, Bible readings, a literary club, and a Saturday evening sociable, see *Minutes of Executive Board Meetings of the WNIA from November 17, 1883 to October 21, 1890*, box 1, folder 3, Collection No. 9237, Division of Rare and Manuscript Collections, Carl A. Kroch Library, Cornell University, Ithaca, NY (hereafter cited as WNIA Papers, Cornell).
16. Foote to Atkins, October 25, 1886, LR #28678–1886; ASQ to Atkins, December 10 and 17, 1886, LR #32860–1886, and LR #33553–1886; and Acting Interior Secretary to Atkins, December 23, 1886, LR #14459–1886, all in #14459–1886; for her thanks see ASQ to Atkins, January 23, 1887, LR #2319–1887, all in RG 75, BIA, NA.
17. "Friends of the Indians. Work of the Lake Mohonk Indian Conference," *New York Times*, October 14, 1886, 4; and "Rights of the Red Man. Friends of the Indian Agitate for His Immediate Relief," *New York Herald*, October 14, 1886, 4. See also "The Fourth Mohonk Conference," *Lend a Hand*, November 1886, 672–81, ASQ on 673.
18. BIC, "Proceedings of the Mohonk Lake Conference," *Eighteenth Annual Report, 1886* (Washington, DC: Government Printing Office, 1887), 88–90. For more on home building see W. Roger Buffalohead and Paulette Fairbanks Molin, "A Nucleus of Civilization"; "American Indian Families at Hampton Institute in the Late Nineteenth Century," *Journal of American Indian Education* 35, no. 3 (Spring 1996): 59–94.
19. "Friends of the Red Men. Work of the Woman's [*sic*] National Indian Association," *New York Times*, November 19, 1886, 3.
20. See WNIA, "Meetings Addressed," *Annual Report, November, 1886*, 14–15. The prior year she also spoke at Homer, see the *Homer Republican*, February 5, 1885, which described a well-filled church as she addressed the object and work of the WNIA.
21. From January 1 to May 24, 1886, her clerical assistant sent out 2,380 letters, mostly Hektograph letters (copies from a prepared gelatin surface, much like a ditto master)

with petition forms, and 1,742 parcels of association literature, see "36th Meeting," *Minutes of Executive Board Meetings of the WNIA from November 17, 1883 to October 21, 1890*, 88, box 1, folder 3, WNIA Papers, Cornell.

22. For 1886 see WNIA, "Our Association's Chronology: Number Thirteen," *Indian's Friend*, March 1898, 2; for their arrival, see "Round Valley Agency," *Annual Report of the CIA to the SI for the Year 1886* (Washington, DC: Government Printing Office, 1886), 47. Also "The Women's National Indian Association," *Southern Workman* (March 1886), 31.
23. ASQ, *Indians and Their Helpers* (Philadelphia, 1886), 8, reprinted in *The Woman's Magazine.*
24. Welsh to ASQ, June 2, 1886, The Indian Rights Association Papers, 1864–1973, reel 68, series 1-A, Incoming Correspondence, 1864–1968, microfilm edition (hereafter cited as IRA Papers); and Welsh to ASQ, May 4, 1888, reel 69, IRA Papers.
25. BIC, "Remarks of Mrs. A. T. [*sic*] Quinton," in "Journal of the Sixteenth Annual Conference with Representatives of Missionary Boards and Indian Rights Associations," *Eighteenth Annual Report, 1886*, 114–15.
26. They did so "to provide and secure for Indians the facilities for and benefits of industrial training, self-support, education, civilization, citizenship and Christianization," WNIA, *Annual Report, 1887*, 7; see also *Minutes of the Trustees of the WNIA, March 11, 1887-November 22, 1893*, box 1, folder 2, WNIA Papers, Cornell.
27. "A Card: From the Women's Indian Association" [West Virginia branch], *Wheeling Register*, October 14, 1887, 4, reported that with the cooperation of the local press, the West Virginia Indian Association would publish facts showing that "our American Indians are capable of being made intelligent, self-support and law abiding citizens."
28. Initially she filled Dickinson's unexpired term, see WNIA, "Our Association's Chronology: Number Fourteen," *Indian's Friend*, April 1898, 2. For his death on November 8, 1887, see WNIA, *Annual Report, 1887*, 24, for presidency, see "Church Gleanings," *Christian Union*, October 27, 1887, 441.
29. For the text see "General Allotment Act (Dawes Act), in Prucha, *Documents of United States Indian Policy*, 171–74.
30. See Francis Paul Prucha, *American Indian Policy in Crisis: Christian Reformers and the Indians, 1865–1900* (Norman: University of Oklahoma Press, 1976), 227–64 for discussion on the legislation. See also Prucha, *The Great Father: The United States Government and the American Indians*, vol. 2 (Lincoln: University of Nebraska Press, 1984), 659–861. For a contemporary discussion see "The Severalty Indian Act," and "The 'Land in Severalty' Law," in *The Gospel in All Lands*, ed. Eugene R. Smith (New York: Missionary Society of the Methodist Episcopal Church, December, 1887), 531–35.
31. For Gates and the IRA, Prucha, *American Indian Policy in Crisis*, 227, 257; and for ASQ, see WNIA, *Address of the President on Current Indian Legislation, Work Needed, Etc., November 30, 1887* (Philadelphia: Royal Printing Company [1887]), 7–8. For ASQ comment about Dawes, see ASQ, "Care of the Indian," 387. ASQ worked closely with Welsh to promote this legislation, see ASQ to Welsh, April 28, 1886, reel 1, IRA Papers.

32. BIC, "Proceedings of the Fifth Annual Meeting of the Lake Mohonk Conference," *Nineteenth Annual Report, 1887* (Washington, DC: Government Printing Office, 1888), 49, 50. And, see for example, "To Uplift the Red Men. Miss Alice Longfellow of Cambridge is President of the Massachusetts Indian Association," *Boston Daily Globe*, August 3, 1902, 33.
33. BIC, "Proceedings of the Fifth Annual Meeting of the Lake Mohonk Conference," 78–79. Other WNIA members expanding on the association's work included Mrs. Osia Jane Joslyn Hiles, Kinney, Mary Dewey, Elizabeth Crannell, and Mrs. G. W. Owen, member of the WNIA press committee and president of the Ypsilanti Indian Association. For their addresses, see 79–82; and 104–5 for Hiles.
34. "Mrs. Quinton's Address on the Indians," *Brooklyn Eagle*, January 8, 1888, 14.
35. WNIA, *Annual Report, 1887*, 14 for her October addresses; reprinted as ASQ, *Address of the President on Current Indian Legislation*, quotes 7, 9; see also "Woman's National Indian Association," *Brooklyn Eagle*, November 30, 1887, 6; and "To Assist the Indian," *New York Times*, December 1, 1887, 4.
36. WNIA, "Our Association's Chronology. Number Fourteen," *Indian's Friend*, April 1898, 2.
37. WNIA, "Our Association's Chronology: Number Fourteen," 2, for Dawes; and BIC, "Journal of the Seventeenth Annual Conference, with Representatives of Missionary Boards and Indian Rights Associations, *Nineteenth Annual Report, 1887*, 129.
38. Lori Jacobson, "Shall We Have a Periodical?" in Mathes, *The WNIA: A History*, 46–61, 50–51. See also NIA, "The Indian's Friend and its Three-Fold Mission," *Indian's Friend*, October 1909, 7.

    Daniel F. Littlefield Jr. and James W. Parins, *American Indian and Alaska Native Newspapers and Periodicals, 1826–1924* (Greenwood Press, 1984), 242–45, lists her dates as editor from 1888–1889 with Helen R. Foote; from 1889–1892 with C. M. Rockwell, taking over again with Rockwell from 1893–94; and sole editor from 1896 to 1902.
39. ASQ, "The Work and Objects of the Woman's National Indian Association," *Report of the International Council of Women, Assembled by the National Woman Suffrage Association, March 25 to April 1, 1888* (Washington, DC: Rufus H. Darby, 1888), 100–101.

    There was a controversy in 1888 when the WNIA Board accepted an invitation to join the National Council of Women. Opposition came from the MIA, which feared that membership would diminish their resources, and from Cranell, who feared the Council would promote prohibition and suffrage. To avoid dissention, the Board retracted their membership. See WNIA, "An Open Letter," *Indian's Friend*, December 1888, 5–6; and WNIA, "The Annual Convention," *Indian's Friend*, November 1888, 3.
40. ASQ to Welsh, May 16, 1888, reel 3, IRA Papers.
41. WNIA, "Historical," *Indian's Friend*, October 1888, 4; and Thomas A. Askew, "The 1888 London Centenary Missions Conference: Ecumenical Disappointment or American Missions Coming of Age?" *International Bulletin of Missionary Research*, July 1994, 113–18. He wrote that the conference "elevated British respect for the Americans present"; and LMC, *Proceedings of the Sixth Annual Meeting* (LMC, 1888), 21.

42. For Civil Service, see BIC, "Remarks of Mrs. A. T. [*sic*] Quinton," in "Journal of the Sixteenth Annual Conference with Representatives of Missionary Boards and Indian Rights Associations," 115. Her address was reprinted as ASQ, "The Annual Address of the President, Mrs. A. S. Quinton," (Philadelphia: Publications of the WNIA, 1888).
43. LMC, *Proceedings of the Ninth Annual Meeting*, 1891 (LMC, 1891), 77–78.
44. "Lo! The Poor Indian. Enthusiastic Ladies Working in His Behalf," *Philadelphia Inquirer*, November 8, 1888, 2. See also WNIA, "The Annual Convention," *Indian's Friend*, November 1888, 1, 3.
45. "Work for Christian Women. The Moral and Physical Improvement of the Indian," *New York Times*, November 28, 1888, 6. On April 13, 1891, Harrison would extend Civil Service rules to some Indian Service positions. Agents were not included until Roosevelt's administration. See IRA, "The Extension of the Civil Service Reform Rules to the Indian Service," *The Ninth Annual Report of the Executive Committee of the IRA* (Philadelphia: Office of the IRA, 1892), 4–9.
46. BIC, "Journal of the Eighteenth Annual Conference with Representatives of Missionary Boards and Indian Rights Associations," *Twentieth Annual Report, 1888* (Washington, DC: Government Printing Office, 1889), 108, 119, and ASQ to Welsh, February 15, 1890, reel 5, IRA Papers, informing him the Kiowa mission just opened.
47. See "Meeting Addressed by Mrs. Quinton," *Annual Report, November, 1889* (Philadelphia: Press of J. A. Wilbour, 1889), 21–22; and "International Department. The Sixth Annual Meeting of the International Missionary Union," *The Missionary Review of the World, April 1889 to December 1890* (Cleveland: Charles W. Wason Collection, 1919), 695.
48. ASQ to Welsh, December 8, 1889, reel 5, IRA Papers. Francis Paul Prucha, in "Thomas Jefferson Morgan, 1889–93," *The Commissioners of Indian Affairs*, 196–97, writes that Morgan was developing a systematized co-educational universal national educational system to accommodate all Indian children. See also "The Red Man's Friends. Annual Meeting of the Massachusetts Indian Association," *Boston Daily Journal*, November 6, 1889, 1.
49. ASQ, "The Annual Address, November 20th, 1889," in *What It Has Done, What It Ought to Do* (Philadelphia, 1889), 6, 8–9. See also, WNIA, "The Annual Convention," *Indian's Friend*, December 1889, 1, 3–4, and "The Indian Association. Its Annual Meeting in Newark Yesterday," *New York Times*, November 21, 1889, 2.
50. Lori Jacobson, "Environed by Civilization' WNIA Home-Building and Loan Department," in Mathes, *The WNIA: A History*, 71.
51. BIC, "Journal of the Nineteenth Annual Conference with Representatives of Missionary Boards and Indian Rights Associations," *Twenty-First Annual Report, 1889* (Washington: Government Printing Office, 1890) 132, 143–44 for ASQ.
52. WNIA, "Meetings Addressed by Mrs. Quinton," *Annual Report, November 1890* (Philadelphia: J. A. Wilbour, 1890), 16.
53. ASQ, *The Ute Question* (Philadelphia: WNIA, [1890]). To Welsh on March 16, 1890, reel 5, IRA Papers, she described the case as "so flagrant" that "it would be infamous to remove them." She was sending anti-removal literature to members

and auxiliaries to disseminate, and also supporting Morgan's confirmation. See ASQ to Welsh, March 18, and April 1, 1890, reel 5, IRA Papers. On January 28, 1892, reel 8, she remarked to Welsh that the WNIA machinery "was pushing the [Ute] matter through the local press, letters, petitions, etc.," concluding that last year her association had gotten enough votes "we felt quite sure, to spoil the bill, and I hope we can all do the same again."

54. WNIA, "ASQ to Kerr, March 18, 1890," *Indian's Friend*, April 1890, 3.
55. ASQ, "A Proposed Criminal Extravagance," *Indian's Friend*, April 1890, 2.
56. BIC, "Journal of the Eighteenth Annual Conference with Representatives of Missionary Boards and Indian Rights Associations," 111–14, 126. For opposition see IRA, "Mr. Painter's Work," *The Fourth Annual Report of the Executive Committee of the IRA* (Philadelphia: Office of the IRA, 1887), 14.

    Childs had conferred with the Indians and the local citizenry, crisscrossed the reservation, escorted some Utes to examine their new home, and negotiated treaty modifications with the three Southern Ute Bands, the Mauches, Capotes, and Weeminuches. See "Journal of the Southern Ute Commission, by T. S. Childs, Secretary," *The Executive Documents of the Senate of the United States*, vol. 2 (Washington, DC: Government Printing Office, 1889), 1–83.
57. ASQ to Welsh, February 21, 1892, reel 8, IRA Papers; Hagan, *The IRA*, 129–30; and Mathes, *Charles C. Painter*, 136–45. WNIA, "Our Association's Chronology. Number Seventeen," *Indian's Friend*, July 1898, 10, reported that during 1892 the WNIA's legislative work carried out by Myra H. Avery and the Committee of Legislative Work was largely on behalf of the Colorado Utes.
58. "Women's Home Mission Meeting," *New York Times*, May 9, 1890, 3. See WNIA, *Annual Report of the WNIA, 1890*, 17.
59. LMC, *Proceedings of the Eighth Annual Meeting, 1890* (Published by the LMC, 1890), 7, 35, 98–101, 112. See also "The Mohonk Conference. The Platform of the Conference for 1890," *Boston Evening Journal*, October 11, 1890, 6.
60. "Woman's National Indian Association," *Philadelphia Inquirer*, November 20, 1890, 1; "Help for the Red Man. The Woman's National Indian Association Meets," *Boston Daily Advertiser*, November 20, 1890, 8; WNIA, *Annual Report, November 1890*, 23–24; and WNIA, "The Annual Convention," *Indian's Friend*, December 1890, 1–3.
61. "Friends of the Indian. The Annual Meeting of the New York Association," *New York Times*, November 25, 1890, 8.
62. WNIA, "Meetings Addressed, by Mrs. Quinton" *Annual Report, November 1891* (Philadelphia: J. A. Wilbour, 1891), 16.
63. ASQ, "The Original Indian Association," *Christian Union*, October 6, 1887, 346.
64. ASQ to Mathew Sniffen, December 4, 1906, reel 19, IRA Papers.

Chapter 5

1. ASQ, "Through Southern California: Letter Number Seven," *Indian's Friend*, October 1891, 1. For this trip see Mathes, *Divinely Guided*, 204–10.

2. ASQ, "Care of the Indian," 374–75.
3. See for example, ASQ, "Law for Indians, and Work for it," *Indian's Friend*, February 1891, 1.
4. Wovoka, a Paiute Indian, fell into a trance, was transported to Heaven, and met God, who directed him to teach the Indian people to live in peace and perform a special dance with the promise of a return of the buffalo and the old way of life. When the Lakotas embraced it, Daniel F. Royer, the inexperienced agent at Pine Ridge, demanded additional troops. When Sitting Bull was killed by Indian police on December 15, frightened Lakota Indians, including Big Foot's band of Miniconjou, fled and were pursued and massacred.

   For a contemporary explanation, see IRA, "The Sioux Outbreak: Its causes and the reforms in Indian management to which it should lead," *The Eighth Annual Report of the Executive Committee of the IRA*, 4–8; see also WNIA "The Threatened Danger," *Indian's Friend*, December 1890, 1; "The Present War," *Indian's Friend*, January 1891, 2; and "From a Pine Ridge Teacher," *Indian's Friend*, March 1891, 3.
5. Eastman, a physician, treated Wounded Knee casualties, meeting future wife Elaine Goodale, who had attended one of the dances, see Elaine Goodale Eastman, "The Ghost Dance War and Wounded Knee Massacre of 1890–91," *Nebraska History* 26 (January 1945): 26–42. For a contemporary account see James Mooney, *The Ghost Dance Religion and the Sioux Outbreak of 1890*, ed. Anthony F. C. Wallace (Chicago: University of Chicago Press, 1965).
6. BIC, "Journal of the Twentieth Annual Conference, with Representatives of Missionary Boards and Indian Rights Association," *Twenty-Second Annual Report, 1890* (Washington, DC: Government Printing Office, 1891), 165.
7. "Woman's Indian Association. Mrs. A. S. Quinton Delivers an Address before the Brooklyn Society," *Brooklyn Eagle*, January 14, 1891, 6.
8. For address, see "The Indian question. Address in Strong Place Baptist Church by Mrs. A. S. Quinton," *Brooklyn Eagle*, February 6, 1891, 1. For her schedule, see WNIA, "Meetings Addressed by Mrs. Quinton," *Annual Report, November 1891* (Philadelphia: J. A. Wilbour, 1891), 16–19.
9. Elizabeth Dustin, "Doings of Women. Mrs. Quintan [*sic*] of the Indian Association," reprinted in the February 22, 1891, *Los Angeles Times*, 14, and *Galveston Daily News*, 11.
10. For her departure, see *Indian's Friend*, March 1891, 2. No mention of a companion was made in this notice, but throughout her reports of the trip she used "we," leading this reader to conclude that someone was traveling with her.
11. WNIA members first read about the Seminoles in WNIA, "The Story of the Florida Seminoles," *Indian's Friend*, November 1889, 3. The December issue followed with "A Plea for the Seminoles of Florida," 2. See also WNIA, "The Seminole Mission," *Report of the Missionary Department of the WNIA, November 1890* [Philadelphia, 1890], 14–16; and Wanken, "The Seminole Mission," in "Woman's Sphere and Indian Reform," 277–99.

12. ASQ to Welsh, February 15, 1890, reel 5, IRA Papers, noted that Thompson was now a WNIA "coworker & helper" for their Seminole work. See ASQ to Welsh, February 19, 1890, for quote and notice of the published letter, WNIA, "A Sprightly Florida Letters," signed by L. J. T., *Indian's Friend*, February 1890, 3–4. In ASQ to Welsh, February 20, 1891, reel 7, she remarked that since the Seminoles "hated & feared" the government, she was fearful that their new agent "may make them confound *us* with *Gov't*."
13. Wanken, "Woman's Sphere and Indian Reform," 282–83, wrote that "only a confirmed optimist could find joy in sleeping on an oilcloth with insects buzzing overhead," leaving her to view ASQ and the WNIA as interested in "evoking sympathy for their cause" rather than presenting the facts.
14. ASQ, "A Visit to the Seminoles," April 1891, 1; and for a later report, see WNIA, "The Seminole Mission," in the December issue, 14.
15. For branch work, see WNIA, "Meetings Addressed by Mrs. Quinton," *Annual Report, November 1891*, 17; and WNIA, "The Seminole Mission," *Indian's Friend*, July 1891, 2, for Brecht's letter. The October 1891 issue, 6, reported that a store had opened.
16. ASQ to Morgan, August 10, 1891, LR #30120–1891; and ASQ to Morgan, January 25, 1892, LR #3170–1892, in RG 75, BIA, NA.
17. ASQ, "A Visit to the Apache Prisoners," *Indian's Friend*, May 1891, 1. See also WNIA, "The Massachusetts Mission for the Apache Prisoners in Alabama," *Sketches of Delightful Work* (Philadelphia: WNIA, 1893), 60–62, and Rose Stremlau, "WNIA Missions in the South," 111–13, 15, 117–18; and Mathes, "The Banner Association: Twenty- Five Years in Massachusetts," 159–60, both in Mathes, *The WNIA: A History*.
18. ASQ, "Prisoners Still," August 1890, 2; and ASQ, "A Visit to the Apache Prisoners," May 1891, 1. See also "Justice to the Apaches," *Indian's Friend*, April 1890, 3; and "The disposition of the Apaches," *Indian's Friend*, October 1890, 2.
19. ASQ, "A Visit to the Apache Prisoners," 1. Stremlau in "WNIA Missions in the South," wrote that the missionary work at Mt. Vernon led to "an extreme makeover of the controversial warrior [Geronimo]" at least in WNIA literature (111). In a letter to the *New York Post*, reprinted in *Indian's Friend*, August 1889, 3, General Samuel C. Armstrong shared letters from Marion Stephens of Hampton Institute and Vincentine Tilyon Booth of Carlisle Indian School, portraying Geronimo as the first in Sunday school, ringing the bell, seating students, and keeping order. When Booth resigned, the MIA replaced her with Alabama native Sophie Shepard.
20. ASQ, "From Texas to Arizona: Letter Number Three," *Indian's Friend*, June 1891, 1–2.
21. ASQ, "En route and in Arizona: Letter Number Four," *Indian's Friend*, July 1891, 1.
22. ASQ, "En route and in Arizona: Letter Number Four," 2–3.
23. Drastic measures had been undertaken to gather students after Superintendent Ralph P. Collins had learned that the village of Oraibi refused to send any students to the school. Learning from Morgan that each village had a quota, Collins, with the support of a special agent and Thomas V. Keam, the trader, arrested opposition leaders, calling on troops to fill the school. See Collins, August 27, 1891, in "Report

of Moqui (Hopi) School, Keam's Cañon, Ariz.," *Sixtieth Annual Report of the CIA to the SI, 1891* (Washington, DC: Government Printing Office, 1891), 552. (Hereafter, Keams Canyon appears as Keam's only when quoting previously published material.)

24. ASQ, "Arizona Tarrying. Letter Number Five," *Indian's Friend*, September 1891, 1.

    The Keams Canyon Indian School for Hopi children opened in late 1887 under James Gallaher, a special disbursing agent, see his September 5 report in "Reports of Indian Schools," *Annual Report of the CIA to the SI for the Year 1887* (Washington, DC: Government Printing Office, 1887), 235. The March 2, 1889, Indian appropriations bill included $10,000 for the purchase of the buildings and other improvement, and on July 13, 1889, Thomas Keam quit claimed the tract known as Keams Canyon to the government. See "Keam's Cañon, Arizona," in "Indian School Sites," *Sixty-First Annual Report of the CIA to the SI, 1892* (Washington: Government Printing Office, 1892), 897. In the sixty-first report, Superintendent, Collins, in "Reports of Superintendents of Schools," 652–53, noted an enrollment of 115.

25. ASQ, "To See the Apaches. Letter Number Six," *Indian's Friend*, September 1891, 2.
26. ASQ to Welsh, June 10, 1891, reel 7, IRA Papers
27. ASQ, "To See the Apaches," 2,
28. ASQ to Morgan, June 17, 1891, LR #22577–1891, RG 75, BIA, NA. Lawrence was the site of Haskell Indian School, founded in 1884, which unlike other off-reservation boarding schools, offered training beyond the usual eight-year program. The Grand Junction Indian School or the Teller Institute, named after Colorado Senator Henry Teller, was open from 1886–1911 when it became a home for the disabled.
29. ASQ, "To See the Apaches," 3. In ASQ to Morgan, June 20, 1891, LR #22739–1891, RG 75, BIA, NA, she noted her arrival in Tucson at 4 A.M.
30. ASQ, "Through Southern California: Letter Number Seven," 1.
31. The first telegram from Yuma was undated, LR #22251–1891. In the second, dated June 24, she noted mailing the deed that day, LR #22511–1891, in RG 75, BIA, NA.
32. WNIA, "The Cohuilla (Cahuilla) Indians," *Indian's Friend*, October 1888, 4. Although not associated with any of the Franciscan missions, they were grouped together with a number of Southern California tribes under the designation of Mission Indian. See George Harwood Phillips, *Chiefs and Challengers: Indian Resistance and Cooperation in Southern California, 1769–1906* (Norman: University of Oklahoma Press, 2014), 17–20.
33. ASQ to Oberly, February 18, 1889, LR #4927–1889, RG 75, BIA, NA, and Oberly to ASQ, February 28, 1889, LS: Education Division, vol. 6, LB, pg. 32–33, RG 75, BIA, NA. See Floyd A. O'Neil, "John H. Oberly, 1888–89," *The Commissioners of Indian Affairs*, 189–91.
34. ASQ to Oberly, March 1, 1889, LR #5839–1889 enclosed in LR #19602–1889 [Special Case (SC) 143]; and ASQ to Oberly, April 12, 1889, LR #9615–1889, RG 75, BIA, NA. Interior Secretary John W. Noble on March 20 had written Oberly accepting his recommendation to grant the WNIA five acres of reservation land, [LR #19602–1889].

    For Preston see Valerie Sherer Mathes and Phil Brigandi, *Reservations, Removal, and Reform: The Mission Indian Agents of Southern California 1878–1903* (Norman: University of Oklahoma Press, 2018), 85–97.

35. ASQ to WHW, June 4, 1889, box 7, Papers of William Henry Weinland, Huntington Library, Art Museum, and Botanical Gardens, San Marino, CA (hereafter cited as WHW Papers).
36. Edmund de Schweinitz Brunner, "History of the Moravian Mission to the Indians of Southern California," *Proceedings of the Society for Propagating the Gospel Among the Heathen as a Survey of the first Twenty-five Years of the Mission* (Bethlehem, PA: Times Publishing, 1923), 9, writes that Quinton was "well acquainted with the Moravian Church and believed that our liturgical forms fitted us in a peculiar manner for work among these Indians who had never known anything except the elaborate ritual of the Roman Church [Catholic]."
37. "The Moravian Mission in Alaska," *New York Times*, November 29, 1885, 5; for arrival see WHW, "Ramona Mission Diary, 1889–1899," and WHW, "Report of Ramona Mission for Decade 1889–1899," boxes 15 and 18, WHW Papers; "Our New Remona [*sic*] Mission," June 1889, 2, and "A Letter From Our New Ramona Mission," July 1889, 1, *Indian's Friend*. See also Brunner, "A History of the Moravian Mission to the Indians of Southern California," *Proceedings of the Society for Propagating the Gospel Among the Heathen: For the Year Ending August 19, 1914* (Bethlehem: Published by the Society, 1914), 63–89; WNIA, *The Ramona Mission and the Mission Indians* (Philadelphia: May 1889); Mathes, "The WNIA Carries on Helen Hunt Jackson's Legacy," in Mathes, *Divinely Guided*, 177–203; and Wanken, "Woman's Sphere and Indian Reform," 305–8, 311, 319.
38. ASQ to WHW, June 4 and 26, 1889, box 7, WHW Papers.
39. Jackson to ASQ, January 31, 1883; July 18, 1883, for Brunson & Wells, and December 7, 1883, for her Indian story. On August 19, 1881, Jackson had written that she was "greatly disheartened by the entire failure" of her *A Century of Dishonor*, all in BANC MSS 99/279 cz, Bancroft Library, University of California, Berkeley.

    See "Report on the Condition and Needs of the Mission Indians of California, Made by Special Agents Helen Jackson and Abbot Kinney, to the Commissioner of Indian Affairs," in *A Century of Dishonor*, 458–514. For more on Brunson and Wells and Jackson as official agent see Mathes, *Helen Hunt Jackson and Her Indian Reform Legacy*, 55–75.
40. Jackson to ASQ, April 2, 1884, MA 4571, Pierpont Morgan Library, New York, New York, reprinted in Mathes, *The Indian Reform Letters of Helen Hunt Jackson*, 319, and Valerie Sherer Mathes, "Helen Hunt Jackson and Southern California's Mission Indians," *California History* 78, no. 4 (Winter 1999/2000), 271.
41. For more on Painter, see Valerie Sherer Mathes and Phil Brigandi, "Charles C. Painter, Helen Hunt Jackson and the Mission Indians of Southern California," *Journal of San Diego History* (Summer 2009), 89–118. For example, see Osia J. Hiles, "The Mission Indians," *Indian's Friend*, November 1888, 4, and articles written by an Eina (unknown) from March through June issues, 1889.
42. ASQ to WHW, July [?] 1889, box 7, WHW Papers.
43. See WHW, "Report of Ramona Mission for Decade 1889–1899," 1, and WHW, "Ramona Mission. 1889," 12, box 15, WHW Papers. Mary Watkins, the government

schoolteacher at the Indian village of Mesa Grande, on March 7, 1900, wrote reformer Constance Goddard DuBois, that "Mr. Wineland [Weinland] who is a Moravian missionary hates Catholics with a bitterness that poisons his own better judgment," box 1, folder 6, #9167, Constance Goddard DuBois Papers, Division of Rare and Manuscript Collections, Carl A. Kroch Library, Cornell University, Ithaca, NY.

44. ASQ to WHW, July [?] 1889, box 7, WHW Papers.

45. Morgan to Quinton, July 27, 1889, LS: Land Division, vol. 94, LB 187, 363–64; copy in box 8, WHW Papers. Four days earlier on July 23, ASQ had suggested to WHW that if the Soboba Indians "cordially consent you *might* perhaps built a cottage there & take the rest of our getting the government permission later," box 7, WHW Papers.

46. ASQ to Welsh, July 5, 1889, reel 4, IRA Papers. Ward, the son of former Mission Agent John S. Ward, struggled to get government reimbursement for his work, see Ward to Atkins, June 10, 1886, LR #15947–1886, RG 75, BIA, NA. Instead he turned to the IRA for financial support. See also Mathes and Brigandi, *Reservations, Removal, and Reform*, 79, 82, 94.

47. For lawsuit, see Mathes and Brigandi, *Reservations, Removal, and Reform*, 58, 76–77, 79, 93–94; and Van H. Garner, "Soboba," in *The Broken Ring: The Destruction of the California Indians* (Tucson: Westernlore Press, 1982), 75–95.

48. ASQ to WHW, July 29, 1889; see also December 20, 1889, in box 7, WHW Papers. For Soboba work see Mathes, *Divinely Guided*, 191, 193–94, 196, 198–202, 210, 224, 230, 239, 246, and Mathes, "The WNIA at Cahuilla, El Potrero, and Saboba," in *Helen Hunt Jackson and Her Indian Reform Legacy*, 119–39.

49. WHW, "Ramona Mission. 1889," 13, box 15, WHW Papers; and Brunner, "History of the Moravian Mission to the Indians of Southern California" (1923 edition), 12–14, 18–19. Morris began teaching at the Potrero village in 1888. In 1889 the Indians built her a comfortable schoolhouse with living quarters where she remained until her 1899 marriage to Marshall French Gilman. See "A Retrospection," Gilman Family Papers, boxes 24–26, WHW Papers.

50. WNIA, *Report of Missionary Work, November 1889* (Philadelphia: Wilbour, 1889) 12, 14–16, for letters from the Weinlands, see 8–13, 16–19. See also WNIA, "From the Ramona Mission," *Indian's Friend*, January 1890, 2, for his work at Potrero.

51. ASQ to WHW, January 17, and February 5, 1890, box 7, WHW Papers. In an undated letter, identified by address and receipt of his Feb. 26 letter, she told him to spend the entire $500 on the chapel; "we certainly want a comfortable and nice looking little chapel where your home is and the headquarters are." In a second letter marked "dictated," she wrote "to go straight on and build" the chapel, both in box 7.

52. For their move see WNIA, "From the Ramona Mission," *Indian's Friend*, March 1890, 1 and "Mrs. Weinland's Letter," *Indian's Friend*, March 1890, 3; for cottage see "Association News," "Pittsburg and Allegheny Honors," *Indian's Friend*, January 1890, 1; and "Our New California Chapel," *Indian's Friend*, May 1890, 3.

53. ASQ to WHW, February 5, and May 23, 1890, box 7, WHW Papers.

54. See WNIA, "The Saboba Station," *Report of the Missionary Department of the WNIA, November 1890*, 12, and WNIA, "The New York City Mission," *The Report of the*

Missionary Department, November 1891 (Philadelphia: Wilbour, n.d.), 7–8. See also WNIA, "Association News and Notes," September 1890, 3, and October 1890, 1, *Indian's Friend* for letters from Fowler. In late October, WHW visited her, writing ASQ she was "doing a great good," see "Association News and Notes," 3, in November 1890 issue. On October 25, 1890, ASQ responded to WHW: "Am so glad to hear so well of Mrs. Fowler. God bless your all & your fields," in WHW Papers, Box 7. For more on Fowler, see Mathes, *Helen Hunt Jackson and Her Indian Reform Legacy*, 48–50, 58–59, 68–69, 71, 78, 90, 123; Mathes, *Divinely Guided*, 178, 189, 200–203; and *Call for Reform*, 23, 29, 37, 44, 46, 126–27, 149, 154–55, 157–60, 177.

55. For Jordan, see "Three Pennsylvania Women," in *A Call for Reform: The Southern California Indian Writings of Helen Hunt Jackson*, ed. Valerie Sherer Mathes and Phil Brigandi (Norman: University of Oklahoma Press, 2015), 149–50; and "Death Calls Mrs. Jordan, *San Jacinto Register*, March 11, 1909.
56. Mrs. Frank H. Fowler, "The San Jacinto Valley," in Elmer W. Holmes, *History of Riverside County, California* (Los Angeles: Historic Record Company, 1912), 242, described this meeting based on the historical sketch provided by her mother-in-law, Mary Sheriff Fowler that she included in her article on pages 235–44. See also "Mrs. Mary Fowler is Called Home," *Hemet News*, September 30, 1921, 1.
57. Stockman to Morgan, August 2, 1890, LR #24390–1890, SC 143, RG 75, BIA, NA; and ASQ to WHW, September 5, 16, and December 9, 1890, box 7, WHW Papers.

    Stockman, pastor at St. Bernardine (the oldest parish in the Diocese) founded St. Francis De Sales in Riverside as a mission to St. Bernardine.
58. WNIA, "The New York City Mission," *The Report of the Missionary Department, November 1891*, 7–8.
59. U.S. Department of the Interior, Office of Indian Affairs, "Field Matrons," *Annual Report of the Commissioner, 1892* (Washington, DC: Government Printing Office, 1892), 101; Lisa E. Emmerich, "To Respect and Love and Seek the Ways of White Women: Field Matrons, the Office of Indian Affairs, and Civilization Policy, 1890–1938" (PhD diss., University of Maryland, College Park, 1987).
60. ASQ to Patterson, June 26, 1891, LR #23501–1891, RG 75, BIA, NA. The second quote is from a memorandum, probably written by Morgan, included with her letter. Belt, an attorney and government employee, often served as assistant Indian commissioner. The May 1897 issue of *Indian's Friend* reported he was a resident of Maryland and had been employed in the Indian service for thirty years; five of his letter books (1885–98) are in the Western History Collection of the University of Oklahoma.
61. ASQ to Morgan, September 1, 1891, LR #40821–1891, RG 75, BIA, NA.
62. WNIA, "Field Matrons," *Indian's Friend*, December 1892, 2; and Helen M. Bannan, "True Womanhood on the Reservation: Field Matrons in the United States Indian Service," *Southwest Institute for Research on Women*, Working Paper No. 18 (Women's Studies, University of Tucson: 1984), 1–25.
63. For Rust's tenure, see Mathes and Brigandi, *Reservations, Removal, and Reform*, 98–132.

64. ASQ, "Though Southern California. Letter Number Seven," *Indian's Friend*, October 1891, 1.
65. ASQ, "Though Southern California. Letter Number Seven," 1.
66. Phil Brigandi and John W. Robinson, "The Killing of Juan Diego: From Murder to Mythology," *Journal of San Diego History* 40, nos. 1–2 (Winter/Spring 1994): 1–22; and Phil Brigandi, "Debating the existence of a 'Real' Ramona," *Valley Chronicle* (Hemet, CA), February 9, 2002.
67. ASQ to Morgan, June 28, and August 4, 1891, LR #24191–1891, and LR #29440–1891, RG 75, BIA, NA. For WHW as overseer see ASQ to WHW, August 4, 1891, box 7, WHW Papers. WHW in "From a Missionary Report," *Indian's Friend*, July 1892, 45, reported that during August and September of 1891 he had traveled by horseback to Cahuilla to start the cottage. See also, Mathes, "WNIA Missionary work Among the Cahuillas and at Martinez," in *Divinely Guided*, 191–92, 204–30.
68. ASQ to Morgan, September 1, 1891, LR #40821–1891, RG 75, BIA, NA.
69. ASQ, "Though Southern California. Letter Number Seven," 6. Babbitt, the wife of Henry W. Babbitt, a clerk in the Interior Department, had begun her teaching career at the Omaha and Winnebago Agency in Nebraska in 1884.
70. Born in Ireland, Downey came to California in 1849, opened a drugstore in Los Angeles and engaged in ranching and real estate, establishing the town of Downey and co-founding the Farmers and Merchants Bank. The seventh state governor, he was a founder of the University of Southern California and of the Historical Society of Southern California. See H. Brett Melendy and Benjamin F. Gilbert, *The Governors of California: Peter H. Burnett to Edmund G. Brown* (Georgetown, CA: Talisman, 1965), 100–113.
71. Mission Indian Agent Samuel S. Lawson to [Roland E.] Trowbridge, August 17, 1880, *Annual Report of the CIA to the SI, 1880* (Washington, DC: Government Printing Office, 1880), 12, noted he had received a copy of this order and that Downey had informed him of his intent to sell. For Lawson's tenure see Mathes and Brigandi, *Reservations, Removal, and Reform*, 29–52.
72. ASQ, "Though Southern California. Letter Number Seven," 6.
73. ASQ, "Though Southern California. Letter Number Seven," 6; for rebuilding see WNIA, "Association News and Notes," *Indian's Friend*, July 1892, 45. In September 1894 Platt was murdered; see for example, "It Was Murder: The Indians Undoubtedly Killed Mrs. Platt," *Los Angeles Times*, September 24, 1895, 4.
74. Mathes and Brigandi, *Reservations, Removal, and Reform*, 11, 13.
75. ASQ, "Though Southern California. Letter Number Seven," 6.
76. At Mohonk, Joseph B. Moore, who served with Smiley and Painter on the 1891 California Mission Indian Commission, noted that Salmons and her mother had bought a small ranch off the Rincon reservation to use the house and its flower gardens and fruit orchard as an "object-lesson" for Indian adults and children. See LMC, "Our Policy Toward the Mission Indians," *Proceedings of the Tenth Annual Meeting, 1892* (LMC, 1892), 115. Salmons had a thirty-seven-year teaching career in government schools, beginning around 1885 at Rincon, and at Pala from 1904 to

1922. See Joel R. Hyer, *"We are Not Savages: Native Americans in Southern California and the Pala Reservation, 1840–1920* (East Lansing: Michigan State University Press, 2001), 151, 154–67, 169–70.

77. ASQ, "Though Southern California. Letter Number Seven," 7. ASQ mistakenly calls this mission Jesuit; all California missions are Franciscan.
78. See Mathes, "The Redlands Indian Association: The WNIA in Southern California," in *The WNIA: A History*, 192–210.
79. On July 12, Quinton, described as "a talented and eloquent speaker," gave an address at the Methodist Tabernacle, see "Pasadena. The Indian Question. Discussed by a Lady Missionary," July 14, 1891, 7; then on July 16, at the end of a WCTU meeting, she addressed the Indian issue and formed an Indian association, see "Pasadena. Lo, the Poor Indian. His Rights, Accomplishments and Advantages," July 18, 1891, 7, both in *Los Angeles Times*.
80. For Potrero under the Moravians, see WHW, "The Indian Mission," February 1, 1893, 72; and WHW, "Report of the Moravian Indian Mission work in Southern California, July 1906," 553; in *The Moravian*, copies in box 18, WHW Papers.
81. WNIA, "Missions Transferred," *Indian's Friend*, May 1890, 2; and ASQ to WHW, May 3, 1890; for traveling missionary see ASQ to WHW, August 7, 1891, both in box 7, WHW Papers.
82. "The Chautauquans," *Los Angeles Times*, July 21, 1891, 6.
83. "Temperance Folks. St. Mary's Total Abstinence Society—Mrs. Amelia S. Quinton's Work," *San Francisco Chronicle*, August 10, 1891, 10. On August 4, ASQ informed WHW that she had found fifty-two letters waiting and had to write two long overdue press articles, box 7, WHW Papers.
84. "Ministers' Meetings," *San Francisco Chronicle*, August 11, 1891, 6.
85. "Women's Indian Association," *Daily Evening Bulletin* (San Francisco), August 12, 1891, 1; and "For the Indians. An Address by Mrs. Amelia S. Quinton. The Northern California Women's Indian Association Organized," *San Francisco Chronicle*, August 12, 1891, 10. See also ASQ, "In Northern California. Letter Number Eight," *Indian's Friend*, November 1891, 9, and Mathes, "Northern California Members and their work at the Hoopa Reservation," in Mathes, *Divinely Guided*, 78–100.
86. WNIA, "Another Dark Region," *Indian's Friend*, January 1890, 1. Spencer also wrote Welsh, who forwarded her letter to Morgan. See Spencer to Welsh, November 10, 1889, and Morgan to Spencer, November 20, 1889, reel 5, IRA Papers. Spencer, who lived in Alameda, was the state superintendent of scientific temperance instruction for the WCTU and author of *A History of the Woman's Christian Temperance Union of Northern and Central California* (Oakland: West Coast Printing, 1911).
87. On February 21, 1891, Walker described those in charge of Hoopa Valley as "godless men, caring for nothing except the money they can pocket," in WNIA, "Concerning Hoopa Valley." See also "Who is Billy Beckwith?" *Indian's Friend*, April 1891, 3.
88. ASQ, "In Northern California. Letter Number Eight," *Indian's Friend*, November 1891, 9.

89. ASQ, "In Northern California. Letter Number Eight," 9, 11. See also WNIA, "Hoopa Valley," and "Another Testimony," in *Indian's Friend*, July 1892, 45; and WNIA, "The California or Hoopa Valley Mission," *Sketches of Delightful Work*, 62–65.
90. ASQ to WHW, August 24, 1891, box 7, WHW Papers.
91. ASQ, "In Northern California. Letter Number Eight, 11; "The Hoopa Indians. A Ladies' Society Discusses Their Condition," *San Francisco Chronicle*, August 29, 1891, 8. WNIA work did not begin until July 1900 when the Presbyterian Board in New York voted to adopt it. See WNIA, "Missions Transferred During 1900," *Report of Missions for 1900–1901* [WNIA, 1901], 2. See also "Now It Is the Indian. The Northern California Women's Indian Association," *San Francisco Call*, August 28, 1891, 8.
92. ASQ, "In Northern California. Letter Number Eight, 11; see Mathes, "The Indian Reform Work of Annie Ellicott Kennedy Bidwell," in *Divinely Guided*, 153–76; Mathes, "Annie E. K. Bidwell: Chico's Benefactress," *California History* (Spring/Summer 1989): 14–25; notes 60–64; and Mathes, "Indian Philanthropy in California: Annie Bidwell and the Mechoopda Indians," *Arizona and the West* (Summer 1983): 153–66.
93. ASQ, "In Northern California. Letter Number Eight, 11; and WNIA, "Another Appeal," November 1889, 2; and "The Digger Indians," May 1890, 1, *Indian's Friend*. See Mathes, "Greenville Indian Industrial School," in *Divinely Guided*, 101–26. There was no Digger tribe. Tourgée, a lawyer, civil rights advocate, magazine founder, editor, and novelist, wrote *Fool's Errand* (1879) about his experiences as a Southern judge during Reconstruction.
94. ASQ to Morgan, April 29, 1890, LR #13351–1890, RG 75, BIA, NA, and Morgan to ASQ, May 3, 1890, LS Education Division, vol. 23, LB 469, RG 75, BIA, NA. Among the eight enclosures with ASQ's letter was a detailed questionnaire about local Indians filled out by Hall at Morgan's request. See also WNIA, "The Digger Indians Mission," February 1891, 3; and WNIA, "The Digger Indians Mission," *Indian's Friend*, March 1891, 1.
95. WNIA, "The Digger Indians," *Report of the Missionary Department of the WNIA, November 1890* (Philadelphia: 1890), 13–14. For Ament, see WNIA, "Association News and Notes," December 1891, 1; and WNIA, "Our Digger Mission," *Indian's Friend*, January 1892, 21.
96. ASQ to Morgan, October 21, 1891, LR #38097–1891, RG 75, BIA, NA.
97. ASQ to Morgan, February 29, 1892, LR #8400–1892, RG 75, BIA, NA. In ASQ to Morgan, August 11, 1892, LR #29371[31921]-1892, RG 75, BIA, NA, she requested $25 per quarter rent for Hall, noting since October 1890 the government had free use. In ASQ to Belt, September 6, 1892, included in LR #33277–1892, RG 75, BIA, NA, she agreed to send the vouchers to Hall.
98. ASQ, "In Northern California. Letter Number Eight," 11; for the first reference to her work, see "Association News and Notes," December 1890, 3; see also WNIA, "A Letter From a New Missionary," *Indian's Friend*, March 1891, 3; and Amelia Martin, "She is Doing what She Can," *Indian's Friend*, July 1891, 4. For more on Hall and Martin see WNIA, "The Digger Mission in California," *Sketches of Delightful Work*, 2–15.

99. ASQ, "In the Northwest. Letter Number Nine," 1.
100. ASQ, "In the Northwest. Letter Number Nine," 1.
101. For text see U.S. Department of the Interior, OIA, "Indian Legislation Passed During the Second Session of the Fifty-First Congress," *Sixtieth Annual Report of the CIA to the SI, 1891* (Washington, DC: Government Printing Office, 1891), 47–48, 612–14; and Mathes and Brigandi, "The California Mission Indian Commission," in *Reservations, Removal, and Reform*, 112–14.
102. LMC, *Proceedings of the Ninth Annual Meeting*, 1891 (LMC, 1891), 24–25. For the commission from Painter's perspective, see Valerie Sherer Mathes, "The California Mission Indian Commission of 1891: The Legacy of Helen Hunt Jackson," *California History* 73, no. 4 (Winter 1993/94): 339–59, notes on 390–95; and from Smiley's perspective, see Larry E. Burgess, "Commission to the Mission Indians: 1891," *San Bernardino County Museum Association Quarterly* 35, no. 1 (Spring 1988): 2–47.
103. In 1890 Foote had been appointed to make a Mission Indian Census, sending her report to be read before that year's conference, see LMC, "Fifth Session," *Proceedings of the Eighth Annual Meeting*, 96–97; and "Journal of the Twentieth Annual Conference, with Representatives of Missionary Boards and Indian Rights Association," *The Executive Documents of the House of Representatives for the Second Session of the Fifty-First Congress, 1890–91* (Washington: Government Printing Office, 1891), 954. For her 1891 presentation, see "The Indian Conference. Encouraging Reports of Work Among the Red Men," *New York Times*, October 8, 1891, 3; and "The Indian Conference. Dr. Gates Chosen President—Papers and Reports Read," *Springfield Republican*, October 8, 1891, 4. ASQ was mentioned in both accounts, advocating for an Indian hospital at Agua Caliente.
104. LMC, *Proceedings of the Ninth Annual Meeting*, 1891, 25–27.
105. LMC, *Proceedings of the Ninth Annual Meeting*, 1891, 84. A graduate of Yale and its divinity school, Whittlesey, served as a Congregational minister, taught at Bowdoin College and later at Howard University, and served on General Oliver O. Howard's staff during the Civil War. He was an assistant commissioner and adjutant of the Freedmen's Bureau and BIC secretary from 1875–1899. See "Eliphalet Whittlesey," *Men of Mark in America: Ideals of American Life Told in Biographies of Eminent Living Americans*, vol. 2, ed. Merrill Edwards Gates (Washington, DC: Men of Mark, 1906), 394–96.
106. *The Constitution of the Cambridge Branch of the Massachusetts Indian Association* (Cambridge, MA: John Ford & Son, 1893), 12.
107. "Old Cambridge," *Cambridge Tribune*, October 31, 1891, 4; see also "Lo, The Poor Indian! Annual Meeting of the Cambridge Branch of the Massachusetts Indian Association," *Boston Journal*, November 3, 1891, 10.
108. "Massachusetts Indian Association," *Boston Evening Journal*, January 23, 1883, 3.
109. "Indians' Champions. Annual Meeting of the Massachusetts Indian Association Reports Effective Work during the Year," *Boston Daily Advertiser*, November 5, 1891, 4; see also "The Indian's Friends. Massachusetts Indian Association Meets," *Boston Journal*, November 5, 1891, 9.

110. WNIA, "Meetings Addressed by Mrs. Quinton," *Annual Report, November 1891*, 19, and WNIA, "Meetings Addressed by Mrs. Quinton," *Annual Report, December 1892* (Lancaster: Examiner Publishing House, 1892), 13. "The Work for the Indian," *Poughkeepsie Daily Eagle*, December 11, 1891, 3, alerted the public to the upcoming meeting on the 14th.
111. ASQ to Morgan, December 18, 1891, LR #44976–1891, RG 75, BIA, NA. In ASQ to Morgan, September 1, 1891, LR #40821–1891, RG 75, BIA, NA, she wrote of two women who could be sent to Agua Caliente, one as field matron, the other, a physician in San Francisco, who could run "the small & inexpensive hospital" she was envisioning. It "would be of inestimable value it seems to me," she concluded.
112. "Mischief Record of 'La Gobernadora.' Former Indian Agent Tells of Devil She Raised," *Los Angeles Times*, May 26, 1902, 9.
113. WNIA, "Our Association's Chronology, Number Seventeen," *Indian's Friend*, July, 1898, 2.

Chapter 6

1. WNIA, "Meetings Addressed by Mrs. Quinton," *Annual Report, December 1892*, 13–14.
2. For details see WNIA, "Our Association's Chronology: Number Seventeen," *Indian's Friend*, July 1898, 10.
3. BIC, "Journal of the Twenty-First Annual Conference of the United States Board of Indian Commissioners with Representatives of Missionary Boards and Indian Rights' Association," in *Twenty-third Annual Report, 1891* (Washington, DC: Government Printing Office, 1892), 131. In his 1887 annual report, Commissioner J. D. C. Atkins had argued for the exclusive use of the English language, see Prucha, *Documents of United States Indian Policy*, 174–76.
4. BIC, "Journal of the Twenty-First Annual Conference," 146–47. The Genoa Indian Industrial School was the fourth nonreservation government school, operating 1884–1934.
5. Caroline H. Dall, "Concerning Women," *Cambridge Tribune*, January 30, 1892, 6. Dall was a prominent women's rights champion, literary scholar, and founder of the American Social Science Association, which aided the poor, unemployed, and mentally ill.
6. ASQ to Welsh, February 15, 1892, reel 8, IRA Papers.
7. For first quote see WNIA, *Our Work—What? How? Why?* (Philadelphia: WNIA Executive Board, January 1893), 25; for the rest, see Wanken, "Woman's Sphere and Indian Reform," 144–46. For example, see WNIA, Miss Kate Foote, *The Indian Legislation of 1888* (Philadelphia: J. F. Dickson, 1888), and Miss Kate Foote, *Indian Legislation-As Far as it Goes* (Philadelphia: WNIA, November 1891).
8. ASQ to Welsh, February 15 and 21, 1892, reel 8, IRA Papers.
9. ASQ to WHW, January 1, 1892. ASQ was dealing with a Mr. Barker who failed to send her the necessary paperwork. She explained to WHW that she refused to expend

any more money until the land was legally hers. See also ASQ to WHW, August 4, 19, and 24, and December 10, 1891, box 7, WHW Papers.

10. ASQ to Morgan, March 21, 1892, LR #10792–1892, RG 75, BIA, NA. In "An Important Work in Good Hands," the May 1892 issue of *Indian's Friend*, 1, praised Morgan, noting he was corresponding secretary of the Providence branch of the Rhode Island IRA.
11. ASQ to Morgan, April 2, 1892, LR #12413–1892, RG 75, BIA, NA. See also, WNIA, "The Seminole Mission in Florida," *Sketches of Delightful Work*, 15–33. At Mohonk she explained that the WNIA had bought 400 acres, selling 80 acres to the government upon which Brecht had "put up buildings and did preparatory work," see BIC, "Proceedings of the Board of Indian Commissioners at the Twelfth Lake Mohonk Indian Conference," *Twenty-Sixth Annual Report, 1894* (Washington, DC: Government Printing Office, 1895), 113. See also, WNIA, "A New Seminole Visit," *Indian's Friend*, May 1894, 7–9; and WNIA, "Our Seminole Mission," *Our Missions, for the Year, 1895* (WNIA Executive Board: December 1895), 18–24.
12. ASQ to Morgan, March 24, 1892, LR #11142–1892; see also ASQ to Morgan, April 22, 1892, LR #15055–1892, RG 75, BIA, NA.
13. ASQ to Morgan, December 21, 1892, LR #45356–1892; Morgan to ASQ, January 4, 1893, [Education] LR #45356–1892; Ament to Morgan, January 21, 1893, LR #3794–1893 all in George Chandler, first Assistant Secretary, to Morgan, February 11, 1893, LR #6101–1893, RG 75, BIA, NA. See also ASQ to Morgan, January 7, 1893, LR #1022–1893, notifying him of her forwarding the letter to Ament.
14. ASQ to Morgan, February 3, 1893, LR #4495–1893, RG 75, BIA, NA. See also WNIA, "The Greenville School and Mission," *Sunshine Work* (Philadelphia: December 1894), 2–7.
15. ASQ to Browning, November 4, 1893, LR #41141–1893; ASQ to Browning, December 8, 1893, LR #45410–1893; and Acting Commissioner to Ament, December 8, 1893, LS: Education Division, vol. 55, LB 214, 389, RG 75, BIA, NA. See also, WNIA, "Ring the Bells," *Indian's Friend*, January 1893, 5.
16. Prucha, *American Indian Policy in Crisis*, 290–91, explains government funding to "contract schools" established by religious groups on Indian reservations.
17. ASQ to Morgan, January 8, 1892, LR #904–1892; and January 30, 1892, LR #3897–1892, RG 75, BIA, NA.
18. ASQ to Morgan, February 29, 1892, LR #8669–1892, RG 75, BIA, NA. In Rust to ASQ, May 5, 1892, he informed her he had received authorization, and a letter from WHW "that the Indians were ready to sign the articles." He had written Babbitt to inform the village captain that they had his consent and approval, box 6, WHW Papers.
19. Rust to ASQ, March 22, 1892, and Rust to Morgan, May 6, 1892, WHW Papers, Box 6. According to his letter, ASQ had written him on March 8. See also Rust to ASQ, May 5, 1892, box 6, WHW Papers.
20. ASQ to WHW, April 4, 1892, box 7, WHW Papers.
21. This number was repeated in WNIA, "Association News and Notes," *Indian's Friend*, June 1892, 2. They collected $60.

22. ASQ to WHW, April 11, 1892, box 7, WHW Papers.
23. ASQ to WHW, April 21, 1892, box 7, WHW Papers.
24. ASQ to WHW, May 16, and 22, 1892, box 7, WHW Papers.
25. ASQ to Rust, May 23, 1892, box 7, WHW Papers.
26. ASQ to WHW, May 30, 1892, box 7, WHW Papers.
27. ASQ to WHW, July 19, 1892, box 7, WHW Papers.
28. ASQ to WHW, July 28, 1892, box 7, WHW Papers.
29. WNIA, "Association News and Notes," August 1892, 48; for suit see WNIA, "Association News and Notes," October 1892, 2, in *Indian's Friend.*
30. ASQ to WHW, September 29, and October 3, 1892, box 7, WHW Papers.
31. ASQ to WHW, October 3, 1892, box 7, WHW Papers.
32. ASQ to Babbitt, October 3, 1892, and ASQ to WHW, October 21, 1892, box 7, WHW Papers.
33. ASQ to Babbitt, November 23, 1892, and ASQ to WHW, November 16, 1892, in box 7, WHW Papers.
34. WNIA, "Agua Caliente," *Sketches of Delightful Work*, 43–46. Hallowell was a graduate of the Woman's Medical College of Pennsylvania. See Clara Marshall, *The Woman's Medical College of Pennsylvania* (Philadelphia: R. Blakiston, 1897: 91, 127, 132, 133.
35. ASQ to Morgan, November 24, 1892, LR #42167–1892, RG 75, BIA, NA. ASQ mentioned WHW's November telegram in ASQ to Babbitt, November 23, 1892, box 7, WHW Papers.
36. ASQ to WHW, November 25; see also, December 2, and 19, 1892. In ASQ to WHW, January 1, 1893, she wrote that Hallowell would start on January 4 from Philadelphia, box 7, WHW Papers.
37. ASQ to WHW, October 3, 1892, Box 7, WHW Papers. See also, WNIA, "Association News and Notes," *Indian's Friend*, December 1892, 3. The February 1893 issue, 5, reported her arrival at Cahuilla.
38. For itinerary, see WNIA, "Meetings Addressed by Mrs. Quinton," *Annual Report, December 1892* (Lancaster: Examiner Publishing House, 1892), 13–14; ASQ, "The Hampton Commencement," *Indian's Friend*, June 1892, 40; and "A Great Man Fallen," *Indian's Friend*, June 1893, 2, for his May 11, 1893 death.
39. WNIA, "Washington," *Indian's Friend*, June 1892, 41; the May issue, 37, included Picotte's medical report. For her article see WNIA, "The Home Life of the Indian," *Indian's Friend*, June 1892, 1. See also ASQ to WHW, May 15, 1892, box 7, WHW Papers, mentioning five meetings in row, and then off to Hampton and Richmond.
40. ASQ to Morgan, September 1, 1892, LR #33277–1892, RG 75, BIA, NA.
41. WNIA, "Association News and Notes," July 1892, 1; and WNIA, "Good News," September 1892, 1, 3, in *Indian's Friend.* Mrs. Collins provided a list of items for Christmas boxes. Superintendent Collins in his August 27, 1891, "Report of Moqui School, Keam's Cañon, Arizona," *Sixtieth Annual Report of the CIA, 1891*, 553, noted some fifty homes were underway, twenty to be built at Oraibi. Superintendent G. W. Goodman in his July 31, 1894, "Report of School at Keams Canyon, Arizona," *Annual Report of the CIA, 1894* (Washington: Government Printing Office, 1895),

368, explained that if the Indians built the stone walls, the government would provide, roofs, floors, and doors and windows, See also WNIA, "Work Among the Moquis," *Sketches of Delightful Work*, 65–68. The total expenditure that year on missionary work was $11,540.35.

42. ASQ to WHW, September 21, 1892, box 7, WHW Papers.

ASQ's property included a nine-room home overlooking an orange grove on the western slope of Perris Valley, with forty-five acres, five in olives and ten in oranges, managed by her stepson, George, see J. H. Tigner, *The Italy of America* (Los Angeles: Home Printing Company, ca. 1908), 40. George, born on November 6, 1866, in England, became a naturalized U.S. citizen. He was living in Perris in the 1910 federal census, occupation, farm laborer, owning his home. He died on January 12, 1941, and was buried in the Perris Valley Cemetery, Riverside.

43. ASQ at WHW, September 29, 1892, box 7, WHW Papers.
44. ASQ to WHW, October 22, 26, and 29; November 16; December 19, 1892; and January 3, 1893, box 7, WHW Papers.
45. For her schedule, see WNIA "Meetings Addressed by Mrs. Quinton," *Annual Report December 1892*, 14; and LMC, Hon. Joseph B. Moore, "Our Policy Toward the Mission Indians," *Proceedings of the Tenth Annual Meeting, 1892* (LMC: 1892), 113–17. Moore, a prosecuting attorney and Michigan state senator, was elected circuit court judge in1888. In 1896 he began a thirty-year career as a Michigan State Supreme Court justice.
46. LMC, "Mrs. Quinton," *Proceedings of the Tenth Annual Meeting, 1892*, 67–68, 95; and WNIA, "The Mohonk Indian Conference," *Indian's Friend*, November 1892, 2.
47. LMC, "Report of Committee on Mission Indians," *Proceedings of the Tenth Annual Meeting, 1892*, 109–110.
48. For Hiles, see "Wrongs of the Redskins. The Mohonk Conference Discusses Methods of Redressing Them," *New York Herald*, October 15, 1886, 5; "To Protect the Indians. Steps Taken to Help the Indians of South California," *New York Times*, October 16, 1886, 5; and Francis Paul Prucha, "A 'Friend of the Indian' in Milwaukee: Mrs. O. J. Hiles and the Wisconsin Indian Association," *Historical Messenger of the Milwaukee County Historical Society* (Autumn 1973): 78–95. See also, Mathes, *Helen Hunt Jackson and her Indian Reform Policy*, 92, 95, 101–106; and Mathes, *Divinely Guided*, 183–89, 191, 194.
49. Members were Philip C. Garrett, Philadelphia; Moses Pierce, Norwich, Connecticut; Joshua W. Davis, Boston and member of the Boston Indian Citizenship Committee; and Austin Abbot and Elliott F. Shepard, New York City.
50. BIC, "The Mission Indians of California," in "Proceedings of the Lake Mohonk Conference," *Eighteenth Annual Report, 1886* (Washington, DC, Government Printing Office, 1887), 79–82 for Hiles's report, and 83 for the committee; and Prof. Charles C. Painter, *A Visit to the Mission Indians of California* (Philadelphia: IRA,1887), 4. See also "The Case of the Mission Indians," *Springfield Republican*, October 16, 1886, 5.
51. Born in Wisconsin, Lewis attended law classes at the National University in Washington, DC. After passing the bar in 1888, he moved to California. See Holmes, *History*

of Riverside County, 575–76, and "Indians Who Will Vote," *San Francisco Chronicle*, September 26, 1888, 6.

52. On May 20, 1891, he had been appointed clerk of the Mission Indian Commission, serving alongside Painter when Smiley and Moore temporarily returned home. See George Chandler, Acting Secretary, to Lewis, May 20, 1891, LR #18465–1891, RG 75, BIA, NA.
53. On September 10, 1892, Lewis informed Morgan that an action had been brought against the Warner Ranch Indians by Downey and the Merchants' Exchange Bank in the California State Superior Court, in LR #33961–1891, RG 75, BIA, NA.
54. LMC, "Frank D. Lewis," *Proceedings of the Tenth Annual Meeting, 1892*, 110–12.
55. ASQ to WHW, April 1, 10, and September 29, 1892, and ASQ to Babbitt, October 3, 1892, box 7, WHW Papers. Following Lewis's Lake Mohonk presentation, Quinton never again mentioned him, although earlier she had been extremely critical of him to Weinland.
56. ASQ to Morgan, November 1, 1892, LR #39462–1892, RG 75, BIA, NA. It can only be assumed that the Indian Office paid all of Johnson's salary.
57. WNIA, "The Annual Convention," *Indian's Friend*, January 1893, 1, 2, 3. See also WNIA, *Annual Report, December 1892* (Philadelphia: Examiner Publishing House, 1892); "Friends of the Red Men. Annual Meeting of the Women's National Indian Association," *Brooklyn Daily Eagle*, December 7, 1892, 12; and "The Care of the Red Men. Meeting of the Women's National Indian Association," *New York Times*, December 8, 1892, 2.

Chapter 7

1. William T. Hagan, "Daniel M. Browning, 1893–97," *The Commissioners of Indian Affairs*, 205–9; and for the conflict between Estudillo and ASQ see Mathes and Brigandi, *Reservations, Removal, and Reform*, 133–59.
2. WNIA, *Annual Report, December 1893* (Lancaster, PA: Examiner Printing House, 1893), 12–14, 36–37, 45. Both the annual reports and *Indian's Friend* tended to avoid the mention of conflicts or difficulties.
3. BIC, "Journal of the Twenty-Second Annual Conference of the United States BIC with Representatives of Missionary Boards and Indian Rights Associations," *Twenty-Fourth Annual Report, 1892* (Washington, DC: Government Printing Office, 1893), 121, 133.
4. For his plan, see Prucha, "Supplemental Report on Indian Education, December 1, 1889," *Documents of United States Indian Policy*, 179, 180.
5. BIC, "Journal of the Twenty-Second Annual Conference of the United States BIC," 137–38.
6. WNIA, "Indian Commissioners' Meeting," *Indian's Friend*, February 1893, 2.
7. BIC, "Journal of the Twenty-Second Annual Conference of the United States BIC," 156 for ASQ's appointment. For mention of their proposed meeting with Cleveland, see WNIA "The New Commissioner," *Indian's Friend*, February 1893,

5. Her conference with Cleveland was listed as January 31, in "Meetings Addressed, by Mrs. Quinton," (12).

8. WNIA, "Association News and Notes," *Indian's Friend*, February 1893, 1.

9. ASQ to Morgan, January 11, 1893, LR #1404–1893, RG 75, BIA, NA; and ASQ to WHW, January 15, 1893, box 7, WHW Papers; and WHW to Rust, January 23, 1893, box 10, WHW Papers.

10. ASQ to Morgan, January 16, 1893, LR #2241–1893, RG 75, BIA, NA; and ASQ to WHW, January 19, 1893, box 7, WHW Papers.

11. ASQ to Morgan, February 4, 1893, LR #4665–1893. Rust complained more than once; see Rust to Morgan, February 20, 1893, LR #7381–1893, in which he claimed the cottage was eighty miles from his agency, both in RG 75, BIA, NA.

12. ASQ to Morgan, February 4, 1893.

13. ASQ to WHW, January 30, and February 4, 1893, box 7, WHW Papers. A reference to the seven Southern California branches, organized into a state association on May 4, 1892, in Pasadena; see WNIA, "Association News and Notes," *Indian's Friend*, June 1892, 1, and Mathes, *Divinely Guided*, 84, 209–10, 212, 214–15, 223.

14. WNIA, "Progress at Cahuilla, *Indian's Friend*, April 1893, 1.

15. Rust to Morgan, February 20, 1893, LR #7381–1893, RG 75, BIA, NA. In an undated "Copy of letter sent the Comm replying to Mrs. Quinton's charge," in the Papers of Horatio Nelson Rust, RU-1–1231, Box 9 (1889–1892), Huntington, he wrote that Johnson had come to the agency on December 17; they went to Cahuilla, viewed the cottage, and contacted the Indian lad, whose father had died on the property. Unwilling to sell, he would rent.

16. ASQ to WHW, February 14, 1893, box 7, WHW Papers.

17. ASQ to WHW, April 13, 1893, box 7, WHW Papers. In ASQ to Belt, March 22, 1893, LR #10514–1893, she thanked him for his March 10 response and for sending instructions to Rust; see also ASQ to Belt, April 3, 1893, LR #11818–1893, RG 75, BIA, NA.

18. WNIA, "Association News and Notes," February 1893, 5; and WNIA, "Progress at Coahuilla," April 1893, 1, *Indian's Friend*.

19. WNIA, *Annual Report, 1894* (Lancaster, PA: Examiner Publishing House, 1894), 19; WNIA "The New York City Indian Mission," *Indian's Friend*, May 1895, 7; WNIA, *Sunshine Work;* and Mathes, "New York Women and Indian Reform," 102–4.

20. Wm. H. Weinland, "The Indian Mission," *Moravian*, February 1, 1893, 72; and WNIA, "Association News and Notes," March 1893, 3; and WNIA, "Progress at Coahuilla," April 1893, 1, *Indian's Friend*. Costo's letter to ASQ praising Johnson as a "good and true friend to all us Indians," *Indian's Friend*, May 1893, 4.

21. WHW, "The Indian Mission," 72.

22. In WNIA, "Letter from the New Mission," *Indian's Friend*, March 1893, 2, they arrived on January 18 not 17. See also WNIA, "From Agua Caliente," April 1893 issue, 2, for their work and "From a New Correspondent," [French], in May 1893, 3.

23. ASQ to WHW, January 30, and February 14, 1893, box 7, WHW Papers.

24. For a positive article on Morgan see WNIA, "Department of the Interior," *Indian's Friend*, March 1893, 1.

25. ASQ to Smith, March 29, 1893, box 7, WHW Papers, enclosing March 16 letters by French, Hallowell, and Fowler. On March 4, Isabella Cadwallader, a WNIA-sponsored missionary worker in Fall River Mills and a representative of the Southern California branches wrote Cleveland in support of, box 1, WHW Papers.
26. Salisberry and Salmons letters, box 6, WHW Papers; Johnson letter, box 4, WHW Papers.
27. Weinland to Smith, March 15, 1893, box 10, WHW Papers. For Estudillo's appointment see *Journal of the Executive Proceedings of the Senate of the United States of America*, vol. 28 (Washington, DC: Government Printing Office, 1909), 461.
28. ASQ to WHW, April 13 and 15, box 7, WHW Papers. ASQ provides no incriminating evidence.
29. ASQ to WHW, April 16, 26, and May 7, 1893, box 7, WHW Papers.
30. ASQ to Browning, May 8, 1893, LR #17196–1893, RG 75, BIA, NA; and ASQ to WHW, May 19 [1893], box 7, WHW Papers, date determined by content. Armstrong, who served in the Confederate Army, was a U.S. Indian Inspector from 1885 to 1889, and then assistant commissioner of Indian Affairs from 1893 to 1895 see https://elmsprings.scv.org/id16.php, and according to "The Commission to the Five Civilized Tribes," *Annual Reports of the Department of the Interior: Indian Affairs: Report of Commissioner and Appendixes* (Washington, DC: Government Printing Office, 1900), 142–43, served on the commission from 1895 to 1898.
31. ASQ to Browning, June 2, 1893, LR #20529–1893, SC 143, RG 75, BIA, NA.
32. ASQ to WHW, June 17, 1893, box 7, WHW Papers.
33. Estudillo to Browning, July 12, 1893, LR #26444–1893, SC 143, RG 75, BIA, NA.
34. ASQ to Browning, July 13, 1893, LR #25849–1893 [in LR #28670], SC 143, RG 75, BIA, NA.
35. Estudillo to Browning, July 28, 1893, LR #28670–1893, SC 143, RG 75, BIA, NA.
36. Estudillo to ASQ, July 25, 1893, LR #34301–1893, RG 75, BIA, NA.
37. ASQ to WHW, August 5, 1893, box 7, WHW Papers.
38. ASQ to Estudillo, August 9, 1893, LR #34301–1893, RG 75, BIA, NA.
39. Estudillo to ASQ, August 18, 1893, LR #34301–1893, RG 75, BIA, NA.
40. ASQ to Estudillo, August 24, 1893, LR #34301–1893, RG 75, BIA, NA.
41. Browning to ASQ, August 14, 1893, LR #28670–1893, SC 143, RG 75, BIA, NA; and ASQ to WHW, August 17, 1893, box 7, WHW Papers.
42. ASQ to Browning, August 17, 1893, LR #31665 [#34928]-1893, SC 31, RG 75, BIA, NA. In an undated letter to WHW, box 7, WHW Papers, ASQ noted that since Indians would get their land in severalty soon, the WNIA could wait.
43. Estudillo to Browning, September 11, 1893, LR #34928–1893, SC 31, RG 75, BIA, NA.
44. ASQ to Browning, November 23, 1893, LR #43864–1893, RG 75, BIA, NA; and ASQ to WHW, December 23, 1893, box 7, WHW Papers.
45. ASQ to Browning, August 22, 1893, LR #31667–1893, SC 31, RG 75, BIA, NA. For text of the telegram see ASQ to Browning, September 4, 1893, LR #34301–1893, RG 75, BIA, NA.

46. Estudillo to ASQ, August 29, 1893, LR #34301–1893, RG 75, BIA, NA; copy in box 8, WHW Papers; see ASQ to the Weinlands, September 4, 1893, enclosing Estudillo's letter, box 7, WHW Papers.
47. ASQ to Browning, September 4, 1893, LR #34301–1893, RG 75, BIA, NA; see also ASQ to WHW, September 4, 1893, box 7, WHW Papers.
48. ASQ to Estudillo, September 6, 1893, LR #34301–1893, RG 75, BIA, NA.
49. ASQ to WHW, October 31, 1893, box 7, WHW Papers.
50. For meetings addressed see WNIA, *Annual Report, December 1893*, 12–14.
51. "The Coming Congress of Women," *New York Times*, May 7, 1893, 12.
    For ASQ, see "Growing Influence of Women in Literature and Business," *Brooklyn Eagle*, October 15, 1893, 4; a review of a book with her article in it, *New York Times*, September 3, 1893, 19; see also Mrs. Amelia S. Quinton, "Women's Work for Indians," *The National Exposition Souvenir: What America Owes to Women*, 293–304.
52. For booth work see WNIA, "82nd Meeting," *Minutes of the Executive Board, November 20, 1890, to October 29, 1913*, 112, box 1, folder 4, WNIA Papers, Cornell. See also Lori Jacobson, "Indians Can be Educated:" The WNIA at the 1893 World's Columbian Exposition," in Mathes, *Gender, Race, and Power in the Indian Reform Movement*, 209–25.
53. See for example, WNIA, "The United States Indian Exhibit," 1; WNIA, "Hampton's Exhibit at Chicago," 2; and WNIA, "An Indian School at the World's Fair," *Indian's Friend*, July 1893, 3.
54. WNIA, "Association News and Notes," May 1893, 1, and June 1893, *Indian's Friend*. For one speech see ASQ, "The Woman's National Indian Association," *The Congress of Women Held in the Woman's Building, World's Columbia Exposition, Chicago, U.S.A., 1893*, vol. 1, ed. Mary Kavanaugh Oldham Eagle (Chicago: W. W. Conkey, 1894), 71–73. See also *The World's Congress of Representative Women*, ed. May Wright Sewall, vol. 1 (Chicago: Rand, McNally & Company, 1894), 141, 240–41.
55. WNIA, *Indian's Friend*, July 1893, 2; and ASQ to WHW, April 16, and 26, 1893, box 7, WHW Papers.
56. WNIA, "From Agua Caliente," *Indian's Friend*, July 1893, 4.
57. ASQ to WHW, August 15, September 4, and October 31, 1893, box 7, WHW Papers.
58. See Mathes, "New York Women and Indian Reform," 98–102.
59. For early history, see WNIA, "The Brooklyn Mission for the Piegans of Montana," *Sketches of Delightful Work*, 56–60; and WNIA, *Sunshine Work*, 26–29. In "Report of Blackfeet Agency, August 15, 1893," *Sixty-Second Annual Report of the CIA to the SI, 1893* (Washington: Government Printing Office, 1893), 174, Agent Steell reported that the Dutchers had arrived on April 2, and that the acreage had been selected on Willow Creek, adjoining the government boarding school. For value at transfer, see WNIA, "What it Cost," *Indian's Friend*, October 1894, 4.
60. ASQ, "A Visit to the Piegans," *Indian's Friend*, August 1893, 1.
61. ASQ, "A Visit to the Piegans," *Indian's Friend*, August 1893, 1. For more see W. H. Matson, July 18, 1893, "Report of Superintendent of Blackfeet School," in *Sixty-Second Annual Report of the CIA to the SIC*, 174–77.

62. ASQ, "A Visit to the Piegans," *Indian's Friend*, August 1893, 2; and ASQ, "A Visit to the Piegans. (Continued)," *Indian's Friend*, September 1893, 1.
63. WNIA, "A Visit to the Piegans. (Continued)," *Indian's Friend*, September 1893, 3; and ASQ "A Visit to the Piegans. (Concluded), *Indian's Friend*, October 1893, 1–3. What was not mentioned was the circumstances a decade earlier when a quarter of the tribe starved to death, see Helen B. West, "Starvation Winter of the Blackfeet," *Montana: The Magazine of Western History* 9, no. 1 (Winter, 1959), 2–19. In his August 15, 1893, report (174), Steell reflected the Piegans continued dependence upon weekly rations, which he described as still insufficient. That year he reported only 85 deaths out of some 2,000 residents.
64. Cook took over on July 22, 1893, just weeks after ASQ's visit, see "Report of Blackfeet Agency, August 15, 1894, *Annual Report of the CIA, 1894* (Washington, DC: Government Printing Office, 1895), 156. Civil service reform was important to ASQ and Welsh. See "Mr. Welsh's Address at Mohonk" on civil service reform in *Indian's Friend*, November 1893, 1, 3, where he noted that President Harrison had extended the rules to cover 700 positions in the Indian Service but not yet that of agent. For extension see "Civil Service Classification in the Indian Service, April 13, 1891," in Prucha, *Documents of United States Indian Policy*, 185–86.
65. LMC, *Proceedings of the Eleventh Annual Meeting, 1893* (LMC, 1893), 19–22 for the Piegans, 71 for WNIA missions. See also "Friends of the Indian in Session," *New York Times*, October 12, 1893, 10.
66. WNIA, "The Annual Meeting," *Annual Report, December 1893*, 9, 14, 35–36. See also, WNIA, "The Annual Convention," *Indian's Friend*, December 1893, 1–2.
67. BIC, "Journal of the Twenty-Third Annual Conference of the United States BIC, with Representatives of Missionary Boards and Indian Rights Associations," *Twenty-Fifth Annual Report, 1893* (Washington, DC: Government Printing Office, 1894), 125.
68. BIC, "Journal of the Twenty-Third Annual Conference," 126; and WNIA, "Meeting of the BIC," *Indian's Friend*, January 1894, 3.
69. WNIA, "Our Association's Chronology. Number Eighteen," *Indian's Friend*, August 1898, 2.

Chapter 8

1. ASQ, "From California," *Indian's Friend*, May 1895, inside front cover.
2. ASQ to WHW, January 9, 1894, box 7, WHW Papers. Advertisements reflected she had backing from the National Institute; Hotel Fredonia; Moravian Ladies' Sewing Society rag dolls; Boyce Brothers, importers and grocers; and O'Neill's importers and retailers.
3. ASQ to WHW, February 17, and March 30, 1894, box 7, WHW Papers. In May 1890, the Perris Irrigation District was organized and made responsible for covering 13,000 acres with water delivered through steel pipes. They also had the power to tax. See, for example, advertisement for "First Irrigation District in San Diego county to

secure water under the Wright Act," in a "Perris Grand Water Festival," *Los Angeles Herald*, October 1891, 12.

4. ASQ to WHW, May 31, July 30, October 13, November 14, and 20, 1894, box 7, WHW Papers. In a May 31 letter, she wrote that Commissioner Morgan, who owned land in Perris Valley, had warned her to make sure she had road access to her property. For their real estate transfer, see *Riverside Enterprise*, June 28, 1893, and *Riverside Daily Press*, November 7, 1893. Her name was mentioned in connection with a legal action filed against the Perris Irrigation District, see "Perris District Bonds Involved in New Case," *Los Angeles Herald*, September 24, 1910, 1.
5. ASQ to WHW, January 9, 1894, and ASQ to Welsh, January 13, 1894, reel 11, IRA Papers.
6. ASQ to Welsh, October 31, 1893, reel 10, IRA Papers.
7. BIC, "Journal of the Twenty-Third Annual Conference of the United States BIC, with Representatives of Missionary Boards and Indian Rights Associations," *Twenty-Fifth Annual Report, 1893* (Washington, DC: Government Printing Office, 1894), 125–27, 131–32.
8. BIC, "Journal of the Twenty-Third Annual Conference," 149–50. For a summary see WNIA, "Platform of the Indian Conference," *Indian's Friend*, January 1894, 6.
9. ASQ to WHW, December 23, 1893, box 7, WHW Papers.
10. "For Better Indian Agents," *New York Times*, January 1, 1894, 11; and "Working for the Indians," *Otsego Farmer*, January 19, 1894, 1.
11. ASQ to Browning, January 26, 1894, LR #3843–1894; Browning to ASQ, January 27, 1894, LS: Education Division, Volume 56, LB 217, 140; and ASQ to Browning, January 30, 1894, LR #4413–1894, all in RG 75, BIA, NA.
12. ASQ to Browning, March 3, 1894, LR #8976–1894, and ASQ to Browning, March 9, 1894, LR #9750–1894, in RG 75, BIA, NA.
13. ASQ to Armstrong, June 18, 1894, LR #23099–1894, RG 75, BIA, NA.
14. Ament, July 1, 1894, "Report of School at Greenville, Cal.," *Annual Report of the CIA, 1894* (Washington, DC: Government Printing Office, 1895), 371–72. See also WNIA, "The Work of Edward N. Ament," *Indian's Friend*, September 1894, 9–10.
15. ASQ to Browning, August 27, 1894, LR #35362–1894. RG 75, BIA, NA.
16. ASQ to WHW, May 31, 1894, box 7, WHW Papers. For her departure, see the February 1895 *Indian's Friend*, 9, and for Ritter's arrival see the March 1895 issue, 2.
17. "Anna Hayward Johnson, From the Indian School at Cahuilla," *Riverside Press and Horticulturist*, December 22, 1894.
18. ASQ to WHW, July 30, 1894, box 7, WHW Papers. For an Agua Caliente missionary report, see WNIA, *Indian's Friend*, March 1894, 6.
19. WNIA, February 1894, 5, and March 1894, 7, in *Indian's Friend.*
20. ASQ to Welsh, February 17, 1894, reel 11, *IRA Papers.*
21. WNIA, March 1894, 4; and ASQ, "The Carlisle Commencement," April 1894, 6–7, in *Indian's Friend*. For her schedule see WNIA, "Meetings Addressed, by Mrs. Quinton," *Annual Report, December 1894* (Lancaster, PA: Examiner Publishing House, 1894), 14.

22. "Are Interested in Indians," *Brooklyn Eagle*, March 16, 1894, 1. See also WNIA, "The Transferred Piegan Mission," *Our Missions, for the Year, 1895*, 41–42.
23. ASQ, "Finding Sisters," *Indian's Friend*, May 1894, 9–10.
24. WNIA, "Meetings Addressed, by Mrs. Quinton," 14–15; "City and Vicinity," *New York Times*, April 28, 1894, 8; and "Indians Becoming Civilized," *New York Times*, April 30, 1894, 5.
25. WNIA, "Meetings Addressed, By Mrs. Quinton,"15; and "Homer and Vicinity," *Homer Republican*, September 27, 1894.
26. ASQ, "The Mohonk Indian Conference," *Indian's Friend*, November 1894, 6–9; and ASQ, "The Mohonk Conference (Concluded)," *Indian's Friend*, December 1894, 7–8.
27. LMC, *Proceedings of the Twelfth Annual Meeting, 1894* (LMC: 1894), 25–26, 76, 82–84, 137–38.
28. For transfer, see WNIA, November 22, 1893, Board of Directors meeting, *Minutes of the Trustees of the WNIA, March 11, 1887–November 22, 1893*, box 1, folder 2, WNIA Papers, Cornell. For a report by Gray see WNIA, "Florida Work," *Indian's Friend*, March 1900, 9–10. See Harry A. Kersey and Donald E. Pullease, "Bishop William Crane Gray's Mission to the Seminole Indians in Florida, 1893–1914," *Historical Magazine of the Protestant Episcopal Church* 42, no. 3 (September 1973): 257–73.
29. LMC, *Proceedings of the Twelfth Annual Meeting, 1894*, 73; 134–35; and ASQ, "The Mohonk conference. (Concluded.)," *Indian's Friend*, December 1894, 7.
30. WNIA, "Meetings Addressed, By Mrs. Quinton," *Annual Report, 1894*, 15–16; and "In Behalf of the Indians. Chauncey M. Depew and Mrs. A. S. Quinton Address a Large Meeting at John D. Rockefeller's Home," *New York Times*, November 27, 1894, 6. WNIA, "News and Notes," *Indian's Friend*, January 1895, 2, included a description, noting 300 had attended. Depew, a lawyer, railroad executive and later a U.S. Senator from New York, had served in 1863 as the Secretary of State of New York and in the New York state legislature.
31. WNIA, *Annual Report, December, 1894* (Lancaster, PA: Examiner Publishing House, 1894), 9, 11; and WNIA, "Our National Convention," *Indian's Friend*, January 1895, inside front cover.
32. "Women's Indian Association," *New York Times*, December 7, 1894, 8; and "Indian Association," *Bangor Daily Whig & Courier*, December 22, 1894. The WNIA representative in Washington, DC, was Kate Foote Coe, president of the Washington branch and chair of the WNIA Committee on Indian legislation, who had taken over the presidency of the auxiliary following the death of her sister, Harriet, in 1886. See "Kate Foote Coe," *A Century of Meriden, Part II* (Meriden, CT: Journal Publishing Company, 1906), 320–22.
33. BIC, "Journal of the Twenty-Fourth Annual Conference of the United States BIC with Representatives of Missionary Boards and Indian Rights Associations," *Twenty-Sixty Annual Report, 1894* (Washington, DC: Government Printing Office, 1895), 38. For a summary, see WNIA, "The Meeting of the Commissioners," *Indian's Friend*, February 1895, inside front cover, 8–9; for a tribute to both, see "A Great Loss," 4, same issue.
34. ASQ to Welsh, January 24, 1895, reel 12, *IRA Papers.*

35. BIC, "Journal of the Twenty-Fourth Annual Conference," 66–67.
36. BIC, "Resolutions of the Indian Commissioners," in "Journal of the Twenty-Fourth Annual Conference," 68–69; for ASQ on committees see WNIA, "The Meeting of the Commissioners," *Indian's Friend*, February 1895, 9; for meeting with Cleveland, see WNIA, "Meetings Addressed, by Mrs. Quinton," *Annual Report, December, 1894*, 13.
37. For Garrett, see "Journal of the Twenty-Fifth Annual Conference of the United States BIC with Representatives of Missionary Boards and Indian Associations," *Report of the Secretary of the Interior; Being Part of The Message and Documents Communicated to the Two Houses of Congress*, vol. 2 (Washington, DC: Government Printing Office, 1896), 1082; and WNIA, *Indian's Friend*, March 1895, 4–5.
38. "National Council of Women," *Syracuse Evening Record*, February 18, 1895, 1; "The Progressive Women. Opening session of the National Council in Washington," *New York Times*, February 19, 1895, 16; "Seeking Woman's Sphere. Work of the National Council Sitting in Washington," *New York Times*, February 20, 1895, 16; and "Women's National Council. The Work of the Sex in Religious Fields Discussed," *Philadelphia Inquirer*, February 20, 1895, 3.
39. Her departure was noted in WNIA, *Indian's Friend*, April 1895, 4.
40. According to "For Sale—Real Estate," *Los Angeles Herald*, July 14, 1895, 14, "all trains stop at Val Verde; [the] brick depot, U.S. post office." ASQ often posted her letters from there.
41. ASQ, "From California," *Indian's Friend*, May 1895, inside front cover, and ASQ to WHW, March 18, 1895, box 7, WHW Papers, for her address. See also An Interested Worker, "The Coming Meeting of the Redlands Indian Association," *Citrograph*, March 9, 1895; and "Indian Work," *Citrograph*, March 23, 1895 (for ASQ); and "Redlands," *Los Angeles Times*, March 17, 1895, 15.
42. For background and site selection attributed to Rust, see Mathes, *Divinely Guided*, 216.
43. Founded in 1888 by Theodore Bailey, the Bailey's Palomar Resort is still in operation.
44. ASQ, "From California," 3, 6. For a school report from Salmons, see WNIA, *Indian's Friend*, November 1896, 4. As late as 1899, WNIA auxiliaries were still sending her money, see WNIA, "News and Notes," *Indian's Friend*, March 1899, 9–10.
45. ASQ, "From California. No. 2," *Indian's Friend*, June 1895, 8; for improvements see "News and Notes," *Indian's Friend*, July 1895, 3.
46. ASQ, "From California. No. 2," 8.
47. WNIA, "New and Notes," *Indian's Friend*, May 1895, 3.
48. A Serrano tribal leader who served as interpreter for Mission Indian agents Lawson and Rust and for WHW. See Mathes, *Divinely Guided*, 196–98, 225–26, 246–47; and Mathes and Brigandi, *Reservations, Removal, and Reform*.
49. When WHW drew up a second petition in the fall of 1901, the Indians commented: "If only Mrs. Quinton would help." He promised to ask if she would write the commissioner on their behalf. See WHW to ASQ, November 30, 1901, Amelia Stone Quinton Papers, Division of Rare and Manuscripts Collection, Cornell University (hereafter, Quinton Papers, Cornell).

50. ASQ, "From California. No. 3." *Indian's Friend*, July 1895, 6–8.
51. WNIA, "A New Desert Mission," *Our Missions, for the Year 1895*, 17–18. In WNIA, "From Rev. Wm. H. Weinland," *Indian's Friend*, January 1896, 3, he reported that on his last trip to the Desert Cahuilla, they asked when they would get their resident missionary. For water see WNIA, "News and Notes," *Indian's Friend*, April 1896, 4.
52. WNIA, "Meetings Addressed, by Mrs. Quinton," *Annual Report, December 1895* (Lancaster, PA: Examiner Publishing House, 1895), 13–14; and ASQ to WHW, April 25, 1895, box 7, WHW Papers.
53. WNIA, "Meetings Addressed, by Mrs. Quinton," 13; and ASQ to Browning, May 21, 1895, LR #22576–1895; ASQ to Hailmann, May 21, 1895, LR #22576–1895; and also ASQ to Browning, June 15, 1895, LR #25833–1895, all in RG 75, BIA, NA.
54. WNIA, "Meetings Addressed, by Mrs. Quinton," 13; for reorganization, see WNIA, "The San Jose Association," *Annual Report, December 1894* (Lancaster, PA: Examiner Publishing House, 1894), 24. See also, WNIA, "News and Notes," *Indian's Friend*, July 1895, 2, 5.
55. On June 9 she addressed the First Baptist Church, see "Church Notices," June 9, 1895, 12; and "City Items in Brief," *San Francisco Call*, June 10, 1895, 7.
56. WNIA, "News and Notes," *Indian's Friend*, August 1895, 3.
57. "The American Indians. Mrs. A. S. Quinton Tells Strange Truths About Them." *San Francisco Chronicle*, June 20, 1895, 7.
58. ASQ to Smith, June 22, 1895, LR #27520–1895, RG 75, BIA, NA.
59. ASQ, "In California—No. 4. The Greenville Visit," *Indian's Friend*, August 1895, inside front cover.
60. For Newell see Mathes, *Divinely Guided*, 113–114.
61. WNIA, "News and Notes," *Indian's Friend*, August 1895, 3.
62. ASQ, "In California—No. 4. The Greenville Visit," inside cover page; and ASQ to WHW, June 30, 1895, box 7, WHW Papers.
63. ASQ to Browning, July 1, 1895, LR #27998 [44886]-1895 and ASQ to Browning, July 5, 1895, LR #28706–1895, in RG 75, BIA, NA.
64. Moss to Browning, July 2, 1895, LR #27998–1894, RG 75, BIA, NA.
65. ASQ, "In California—No. 4. The Greenville Visit," 9; and ASQ, "An Indian Fourth of July," *Indian's Friend*, August 1895, 8; and "Studying Indians," *Oroville Weekly Mercury*, July 12, 1895, 2.
66. ASQ, "On the Wing-No. 5-Pacific Coast Visits," *Indian's Friend*, September 1895, inside cover.
67. For a history of Chief Lot see Rev. Jonathan Edwards, *An Illustrated History of Spokane County, State of Washington* (n.p.: W. H. Lever, 1900), 25–26.
68. ASQ, "On the Wing-No. 6- The Visit to Our Spokane Mission," *Indian's Friend*, October 1895, inside front cover. Robert H. Ruby and John A. Brown, *The Spokane Indians: Children of the Sun* (Norman: University of Oklahoma Press, 2006), write that Clark, who was born in Kensington, Quebec, had arrived at Wellpinit on October 25, 1894 (210–16). The authors describe her as teacher and a protector who the WNIA had

moved to Heal Bay when the government converted Fort Spokane into a boarding school for Colville and Spokane reservation children (215).

69. "Report of Colville Agency, August 16, 1895," *Annual Report of the SI, 1895*, vol. 2 (Washington, DC: Government Printing Office, 1896), 313.
70. Edwards, *An Illustrated History of Spokane County*, 117–23. The Indian war following the Whiteman Mission attack forced Eells to move to Washington, where, in addition to his continued missionary work, he founded Whitman College. See the Cushing Eells Collection, Northwest Archives, Whitman College, Walla Walla, Washington.
71. The American Board (Presbyterian and Congregational churches) worked in foreign lands, transferring in 1882 these few missions to the American Missionary Association (AMA), which with the exception of their West African mission, were within the United States. This transfer unified the AMA work. See AMA, "Our Indian Work," *American Missionary*, October 1883, 291; and "Report of Committee on Indian Missions," *American Missionary*, December 1883, 370.
72. Edwards, *An Illustrated History of Spokane County*, 24; and Ruby and Brown, *The Spokane Indians*, 188.
73. ASQ [?], "The Spokane Mission," *Indian's Friend*, February 1895, 7–8; and H. W. C., "Notes of Work Among the Spokanes," *Indian's Friend*, May 1895, 8–9.
74. WNIA, "The Spokane Mission," *Our Missions, for the Year, 1895*, 31–37. For a Clark report, see WNIA, "A Year's Work for the Spokanes," *Indian's Friend*, April 1896, inside front cover, 8.
75. WNIA, "News and Notes," *Indian's Friend*, November 1895, 5, reported a new room to the schoolhouse, a Sunday school started by Clark, and the hiring of an interpreter and new missionary workers, Mr. and Mrs. Gow, sent by the Presbyterian Board in New York City. See also WNIA, "News and Notes," *Indian's Friend*, December 1895, 2–3, for more on the Gows.
76. ASQ, "On the Wing-No. 6-The Visit to Our Spokane Mission," inside front cover, 9; and ASQ to WHW, August 6, 1895, box 7, WHW Papers.
77. ASQ to WHW, August 19, 1895, box 7, WHW Papers.
78. ASQ to WHW, October 5, 1895, box 7, WHW Papers.
79. WNIA, "Committee on Resolutions," *Annual Report of the WNIA, December 1895* (Lancaster, PA: Examiner Publishing House, 1895), 39.
80. LMC, "Mrs. A. S. Quinton," *Proceedings of the Thirteenth Annual Meeting, 1895* (LMC, 1896), 89–91; see also ASQ, "The Mohonk Conference, Oct. 9th, 10th, and 11th," *Indian's Friend*, November 1895, inside front cover, 8–10.
81. WNIA, "The Pioneers' Reunion," *Indian's Friend*, December 1895, 8–9; see also "Three Thousand Women: Assemble in Honor of Mrs. Stanton's Birthday," *Brooklyn Eagle*, November 13, 1895, 5.
82. "In Behalf of the Red Men," *New York Herald*, November 25, 1890, 4.
83. ASQ, "Our Annual Convention," *Indian's Friend*, January 1895, inside front cover, 5–9.
84. ASQ to Weinland, December 7, 1895, box 7, WHW Papers.
85. See WHW, "From a Late Report," *Indian's Friend*, June 1896, 8–9.

86. For a more detailed summary see WNIA, "Our Association's Chronology, Number Nineteen," *Indian's Friend*, September 1898, 2, 11; and WNIA, "Our Association's Chronology, Number 20, *Indian's Friend*, May 1899, 2, 11.

Chapter 9

1. WNIA, "Meetings Addressed, by Mrs. Quinton," *Annual Report, December 1896* (Lancaster, PA: Examiner Publishing House, 1896), 23–24.
2. An early women's club, see https://philadelphiaencyclopedia.org/archive/womens-clubs/.
3. See WNIA, *The Case of the Florida Seminoles* (WNIA: ca. 1897); and WNIA, "Help the Seminole," *Indian's Friend*, June 1899, 7–8.
4. BIC, "Mrs. Quinton," "Journal of the Twenty-Fifth Annual Conference of the United States BIC with Representatives of Missionary Boards and Indian Associations," *Report of the Secretary of the Interior; Being Part of The Message and Documents Communicated to the Two Houses of Congress*, vol. 2 (Washington, DC: Government Printing Office, 1896), 1077–1078. For the missions, see WNIA, "Our Association's Chronology. Number 20," *Indian's Friend*, May, 1899, 2, 11.
5. BIC, "The Teller Bill," in "Journal of the Twenty-Fifth Annual Conference," 1082. For Smith see WNIA, "Report of the Secretary of the Interior," *Indian's Friend*, January 1896, 4; WNIA, "The Teller Bill," *Indian's Friend*, February 1896, 6–7; and WNIA, "A Continuous, Non-Partisan Indian Commission," *Indian's Friend*, February 1897, 7.
6. Leupp, who temporarily replaced IRA Agent Painter after he died, served from 1905 to 1909 as Indian commissioner, see Donald L. Parman, "Francis Ellington Leupp, 1905–1909," *The Commissioners of Indian Affairs*," 221–32.
7. WNIA, "A Needed Amendment," *Indians' Friend*, March 1896, 6–7.
8. BIC, "Mrs. Quinton," "Journal of the Twenty-Fifth Annual Conference," 1080–81.
9. BIC, "The Teller Bill," 1082, 1096; and ASQ, "Meeting of the Indian Commissioners," *Indian's Friend*, February 1896, 9–10.
10. WNIA, "The Non-Partisan Commission Bill," *Indian's Friend*, March 1897, 6–7; for text, see "Bill," *Indian's Friend*, April 1897, 6.
11. WNIA, "Meetings Addressed by Mrs. Quinton," *Annual Report, December 1896*, 23, and "Work Among the Indians. Mrs. A. S. Quinton and Miss Howard Tell their Experiences," *Brooklyn Eagle*, January 23, 1896, 5.
12. ASQ to Browning, January 29, 1896, LR #4506–1896, RG 75, BIA, NA.
13. WNIA, "From Hoopa Valley, California," *Indian's Friend*, December 1895, 7–8; and Mathes, "Northern California Members and The Work at the Hoopa Reservation," in *Divinely Guided*, 89–100.
14. Denton to Taber, January 12, 1896; Taber to ASQ, January 17, 1896; and ASQ to Browning, January 30, 1896, all in LR #4632–1896, RG 75, BIA, NA.
15. ASQ to Browning, March 4, 1896, LR #8859–1896, RG 75, BIA, NA; see also, WNIA, "In the Hoopa Valley," *Indian's Friend*, March 1896, 9. For his departure, see May

1896, 9, and for letter extracts see WNIA, "From the New Mission," *Indian's Friend*, June 1896, 2.

16. Eyster to Browning, November 10, 1895, LR #46735–1895 [in #49516–1895]; Dougherty to Browning, November 30, 1895, LR #49516–1895; and ASQ to Browning, May 10, 1896, LR #18070–1896, all in SC 143, RG 75, BIA, NA.
17. ASQ to Browning, October 24, 1896, LR #40999–1896, RG 75, BIA, NA. WNIA, "News and Notes," *Indian's Friend*, August 1896, 4, reported that Dougherty had received instructions to set aside a tract of land.
18. Dougherty to Browning, November 11, 1896, and Dougherty to Jones, May 8, 1897, in LR #19593–1897, SC 143, RG 75, BIA, NA. WNIA, "News and Notes," *Indian's Friend*, October 1896, 4, reported Hearst's pledge. For a letter from Armstrong see WNIA, "News and Notes," *Indian's Friend*, December 1896, 5. See also WNIA, "The Mission of the Northern California Auxiliary," *Our Missionary Report for 1896*, 33–38.
19. For appointment see WNIA, "News and Notes," April 1897, 5; see also WNIA, "Hoopa Valley Notes," *Indian's Friend*, July 1897, 9–10; and Mathes, *Divinely Guided*, 92–93, 95–97, 262, 302n57, for Goddard's biography. For his report, see WNIA, "News and Notes," *Indian's Friend*, May 1899, 9. It is unknown why Armstrong left.
20. ASQ to WHW, February 21, see also April 28, 1896, box 7, WHW Papers.
21. ASQ to WHW, March 15, 1896; on June 8, 1896, she recommended the bedroom be 12 x 12 feet, and the large room 12 x 20 feet with a folding door between to open at night, box 7, WHW Papers.
22. ASQ to WHW, September 21, 1896, box 7, WHW Papers.
23. ASQ to WHW, February 24, 1896, box 7, WHW Papers, and ASQ to Browning, April 17, 1896, LR #18032–1896, RG 75, BIA, NA.
24. ASQ to WHW, September 28, October 1, and October 10, 1896, box 7, WHW Papers, A notice in WNIA, "News and Notes," *Indian's Friend*, May 1897, 5, encouraged members to support her work.
25. ASQ to WHW, March 15, and June 6, 1896; see also ASQ to WHW, June 22 and September 4, 1896, box 7, WHW Papers. Charles F. Larrabee was former chief of the land division and later an assistant commissioner.
26. Copy of Browning to ASQ, June 17, 1896, in WHW Papers, Box 8. ASQ, "From our Old Desert Museum," *Indian's Friend*, November 1905, 5, reported that according to Mrs. Robert Staveley (the Staveleys were the current missionaries) the new wells had enabled subsistence agriculture.
27. Copy of Sims to Browning, June 20, 1896, [Authority 48694, 3864 Ind. Div. '96] in box 7, WHW Papers.
28. The June, 1896, *Indian's Friend*, 6, reported the president had signed legislation bringing most teaching positions, chief clerks, and all high-grade department officials under such rules. ASQ to WHW, June 6, 1896, box 7, WHW Papers. For legislation, see Prucha, "Extension of Civil Service Rules," *Documents of United States Indian Policy*, 195–97.

29. ASQ to Browning, June 27, 1896, LR #24445–1896; and ASQ to Browning, July 24, 1896, LR #28250–1896; see also ASQ to Browning, August 14, 1896, LR #31255–1896, in RG 75, BIA, NA.
30. ASQ used Clifton Springs as a return address for several letters to WHW and Browning. For Saratoga Springs see ASQ to WHW, June 28, 1896, box 7, WHW Papers. In a July 8 letter she wrote she was under a doctor's care, trying to rest.
31. ASQ to WHW, July 23, 1896, box 7, WHW Papers.
32. ASQ to WHW, September 4, 10, and 14, 1896, box 7, WHW Papers. Woosley attended the Moravian Theological Seminary in Bethlehem, see Mss HM 66349–66358, David Woosley. Diaries and Correspondence, 1896–1940. Record no. b1630460. Huntington Library, Art Museum, and Botanical Gardens, San Marino, CA.
33. WHW, "The Desert Mission," *Indian's Friend*, November 1896, 2. See also WNIA, "The Mission of the Brooklyn Auxiliary," *Our Missionary Report for 1896* (WNIA, 1896), 24–27.
34. ASQ to WHW, September 28, 1896, box 7, WHW Papers. In WNIA, "News and Notes," *Indian's Friend*, October 1896, 5, it was reported that papers had been signed and adobe bricks made. The Woosleys were staying with WHW.
35. ASQ to WHW, December 22, 1896, box 7, WHW Papers; and WNIA, "Dedication of the New Mission Church," *Indian's Friend*, February 1897, 7, and WNIA, "The Mission of the Brooklyn Indian Association," *Our Missionary Report for 1897*, 35–38.
36. ASQ to WHW, October 1, and 10, 1896, box 7, WHW Papers.
37. For Eldridge, see Mathes, "The Banner Association: Twenty-Five Years in Massachusetts," 160–61, 163–66, 306–9.
38. LMC, "Third Session," *Proceedings of the Fourteenth Annual Meeting, 1896* (LMC, 1897), 64; and "The Troubles of Poor Lo. Mohonk Conference Discusses Means of Aiding Indians," *New York Times*, October 16, 1896, 7.
39. ASQ to WHW, October 21, and 24, 1896, box 7, WHW Papers.
40. WNIA, *Annual Report, December, 1896*, 40. See also "Work Among the Indians: What Has Been Accomplished by the National Association," *New York Times*, December 10, 1896, 6; and "Working for the Indians. Annual Meeting of the WNIA," *Rocky Mountain News*, December 10, 1896, 4.
41. ASQ to WHW, October 31, 1896, and March 15, and April 15, 1897, box 7, WHW Papers.
42. For Elizabeth Haddon see https://www.womenhistoryblog.com/2008/08/elizabeth-haddon-estaugh.html. For Quinton's addresses see WNIA, "Meetings Addressed," *Annual Report of the WNIA, December 1897* (Philadelphia: Hudson Wagenseller, 1897), 13–14.
43. ASQ to WHW, January 6, 1897, box 7, WHW Papers.
44. BIC, "Journal of the Twenty-Eight annual Meeting of BIC and the Secretaries of the Religious Missionary Societies," *Twenty-Eight Annual Report, 1896* (Washington: Government Printing Office, 1897), 106–106. See also WNIA, "The Meeting of the BIC," *Indian's Friend*, February 1897, 6.
45. ASQ to WHW, February 4, 15, 17, and March 6, 13 [for telegram] 1897; see also WNIA, "News and Notes," *Indian's Friend*, March 1897, 5.

46. Ament to ASQ, September 7, 1896, and ASQ to Browning, October 1, 1896, both in LR #37382–1896, and ASQ to Browning, December 23, 1896, LR #48133–1896, in RG 75, BIA, NA. For corrections see Browning to Quinton, September 19, 1896, General Correspondence 1894–1921, Greenville (Box 67) 1894–1900, Letter Sent #23250–1896 [35959], RG 75, BIA, NA, San Bruno, California. For transfer see WNIA, "Annual Report of the Trustees for year ending December 1, 1896," in *Minutes of the Trustees of the WNIA, March 11, 1887–November 22, 1893*, box 1, folder 2, WNIA Papers, Cornell.
47. ASQ to Browning, March 2, 1897, LR #8348–1897; and March 25, 1897, LR #11206–1897, RG 75, BIA, NA.
48. ASQ to Browning, March 26, 1897, LR #11368–1897, RG 75, BIA, NA.
49. For NYCIA see "Society Notes," *New York Times*, March 28, 1897, 5.
50. ASQ to Browning, April 3, 1897, LR #12503–1897, in RG 75, BIA, NA.
51. WNIA, "A Disaster to Greenville School," May 1897, 10, and WNIA, "Greenville after the Fire," July 1897, 8 in *Indian's Friend*. WNIA auxiliaries continued their support once the government took over, see WNIA "A Noble State Work," *Indian's Friend*, March 1899, 11.
52. Browning to ASQ, April 9, 1897, LS #13010–1897, Education Division, vol. 84, LB 272, pg. 79 and 80; ASQ to Browning, April 12, 1897, LR #13828–1897; and ASQ to Smith, May 22, 1897, LR #20234–1897, RG 75, BIA, NA.
53. ASQ to Jones, July 1, 1897, LR #26160–1897; ASQ to Smith, July 8, 1897, LR #27439–1897; and ASQ to Smith, July 14, 1897, LR #28743–1897, RG 75, BIA, NA. See WNIA, "News and Notes," *Indian's Friend*, August 1897, 4.
54. WNIA, "99th Meeting," *Minutes of the Executive Board, November 20, 1890 to October 39, 1913*, 226, box 1, folder 4, WNIA Papers, Cornell.
55. For Hailmann see ASQ to Welsh, April 7, 1897, reel 13, IRA Papers; ASQ to WHW, April 30, 1897, box 7, WHW Papers; and WNIA, "Superintendent Hailmann," *Indian's Friend*, April 1897, 7. McKinley appointed Reel, who was active in the Republican Party and had assured his winning in Wyoming, see K. Tsianina Lomawaimi and T. Tsianina Lomawaima, "Estelle Reel, Superintendent of Indian Schools, 1898–1910: Politics, Curriculum, and Land," *Journal of American Indian Education* 35, no. 3 (Spring 1996), 8.
56. For Jones' tenure see W. David Baird, "William A. Jones, 1897–1904," *The Commissioners of Indian Affairs*, 211–20; and ASQ to WHW, April 30, 1897, box 7, WHW Papers; and WNIA, "The New Secretary of the Interior," *Indian's Friend*, March, 7–8.
57. Bliss to Welsh, July 1, 1897, reel 13, IRA Papers; and Bliss to ASQ, June 15, 1897, copy in box 8, WHW Papers.
58. ASQ to WHW, June 9, see also June 12 and July 3, 1897, box 7, WHW Papers.
59. Hallowell to Quinton, May 24, 1897, and ASQ to Sniffen, June 1, 1897, Herbert Welsh Collection (#702), Box 41, Historical Society of Pennsylvania, Philadelphia. See WNIA, "News and Notes," *Indian's Friend*, July 1897, 5, for Hallowell's letter.
60. WNIA, *Indian's Friend*, March 1894, 1.

61. For the lawsuit see Mathes and Brigandi, *Reservations, Removal, and Reform*, 144–48; WNIA, "A Most Unjust Decision," February 1897, 1, and "Agua Caliente, July 1897, 1, *Indian's Friend*.
62. Ward to Welsh, June 19, 1897; see also Ward to Welsh, July 1, 1897, thanking him for the bond, reel 13, IRA Papers.
63. WNIA, "News and Notes," *Indian's Friend*, August 1897, 6. See also, Mathes, *Divinely Guided*, 244–45; and Mathes and Brigand, *Reservations, Removal, and Reform*, 167–68.
64. WNIA, "The Mission of the New York City Indian Association," *Our Missionary Report for 1897* (WNIA, 1897), 29–34.
65. "Homer: Gleanings of News from Our Town Village," *Cortland Evening Standard*, July 31, 1897, 6. On August 1 she conducted a Bible reading at the Old Ladies Home.
66. For transfer see WNIA, "The Mission of the Brooklyn Association," *Our Missionary Report for 1897*, 37; and ASQ to WHW, July 3, 1897, and September 26, 1897, box 7, WHW Papers.
67. ASQ to WHW, July 3, 1897, and September 26, 1897, box 7, WHW Papers; and ASQ to Sniffen, July 8, and July 10, 1897, Herbert Welsh Collection (#702), Box 41, Historical Society of Pennsylvania. For itinerary, see WNIA, "Meetings Addressed by Mrs. Quinton," *Annual Report, December 1897* (Philadelphia: Hudson Wagenseller, 1897), 14.
68. LMC, "Third Session," *Proceedings of the Fifteenth Annual Meeting, 1897* (LMC: 1897), 50–52. This unidentified friend was Mary Dewey, who with other members of the MIA, had raised half of the $6100. See Welsh to Mrs. James S. Howe, MIA executive board member, June 28, 1897, reel 13, IRA Papers.
69. LMC, Mrs. A. S. Quinton, "The Abolition of Unnecessary Agencies," *Proceedings of the Fifteenth Annual Meeting, 1897*, 84–86. See also WNIA, "The Mohonk Indian Conference," 6 and "The Lake Mohonk Platform," 6–7, *Indian's Friend*, November 1897.
70. For absence, see "Our Red Men: Women's Indian Association in Session," *Brooklyn Daily Eagle*, December 13, 1897; and ASQ to WHW, December 18, 1897, box 7, WHW Papers.
71. ASQ to WHW, March 22, 1898, box 7, WHW Papers; and WNIA, "News and Notes," *Indian's Friend*, May 1898, 4–5.
72. ASQ to WHW, April 28, 1898, box 7, WHW Papers for Smiley's presentation of the library; and WNIA, "News and Notes," *Indian's Friend*, June 1898, 4.
73. WNIA, "News and Notes," *Indian's Friend*, July 1898, 4. Home on the 14th in ASQ to WHW, July 6, 1898, box 7, WHW Papers, she explained she was busy with fruit canning and her Indian work.
74. In Hallowell to WHW, October 6, 1899, box 1, WHW Papers, she congratulated Weinland on his new home. He now was no longer affiliated with the WNIA. In de Schweinitz to WHW, July 24, 1900, box 2, WHW Papers, he was informed that his official position was as the Superintendent of the Southern California Mission, now

obligated to submit annual reports to the Moravian Mission Board. See WNIA, "News and Notes," *Indian's Friend*, September 1898, 4.

75. ASQ to WHW, August 1, 12, and 26, 1898 , box 7, WHW Papers. For her schedule, see WNIA, *Annual Report, December 1898* (Philadelphia: George Dukes, 1898), 14.
76. WNIA, "Our Association's Chronology. Number 25," *Indian's Friend*, October 1899, 2, for quote; and LMC, "Miss Dewey," *Proceedings of the Twelfth Annual Meeting, 1894*, 82–84, quote on 83. For background see MIA, "Secretary's Report," *Thirteenth Annual Report, 1895* (Boston: J. Stilman Smith, 1895), 6–11; and for a report from Calfee see WNIA, "The Hualapais," *Indian's Friend*, July 1898, 7–8.
77. First quote, WNIA, "The Massachusetts Mission," *Indian's Friend*, October 1898, 6; and LMC, "Mrs. Quinton," *Proceedings of the Sixteenth Annual Meeting, 1898* (LMC, 1898), 31. In Dewey to ASQ, October 9, 1903, she noted the MIA's meeting was "thrown into such confusion & discomfiture" when Calfee resigned as field matron, Quinton Papers, Cornell.
78. WNIA, *Minutes of the Executive Board, November 20, 1890, to October 29, 1913*, 245, box 1, folder 4, WNIA Papers, Cornell. See also WNIA, "Our New Mission," *Indian's Friend*, May 1898, 7; and WNIA, "The Thursday Morning Session," *Annual Report, December 1898*, 26–28.
79. A donation by Mary S. Crozer, a WNIA executive board member from Philadelphia, to honor her husband J. Lewis Crozer who died in 1897. See "J. Lewis Crozer," *History of the Delaware County National Bank* (Chester: Press of the Chester Times, 1914), 129.
80. ASQ, "Among the Bears," *Indian's Friend*, October 1892, 2.
81. ASQ, "Among the Bears," 10, and WNIA, "Our Association's Chronology. Number 26," *Indian's Friend*, November 1899, 1.
82. LMC, "Mrs. Quinton," *Proceedings of the Sixteenth Annual Meeting*, 30–32.
83. See Louis H. Roddis, "The Last Indian Uprising in the United States," *Minnesota History Bulletin* 3, no. 5 (February 1920): 273–90. For quote, see "Thirtieth Annual Report of the BIC," in *Annual Reports of the Department of the Interior,1898* (Washington, DC: Government Printing Office, 1898), 1091.
84. LMC, "Platform of the Sixteenth Annual Lake Mohonk Indian Conference," *Proceedings of the Sixteenth Annual Meeting, 1898*, 7–8, reprinted in WNIA, "The Platform Adopted at Lake Mohonk, Oct., 1898," *Indian's Friend*, November 1898, 6–7. Gilfillan's entire address was reprinted, 2, 10–12.
85. WNIA, "Chippewas were Wronged," *Indian's Friend*, February 1899, 1.
86. See "Women's National Indian Association," *New York Times*, December 8, 1898, 1; "Justice for the Indian. Woman's National Indian Association Meets at Portland," *Boston Daily Globe*, December 8, 1898, 7. Also WNIA, *Annual Report, December 1898*, 9, for quote; for a summary see WNIA, "The Annual Meeting," *Indian's Friend*, January 1899, 2–5, 7–12; and Walter V. Hickey, "The Final Voyage of the Portland," *Prologue* 38, no. 4 (Winter 2006).
87. ASQ, "Our War Lesson," *Indian's Friend*, January 1899, 2, 6–7, also printed as a pamphlet.

88. Susan L. Webb, *Indian Appropriations Act of 1896* [electronic resource] The First Amendment Encyclopedia, Middle Tennessee State University (accessed March 17, 2019). http://www.mtsu.edu/first-amendment/article/1039/indian-appropriations-act-of1896. In 1897 the LMC recommended the immediate cessation of government appropriations for religious contract schools, *Proceedings of the Fifteenth Annual Meeting, 1898*, 116. For more, see WNIA, "Indian Schools," *Indian's Friend*, June 1899, 10–11.
89. See WNIA, "The Meetings of the Year," *Annual Report, December 1899* (Philadelphia: George Dukes, 1899), 14. "The Indian Association," *Cambridge Chronicle*, January 28, 1899, 11, reported the warm welcome ASQ was given as she spoke "with all her old ease and readiness, and with an unusual degree of emphasis and force."
90. For aunt see ASQ to WHW, February 23, and July 17, 1899, box 7, WHW Papers; and for editor, Littlefield and Parins, *American Indian and Alaska Native Newspapers and Periodicals*, 243. Beginning with the February 1897 issue, the editorial page under the paper's title read "Published by Mrs. A. S. Quinton."
91. ASQ to Hitchcock, May 27, 1899, and Tonner to Wright, June 17, 1899 (Land Authority 61540), copies in boxes 7, 8, WHW Papers. See WNIA, *Indian's Friend*, March 1899, 1, for Hitchcock.
92. Paul de Schweinitz to WHW, July 28, 1899, box 2, WHW Papers. For his three- issue article see WHW, "The Indians of Southern California," *Indian's Friend*, December 1899, 2; "Indians of Southern California, No. 2," *Indian's Friend*, February 1900, 2; and "The Indians of Southern California. No. 3," *Indian's Friend*, April, 1900, 2.
93. ASQ to WHW, August 24, 1899, box 7, WHW Papers.
94. Smiley to ASQ, September 1, 1899, Quaker Collection. She arrived on October 11, see WNIA, "The Meetings of the Year," *Annual Report, December 1899*, 15.
95. F. H. Hendry, a member of the Florida state legislature, who called their attention to the Seminoles, authored a bill setting aside this land. It passed in May 1899, see WNIA, "News and Notes," *Indian's Friend*, October 1899, 6–7. For the Rebecca Collins Hospital, see WNIA, "The New York Missionary Work," *The Report of Missions for 1900* (Philadelphia: 1900), 17.
96. Foote had served as WNIA treasurer for fourteen years. See NIA "The Helen R. Foote School and Mission," *Report of Missions for 1900–1901* (Philadelphia, 1901), 3–6; and WNIA, "From Our Helen R. Foote Mission," *Indian's Friend*, February 1900, 7. Isabella M. Cadallader had initiated the work at Fall River Mills.
97. LMC, "Mrs. Quinton," *Proceedings of the Seventeenth Annual Meeting, 1899* (LMC, 1900), 78.
98. WNIA, "The Mohonk Indian Conference," *Indian's Friend*, November 1899, 8–9.
99. ASQ to WHW, October 18, 1899, box 7, WHW Papers; and LMC, *Proceedings of the Seventeenth Annual Meeting*, 13, 30–33.
100. ASQ to WHW, November 7, 1899, box 7, WHW Papers.
101. WNIA, *Annual Report, December 1899*, 9, 23. See also WNIA, "The Annual Meeting," *Indian's Friend*, January 1900, 2, 8–11; and "Woman's Indian Association," *New York Times*, December 7, 1899, 3.
102. WNIA, "The Annual Address," *Indian's Friend*, January 1900, 2, 6–7.

Chapter 10

1. WNIA, "The Meetings of the Year," *Annual Report, December 1900* (Philadelphia: George Dukes, 1900), 15–16; and ASQ to Smiley, July 14, 1900, Quaker Collection.
2. ASQ to WHW, July 24 and August 1, 1900, box 7, WHW Papers. In ASQ to Alfred Homas Smiley [A. K. Smiley's twin brother], August 11, 1900, Quaker Collection, she wrote she would remain in Hamilton for the summer. See WNIA, "News and Notes," 4, for notification of death; WNIA, "Entered into Rest," 6; "Mrs. Mary L. Bonney Rambaut," 8–9, all in the August 1890 *Indian's Friend;* also "Well-Known Educator Dead," *Philadelphia Times*, July 26, 1900, 1.
3. ASQ to Mr. and Mrs. A. K. Smiley, September 14, 1900, Quaker Collection. Their addition at the end of the Spanish-American war prompted a new name, the Lake Mohonk Conference on the Indian and Other Dependent Peoples. See "Our Dependent Races," *Indian's Friend*, October 1900, 6.
4. ASQ to Jones, October 11, 1900, LR #50368–1900, RG 75, BIA, NA. Jones' agreement letter was printed in WNIA, "News and Notes," *Indian's Friend*, November 1900, 4. Ament instead moved to Berkeley, became the proprietor of the Ashby Furniture Company and mayor from 1932 to 1939.
5. LMC, "Fifth Session," *Proceedings of the Eighteenth Annual Meeting, 1900* (LMC, 1901), 106–107; see also WNIA, "The Eighteenth Mohonk Indian Conference," November 1900, 6–7; and WNIA, "The Lake Mohonk Indian Conference (concluded)," December 1900, 6–9 in *Indian's Friend.*
6. The congregation of the Beth Eden Baptist Church and the First Baptist Church merged, sold their properties, and constructed a new church, dedicated on October 14, 1900. For merger, see *The Bi-Centennial Celebration of the Founding of the First Baptist Church*, 7, 146–47.
7. WNIA, "Anniversary and Annual Meeting," *Indian's Friend*, January 1901, 2, 9–12. See also "Red Man Ready for Citizenship, so Declares President Quinton of the Woman's National Indian Association," *Philadelphia Inquirer*, December 11, 1900, 2.
8. WNIA, "In Memory of the Honorable President," A*nnual Report, December 1900*, 21–23.
9. For her schedule, see WNIA, *Annual Report, December 1901* (Philadelphia: George Dukes, 1901), 20; for her editorials, see ASQ to WHW, January 17, 1901, box 7, WHW Papers; and WNIA "The Mission Indians," January 1901 6–7; and WNIA, "The Mission Indians Again," February 1901, 7–8, in *Indian's Friend.* See "Starving Indians at La Posta. Bishop Johnson and Rev. H. B. Restarick Home From Long Trip," *San Diego Union and Daily Bee*, December 1900, 6.
10. ASQ to WHW, January 17 and 22 and February 7, 1901, the latter enclosing Gates' letter, box 7, WHW Papers.
11. ASQ to WHW, February 13 and 22, 1901, box 7, WHW Papers.
12. Johnson to ASQ, February 28, 1901, Quinton Papers, Cornell.

13. ASQ to WHW, March 2 and 19, and May 13, 1901 [for quote], box 7, WHW Papers, Huntington; for Yuma work, see WNIA, "News and Notes," *Indian's Friend*, April 1901, 4.
14. ASQ to Jones, March 26, 1901, LR #16352–1901, RG 75, BIA, NA; and ASQ to WHW, May 13, 1901, box 7, WHW Papers.
15. WNIA, Constance Goddard DuBois, "The Mission Indians Again," September 1901, 8; and a notice on her pamphlet in WNIA, "News and Notes," March 1901, 6 in *Indian's Friend*.
16. Constance Goddard DuBois, "Our American 'Reconcentrados,'" *City and State*, November 8, 1900, 297–299, later reprinted in IRA, *The Eighteenth Annual Report of the Executive Committee of the IRA* (Philadelphia: Office of the IRA, 1901), 23–30. See also *Listening to the Raven: The Southern California Ethnography of Constance Goddard DuBois*, ed. Don Laylander (Salinas, CA: Coyote Press, 2004); and Don Laylander, "Early Ethnographic Notes from Constance Goddard DuBois on the Indians of San Diego County," *Journal of California and Great Basin Anthropology* 26, no. 2 (2006), 205–14.
17. ASQ to WHW, January 17, 1901, box 7, WHW Papers.
18. WNIA, "The Report of Charles L. Partridge, Esq.," September 1901, 9–10, and WNIA, "Redlands Association," June 1901, 9–10 in *Indian's Friend*. See also "Women Discuss Indian Matters. Redlands Association Holds an Interesting Meeting," *Los Angeles Herald*, April 25, 1901, 10.
19. WNIA, "News and Notes," *Indian's Friend*, June 1901, 10.
20. WNIA, "Editorial Page," July 1901, 7; and WNIA, "Editorial Page," August 1901, 7–8, both in *The Indian's Friend*. The youths were Sortero Amago of La Jolla, who explained her family had 200 acres under cultivation, and Ramaulda Le Chuza, of Mesa Grande, explaining that some residents of her village were even citizens and had voted, 8.
21. On October 25, 1899, Brosius wrote Welsh that the law clerk had written a formal letter to the IRA recommending that the case be appealed, see reel 14, IRA Papers. See also Brosius to Welsh, October 28, 1899.
22. Brosius to Weinland, February 27, 1901, box 5, WHW Papers.
23. ASQ to WHW, June 3, and July 5, 1901, box 7, WHW Papers.
24. WNIA, "Help for Agua Caliente Indians," *Indian's Friend*, September 1901, 6.
25. WNIA, "Editorial Page," *Indian's Friend*, July 1901, 6.
26. ASQ to WHW, August 5, 1901, box 7, WHW Papers.
27. ASQ to WHW, August 20, 1901, box 7, WHW Papers.
28. WNIA, Constance Goddard DuBois," The Mission Indians—A Crisis," *Indian's Friend*, October 1901, 2.
29. ASQ to WHW, June 3, and July 5, 1901, box 7, WHW Papers.
30. ASQ to WHW, August 20, 1902, box 7, WHW Papers; and "Annual Report for 1902," Minute Books, Redlands Indian Association Collection, Heritage Room Archives, A. K. Smiley Public Library, Redlands, CA.

31. Tonner to ASQ, August 9, 1901 (Land #36865–1901), Quinton Papers, Cornell. See also WNIA, "Editorial page," *Indian's Friend*, October 1899, 7, also 6.
32. WNIA, "Land for the Florida Seminoles," *Indian's Friend*, October 1901, 7.
33. WNIA, "Land for the Florida Seminoles," 7.
34. Brecht to ASQ, September 4, 1901, and Hendry to Brecht, September 5, 1901, Quinton Papers, Cornell. On May 9, 1917, a state reservation was established with IRA's Matthew Sniffen playing a role. See James M. Covington, "Formation of the State of Florida Indian Reservation," *Florida Historical Quarterly* 64, no. 1 (July 1985): 62–75.
35. ASQ to WHW, September 12, 1901, box 7, WHW Papers; WNIA, *Annual Report, December 1901*, 20 for her schedule; LMC, "Quinton," *Proceedings of the Nineteenth Annual Meeting, 1901* (LMC, 1902), 78–79, 113–114 for DuBois; and WNIA, "The Lake Mohonk Indian Conference," *Indian's Friend*, November 1901, 2, 10–11.
36. WNIA, "News and Notes," *Indian's Friend*, December 1901, 10.
37. WNIA, "The Address of the President," *Annual Report, December 1901*, 12–14, 21. For a summary see NIA, "The Annual Meeting," *Indian's Friend*, January 1902, 2, 7–11.
38. For letter see NIA, "The Annual Meeting," 6.
39. NIA, "Vale-Salve," *Indian's Friend*, January 1902, 6; and ASQ to WHW, December 11, 1901, box 7, WHW Papers.
40. *Indian's Friend*, February 1902, 6.
41. For schedule, see NIA, *Annual Report, December 1902* (Philadelphia: 1902), 18; NIA, "News and Notes," *Indian's Friend*, April 1902, 4 (reception), 5 (DAR); see Mrs. Amelia Stone Quinton, DAR ID No. 19525, *The National Society of the Daughters of the American Revolution*, vol. 20, 196; and for conference with the commissioner see ASQ to WHW, February 3, 1902, box 7, WHW Papers.
42. NIA, ASQ, "Westward Ho," *Indian's Friend*, April 1902, 2.
43. ASQ to WHW, January 25, 1902, box 7, WHW Papers. According to Sister Alberta Cammack, the school had been founded by the Sisters of St. Joseph of Carondelet in 1886. See parentseyes.arizona.edu/carondelet/cammack_fortyuma.html.
44. ASQ to WHA, February 3 and 12, 1902, box 7, WHW Papers.
45. ASQ, "A Visit to the Yumas," *Indian's Friend*, May 1902, 2. See also NIA, "The Yuma Mission," *Missionary Report for 1903* (Philadelphia, 1903), 11–12; and NIA, "The Yuma Mission," *Missions of 1904* (Philadelphia, 1904), 22–25. Her promise of a cottage and permanent missionaries became a reality in1904 with the appointment of Rev. Frank T. Lea and his wife.
46. NIA, "Work Among the Yumas," *Indian's Friend*, July 1902, 10.
47. ASQ to Jones, April 3, 1902, LR #21137–1902, RG 75, BIA, NA.
48. ASQ, "A Visit to the Desert Indians," *Indian's Friend*, June 1902, 2, 7.
49. For addresses see NIA, *Annual Report, December 1902* (Philadelphia, 1902), 19; NIA, "News and Notes," June 1902, 4–5; and for San Francisco addresses, ASQ, "Dear Friends of the Indian's Friend," *Indian's Friend* September 2, 1902, 2.
50. NIA, "At Agua Caliente," 2, and NIA, "News and Notes," *Indian's Friend*, July 1902, 5.

51. NIA, "The Warner's Ranch Indians," *Indian's Friend*, June 1902, 6–7; and NIA, "News and Notes," *Indian's Friend*, August 1902, 6.
52. Lummis had invited Smiley to serve on his advisory board. Smiley to Lummis, January 20, 1902, Alfred K. Smiley, MS 1.1.4048, Charles F. Lummis Manuscript Collection, Braun Research Library, Southwest Museum, Autry Museum of the American West, Los Angeles (hereafter cited as Lummis Collection), Smiley described the upcoming eviction as one of the "saddest and most shameful events connected with the Indian Service."
53. "Final Report of the Warner's Ranch Indian Advisory Commission," Lummis Collection. See "New Home for Mission Indians," *San Francisco Call*, May 30, 1902, 2; ASQ, "The Agua Calientes," *Indian's Friend*, October 1902, 2; Mark Thompson, "Showdown at Warner's Ranch," *American Character: The Curious Life of Charles Fletcher Lummis and the Rediscovery of the Southwest* (New York: Arcade Publishing, 2001), 213–43.
54. Lummis to ASQ, May 23, 1902, Amelia S. Quinton MS 1.1.3648, Lummis Collection.
55. Lummis to Babbitt, May 23, 1902, Josephine H. Babbitt, MS 1.1.161, Lummis Collection. Learning from the *Los Angeles Times* that Lummis was going to confer with Roosevelt, Babbitt had written to him expressing hope that the Indians would be able "to retain their present homes."
56. Wright to Lummis, May 26, 1902, Wright MS1.1.4763A, Lummis Collection.
57. "Poor Indians Victimized. Female False Pretender Among Them," *Los Angeles Times*, May 23, 1902, A1; and Babbitt to Lummis, May 25, 1902, Babbitt MS 1.1.161, Lummis Collection. For details, see Valerie Sherer Mathes and Phil Brigandi, "The Mischief Record of 'La Gobernadora': Amelia Stone Quinton, Charles Fletcher Lummis, and the Warner Ranch Indian Removal," *Journal of San Diego History* 57, no. 1–2 (Winter/Spring 2011): 69–96.
58. ASQ to WHW, May 24, 1902, box 7, WHW Papers.
59. "Says She is Blameless," *Los Angeles Times*, May 30, 1902, 5.
60. Jones to ASQ, June 5, 1902, Quinton Papers, Cornell.
61. "Mischief Record of 'La Gobernadora.' Former Indian Agent Tells of Devil, She Raised," *Los Angeles Times*, May 26, 1902, 9.
62. "Mrs. Quinton Explains," *Los Angeles Times*, May 28, 1902, 5; and ASQ, "Dear Friends of the Indian's Friend," *Indian's Friend*, September 1902, 2.
63. ASQ to Lummis, June 3, 1902; and "Mrs. Quinton's Reply, To the Slanderous report of May 23rd," Amelia S. Quinton MS 1.1.3648, Lummis Collection.
64. "Fight Till Last Ditch. Trouble is Brewing at Warner's Ranch," *Los Angeles Times*, July 26, 1902, A1.
65. For itinerary see NIA, *Annual Report, December 1902* (Philadelphia, 1902), 19; and "Champions the American Indian. Mrs. Quinton, President of National Association to Speak," *San Francisco Chronicle*, August 22, 1902, 13; and "Aiding Indians is Her Mission; Address by the President of the National Association," *San Francisco Chronicle*, September 1, 1902, 3; and "To Discuss the Work of Indian Association; Mrs. Amelia Quinton of Philadelphia Will Talk at Calvary Presbyterian Church," *San Francisco Call*, August 31, 1902, 21.

66. Bidwell to ASQ, July 31, 1902, Quinton Papers, Cornell.
67. For more on the school, see ASQ, "Over the Siskiyou Range and Eastward," *Indian's Friend*, November 1902, 2; and Valerie Sherer Mathes, "The Women's National Indian Association in 19th Century Northern California," *Aloha, Amigos! The Richard H. Dillon Memorial Volume Brand Book 24* (Los Angeles: Westerners International, 2020), 450–53.
68. ASQ, "Over the Siskiyou Range and Eastward," 2, 8; and ASQ to Smiley, September 26. 1902, Quaker Collection.
69. ASQ to Smiley, October 14, 1902, Quaker Collection.
70. LMC, *Proceedings of the Twentieth Annual Meeting, 1902* (LMC: 1903), 29–31; NIA, "The Mohonk Indian Conference," *Indian's Friend*, November 1902, 6–7, 10–11.
71. Stone to ASQ, December 31, 1902, Quinton Papers, Cornell. A layman in Wilmington, Delaware's First Unitarian Society from 1866 to 1895, he was ordained in 1898, serving parishes in Kansas City and in Oakland, San Francisco, Santa Barbara, and Santa Cruz, California. From 1911 to 1913 he was mayor in Santa Cruz. See Susan Mulchaney Chase, Ruth Mette, Peggy Rawheiser, *150 Years of History, Roots and Branches, Continuity and Change* (First Unitarian Church of Wilmington, Delaware, 2016), 11; "In Memoriam, George Whitefield Stone," *Pacific Unitarian* 32, no. 4 (April 1923): 99; *California Blue Book or State Roster, 1913–1915* (California State Printing Office, 1915), 492; and "A Progressive Golden Wedding," *California Outlook* 18, no. 5 (January 30, 1915), 9–10.

Chapter 11

1. George W. Stone to ASQ, February 21, 1903, Quinton Papers, Cornell, described Redlands as physically quite beautiful but "theologically" more orthodox than any eastern place he had worked. He wrote on June 23 that he had revived the Redlands Church and was looking for a minister to take over. He was now preaching at the First Church in San Francisco, hoping to move to Palo Alto to start up another congregation
2. For addresses, see NIA, "Meetings Addressed by Mrs. Quinton," *Annual Report, December 1903* (Philadelphia: Times Printing House, 1903), 20; and "Deprecates the Attitude of National Government Toward its Wards—Other Topics Discussed," *Evening Star* (Washington, DC), March 4, 1903, 7.

   In Seymour Stone to ASQ, May 10, he cautioned her to rest "as the years go & we linger superfluous," Quinton Papers, Cornell. Seymour, who lived in Syracuse, was a trustee of the parochial fund of the Protestant Episcopal Church in the Diocese of Central New York and managed the Syracuse chapter of the Sons of the American Revolution. See *A National Register of the Society Sons of the American Revolution* (New York: Andrew M. Kellogg, 1902), 737; and *Journal of the Thirtieth Annual Convention of the Protestant Episcopal Church in the Diocese of Central New York, 1898* (Utica, NY: Herald Job Department, 1898), 87
3. Boardman to ASQ, March 19, 1903, Quinton Papers, Cornell.

4. Gray to ASQ, April 30, 1903, Quinton Papers, Cornell; and NIA, "The Waiting Seminoles," *Indian's Friend*, June 1903, 2. It was reported that during his annual visit to the Everglades, he expressed the hope of opening a small school for the Indian trader's children to encourage Indian attendance, *Indian's Friend*, July 1903, 10.
5. Jones to ASQ, May 2, 1903, Quinton Papers, Cornell; and ASQ, "Our Missionary News," *Indian's Friend*, June 1903, 9, for Weinland's comments. See also NIA, "News and Notes," 5.
6. For itinerary see ASQ, "Summer Notes," *Indian's Friend*, October 1903, 8–9.
7. The previous were (1) Two Gray Hills, New Mexico; (2), the Rebecca Collins Memorial Hospital at Jewett, New Mexico; and (3) near Tuba, Arizona, which opened in January 1903. For Cole, see ASQ, "Getting Ready for Work," September 1903, 9. For Tuba, see ASQ, "The New Navajo Mission," July 1903, 8–9; NIA, "Tuba News," August 1903, 8–9; ASQ, "The Tuba Letter," September 1903, 8–9; and ASQ, "Tuba News," April 1904, 8, which gave a transfer date of March 1, 1904, to the NYCIA, all in *Indian's Friend.* In September 1903 the Indian Office granted the NIA the use of four acres and buildings near Tuba, see A. C. Tonner, Acting Commissioner to ASQ, May 6, 1904, Quinton Papers, Cornell.
8. Seymour to ASQ, July 7 and July 27, 1903, Quinton Papers, Cornell. For her Homer address see *Cortland Evening Standard*, July 7, 1903, and for her schedule see NIA, *Annual Report, December 1903* (Philadelphia: Times Printing House, 1903), 20.
9. ASQ, "Waste Places," *Indian's Friend*, July 1903, 2, included text of the Indian's petition; see also ASQ, "Waste Places," *Indian's Friend*, August 1903, 2; ASQ, "News of Our Mohave-Apaches," *Indian's Friend*, December 1903, 6–7; NIA, "The Mohave-Apache Mission," *Missions of 1904* (Publication of the NIA, 1904), 17–22; and ASQ, "From the National Headquarters: Work at Camp McDowell," *Indian's Friend*, May 1905, 10. See also Gill to ASQ, November 10, 1905, Quinton Papers, Cornell. In ASQ to Leupp, December 12, 1905, she requested Gill's appointment as a field matron, LR #99692–1905, RG 75, BIA, NA.
10. ASQ, "From Agua Caliente to Pala," August 1903, 6–7, and NIA, "News from Pala, Cal.," December 1903, 11, *Indian's Friend;* for removal see Mathes and Brigandi, *Reservations, Removal, and Reform*, 176–79. Jenkins, one of eight special inspectors, served from 1918 to 1919 as agent at the Morongo Reservation. Babbitt later transferred to Santo Domingo Pueblo as a field matron, then to Algodones, New Mexico, before moving to the Panama Canal Zone in 1916 to live with her son, see "Mrs. Josephine Babbitt," *New York Times*, July 14, 1940, 33. In NIA, "Missionary Exigencies," *Indian's Friend*, March 1910, 8, they reprinted her January 10 letter describing her work at Algodones. She was working among more than five hundred Indians, "very much uncivilized and with no wish to be civilized, having almost continuous dances and opposed to everything but having their own way," she wrote.
11. Weinland to ASQ, August 21, 1903, Quinton Papers, Cornell. The text of the petition is not known.
12. Weinland to ASQ, September 6, 1903, Quinton Papers, Cornell.

13. Smiley to ASQ, September 5, 1903, Quinton Papers, Cornell for invitation. LMC, "Mrs. Amelia S. Quinton," *Proceedings of the Twenty-first Annual Meeting, 1903* (LMC Conference, 1904), 134–36; and NIA, "The Mohonk Conference," *Indian's Friend*, November 1903, 6–7, 9–11.
14. "Headquarters Changed," *Rochester Democrat and Chronicle*, December 10, 1903, 17. They rented a room in the Presbyterian Building on Fifth Avenue. See also NIA, "Our New Headquarters," *Indian's Friend*, March 1904, 7.
15. NIA, *Annual Report, December 1903* (Philadelphia: Times Printing House, 1903), 32; NIA, "The Annual Meeting," *Indian's Friend*, January 1904, 2, 6–7, 8–11.
16. "Helen Edith Ainsworth Wakeman," *Woman's Who's Who of America, 1914–1915* (New York: American Commonwealth Company, 1914), 845. In Wakeman to ASQ, October 31, 1903, Quinton Papers Cornell, she accepted the new position, "trusting in God for inspiration."
17. NIA, *Indian's Friend*, January 1904, 6 for quote; Reel to ASQ, January 9, 1904, and Dewey to ASQ, January 12, 1904, Quinton Papers, Cornell.
18. For example, see ASQ, "From Kin Hoyhony," May 1904, 9; ASQ, "Moencopi News," September 1904, 8; and ASQ, "Our Mojave-Apache Mission," *Indian's Friend*, September 1904, 8–9.
19. For schedule see NIA, "Meetings Addressed by Mrs. Quinton," *Annual Report, December 1904* (New York: 1904), 22–23; and NIA, "News and Notes," June 1904, 4, for Washington visit; and NIA, "News and Notes," August 1904, for his visit, in *Indian's Friend;* and ASQ to WHW, July 6 and 15, 1904, box 7, WHW Papers.
20. ASQ to Smiley, September 8, 1904, Quaker Collection, for acceptance of invitation; LMC, "Mrs. Amelia S. Quinton," *Proceedings of the Twenty-Second Annual Meeting, 1904* (LMC, 1904), 152–53, 163 for resolution; and NIA, "The Mohonk Conference," *Indian's Friend*, November 1904, 2, 7–9, 11.
21. NIA, *Annual Report, December 1904*, 24 (nominating committee); and NIA, "The Annual Meeting," *Indian's Friend*, January 1905, 7–9.
22. Leupp, an IRA member, was welcomed by the association, see NIA, *Indian's Friend*, January 1905, 6; and Donald L. Parman, "Francis Ellington Leupp, 1905–1909," *The Commissioners of Indian Affairs*, 221–32.
23. ASQ to Jones, December 9, 1904 (copy), Quinton Papers, Cornell; for response see NIA, "Letter from Commissioner Jones," *Indian's Friend*, February 1905, 7.
24. ASQ to Roosevelt, December 21, 1904 (copy). On January 17, 1905, Larrabee responded that he had received her letter to the president and hoped all the subjects she covered would "receive such attention as they merit," in Quinton Papers, Cornell.
25. ASQ, "Regarding Indian Trust Funds," *Indian's Friend*, March 1905, 6–7. See also her article "The Coming Reform," June issue, 6–7.
26. ASQ "Field Matron Work," *Indian's Friend*, March 1905, 8–9. See also, Tonner to ASQ, May 20 and June 2, 1904, and Larabee to ASQ, February 17, 1905, Quinton Papers, Cornell.
27. ASQ, "From Yuma," *Indian's Friend*, June 1905, 9; and NIA, "The Yuma Mission," *Missions of 1904*, 22–25.

28. ASQ, "From the National Headquarters," *Indian's Friend*, June 1905, 10.
29. NIA, "Meetings addressed by Mrs. Quinton," *Annual Report, December 1905* (New York, NY: 1905), 24; and NIA, "The Indian Institute," *Indian's Friend*, July 1905, 7–8, and NIA, "The Indian Institute," *Indian's Friend*, August 1905, 6. For the Cortland and Homer addresses see "News and Notes," *Indian's Friend*, September 1905, 4–5.
30. "Local News," *Homer Republican*, September 7, 1905; "Homer," *Cortland Standard*, September 8, 1905, 8; and "Mrs. Quinton Resigns," *Cortland Standard*, December 14, 1905, 12.
31. ASQ, "Greenville Work Again," *Indian's Friend*, September 1905, 10; and Wentzell to ASQ, February 5, 1904, and December 19, 1904, Quinton Papers, Cornell. See NIA, "News and Notes," *Indian's Friend*, March 1904, 5.
32. Wentzell to ASQ, May 5, 1905, Quinton Papers, Cornell.
33. ASQ, "Greenville Work Again," *Indian's Friend*, September 1905, 10; ASQ to Wentzell, August 23, 1905; and Wetzell to ASQ, August 8, 1905, in Quinton Papers, Cornell.
34. ASQ to Truebody, October 25, 1905, Quinton Papers, Cornell.
35. ASQ to Smiley, September 9, 1905, Quaker Collection; and LMC, "Mrs. Quinton," *Proceedings of the Twenty-third Annual Meeting, 1905* (LMC, 1905), 208–9. See NIA, "Indians and Other Dependent Peoples," *Indian's Friend*, October 1905, 2, 8–9; and NIA, "The Mohonk Conference," *Indian's Friend*, November 1905, 2, 8–11.
36. A graduate of the Chicago Theological Seminary, he held pastorates in Illinois and New York, see "Humphrey, William Brewster," *Who's Who in New York, 1914, a Biographical Dictionary of Contemporaries*, ed. William F. Mohn (New York: Who's Who in New York City and State, 1914), 377–78.
37. NIA, *Annual Report, December 1905* (New York, 1905), 25–26; and ASQ, "From the National Headquarters," *Indian's Friend*, November 1905, 7. For Carter's lace work, see Jane E. Simonsen, *Making Home Work: Domesticity and Native American Assimilation in the American West, 1860–1919* (Chapel Hill: University of North Carolina Press, 2006), 105–9; little information exists on Clark.
38. ASQ, "From our Apache-Mojave Field;" ASQ, "Yuma News;" and ASQ, "Mrs. Lea's Letter," 10–11, *Indian's Friend*, February 1906.
39. WNIA, "Christmas in the New Chapel at Greenville," *Indian's Friend*, February 1897, 8–9.
40. ASQ to Leupp, March 7, 1906, LR #21342–1906, RG 75, BIA, NA; see also Leupp to ASQ, March 21, 1906, and Larabee to ASQ, March 10, 1906, in Quinton Papers, Cornell.
41. Johnson to ASQ, February 21, 1906, Quinton Papers, Cornell.
42. Leupp to ASQ, March 21, 1906; ASQ to Leupp, March 27, 1906 (copy); and ASQ to Trubody, March 27, 1906 (copy), in Quinton Papers, Cornell.
43. ASQ to Johnson, March 27, 1906, in response to Johnson to ASQ, March 20, 1906. In Johnson to ASQ, April 5, in Quinton Papers, Cornell, he wrote he had found a five-room house near the chapel at $5 a month. See also ASQ to Johnson, April 10, LR, General Correspondence, 1894–1921, Greenville (Box 69) 1906–1910, RG 75, BIA, NA, San Bruno, California.

44. Larrabee to ASQ, March 30, 1906, Quinton Papers, Cornell.
45. ASQ to Johnson, April 12, 1906, and Johnston to ASQ, April 18, 1906. In Johnson to ASQ, April 5, 1906, Quinton Papers, Cornell, he noted he had visited Trubody earlier that month.
46. Larrabee to ASQ, April 18, 1906; ASQ to Larrabee, April 21, 1906; and ASQ to Johnson, April 21, 1906, in Quinton Papers, Cornell; and ASQ, "Mission and Other News," *Indian's Friend*, April 1906, 8.
47. NIA, "News and Notes," 5, see also ASQ, "Good News from Our Missions," 8–9, *Indian's Friend*, May 1906.
48. ASQ to Rockefeller, April 23, 1906, and ASQ to Mrs. Rockefeller, May 24, 1906, Quinton Papers, Cornell. This person's identity is unknown.
49. ASQ to the Missionary Committee, May 15, 1906; and ASQ to Leupp, May 22, 1906, Quinton Papers, Cornell.
50. ASQ to Larrabee, May 8, 1906, enclosed with a copy of the deed, LR #40607–1906, RG 75, BIA, NA; Larrabee to ASQ, May 16, 1906, and ASQ to Leupp, May 22, 1906 (copy), Quinton Papers, Cornell.
51. Johnson to ASQ, May 14, 16, and 25, 1906; and ASQ to Johnson, May 22, 1906, Quinton Papers, Cornell.
52. ASQ, "Our Mission News," *Indian's Friend*, July 1906, 9; ASQ, "A Vacation Mission Report," *Indian's Friend*, August 1906, 7; and ASQ, "A Missionary's Letter," *Indian's Friend*, October 1906, 8.
53. ASQ to Smiley, September 14, 1906, Quaker Collection; LMC, *Proceedings of the Twenty-Fourth Annual Meeting, 1906* (LMC, 1906), 141–42; and NIA, "The Mohonk Indian Conference," *Indian's Friend*, November 1906, 2, 8–11.
54. NIA, *Report of Missions, 1906* (New York: Volunteer Press Print, 1906), 4–12, 14–20.
55. ASQ, "Progress at Greenville," 7, and ASQ, "Apache-Mojave News," 8, *Indian's Friend*, January 1907. In April 1907 this station was turned over to the Presbyterian Board, see NIA, "Recent Missions," *Report of Missions, 1907* (New York: Volunteer Press Print, 1907), 8.
56. ASQ to WHW, January 9, 1907, box 7, WHW Papers; and ASQ, "Fruitage," *Indian's Friend*, February 1907, 8.
57. ASQ to WHW, March 20, April 11, and June 22, 1907, box 7, WHW Papers; and for talk "Needs Four Acres to Turn Around," *Los Angeles Herald*, June 4, 1907, 7.
58. ASQ to WHW, June 22, 1907, box 7, WHW Papers; NIA, *Annual Report, December 1907* (New York:1907), 11; and in NIA, "Office Notes and Comment," *Indian's Friend*, June 1907, 9, she wrote that her investigation in Moapa, Nevada, disclosed conditions not suitable for a mission.
59. NIA, "Jamaica Plain (MA) Indian Association," *Indian's Friend*, January 1908, 5.
60. ASQ, "Hunting a New Field," *Indian's Friend*, August 1907, 7.
61. ASQ, "A Crowned Entrance," and "A Letter from our New Mission," *Indian's Friend*, November 1907, 6–8.
62. ASQ to WHW, July 12, 1907, box 7, WHW Papers.

63. NIA, "An Indian Conference in California," *Indians Friend*, September 1907, 2, 11–12,; see also Mathes, *Divinely Guided*, 136, 140–45, 151, 160.
64. ASQ to Smiley, September 3, and October 10, 1907, Quaker Collection. See NIA, *Annual Report, December 1907* (New York: 1907), 11. See also "Woman's Missionary Union to Hold All-Day Session," *Los Angeles Herald*, November 4, 1907, 6.
65. ASQ, "The California Conference," *Indian's Friend*, June 1908, 6–7.
66. Valerie Sherer Mathes, "C. E. Kelsey and California's Landless Indians," in Mathes, *Gender, Race, and Power in the Indian Reform Movement*, 163–81; and for the NCIA, see Mathes, *Divinely Guided*, 129–52.
67. ASQ to Smiley, August 13, 1908, Quaker Collection.
68. ASQ, "The Third Zayante Conference," *Indian's Friend*, September 1908, 2, 7–8, and ASQ, "Third Zayante Conference (Concluded from last issue)," October, 10, for quotes. For True see "The Right Woman for Her Work," 5, September issue.
69. NIA, *Annual Report, December 1908* (New York: 1908), 12. See ASQ to WHW, February 17, 1909, box 7, WHW Papers.
70. ASQ, "Progress at the New Mission," 6–7; ASQ, "Our Greenville Mission," *Indian's Friend*, January 1908, 7; and ASQ, "Blessing at Greenville, *Indian's Friend*, March 1908, 7. In September 1908 the Greenville station was transferred to the Woman's Home Missionary Society of the Methodist Episcopal Church; see NIA, "News and Notes," *Indian's Friend*, November 1908, 4.
71. ASQ to Smiley, September 4, and October 13, 1908, Quaker Collection; and NIA, "Miss Sybil Carter," *Indian's Friend*, October 1908, 7–8.
72. NIA, *Annual Report*, December 1908, 26–27.
73. NIA, "News and Notes," *Indian's Friend*, April 4, 1909; and "Unites with Congregational Church," *Homer Republican*, March 18, 1909, 4.
74. ASQ, "A Patriotic Holiday," *Indian's Friend*, July 1909, 6–7.
75. ASQ to Wilson, January 14, 1908, LS: Klamath Agency, Box 21, RG 75, BIA, NA.
76. NIA, "The New Klamath Mission in Oregon," *Report of Missions, 1908*, 15–23.
77. ASQ, "Our First Oregon Mission Work," *Indian's Friend*, January 1909, 7; see also ASQ, "A Klamath Report," 6–7, February issue; and ASQ, "At the Klamath Mission," 6–7, March issue.
78. ASQ to Phillips, August 20, 1909, and ASQ to Smiley, October 5, 1909, in Quaker Collection.
79. NIA, *Annual Report, December 1909* (New York, NY: 1909), 12, 20–21, 24.
80. NIA, "Office Notes and Comment," May 1910, 9; and ASQ, "An Outlook," October 1910, 6, in *Indian's Friend*.
81. ASQ to Smiley, September 3, and October 4, 1910.Quaker Collection.
82. NIA, "The Annual Meeting of the National Indian Association," *Indian's Friend*, December 1910, 2; and NIA, *Annual Report, December 1910* (New York: 1910), 24.
83. ASQ to Smiley, August 27, 1911, Quaker Collection.
84. ASQ to Smiley, October 26, 1911, Quaker Collection; and NIA, "The Lake Mohonk Conference," *Indian's Friend*, November 1911, 12.

85. NIA, *Annual Report, December 1911* (New York: 1911), 14, 29.
86. NIA, *Indian's Friend*, December 1912, 6–7, and NIA, *Annual Report, December 1912* (New York: 1912), 27.
87. NIA, "Office Notes and Comment," *Indian's Friend*, February 1913, 9–10, and *Homer Republican*, January 23, 1913, 5.
88. ASQ to Mr. and Mrs. Daniel Smiley, August 30 and October 14, 1913, Quaker Collection.
89. NIA, "Mrs. Quinton's Greeting to the Annual Meeting," *Indian's Friend*, December 1913, 6; see also NIA, *Annual Report, December 1913* (New York: 1913), 29.
90. LMC, "Members Present," *Report of the Thirty-Second Annual LMC on the Indian and Other Dependent Peoples* (LMC, 1914), 210, and NIA, "The Annual Meeting of the National Indian Association," *Indian's Friend*, December 1914, 2, 10.
91. ASQ to Daniel Smiley, September 2, and October 12, 1915, Quaker Collection. NIA, *The Annual Report* (New York: December: 1915), 34; and ASQ, "Mrs. George Dana Boardman," *Indian's Friend*, November 1915, 6.
92. ASQ to Daniel Smiley, August 30, October 11, and 16, 1916, Quaker Collection.
93. NIA, "Annual Meeting of the National Indian Association," *Indian's Friend*, January 1917, 2; NIA, *Annual Report* (New York: 1916), 28; and NIA, *Annual Report* (New York: 1917), 32.
94. ASQ, "The New Year's Call," *Indian's Friend*, January 1918, 6–7.
95. NIA, "New York City Indian Association," *Indian's Friend*, May 1918, 45; and NIA, "Annual Meeting of the National Indian Association," *Indian's Friend*, January 1920, 7.
96. NIA, "Annual Meeting of the National Indian Association," January 1921, 5; for address see NIA, "Annual Meeting of the National Indian Association," *Indian's Friend*, January 1922, 2, 6.
97. "Brief Personal Paragraph," *Homer Republican*, May 5, 1910, 3; "Homer," *Cortland Standard*, May 7, 1910, 8, and "Commencement Exercises and Alumni Banquet," *Cortland Standard*, June 22, 1910, 8; and "Normal 'Grads' Hold Exercise," *The Post Standard* [Syracuse], June 22, 1910, 13. See also *Cortland Standard*, July 15, 1910.
98. *Homer Republican*, June 8, 1911, 3; and October 12, 1911, 5.
99. *Homer Republican*, May 16, 1912, 3; and *Homer Republican*, August 22, 1912, 3 (death of sister-in-law).
100. *Cortland Democrat*, October 11, 1912, 8; and "Meeting of Sennightly Club," *Homer Republican*, October 10, 1912, 5.
101. "Missionary Lawn Social," *Homer Republican*, July 17, 1913, 5; "Homer," *Cortland Standard*, September 16, 1914, 8; for sale see *Cortland Democrat*, March 19, 1915.
102. "Mrs. Amelia Stone Quinton," *New York Times*, June 25, 1926, 21; and *Cortland Democratic*, July 2, 1926, for burial. See also "Mrs. Amelia Stone Quinton," *Indian's Friend*, July 1926, 6.
103. "Mrs. Quinton Leaves Trust Fund to Churches," *Syracuse* (NY) *Journal*, December 7, 1928, 8.

Conclusion

1. NIA, "The Fiftieth Anniversary Luncheon," *Indian's Friend*, January 1930, 5.
2. NIA, *Fifty-Fourth Annual Report* (New York: December 1933), 2, 8–12.
3. NIA, *Indian's Friend*, June 1951, 2–4.
4. "Constitution of the Indian Treaty-Keeping and Protective Association," (June 3, 1881), 18, ITKPA, WNIA Papers, Cornell.
5. WNIA, "Constitution of the WNIA," *Annual Meeting and Report of the WNIA, October 27, 1883*, 19–20.
6. WNIA, *Annual Report of the WNIA, November 1886*, 9–11.
7. LMC, "President Gates," *Proceedings of the Eighth Annual meeting of the LMC*, 101, reprinted in WNIA, "Well-Deserved Tribute," *Indian's Friend*, August 1891, 2.
8. ASQ, *Seven Ways to Help Indians* (Philadelphia, November 1890), 11.
9. ASQ, "The Indian," in *The Literature of Philanthropy*, ed. Frances Abigale Rockwell Goodale (New York: Harper & Brothers, 1893), 122, 127.
10. ASQ, "The Providential Beginnings" (President's Address of 1894), (N.p.: N.d), 7. However, attached was a listing of NIA officers for 1906.
11. ASQ, "The Annual Address of the President, November 7th, 1888," 2, 3.
12. Lori Jacobson, email message to author, April 1, 2021.
13. ASQ to Welsh, February 21, 1892, reel 8, *IRA Papers*; ASQ, "The Annual Address, November 20th, 1889," in *What It Has Done, What It Ought to Do* (Philadelphia, 1889), 8–9.

Bibliography

Primary Sources

Manuscript Collections

American Baptist Historical Society Archives Center. Mercer University, Atlanta, GA.
Babbitt, Josephine. Letter. MS 1.1.161. Charles F. Lummis Manuscript Collection. Braun Research Library, the Autry Museum of the American West, Los Angeles, CA.
Cambridge Branch, Massachusetts Indian Association. Records. Brinkler Library, Cambridge Historical Society, Cambridge, MA.
Dawes, Henry Laurens. Papers. Manuscript Division. Library of Congress, Washington, DC.
Gilman Family Papers. Boxes 24–26. William Henry Weinland Papers, 1853–1946. Record no. b1526485. Huntington Library, Art Museum, and Botanical Gardens, San Marino, CA.
Indian Rights Association. Annual Report of the Executive Committee. Originally published annually in Philadelphia by the Association they are available at university libraries, digitized on the Internet Archive (https://archive.org/), and reproductions have been published by Nabu Press.
Indian Rights Association. Records, Collection 1523 (1830–1986) [Incoming Correspondence, 1864–1968]. Historical Society of Pennsylvania, Philadelphia, PA. http://www2.hsp.org/collections/manuscripts/i/IRA1523.html.
Indian Rights Association, Cambridge Branch. Secretary's Records. Cambridge Public Library, Cambridge, MA.
Jackson, Helen Hunt. Letters to Amelia Quinton and Abbot Kinney: ALS, 1880 Dec.–1884 Feb. Bancroft Library, University of California, Berkeley, CA.
Jackson, Helen Hunt. Collection 100, Special Collections. UCLA Library, Charles E. Young Research Library, University of California at Los Angeles, Los Angeles, CA.
Kellogg Memorial Research Library. Cortland County Historical Society, Cortland, NY.
Lummis, Charles Fletcher. Manuscript Collection. Braun Research Library, Southwest Museum, Autry Museum of the American West, Los Angeles, CA.
Massachusetts Indian Association. *Annual Reports*. Various years. Originally published annually in Boston by Frank Wood, Printer, for the Association they are available

at some large libraries and digitized versions are on the Internet Archive (https://archive.org/) and Hathi Trust Digital Library (https://babel.hathitrust.org/).
Morgan County Archives. Madison, GA.
National Archives and Records Administration. Bureau of Indian Affairs, Letters Received. Record Group 75. Washington, DC.
Quaker Collection. Haverford College, Haverford, PA.
Quinton, Amelia Stone. Papers. Division of Rare and Manuscript Collections, Carl A. Kroch Library, Cornell University, Ithaca, NY.
Quinton, Amelia Stone. MS 1.1.3648. Charles F. Lummis Manuscript Collection. Braun Research Library, Southwest Museum. Autry Museum of the American West, Los Angeles, CA.
Redlands Indian Association Collection. Minute Books. Heritage Room Archives. A. K. Smiley Public Library, Redlands, CA.
Rust, Horatio Nelson. Papers, 1799–1906. Record no. b1526547. Huntington Library, Art Museum, and Botanical Gardens, San Marino, CA.
Smiley, Alfred K. [MS 1.1.4048] Charles F. Lummis Manuscript Collection. Braun Research Library, Southwest Museum. Autry Museum of the American West, Los Angeles, CA.
Weinland, William Henry. Papers, 1853–1946. Record no. b1526485. Huntington Library, Art Museum, and Botanical Gardens, San Marino, CA.
Welsh, Hebert. Collection. Historical Society of Pennsylvania, Philadelphia, PA.
Women's National Indian Association (WNIA). Papers, 1880–1951. Collection No. 9237. Division of Rare and Manuscript Collections, Carl A. Kroch Library, Cornell University, Ithaca, NY.
Minutes of Executive Board Meetings from November 17, 1883, to October 21, 1890.
Minutes of the Trustees
Records of the Indian Treaty-Keeping and Protective Association from Dec. 1880.
Woosley, David. Diaries and Correspondence, 1896–1940. Record no. b1630460. Huntington Library, Art Museum, and Botanical Gardens, San Marino, CA.

Government Documents

"An Act for the Relief of the Omaha Tribe. . . ." The Statutes at Large of the United States of America from December 1887 to March 1889. Washington: Government Printing Office, 1889: 150–51.
Annual Report of the Commissioner of Indian Affairs to the Secretary of the Interior. Washington, DC: Government Printing Office, various years.
Board of Indian Commissioners. *Annual Reports of Conference with Representatives of Missionary Boards and Indian Rights Associations.* Washington, DC: Government Printing Office, various years.
Executive Documents of the Senate of the United States. Washington, DC: Government Printing Office, 1889.
Journal of the Executive Proceedings of the Senate of the United States of America. Vol. 28. Washington, DC: Government Printing Office, 1909.

"Journal of the Southern Ute Commission, by T. S. Childs, Secretary." *The Executive Documents of the Senate of the United States*. Vol. 2. Washington, DC: Government Printing Office, 1889.

Proceedings on the Occasion of the Presentation of the Petition of the Women's National Indian Association, by Hon. H. L. Dawes, February 21, 1882. Washington, DC, 1882.

Report of the Secretary of the Interior; Being Part of the Message and Documents Communicated to the Two Houses of Congress. Vol 2. Washington, DC: Government Printing Office, 1896.

"Testimony Taken Before the Committee of Indian Affairs," House of Representatives, 44th Congress, 1st sess., Misc. Doc. #167. *Index of the Miscellaneous Documents of the House of Representatives for the First Session of the Forty-Fourth Congress*. Washington, DC: Government Printing Office, 1876.

U. S. Congress. House. Vol. 10, Part 2, 46th Cong., 2nd sess. February 20, 1880. *Congressional Record*, 1044.

U. S. Congress. Senate. "Senator Dawes Presents Petition," 46th Cong., 3rd sess., January 27, 1881. *Congressional Record*, 953–54.

U. S. Congress. Senate. Vol. 13, Part 2, 47th Cong., 1st sess., February 21, 1882. *Congressional Record*, 1326–30.

Primary Sources

Alabama Official and Statistical Register. Montgomery: Brown Printing Company, 1903.

Annual Report of the Association for the Advancement of Women, for 1881. Boston: Cochrane & Sampson, 1882.

Annual Report of the Northern Baptist Convention. Vol. 9. Philadelphia: American Baptist Publication Society, 1916.

Baptist Home Mission Monthly. American Baptist Historical Society Archives, Center, Mercer University, Atlanta, Georgia. Various issues.

Baptist Home Missions in North America, 1832–1882. New York: Baptist Home Mission Rooms, 1883.

Barber, John W., and Henry Howe. *Historical Collections of the State of New York*. New York: S. Tuttle, 1842.

Brunner, Edmund de Schweinitz. "The First Protestant Mission in Southern California. Its Establishment." *History of the Moravian Mission to the Indians of Southern California*. Bethlehem, PA: Times Publishing Co., 1923.

———. "History of the Moravian Mission to the Indians of Southern California." *Proceedings of the Society for Propagating the Gospel Among the Heathen, for the Year Ending August 19, 1914*.

Campbell, Jesse Harrison. *Georgia Baptists; Historical and Biographical*. Macon, GA: J. W. Burke & Company, 1874.

Catalogue of Georgia Female College, 1855–56. Benj. G. Liddon, 1856.

Catalogue of the Officers and Students of Cortland Academy, for the Academic Year 1848–50. Homer, NY: Rufus A. Reed, 1850.

"Catharine Beecher: Circular addressed to Benevolent Ladies of the U. States." In *The Cherokee Removal: A Brief History with Documents*, edited by Theda Perdue and Michael D. Green. Boston: Bedford/St. Martin's 2005: 113–14.

Cathcart, William. *The Baptist Encyclopedia*. Philadelphia: Louis H. Evarts, 1883.

Centennial Temperance Volume: A Memorial of the International Temperance Conference held in Philadelphia, June 1876. New York: New York Temperance Society and Publication House, 1877.

Chesnut [sic] Street Female Seminary, No. 525 Chesnut [sic] Street, Philadelphia. Philadelphia: John Young, 1850.

Chestnut Street Female Seminary. Boarding and Day School, Philadelphia, No. 525 Chestnut Street. Philadelphia: Henry B. Ashmead, 1855.

Chestnut Street Female Seminary. Boarding and Day School, Philadelphia, No. 1615 Chestnut Street. Philadelphia: Henry B. Ashmead, 1860.

Christian Educators in Council: Sixty Addresses by American Educators with Historical Notes Upon the National Education Assembly Held at Ocean Grove, N. J. August 9–12, 1883, compiled by Rev. J. C. Hartzell. New York: Phillips & Hunt, 1884.

Connecticut Indian Association. *Historical Sketch of the Connecticut Indian Association from 1881 to 1888*. Hartford, CT: Fowler & Miller, 1888.

The Constitution of the Cambridge Branch of the Massachusetts Indian Association. Cambridge: John Ford & Son, 1893.

Cortland Academy: Twenty-Seventh Annual Catalogue for the Year Ending July 8, 1846. R. A. Reed, 1846.

The Council Fire and Arbitrator. Various years.

Dewey, Mary E., *Historical Sketch of the Formation and Achievements of the Women's National Indian Association*. National Indian Association, 1900.

DuBois, Constance Goddard. "Our American 'Reconcentrados.'" *City and State: Commonwealth and Party* (November 8, 1900): 297–99.

Eagle, Mary Kavanaugh Oldham, ed. *The Congress of Women Held in the Woman's Building, World's Columbia Exposition, Chicago, U.S.A., 1893*. Vol. 1. Chicago: W. W. Conkey, 1894.

Edwards, Rev. Jonathan. *An Illustrated History of Spokane County, State of Washington*. N.p.: W. H. Lever, 1900. https://archive.org/details/illustratedhistoooedwa/page/n5/mode/2up.

The Family Magazine or Monthly Abstract of General Knowledge, 1837. Cincinnati: Eli Taylor, 1837.

Forty-Seventh Annual Report of the American Baptist Home Mission Society. New York: American Baptist Home Mission Rooms, 1879.

French, J. H. *Gazetteer of the State of New York*. Syracuse: R. Pearsall Smith, 1860.

Gazetteer and Business Directory of Cortland County, New York for 1869. Syracuse: The Journal Office, 1869.

A Gazetteer of the State of New York. Albany: C. Van Benthuysen, 1843.

Georgia Female College. Madison: Published for the Georgia Female College, 1850.

History of Alabama and Dictionary of Alabama Biography. Vol. 4. Chicago: C. J. Clark, 1921.

The Home Mission Monthly. Various issues.
Index of the Miscellaneous Documents of the House of Representatives for the First Session of the Forty-Fourth Congress. Washington, DC: Government Printing Office, 1876.
The Indian Question: Report of the Committee Appointed by Hon. John D. Long. Boston: Frank Wood, 1880.
Jackson, Helen Hunt. *A Century of Dishonor: A Sketch of the United States Government's Dealing with Some of the Indian Tribes*. Boston: Roberts Brothers, 1888.
Journal of the Thirtieth Annual Convention of the Protestant Episcopal Church in the Diocese of Central New York, 1898. Utica: Herald Job Department, 1898.
Lake Mohonk Conference. *Proceedings of the Lake Mohonk Conference of Friends of the Indians*. Various years.
Lend a Hand: A Journal of Organized Philanthropy. Various issues.
Marshall, Clara. *The Woman's Medical College of Pennsylvania*. Philadelphia: R. Blakiston, 1897.
The Missionary Review of the World, April 1889 to December 1890. Cleveland: Charles W. Watson Collection, 1919.
National Indian Association. *NIA Missions of 1904*. NIA, 1904.
———. *Report of Missions, 1906*. New York: Volunteer Press, 1906.
———. *Report of Missions, 1907*. New York: Volunteer Press, 1907.
Official Report of the Thirteenth Universal Peace Congress. Boston: Peace Congress Committee, 1904.
Ogontz, English, French and German Boarding and Day School for Young Ladies. Philadelphia: Henry B. Ashmead, 1883.
Owen, Thomas McAdory. *History of Alabama and Dictionary of Alabama Biography*. Vol. 4. Chicago: S. J. Clark, 1921.
Painter, Prof. Charles C. *A Visit to the Mission Indians of California*. Philadelphia: Indian Rights Association, 1887.
Pancoast, Henry S. *Impressions of the Sioux Tribes in 1882, with Some First Principles in the Indian Question*. Philadelphia: Franklin Printing House, 1883.
Quinton, Amelia Stone. *Address of the President on Current Indian Legislation, Work Needed, Etc*. Philadelphia: Royal Printing Company, 1887.
———. "Care of the Indian." In *Woman's Work in America*, edited by Annie Nathan Meyer, 373–91. New York: Henry Holt, 1891.
———. "The Indian." In *The Literature of Philanthropy*, edited by Francis Goodale, 116–40. New York: Harper & Brothers, 1893.
———. "Indian Territory Exclusion," *Lend a Hand: A Journal of Organized Philanthropy*. Vol. 1. Boston: Lend A Hand Publishing Company, 1886: 74–76.
———. *The Mohonk Indian Conference*. (Leaflets of the Women's National Indian Association [1885]).
———. "The Original Indian Association." *Christian Union*, October 6, 1887.
———. *A retrospect and its Lessons*. WNIA: Annual Address, Dec. 6th, 1894.
———. *Suggestions to Friends of the Women's National Indian Association*. Publications of the WNIA [1886].

———. *What it has Done: What it Ought to Do.* Philadelphia: WNIA, November 1889.

———. "The Woman's National Indian Association." In *The Congress of Women Held in the Woman's Building, World's Columbia Exposition*, edited by Mary Kavanaugh Oldham Eagle, 71–73. Chicago: W. B. Conkey, 1894.

———. "Women's Work for Indians." In *The National Exposition Souvenir: What America Owes to Women*, edited by Lydia Hoyt Farmer, 293–304. Buffalo: Charles Wells Moulton, 1893.

———. "The Work and Objects of the Woman's National Indian Association." *Report of the International Council of Women, Assembled by the National Woman Suffrage Association, March 25 to April 1, 1888.* Washington, DC: Rufus H. Darby, 1888.

———. *The Ute Question.* Philadelphia: WNIA, [1890].

Register of the Empire State Society of the Sons of the American Revolution. Empire State Society, 1899.

The Sailors' Magazine and Seamen's Friend for the Year Ending December, 1873. Vol. 45. New York: American Seamen's Friend Society, 1873.

Sewall, May Wright, ed. *The World's Congress of Representative Women.* Vol. 2. Chicago: Rand McNally, 1894.

Smith, Eugene R., ed. *The Gospel in All Lands.* (New York: Missionary Society of the Methodist Episcopal Church, December 1887).

Southern Workman. Various issues.

Welsh, Herbert Welsh. *Four Weeks Among Some of the Sioux Tribes of Dakota and Nebraska, Together with a Brief Consideration of the Indian Problem.* Germantown, Philadelphia: Horace F. McCann, Steam-Power Printer, 1882.

Willard, Frances E., and Mary A. Livermore, eds. *A Woman of the Century: Fourteen Hundred-seventy Biographical Sketches Accompanied by Portraits of Leading American Women in All Walks of Life.* Buffalo: Charles Wells Moulton, 1893.

Wittenmyer, Mrs. Annie. *History of the Woman's Temperance Crusade.* Philadelphia: Published at the Office of the Christian Woman, 1878.

Woman in Sacred Song: A Library of Hymns, Religious Poems and Sacred Music by Woman. Oakland, CA: Arthur E. Whitney, 1888.

The Women's Baptist Home Mission Society. *The Women's Baptist Home Mission Society, 1877 to 1882: Minutes of Annual and Special Meetings, and Annual Reports of Corresponding Secretary During the First Five Years.* Chicago: R. R. Donnelley, 1883.

Women's National Indian Association. *Address of the President of the Women's National Indian Association. Philadelphia: November 17th, 1885.* Philadelphia: Grant & Faires.

———. *Annual Report.* Various years.

———. *The Case of the Florida Seminoles.* Ca. 1897

———. *Christian Civilization and Missionary Work of the WNIA.* Philadelphia: Royal Printing Company, 1887.

———. *How to Organize an Indian Association (Publications of the WNIA [1888].*

———. *The Indian's Friend.* Numerous issues.

———. *Minutes of the Trustees.* Various years.

———. *Official Pamphlet of the National Indian Association, with Suggestions and Facts for its Helpers*. Philadelphia: Women's National Indian Association: 1882.
———. *Our Missionary Report for 1896*. Philadelphia: WNIA, 1896.
———. *Our Missionary Report for 1897*. Philadelphia: WNIA, 1897.
———. *Our Missions, for the Year 1895*. Philadelphia: December 1895.
———. *Report of Missionary Work, November 1889*. Philadelphia: Wilbour, 1889.
———. *The Report of the Missionary Department, November 1891*. Philadelphia: Wilbour, 1891.
———. *Report of the Missionary Department of the WNIA, November 1890*. [Philadelphia, 1890].
———. *The WNIA Report on Missionary Work*. Philadelphia: November 1888.
———. *Sketches of Delightful Work*. Philadelphia: January 1893.
———. *Sunshine Work*. Philadelphia: December 1894.

Secondary Sources

Books

Adams, David Wallace. *Education for Extinction: American Indians and the Boarding School Experience, 1875–1928*. Lawrence: University Press of Kansas, 1995.
The Ancestry and Descendants of Frank Marion Swanson. Vol. 1. Compiled by Marion Swanson Wattenbarger, 1997.
Andersson, Rani-Henrik. *The Lakota Ghost Dance of 1890*. Lincoln: University of Nebraska Press, 2008.
Bordin, Ruth. *Woman and Temperance: The Quest for Power and Liberty, 1873–1900*. Philadelphia: Temple University Press, 1981.
Burgess, Larry E. *Mohonk: Its People and Spirit: A History of One Hundred Years of Growth and Service*. New York: Purple Mountain Press, 1996.
Campbell, Jesse Harrison. *Georgia Baptists: Historical and Biographical*. Macon: J. W. Burke, 1874.
Carter, Christine Jacobson, ed. *The Diary of Dolly Lunt Burge, 1848–1879*. Athens: University of Georgia Press, 1997.
Chase, Susan Mulchaney, Ruth Mette, and Peggy Rawheiser. *150 Years of History, Roots and Branches, Continuity and Change*. Wilmington, DE: First Unitarian Church, 2016.
Cott, Nancy F. *The Bonds of Womanhood: "Woman's Sphere" in New England, 1780–1835*. New Haven, CT: Yale University Press, 1977.
Daniels, Morris S. *The Story of Ocean Grove: Related to the Year of its Golden Jubilee*. New York: Methodist Book Concern, 1919.
Douglas, Ann. *The Feminization of American Culture*. New York: Alfred A. Knopf, 1977.
Dubois, Constance Goddard. *A Soul in Bronze, A Novel of Southern California*. Chicago: Herbert S. Stone, 1900.
Fox, Norman. *Preacher and Teacher: A Sketch of the Life of Thomas Rambaut*. New York: Fords, Howard & Hulbert, 1892.

Gates, Merrill Edwards, ed. *Men of Mark in America: Ideals of American Life Told in Biographies of Eminent Living Americans*. Vol. 2. Washington, DC: Men of Mark, 1906.

Ginzberg, Lori D. *Women and the Work of Benevolence: Morality, Politics, and Class in the Nineteenth-Century United States*. New Haven, CT: Yale University Press, 1990.

Greene, Jerome A., and Douglas D. Scott. *Finding Sand Creek: History, Archeology, and the 1864 Massacre Site*. Norman: University of Oklahoma Press, 2004.

Hagen, William T. *The Indian Rights Association: The Herbert Welsh Years, 1882–1904*. Tucson: University of Arizona Press, 1985.

Holmes, Elmer W. *History of Riverside County, California*. Los Angeles: Historic Record Company, 1912.

Huntington, Maria. *Harriet Ward Foote Hawley*. BiblioLife, L.L.C. 1923.

Hyer, Joel R. "*We are Not Savages: Native Americans in Southern California and the Pala Reservation, 1840–1920*. East Lansing: Michigan State University Press, 2001.

Jacobs, Margaret. *White Mother to a Dark Race: Settler Colonialism, Maternalism, and the Removal of Indigenous Children in the American West and Australia, 1880–1940*. Lincoln: University of Nebraska Press, 2009.

Johnson, Curtis D. *Islands of Holiness: Rural Religion in Upstate New York, 1790–1860*. Ithaca: Cornell University Press, 1989.

Keen, William Williams, ed. *The Bi-Centennial Celebration of the Founding of the First Baptist Church of the City of Philadelphia, 1698–1898*. Philadelphia: American Baptist Publication Society, 1899.

Knight, Lucian Lamar. *Georgia's Landmarks, Memorials and Legends*. Vol. 2. Atlanta: Byrd Printing Company, 1914.

Kvasnicka, Robert M., and Herman J. Viola, eds. *The Commissioners of Indian Affairs, 1824–1977*. Lincoln: University of Nebraska Press, 1979.

Littlefield, Daniel F., and James W. Parins. *American Indian and Alaska Native Newspapers and Periodicals, 1816–1924*. Westport, CT: Greenwood Press, 1984.

Mark, Joan. *A Stranger in Her Native Land: Alice Fletcher and the American Indians*. Lincoln: University of Nebraska Press, 1988.

Mathes, Valerie Sherer. *Divinely Guided: The California Work of the Women's National Indian Association*. Lubbock: Texas Tech University Press, 2012.

———, ed. *Gender, Race, and Power in the Indian Reform Movement: The Women's National Indian Association*. Albuquerque: University of New Mexico Press, 2020.

———. *Helen Hunt Jackson and her Indian Reform Legacy*. Austin: University of Texas Press, 1990.

———, ed. *The Indian Reform Letters of Helen Hunt Jackson, 1879–1885*. Norman: University of Oklahoma Press, 1998.

———, ed. *The Women's National Indian Association: A History*. Albuquerque: University of New Mexico Press, 2015.

———, and Phil Brigandi, eds. *A Call for Reform: The Southern California Indian Writings of Helen Hunt Jackson*. University of Oklahoma Press, 2015.

———, and Phil Brigandi. *Reservations, Removal, and Reform: The Mission Indian Agents of Southern California 1878–1903*. Norman: University of Oklahoma Press, 2018.

———, and Richard Lowitt. *The Standing Bear Controversy: Prelude to Indian Reform.* Urbana: University of Illinois Press, 2003.

Mattingly, Carol. *Well-Tempered Women: Nineteenth-Century Temperance Rhetoric.* Carbondale: Southern Illinois University Press, 1998.

McLoughlin, William G. *The American Evangelicals, 1800–1900: An Anthology.* New York: Harper and Row, 1968.

Melendy, H. Brett, and Benamin F. Gilbert. *The Governors of California: Peter H. Burnett to Edmund G. Brown.* Georgetown: CA: Talisman Press, 1965.

Mooney, James. *The Ghost Dance Religion and the Sioux Outbreak of 1890*, edited by Anthony F. C. Wallace. Chicago: University of Chicago Press, 1965.

Morgan County, Georgia Heritage: 1807–1997. Walsworth Publishing, 1997.

A National Register of the Society Sons of the American Revolution. New York: Andrew M. Kellogg, 1902.

Newman, Louise Michele. *White Women's Rights: The Racial Origins of Feminism in the United States.* New York: Oxford University Press, 1999.

Nye, Russel Blaine. *Society and Culture in America, 1830–1860.* New York: Harper & Row, 1974.

Phillips, George Harwood. *Chiefs and Challengers: Indian Resistance and Cooperation in Southern California, 1769–1906.* Norman: University of Oklahoma Press, 2014.

Phillips, Kate. *Helen Hunt Jackson: A Literary Life.* Berkeley: University of California Press, 2003.

Portnoy, Alisse. *Their Right to Speak: Women's Activism in the Indian and Slave Debates.* Cambridge, MA: Harvard University Press, 2005.

Prucha, Francis Paul. *American Indian Policy in Crisis: Christian Reformers and the Indian, 1865–1900.* Norman: University of Oklahoma Press, 1976.

———. *American Indian Policy in the Formative Years: The Indian Trade and Intercourse Acts, 1790–1834.* Lincoln: University of Nebraska Press, 1970.

———. *Documents of United States Indian Policy.* 2nd ed. Lincoln: University of Nebraska Press, 1990.

———. *The Great Father: The United States Government and the American Indian.* Vol. 2. Lincoln: University of Nebraska Press, 1984.

———. *Indian Policy in the United States: Historical Essays.* Lincoln: University of Nebraska Press, 1981.

Ragsdale, B. D. *Story of Georgia Baptists.* Vol. 2. Atlanta: Foote and Davies Co., 1935.

Rhea, John M. *A Field of their Own: Women and American Indian History, 1830–1941.* Norman: University of Oklahoma Press, 2016.

Ruby, Robert H., and John A. Brown. *The Spokane Indians: Children of the Sun.* Norman: University of Oklahoma Press, 2006.

Ryan, Mary P. *Womanhood in America: From Colonial Times to the Present.* New York: New Viewpoints, 1979.

Scott, Anne Firor, *Making the Invisible Woman Visible.* Urbana: University of Illinois Press, 1984.

Simonsen, Jane E., *Making Home Work: Domesticity and Native American Assimilation in the American West, 1860–1919*. Chapel Hill: University of North Carolina Press, 2006.

Story of Georgia Baptists. Vol. 2. Atlanta: Foote and Davies Company, 1935.

Thompson, Mark. *American Character: The Curious Life of Charles Fletcher Lummis and the Rediscovery of the Southwest*. New York: Arcade Publishing, 2001.

Tibbles, Thomas Henry. *Buckskin & Blanket Days: Memoirs of a Friend of the Indians*. Lincoln: University of Nebraska Press, 1969.

———. *The Ponca Chiefs: An Account of the Trial of Standing Bear*. Lincoln: University of Nebraska Press, 1972.

Tigner, J. H. *The Italy of America*. Los Angeles: Home Printing Company, ca. 1908.

Tong, Benson. *Susan La Flesche Picotte, M.D.: Omaha Indian Leader and Reformer*. Norman: University of Oklahoma Press, 1999.

Wittenmyer, Annie. *History of the Woman's Temperance Crusade*. Philadelphia: Published at the Office of the Christian Woman, 1878.

Woman's Who's Who of America, 1914–1915. New York: American Commonwealth Company, 1914.

Zaeske, Susan. *Signatures of Citizenship: Petitioning, Antislavery, & Women's Political Identity*. Chapel Hill: University of North Carolina Press, 2003.

Articles and Book Chapters

Askew, Thomas A. "The 1888 London Centenary Missions Conference: Ecumenical Disappointment or American Missions Coming of Age?" *International Bulletin of Missionary Research*, July 1994: 113–118.

Bannan, Helen M. "'True Womanhood' and Indian Assimilation." In *Selected Proceedings of the Third Annual Conference on Minority Studies*, vol. 2, edited by George E. Carter and James R. Parker, 187–94. La Crosse: Institute for Minority Studies, University of Wisconsin, 1976.

———. "True Womanhood on the Reservation: Field Matrons in the United States Indian Service," *Southwest Institute for Research on Women*, Working Paper No. 18 [Women's Studies, University of Arizona, Tucson, 1984]: 1–25.

Brigandi, Phil. "Debating the Existence of a 'Real' Ramona." *Valley Chronicle* (Hemet, CA), February 9, 2002.

Brigandi, Phil, and John W. Robinson. "The Killing of Juan Diego: From Murder to Mythology." *Journal of San Diego History* 40, nos. 1–2 (Winter/Spring 1994): 1–22.

Buffalohead, W. Ruger, and Paulette Fairbanks Molin, "A Nucleus of Civilization: American Indian Families at Hampton Institute in the Late Nineteenth Century." *Journal of American Indian Education* 35, no. 3 (Spring 1996): 59–94.

Burgess, Larry E. "Commission to the Mission Indians, 1891." *San Bernardino County Museum Quarterly* (Spring 1988): 1–47.

———. "What is a Woman Worth?" In Mathes, *The Women's National Indian Association*, 213–39.

Cahill, Cathleen D. "Noble Women not a Few: The Lake Mohonk Conferences." In Mathes, *The Women's National Indian Association*, 213–39.

Covington, James M. "Formation of the State of Florida Indian Reservation," *Florida Historical Quarterly* 64, no. 1 (July 1985): 62–75.

Eastman, Elaine Goodale. "The Ghost Dance War and Wounded Knee Massacre of 1890–91," *Nebraska History* 27 (January 1945): 26–42.

Foster, Sarah Whitmer, and John T. Foster, Jr. "Historical Notes and Documents: 'Harriett Ward Foot Fawley: Civil War Journalist.'" *Florida Historical Quarterly* 83, 4 (Spring 2005): 448–67.

Hershberger, Mary, "Mobilizing Women, Anticipating Abolition: The Struggle Against Indian Removal in the 1830s." *Journal of American History* (June 1999): 15–40.

Hickey, Walter V. "The Final Voyage of the *Portland*," *Prologue* 38, no. 4 (Winter 2006).

Jacobson, Lori. "Environed by Civilization," WNIA Home-Building and Loan Department." In Mathes, *The Women's National Indian Association*, 65–83.

———. "Indians Can be Educated:" The WNIA at the 1893 World's Columbian Exposition." In Mathes, *Gender, Race, and Power in the Indian Reform Movement*, 209–25.

———. "Shall We Have a Periodical?" In Mathes, *The Women's National Indian Association*, 46–61.

Keller Jr., Robert H. *American Protestantism and United States Indian Policy, 1869–82* (Lincoln: University of Nebraska Press, 1983).

Kerber, Linda K. "Separate Spheres, Female Worlds, Woman's Place: The Rhetoric of Women's History. *Journal of American History* 75 (June 1988): 9–39.

Kersey, Harry A., and Donald E. Pullease. "Bishop William Crane Gray's Mission to the Seminole Indians in Florida, 1893–1914." *Historical Magazine of the Protestant Episcopal Church* 42, no. 3 (September 1973): 257–73.

Laylander, Don. "Early Ethnographic Notes from Constance Goddard DuBois on the Indians of San Diego County." *Journal of California and Great Basin Anthropology* 26, no. 2 (2006): 205–14.

Mathes, Valerie Sherer. "Annie E. K. Bidwell: Chico's Benefactress." *California History* (Spring/Summer 1989): 14–25, notes 60–64.

———. "The Banner Association: Twenty-Five Years in Massachusetts." In Mathes, *The Women's National Indian Association*, 153–72.

———. "Baptist Missionary Work at Round Valley, California." *American Baptist Quarterly* (Fall 2010): 172–86.

———. "Boston, the Boston Indian Citizenship Committee, and the Poncas." *Massachusetts Historical Review* 14 (2012): 119–48.

———. "The California Mission Indian Commission of 1891: The Legacy of Helen Hunt Jackson," *California History* 73, no. 4 (Winter 1993/94): 339–59, notes 390–95.

———. "C. E. Kelsey and California's Landless Indians." In Mathes, *Gender, Race, and Power in the Indian Reform Movement*, 163–81.

———. "Helen Hunt Jackson, Amelia Stone Quinton, and the Mission Indians of California." *Southern California Quarterly* 96, no. 2 (Summer 2014): 172–205.

———. "Helen Hunt Jackson and Southern California's Mission Indians." *California History* 78, no. 4 (Winter 1999/2000): 262–73, notes 303–4.

———. "Indian Philanthropy in California: Annie Bidwell and the Mechoopda Indians." *Arizona and the West* (Summer 1893): 153–66.

———. "Iron Eye's Daughters: Susette and Susan LaFlesche, Nineteenth-Century Indian Reformers." In *By Grit and Grave: Eleven Women Who Shaped the American West*, edited by Glenda Riley and Richard W. Etulain, 135–52. Golden, CO: Fulcrum, 1997.

———. "Mary Lucinda Bonney and Amelia Stone Quinton, Founders of the Women's National Indian Association." *American Baptist Quarterly* (Winter, 2009): 421–40.

———. "New York Women and Indian Reform." *New York History* (Winter/Spring 2013): 84–109.

———. "Susan LaFlesche Picotte, MD: Nineteenth-Century Physician and Reformer," *Great Plains Quarterly* (Winter 1993): 172–86.

———. "The Redlands Indian Association: The WNIA in Southern California." In Mathes, *The Women's National Indian Association*, 192–210.

———. "The Women's National Indian Association in 19th Century Northern California," *Aloha, Amigos! The Richard H. Dillon Memorial Volume Brand Book 24* (Los Angeles: Westerners International, 2020): 435–66.

———, and Phil Brigandi. "Charles C. Painter, Helen Hunt Jackson and the Mission Indians of Southern California," *Journal of San Diego History* 55, no. 3 (Summer 2009): 89–118.

———, and Phil Brigandi. "The Mischief Record of 'La Gobernadora' Amelia Stone Quinton, Charles Fletcher Lummis, and the Warner Ranch Indian Removal." *Journal of San Diego History* 57, nos. 1–2 (Winter/Spring 2011): 69–96.

Newman, Louise Michele. "The 'Indian Problem' as a 'Woman Question.'" In *White Women's Rights: The Racial Origins of Feminism in the United States*, 116–31. New York: Oxford University Press, 1999.

Plane, Ana Marie, and Gregory Button. "The Massachusetts Indian Enfranchisement Act: Ethnic Contest in Historical Context, 1849–1869." *Ethnohistory* 40, no. 4 (Autumn 1993): 587–618.

Prucha, Francis Paul. "A 'Friend of the Indian' in Milwaukee: Mrs. O. J. Hiles and the Wisconsin Indian Association," *Historical Messenger of the Milwaukee County Historical Society* (Autumn 1893): 78–95.

———. "Indian Policy Reform and American Protestantism, 1880–1900." In *Indian Policy in the United States*, 229–51. Lincoln: University of Nebraska Press, 1981.

Rhea, John M. "From Indian Territory to Philadelphia: A Critical Reexamination of the Origins and Early History of the Women's National Indian Association, 1877–1881." In Mathes, *Gender, Race, and Power in the Indian Reform Movement*, 27–54.

Roddis, Louis H. "The Last Indian Uprising in the United States," *Minnesota History Bulletin* 3, no. 5 (February 1920): 273–90.

Stremlau, Rose. "WNIA Missions in the South." In Mathes, *The Women's National Indian Association*, 102–25.

Welter, Barbara. "The Cult of True Womanhood, 1820–1860." In *Dimity Convictions: The American Woman in the Nineteenth Century*. Athens: Ohio University Press, 1976.

Dissertations

Bannan, Helen Marie. "Reformers and the 'Indian Problem,' 1878–1887 and 1922–1934." PhD diss., Syracuse University, 1976.

Burgess, Larry E. "The Lake Mohonk Conferences on the Indian, 1883–1916." PhD diss., Claremont, 1972.

Emmerich, Lisa E. "To Respect and Love and Seek the Ways of White Women: Field Matrons, the Office of Indian Affairs, and Civilization Policy, 1890–1938." PhD diss., University of Maryland, College Park, 1987.

Jacobson, Lori L. "Agencies and Associations: Women Write Indian Reform in Nineteenth-Century America." PhD diss., State University of New York, Buffalo, 2007.

Lastowka, Carol Anne Chase, "At Home and Industriously Employed: The Women's National Indian Association." Master's thesis, University of Arizona, 1994.

Romeyn, Sara Northrop. "A Sentimental Empire: White Women's Responses to Native American Policy, 1824–1894." PhD diss., George Washington University, 2003.

Ryan, Mary P. "American Society and the Cult of Domesticity, 1830–1860." PhD diss., University of California at Santa Barbara, 1971.

Thompson, Gregory Coyne. "The Origins and Implementation of the American Indian Reform Movement: 1867–1912." PhD diss., University of Utah, 1981.

Wanken, Helen M. "Woman's Sphere and Indian Reform: The Women's National Indian Association, 1879–1901." PhD diss., Marquette University, 1981.

Newspapers

Bangor (ME) *Daily Whig & Courier*
Boston Daily Advertiser
Boston Daily Globe
Boston Daily Journal
Boston Evening Journal
Brooklyn (NY) *Eagle*
Buffalo (NY) *Evening Courier & Republic*
Cambridge (MA) *Tribune*
Cincinnati Commercial Tribune
Citrograph
Cortland County (NY) *Democrat*
Cortland County (NY) *Republic*
Cortland (NY) *Evening Standard*
Daily Evening Bulletin (San Francisco)
Evening Star (Washington, DC)
Galveston Daily News
Hemet (CA) *News*
Homer (NY) *Republican*
Los Angeles Herald

Los Angeles Times
Lowell (MA) *Daily Courier*
Madison (WI) *Family Visitor*
National Baptist
New York Post
New York Herald
New York Times
Oroville (CA) *Weekly Mercury*
Otsego (NY) *Farmer*
Philadelphia Inquirer
Post Standard (Syracuse, NY)
Poughkeepsie (NY) *Daily Eagle*
Riverside (CA) *Enterprise*
Riverside (CA) *Press and Horticulturist*
Rochester (NY) *Democrat and Chronicle*
Rocky Mountain News (Denver)
San Francisco Chronicle
San Jacinto (CA) *Register*
Southwestern Christian Advocate (New Orleans)
Springfield (IL)*Republican*
Syracuse (NY) *Evening Record*
Valley Chronicle (Hemet, CA)
Weekly Madisonian (WI)
Wheeling (WV) *Register*

Index

References to illustrations appear in italics.

www.ingramcontent.com/pod-product-compliance
Ingram Content Group UK Ltd.
Pitfield, Milton Keynes, MK11 3LW, UK
UKHW011040190826
474455UK00004B/226

9 780806 192918